S0-CMV-334

KARL RAHNER

His Life, Thought and Works

POPE PIUS XII LIB., ST. JOSEPH COLLEGE

3 2528 01261 1127

KARL RAHNER

His Life, Thought and Works

by

HERBERT VORGRIMLER

Translated by
EDWARD QUINN

DEUS BOOKS
PAULIST PRESS
(Paulist Fathers)
Glen Rock, N. J.

A Deus Books Edition of Paulist Press, 1966, by special arrangement with Burns & Oates Ltd., London, S.W.1.

This is a translation of Karl Rahner—Leben, Denken, Werke (*Manz Verlag, Munich*) *originally published by Uitgeverij Lannoo in Tielt under the title* Karl Rahner—Denkers over God en Wereld.

Nihil obstat: Carolus McGowan, B.A.

   Censor deputatus

Imprimatur: Patritius Casey

   Vicarius Generalis

Westmonasterii: die 23a Octobris 1965

The Nihil obstat *and* Imprimatur *are a declaration that a book or pamphlet is considered to be free from doctrinal or moral error. It is not implied that those who have granted the* Nihil obstat *and* Imprimatur *agree with the contents, opinions or statements expressed.*

© Uitgeverij Lannoo, 1963

English translation © Burns & Oates Ltd., 1965

Published by Paulist Press
Editorial Office: 304 W. 58 St., N.Y. 19, N.Y.
Business Office: Glen Rock, N.J.

Printed and bound in the United States of America by Our Sunday Visitor Press

Contents

1 Karl Rahner's Life

In a brief introduction to the life, thought and work of a theologian, a priest and a religious, is it wholly right to begin by naming his birth-place and giving the exact setting of his native-land? For the *theologian*, in the second millennium of the history of the Church of Christ, it is no longer possible to begin to practise theology relying entirely and solely on himself. His spiritual and therefore his first home is the meditation of the Church of all ages on the inexhaustible Word of God. He has to be at home with God's people in the Old Testament, in its covenant-theology, its expectation of ultimate and final salvation in the Messiah, its afflictions from without and its divisions within: the people in which God's Word became flesh. He has to be able to follow the magnificent development of patristic thought in which the last phase of ancient philosophy—neoplatonism—confronted divine revelation and found there its supreme and unexpected confirmation: that finite man comes to share in the divine being itself and returns to his origin in a gradual process of divinization. He will always be indebted to the clear, systematic thought of scholasticism with its firm statement of principles, particularly to St Thomas Aquinas, in whom theological reflection perhaps took the first great step forward from ancient, cosmocentric to modern, personalist philosophy. The theologian finally has to understand his own time, the thinking, hoping, dreaming of men of every "today", to whom he has to relate and expound the Gospel, but who also from their standpoint can assist him to a deeper understanding of the Word of God. And is not the *priest* also, as it were, without an earthly home and ancestors? At least he ought to be so. The priest belongs to the order of Melchisedech, the priest-king of whom it is said in Scripture: "No name of father or mother, no pedigree, no date of birth or of death; there he stands, eternally, a priest, the true figure of the Son of God" (Heb. 7.3). Greater than that of his first home, given him by nature, is the family which the priest calls his own: "If anyone does the will of my Father who is in heaven, he is my brother, and sister, and mother" (Matt. 12.50). That applies most of all to the *religious*.

Here we are concerned with the life of a Jesuit. This involves a paradox: for being a Jesuit means to push private affairs into the background and to regard them as secondary. First and last in the Society of Jesus come service, discipline, obedience, selflessness: not for the sake of the smooth functioning of the institution, but because this is the only way in which man can really bear witness to the infinite grandeur and mystery of God. This absolute service which a man accepts in becoming a Jesuit not only forbids any cult of the person and any parade of himself as a star, but requires him also on entering the order, and at any future time when it seems necessary, to break off all contact with the past. In the foundation of Ignatius of Loyola the Spanish and German conceptions of military service were more or less naturally fused into a remarkable synthesis, a synthesis which of its nature cannot appeal to everyone. Once a person has experienced and obeyed this vocation the description of that man is, strictly speaking, already complete.

These general remarks will explain what is essential in the person of Karl Rahner. He is unreservedly a Jesuit. Why he became one, is not for us to say: it must be accepted as a fact. The essential characteristics of the Society of Jesus are so imprinted upon him that they have become the essential characteristics of his personality. He is first of all wholly and unstintingly the Church's man, a servant of the Catholic Church: her affairs, concerns and problems have become his own most intimate affairs, concerns and problems. It is his aim to serve the Church in that absolute form which is proper to the Society of Jesus: in obedience to his superiors. This means working precisely where one is needed at any particular moment and, once there, in allowing oneself to be used. Undoubtedly such a way of life in our modern society seems, when closely examined, shocking and revolting. Undoubtedly also it provides innumerable opportunities for cheap and silly comment (such as "corpse-like obedience"). No one has explained more finely than Hans Urs von Balthasar how little this implies the annihilation of humanity: "In the last resort, you alone are, and are all in all. And we are not, for what is good in us is already you; and what we are ourselves is not worth considering. In your presence we diminish and want to be nothing but your mirror and a window for our brethren. Our decline before you is your ascendancy over us, our consummation in you and your entry into us." Such a life is scarcely credible in this age and particularly in our world. But it continues to be lived by some.

That had to be said from the beginning, for the reader must not expect to find here details of Karl Rahner's private life. In fact, there would be little enough to relate. He is a theologian, at the service of his order; he has no private property and cannot dispose of his income; he lives in a Jesuit house, in a room furnished with the utmost simplicity and which—like other members of his order—he himself keeps clean and tidy. We can say that he works unceasingly at theology, so that a list of his books and articles already numbers nearly a thousand; that he has chosen to interest the public in these things and has travelled all over Europe, speaking in halls filled to overflowing; that he has addressed cardinals and bishops at the Council; or that his writings have been translated into more than ten languages. What more can be said of his "private life"? He rises after a few hours' sleep, says Mass, makes his prescribed meditation, reads his office, answers letters or applies himself to study, so that he already has a whole day's work behind him when others are just beginning. Only after this come the lectures, visits, and finally writing articles and books until late into the night.

There is simply no place here for the more light-hearted interests. It cannot be said of him, for instance, as it is said of some other theologians, that they are connoisseurs of wine, botanical experts, keen mountaineers or skiers. Yet it would be false to conclude from the absence of these brighter spots that his existence is joyless and heartless. Hundreds of Karl Rahner's listeners can relate how often otherwise dry occasions were studded with examples of his humour, how he enjoys a joke and how gladly he seizes on a forceful expression.

We can—indeed, we must—mention another aspect of his "private" life. There are many poor people in different places who have been helped by him. He possesses nothing himself, but when he hears of a person's need he is able to tap the sources of material aid; I am inclined to think also that he sizes up the people to whom he appeals by their readiness to help. Pastoral care and spiritual aid in the form of letters and interviews lasting for hours also deserve to be mentioned at least briefly here. I have often observed how gladly he finds time for a troubled soul who stops him on the street—at least as willingly as for theologians who come from a distance to consult him.

Here, I think, lie the roots of Karl Rahner's "existential" theology: he is quite literally a "sympathetic" person. "Existential" does not mean only—as I shall explain in the second part of this book—remaining in contact with the thought of the present time. It means first of all that, in his professional work as a theologian and in his "private" life, he is always wholly concerned with the religious basis of the human situation. Seen from this standpoint, his theology may be described as "kerygmatic theology"; but the term is liable to be misunderstood. For Rahner it does not mean that alongside the necessarily abstract and dry, strictly scientific theology, there must be a diluted form "for wider circles"; nor does it mean that he is opposed to subtle, highly specialized theological studies. It is simply a difference of horizon.

He wants to liberate theological formulas and concepts from the rigidity they have acquired as mere tools, without throwing them aside and without questioning their value and importance in the Church's theological tradition—as the modernists of all ages do. Out of consideration for the reader, for man's sake, he restores to the concepts and formulas of text-book theology their dignity as embodiments of the living word, not brandishing them or juggling with them, but seeking out the reality in them (not elsewhere) and then seizing on the reality itself. Because he has first experienced man as a questioner, he has mastered the art of questioning and questions himself ruthlessly. He is opposed to all merely habitual ways of thinking, to intellectual sloth, to self-satisfaction, whose practitioners always know without further thought all that a word implies. Such lifeless apathy will always lack that which is offered in abundance in Karl Rahner's theology and which distinguishes

11

all the great philosophers: wonder at the reality itself
which reveals itself to the questioner and—taking him
by surprise—enlightens him.

In addition to all this, he possesses the unusual gift of
stating what he has thought out. Rahner rightly counts
as one of the few contemporary thinkers who has
acquired an unmistakable style. It is not a style that is
easily accessible: it creates work for hearer and reader.
But a guide to Karl Rahner's work must certainly explore
the peculiarities of his style. We might say that this consists of two components and an "alienating effect", which
secures their sequence and co-ordination.

The first component is an attempt, with the aid of
all the possibilities of language—above all of the participles, otherwise little used in German—so to express
the known truth that the formal repetition of concepts
finally reveals the reality itself, without the concepts
being thereby devalued: in other words in such a
sentence there resounds—so to speak—all the past
achievement of theology, wrapped up in secondary con-
ditional clauses and in innumerable participles. Incidentally, no expert can fail to observe that this resonance
presupposes immense historical and systematic knowledge: in a word, sheer industry. Rahner's definition of
grace and nature provide a good example of this first
component of his style:

> Grace is the *a priori* capacity for the connatural
> reception of God's self-disclosure in word (faith-
> charity) and in the beatific vision. Nature is man's
> permanent state presupposed in his being able to
> listen, in such a form that the sinner and unbeliever
> can close his mind to this persistent self-disclosure of
> God without (as in a culpable denial of his meta-
> physical essence) at the same time implicitly affirm-

ing what is denied; in such a form also that this self-disclosure can appear to man once created as an absolutely free miracle of personal love, which he cannot demand "of himself" (by nature), although it can be addressed to him and he is essentially open to it (nature as a positive *potentia obedientialis* for supernatural grace).[1]

The theologian will find in this lengthy statement a complete summary of doctrine on grace; he will find correctly stated the Church's teaching on the relationship between nature and grace; and yet in Rahner's language the thing itself becomes clearer than before and in his formulation touches the hearer more directly ("God's self-disclosure", "free miracle of personal love"). The statement of course is not simple and a person who cannot understand it at first reading need not think that he is stupid. Nor was the sentence produced in a day, nor even in a year. It has to be read twice, three times, and every word must be kept in mind throughout the process. This naturally presupposes good will and some effort. Theology advances only by retaining what has been previously established and then questioning this anew and more deeply; but many Christians and not a few theologians hesitate to make the effort of constant questioning: they expect rather to perceive in a theological or religious work what they have already known for a long time, and to find those categories within which their thought is accustomed to proceed. But the Word of God, for ever inexhaustible, did not go out into the world merely to confirm theology and the time and energies of a theologian are too precious to be consumed in sterile repetition of the same thing. Karl Rahner's <u>style eludes lazy minds.</u> The genuine listener is fascinated by the perfectly apt, complex statement, because it is almost

13

overflowing with data and queries (the first component
of Rahner's style).

A reader is also directly involved in the *second component*, which I would describe as the element of religious pathos and which in most of Rahner's works is
found interspersed in the midst of rigorously scientific
statements. This sudden turn of style is what I called the
"alienating effect". Thus we read in a technical theological essay on the hypostatic union:

> God's remoteness is the incomprehensibility of his
> all-penetrating proximity: this is the message of
> Christmas. He is tenderly present. He is near. He
> touches the heart gently with his love. He says: "Do
> not fear." In prison he is at hand. If, when we begin to
> seek him, we think that he is not present it is because
> there was never a moment in our life when we did not
> possess him in the unobtrusive sweetness of his in-
> effable love. He is present like pure light, concealed
> because everywhere diffused, as, in the silent humility
> of its nature, his light making everything else visible.
> Christmas tells you in your solitude: Trust your sur-
> roundings, they are not emptiness; let go and you will
> find; renounce and you will be rich.[2]

Sentences like these, full of religious pathos, are not
introduced into Rahner's work as rhetorical tricks; and
it would be offensive to speak of "sentimentality". The
point is that the original pastoral aspect of his theology
becomes visible here: it is his intention, not to provide
theoretical instruction alone, but also to assist man to
experience grace. In a world where technology and industry loom so large that it seems impossible for man to
realize anything unless it is produced and controlled by
hand, Rahner's message is for many a decisive aid to an

experience of their own transcendence and therein to an experience of God.

Here, too, we can see a fundamental "weakness" of Rahner's. Because he knows man's deep religious need and because this is of considerable concern to him, he thinks that every other theologian in the Church must feel the same. And when he finds that their feelings are in no way involved, he cannot easily conceal his disappointment. That is the reason—and that alone—for his occasional harsh comments on the theology of the schools which does not manage to go beyond the mere repetition of the same concepts (rigidly applied and perhaps never properly understood) or to see through them the truths they would express, thus failing to explain them in the form of healing responses to man's need. But once again: this "existential" factor of theology must not be paraded at the expense of scientific exactitude. "In fact the strictest theology, that most passionately devoted to reality alone and ever on the alert for new questions, the most scientific theology, is itself in the long run the most kerygmatic."[3] Thus Rahner imposes on his students a task that is doubly hard: to deal with the content of theology in a strictly scientific way and at the same time always to face the question, "How shall I say this to the man in the street?" If the current theology of the schools provides no answer to this, Rahner treats it not only with contempt and irony, but also with anger.

It is also typical of Karl Rahner that he takes quite seriously the religious problem of man today, often understands it for the first time in its full import and brings all its consequences into the open. In the same spirit he is able to look at the Church and Christianity, as it were, from outside. He shows frankly and plainly what it is in the Church which makes it so difficult for non-Christians today to see in her a foundation of God himself. He sees

15

the consequence and lays his finger on it: non-Christians today will develop their own culture and morality in a reversal of the historical process.

The non-Christian world, which (though we love to assert such things of it) is *not* a sheer mass of decomposition and deterioration, will even seek to develop its own forces, its own institutions of a social, intellectual, educational and moral kind, and these will certainly not be so obliging as to prove a mere series of desperate and unsuccessful efforts. These things will then make an impression on Christians, and refute our cheaply repetitious (and theologically false) propaganda to the effect that anywhere where the Church and the clergy are not in control and do not supply the principles of action, there can be nothing but disintegration and decay.[4]

Because of this honesty in analysis and language and because of his warning against all attempts to confine Christianity to the forms of pious associations, Rahner is regarded by some as a revolutionary. The description does not fit. His theology is just as traditional as it is original; he thinks at least as much with the Church, is quite as truly a man of the Church, as his critics. A frank way of speaking is natural to him, but so also is Ignatius of Loyola's whole-hearted and intimate devotion to the Church. Even when he speaks—as few before him have spoken—of the Church of sinners and the sinning Church, there is never the slightest doubt that he believes the same Church to be the infallible community of Jesus Christ ruled by the Spirit of God.

After this attempt to describe Karl Rahner's general outlook, we must now give a chronological account of his life. He is Swabian. He was born in Freiburg im Breisgau,

March 5, 1904. His parents also, Professor Karl Rahner (1868-1934) and Frau Luise Rahner (née Trescher, still living in Freiburg at the age of 90), came from that neighbourhood. People from these parts (Martin Heidegger, Karl Barth, Bernhard Welte, Max Müller, are among them) are supposed to be reserved, introspective, and ready to work like horses; they are considered to have a deep sense of humour, but no spontaneous and clear-sighted joy in life—only a melancholy irony. However that may be, Karl Rahner spent his youth from 1908-22 in Freiburg: he attended the boys' primary school 1910-13, the grammar school from 1913 until he gained his leaving certificate on March 29, 1922. There is not much to report about those early years. He was an average student, bored during lessons. He was an enthusiastic supporter of the youth movement and a member of "Quickborn".[5] Finally, he became friendly with Pier Giorgio Frassati. The latter was a young Italian student, born 1901, who lived with the Rahners and made a deep impression on Karl. How deep can be seen from his introduction in 1961 to Pier Giorgio's biography (he died of infantile paralysis in 1925):

> Even if there are now and were then many of his calibre, it would still be right to praise the young Christian as represented by Frassati: naturally radiant and virile, open to all that speaks of freedom and beauty, with a deep social sense, having at heart the Church and her destiny. But Frassati was more than this, as the reader ought to discover from this modern life of a saint. At that time there were not yet many who came from upper middle-class liberal circles and who also became Christians as Frassati did, without a trace of the usual psychological mechanism of the sons' protest against their fathers. That is the remark-

17

able thing: what he lacks is precisely this attitude of protest. He is a Christian simply by being there and his only protest consists in the fact that he assumes that this attitude, self-evident to him, is self-evident to everybody. He derives his courage and his power to be a Christian, not from his opposition to his parents' generation, not from cultural diagnoses and prognoses and the like, but from the Christian reality itself: that God is, that prayer is fruitful, that the sacraments nourish the "eternal in man", that all men are brothers. Here particularly the mysterious spontaneity of divine grace becomes perceptible: suddenly a Christian is again present where background and parents suggested that this was wholly a thing of the past. And he is happy simply to be, without adopting a party line and making an effort to be different. Here was a Christian who lived his Christianity as something which he accepted in an almost terrifying way as self-evident, with what to us seemed a dubious and maddening lack of problems (because he—although perhaps with tears —submerged the problems in the grace of faith): praying, eating the bread of death and life, loving his brethren.[6]

We may perhaps apply this catchword also to the youth and the decision of Karl Rahner: these were "self-evident". Self-evident, but as the result of a hard and stubbornly worked out decision which is not manifested by any external "conversion" and is proved by unceasing and selfless service.

On April 20, 1922, three weeks after his school-leaving examination, Karl Rahner entered the novitiate of the North German province of the Society of Jesus. It was then at Feldkirch in the Vorarlberg, in Austria. Three years earlier his brother, Hugo Rahner, had entered the same novitiate.[7] In the novitiate, he devoted himself completely to problems of the spiritual life, without ambitions, without expressing a preference for a particular field of activity: he was interested solely in the fundamentals of the religious life and the study of spiritual writers. He presented to the novitiate magazine the first drafts of some articles, wholly concerned with spirituality, which (as we shall see) later appeared in print.

On April 27, 1924, he took his vows as a scholastic (which in fact bind the religious to the Society of Jesus, but do not bind the Society to him). In accordance with the custom of the order, he spent the first year (1924-5) in studying philosophy at Feldkirch; the second and third year (1925-7) he spent at Pullach, near Munich. A stack of thick notebooks testifies to his industry during these years and reveals his special field of interest. His teachers in philosophy were then K. Frank, K. Frick, B. Jansen, J. B. Schuster, A. Willwoll: reputable and solid pedagogues. But there exists a further stack of notebooks, the evidence of his secret hobby. In these, in his clear, precise handwriting, Karl Rahner made excerpts from the works of Kant and of the Jesuit philosopher, J. Maréchal (d. 1944 in Louvain), who confronted thomism with Kantian philosophy and tried to make Kant's transcendental method fruitful for the thomist theory of knowledge.

During these first years of study, Karl Rahner's superiors in the Order must have intended him for a scholarly career: it seems that they were thinking of the history of philosophy. But, in accordance with the Jesuit rule, a period of practical work had to come before further intellectual formation, between philosophy and theology. For Rahner this consisted in giving Latin lessons in the juniorate in Feldkirch. It is certainly to this activity that he owes his astounding knowledge of Latin, shown in a variety of ways, both in the records of his principal Latin lectures in Innsbruck and in his speeches at the Council or in conversations with foreign theologians.

At that time one of his students was Alfred Delp, born 1907 in Mannheim, who became a Jesuit in 1926. Later he was associated with the monthly, *Stimmen der Zeit*, as sociologist, became one of the conspirators against Hitler, was arrested by the Nazis July 28, 1944, and was hanged in Berlin, February 2, 1945. The writings he left behind him have a right to rank among the modern "acts of the martyrs".[8] In 1938 we find him again as a close assistant of Karl Rahner.

Rahner began his theological studies in 1929 at Valkenburg in Holland. Among his teachers were outstanding scholars, some of them still living: K. Prümm, exegete and patrologist; J. Rabeneck and H. Lange, dogmatic theologians; H. Weisweiler, historian of dogma; F. Hürth, moral theologian; J. Grisar, church historian; E. Raitz von Prentz, ascetic theologian. On July 26, 1932, he was ordained priest in St Michael's church in Munich by Cardinal Faulhaber. His theological studies continued until 1933, after which he went for his tertianship—the year's retreat prescribed by the constitutions of the order —to St Andrä in the Lavant valley (Carinthia). In 1934 he was sent by his superiors to take a degree in philosophy at Freiburg, his birthplace.

For one with such innate gifts for the subject, the Freiburg faculty of philosophy at that time was a particularly interesting and stimulating centre. Normally, in the philosophical faculties and institutes, the student was not taught to philosophize, but instructed in the history of philosophy and restricted to the task of classifying philosophers, epochs, trends, etc. Together with Heidelberg, from 1890 onwards, Freiburg had the good fortune of receiving an uninterrupted succession of "real" philosophers of the so-called "Baden School" of Neo-Kantianism. In 1928 Martin Heidegger came to Freiburg: he had started out from Neo-Kantianism, but since 1927 had made his own radical way. There was, of course, a chair for Catholic philosophy, and this was occupied by Martin Honecker, a naïve, narrow-minded representative of that rationalistic neo-scholasticism which had little more to do with St Thomas Aquinas than had the bearded existentialists of Montmartre with the philosophy of existentialism. Rahner had to take his degree under Honecker's guidance; but as the prescriptions required him to study other subjects also for his doctorate, he was able to count among his real teachers two more well-known Freiburg scholars, the legal philosopher Erik Wolf and the historian Johannes Spörl. But Freiburg meant, above all, Martin Heidegger. Access to his famous seminar was not particularly easy. There Karl Rahner met Catholic students of Heidegger whose names are now everywhere famous: Gustav Siewerth, Bernhard Welte, Max Müller, Johannes B. Lotz, among others. He kept records also of these strenuous studies: notes on Heidegger's interpretation of Plato, Aristotle, Kant and the Pre-Socratics.

But the subject of a dissertation had to be settled with Honecker. It was to deal with thomistic epistemology: "thomistic" being understood here not in the sense of what we call thomism, not as the theories of commentators and imitators, but as the thought of Aquinas himself. Rahner wanted to write a philosophical, not an historical work. That also was the reason for choosing this theme: for Aquinas particularly the metaphysics of finite knowledge is the first approach to philosophical reflection, but —since he is essentially a theologian—it is nowhere completely and systematically worked out. Karl Rahner

21

proves that in this approach the whole of Aquinas' teaching on human knowledge is contained and brought together in an original unity. Man's knowing takes place first and foremost in the world of experience, since the human mind is constantly turned towards the outward appearance. This principle Rahner develops systematically in his interpretation of Aquinas, starting out from the nature of the human question which man poses as soon as he appears in the world and asks about being as a whole. The consequences of this approach are far-reaching.

Being as knowing, occupied with a thing here and now, is called "sensation"; knowledge of being as a whole is called "intellect"; hence there must be a primal unity of both. Thus Aquinas also says that neither sensation nor intellect can ever be found as such in the concrete: the one can be distinguished from the other only in its unity with that other. Therefore the epistemological problem is not at all that of bridging the gap between knowing and object (this "gap" does not exist for Aquinas himself, but is a rationalistic pseudo-problem created by his interpreters): it is rather how the thing known, being identical with the knower, can be confronted with the knower and how therefore there can be any knowledge at all of another as such. From now onwards, Rahner works out this possibility from the fact that sensation originates in the mind—but we cannot follow the stages of this theory of knowledge here. An introduction to his life and work does not require an extensive treatment of this theme. It is sufficient to quote the closing sentences which indicate the point which Rahner has reached at the end of this inquiry:

Aquinas as theologian is concerned with man as the point at which God shows himself in such a way that he can be heard in his revealing word: *ex parte animae.* In order to be able to hear whether God is speaking, we must know that he is; in order that his word should not reach someone who already knows, he must be hidden from us. In order that he should speak to men, his word must reach us where we are always already present, at a point on earth, in earthly time. In so far as man enters into the world, by turning to the phantasm, being as such is always already revealed to him and in it he has already acquired a knowledge of the existence of God; but at the same time also this God always remains concealed as transcending this world. Abstraction is the disclosure of being as such, which places man before God; conversion is an entry into the here and now of this finite world, which makes God the distant Unknown. Abstraction and conversion for Aquinas are the same thing: man. If man is understood in this way, he can hear whether God perhaps is speaking, because he knows that God is; God can speak, because he is the Unknown. And if Christianity is not an idea of the eternal, ever-present spirit, but Jesus of Nazareth, Aquinas' epistemology is Christian in as much as it recalls man to the here and now of his finite world; for the Eternal also entered into it, in order that man should find him and in him once again find himself.[9]

Thus Rahner is right in the midst of the study or—we might say—appraisal of the first principles of theology. As Gottlieb Söhngen once very pointedly remarked, Catholic theology since Aquinas has been marking time on these questions. We have not seized on the suggestions provided by Aquinas himself: we preferred to work with the facts, not troubling to examine more closely the reason behind them. Within the scope of Catholic theology, the theme of fundamental theology ran: If

23

God reveals himself, man must attend; but God has revealed himself, naturally and supernaturally; therefore . . . This is no answer to the pressing questions of modern thought. Why is man able to hear God at all? How does such a reception of a divine revelation take place? More particularly, how can the hearer guarantee that it is a divine revelation and render a credible account of it to others? It was here that Rahner's theological road began: in the tracks of Aquinas; in conversation with Kant, with German Idealism, with Heidegger. The road led him to the elements of a Christian anthropology, a theological doctrine of man. And precisely by reflecting on "conversion", on man's necessary self-commitment to the world, there emerged for Rahner still further ideas essential for his theology: the positive valuation of earthly realities, the discovery of the importance of human time, the new appreciation of matrimony.

The conclusions to be drawn for epistemology, as also the whole vaster horizon thus revealed, were hidden from Martin Honecker. He reproached Rahner for taking up Aquinas' suggestions and then abandoning himself to the dynamism of their content. That was, and indeed remains, a fundamental problem: the question of interpretation, of understanding what an older philosopher really said and meant. Is Aquinas properly interpreted simply by grouping his statements in their original form as a, b, c, by the historical and sterile repetition of his axioms, as had hitherto been the practice of Martin Honecker or Hans Meyer in Germany? As we can see expressly stated in the preface to his work, Karl Rahner from the very beginning was quite clearly opposed to such a method, which does not do justice to real thinking: "If the reader thus gains the impression that this is an interpretation of Aquinas derived from modern philosophy, the author will consider such an observation as indicating not a defect but an advantage of the book: if only because he did not know why he should study Aquinas except for the sake of the questions which stir his philosophy and the philosophy of his time."[10] This of course was the very reason why Honecker refused to accept the work as a philosophical dissertation.

Rahner has never defended himself against Honecker, although it would have been easy for him to do so (it would have sufficed to publish his examiner's inept marginal comments on his dissertation[11]). The work was published by Felizian Rauch of Innsbruck in 1939, with the title, *Geist in Welt* (the foreword explains: "*Geist* is used as the name of a power that reaches beyond the world to grasp the metaphysical; *Welt* is the name of the reality accessible to man's immediate experience").[12] It was promptly described as an "extremely stimulating" book, written "with unusual speculative power: undoubtedly one of the most important books on scholastic philosophy to appear in recent times".[13] In 1957 Kösel-Verlag of Munich published a second edition of 414 pages, revised and augmented by Johannes Baptist Metz (who is certainly Rahner's most speculatively gifted student). No one then in Germany remembered the name of Honecker who had not wanted to grant Rahner his doctorate in philosophy, but about the same time Martin Heidegger made one of his rare journeys in order to pay a visit to his now famous student in Innsbruck.

Before following his career further, we must take a side-glance at Rahner. He has a spontaneous inclination towards pastoral care for the individual, the renewal and deepening of faith: his sermons draw men, not through a display of rhetoric, but because he reads the hearer's secret and open questions as in a book, gives them expression and makes them his own—even if at the end all that remains is a question about the mystery of God and no ready-made recipes have been thundered out. Rahner's sermons are marked by the greatest respect for the individual person as hearer: he has never played upon those instincts which can very easily be roused in any large audience; he has never talked for the sake of talking. In brief: he is by nature what is conventionally called "a spiritual director", of the kind that Ignatius of Loyola would have wanted as director of the Exercises; he is particularly concerned with the human mind (not to be understood in a rationalist sense) and with calling it to real contemplation, but he is inclined to neglect the aesthetic aspect of things. I mention all this here because, at the time of which we are speaking, in Freiburg about the year 1934, he was invited for the first time to give retreats. From that time onwards, he has never refused such requests provided he could somehow snatch time for them.[14]

He returned in 1936 from Freiburg to Innsbruck. At the wish of his superiors he prepared himself for a doctorate in theology, writing a dissertation (still unpublished) on the Church's origin from the wound in the side of Christ as portrayed in the writings of the Fathers: as a result of this, he became doctor of theology at Innsbruck (December 19, 1936). He was expected soon to begin teaching at the university, an appointment that was not difficult to obtain under the laws then prevailing in Austria, provided the candidate could show that he had already published learned works. In fact, he had published in 1932-4 the articles on spiritual theology originally written for the novitiate magazine: in the French *Revue d'Ascétique et de Mystique*, there appeared "Cinq sens spirituels chez Origène" (1932), "Les sens spirituels au Moyen-Age, en particulier chez Bonaventure" (1933) and "Coeur de Jésus chez Origène" (1934); in *Zeitschrift für Aszese und Mystik*, "Die geistliche Lehre des Evagrius Ponticus" (1933) and "Der Begriff Ecstasis bei Bonaventura" (1934). These were accepted and he was appointed to the theological faculty at the university of Innsbruck on July 1, 1937, and in the winter term of that year began his lectures on dogmatic theology.

What was unique in Rahner's theology lay mainly in the continuation of the line of thought begun in Freiburg: his is a metaphysical, not a positive historical theology. Negatively, this means that it contains neither "leaps" nor "twists" and thus that any particular development can be traced back to the "origin".

This first became clear in 1937 at the Salzburg summer-school, when Rahner gave fifteen lectures on "the Foundation of a Philosophy of Religion". These were later worked up into a book, *Hörer des Wortes*, published in 1941. A new edition of this important work, revised by J. B. Metz, appeared in 1963.[15] He is concerned here, not with a "scientific-theoretical" foundation of the philosophy of religion as a branch of theology, but with the objective, basic question of man's relationship to God: whether and how man is positively open to a divine revelation, without there being any necessity that this revelation should take place. The question therefore is metaphysical and not yet definitely theological, but it arises precisely out of the common ground of philosophy (of religion) and theology in which the nature of man himself is in question. Man is spirit, but spirit in space and time. He can be spirit, therefore, only when he applies himself to the phenomenon. To *a* phenomenon? To the greatest possible abundance of phenomena. For the richer and more varied are these phenomena, the more there appears in them the goal of the human spirit: "being as such, that also extends beyond this world".[16] But at the same time man is himself phe-

nomenon, the most spiritual of phenomena. In him,
therefore, being as such can also reach its fullest expression. This in fact takes place at the point where man's
being is most completely realized. For Rahner that is
above all the history of mankind. If absolute, infinite
being were not to speak at all, it would still be present,
and the most essential thing about human history would
then be God's silence in it. But the history of mankind
remains the point at which God may possibly speak and
man in his innermost nature is the one who listens to the
word of God or awaits God's self-disclosure. "Only one
who hears in this way is what he really has to be:
man."[17] That is how Karl Rahner attempts to define
man: "the being of receptive spirituality standing in
freedom before God, who is free in regard to a possible
revelation: a revelation which, if it occurs, takes on the
form of a word spoken in man's history."[18] So far human
thought can reach. To elaborate it, is the function of
theology, attending in faith to the content of the word
thus uttered.

"God's communication of himself to man" thus became a kind of summary of Karl Rahner's theology of
grace, on which he lectured in Innsbruck from 1937
onwards. For him this central point of Christian dogmatic
theology gains its character from his basic reflections on
man as constantly open, attentive, and on God as freely
and without any necessity communicating himself to
man: that is, from his anthropology. Furthermore, it
bears the imprint of a sound and thoroughgoing biblical
theology and of a special understanding of patristic
theology, above all of the Greek Fathers (in which
Rahner made use of modern French studies in patrology,
particularly of the work of Henri de Lubac and Jean
Daniélou), and finally of a broad presentation of the
Tridentine teaching on justification. In all these points
28

Rahner's text on the Catholic theology of grace, which he composed in Latin and in that winter of 1937 had duplicated for the use of his students, is quite different from the usual text-book treatment. This *Codex de Gratia* was four times expanded and appeared with 350 pages in 1954 at Innsbruck. Out of this intense preoccupation with the theology of grace there also resulted a number of important articles: in the history of theology, the essays on the concept of the "supernatural" in Clement of Alexandria (in the Roman review, *Gregorianum*, 1937), on Augustine and Semi-Pelagianism (in *Zeit-schrift für katholische Theologie*, 1938), and on the scholastic conception of uncreated grace (*ibid.*, 1939); in systematic theology, the essay on the theological concept of concupiscence (*ibid.*, 1941).

Something really ought to be said here about the situation of theology generally in those years just before the outbreak of war. I shall try to do this in the second part of the book. For it is only in the light of that situation that we can understand why Rahner has raised so many and such varied theological problems. But there is one aspect that may be mentioned now. Those who belonged to that generation of theologians, then thirty to forty years old, were trying with all their mind and heart to break free from the sad state to which Catholic theology had been reduced. Some wished to free theology from the rigidity which had been caused by the severity of the Roman reaction to heretical modernism, and also to the youthful biblical movement, to Herman Schell, to the liturgical renewal and to inter-confessional discussion (we may recall the banishment of Dom Lambert Beauduin in Belgium). (From one point of view this rigidity could be excused, for there seemed nothing left now to do except to repeat what had already been said constantly for 400 years.) On the other hand, there were some who though wanting to remain Catholic, had set themselves apart from the Church and her teaching office and had published a number of books under pseudonyms and without *imprimatur*, attacking the state of affairs at the time.

Midway between these fronts was a group of young theologians who did not wish to adopt either attitude. As theologians and teachers in the Church, they wanted again to enter into conversation, to discuss; they wanted to bring to an end heresy-hunting and meddling behind the scenes in ecclesiastical politics. As in French theology, they emphasized the importance of friendly co-operation (rejecting professorial high-handedness and trying to meet the needs of the time): they wanted to engage in team work. First of all, Hugo Rahner must be mentioned in this connection: he was professor of early Church history and of patrology in Innsbruck from 1935 and co-operated at that time with his brother Karl on the content (but not on the scientific theory) of a "kerygmatic theology".[19] In Munich, also working in this direction, was a group of theologians which consisted of A. Delp, P. Bolkovac, H. Urs von Balthasar, A. Lieske (all Jesuits), and in Freiburg, Dr Robert Scherer. In 1938 Karl Rahner also joined this group. Particularly important was the new scheme of dogmatic theology which he drew up with the assistance of von Balthasar and which later appeared in the first volume of his *Schriften zur Theologie*.[20] At this time also the idea was conceived of a series of works, *Quaestiones Disputatae*, reviving from the great ages of Catholic theology a tradition of discussion and enquiry.

At first, this work had no outward success. In March 1938 National-Socialist Germany invaded Austria. The Nazis quickly exploited the initial enthusiasm of the Austrians and the cultural inferiority of the Austrian Catholics, interfering with the Church much more than

they had done in Germany itself. On July 20, 1938, they
abolished the theological faculty of the university of
Innsbruck. The professors continued their teaching in
the building of the Jesuit college, where it was possible
for a while to maintain the normal life of the order and
the daily routine. On August 15, 1939, Rahner made his
final vows in the order, taking his vows as a professed
religious in the Austrian Jesuit novitiate at St Andrä in
the Lavant valley (Carinthia).

In October 1939 the Jesuit college in Innsbruck was
closed by the Nazis. War had by now been declared and
in Germany they were preaching loyalty to the "Führer,
Volk und Vaterland". Rahner received a "district pro-
hibition" (*Gauverbot*) and was sent away from the Tyrol.
The Viennese prelate, Karl Rudolf, as the Cardinal's
delegate, offered him refuge in Vienna and took him into
the diocesan administration (with the title of "curial
counsellor") and into the pastoral institute. In his book,
Aufbau im Widerstand (an account of pastoral work in
Austria 1938-45), Rudolf describes the courageous efforts
of this Viennese group against the Nazis, the fearless way
in which they continued their theological and pastoral
activities, and in particular brings out the value of Karl
Rahner's contribution.[21] His lectures, especially in the
pastoral institute and in the church of the Friars Minor,
were concerned with anthropology as the point of depar-
ture for theology and with the philosophy of Martin
Heidegger (even in 1940, the Paris review, *Recherches
de science religieuse*, published Rahner's article on this
subject, "An Introduction to Heidegger's Conception of
Existentialist Philosophy"); but they also formed complete courses of dogmatic theology and seminars on
particular questions, on questions of asceticism and
mysticism, on sexual ethics and other problems of the
layman in the Church. In spite of the dangerous situa-

Karl Rahner

tion, Rahner left Vienna, from 1939 to 1944, to lecture in Leipzig, Dresden, Strasbourg and Cologne. In this way a foundation was established for many later publications, additional stones to be built into the structure of a modern dogmatic theology following the Munich outline.

One thing that happened during the years that Rahner spent in Vienna deserves to be recalled (it is published here for the first time). On January 18, 1943, Conrad Gröber, then archbishop of Freiburg, issued a letter of twenty-one pages addressed to the German (and Austrian) episcopate. In this letter (which lies before me, together with the rest of the material), the archbishop complains bitterly of innovations "in the field of Catholic theology and liturgy", which he sums up in seventeen points:

1. The division within the clergy between old and young (among the reckless young were included also the "liturgical agitators", the supporters of a "kerygmatic theology", the "Viennese activists", who "rush to adopt the new schemes and in the light of these to reorganize their parishes").

2. The decline of interest in natural theology.

3. A new definition of faith (the conception of faith as "becoming conscious of unity with Christ" and other similar ideas).

4. The increasing depreciation of scholastic philosophy and theology.

5. The bold and reckless reversion in practice to early and primitive times, norms and forms.

6. The one-sided preference for the Eastern Fathers, "with their peculiar ideas and forms of expression".

7. The increasing influence of Protestant dogmatic theology on the Catholic presentation of the faith.

8. Throwing open the frontiers in relation to other

Churches in order to fulfil the aims of the *Una Sancta* movement.

9. The modern concept of the Church, "according to which it is no longer the *societas perfecta*, founded by Christ, but a kind of 'biological organism'."

10. The excessive supernaturalism and the new mystical attitude in our theology.

11. The Christ-mysticism, "now flourishing, which I do not know whether to describe as astonishing or shocking".

12. The conclusions drawn from the doctrine of the mystical body of Christ ("people really seem to be forgetting that metaphors such as St Paul uses must not be overworked, but must be explained . . . in the light of the fact—which certainly holds also for St Paul—that all comparisons limp").

13. Over-emphasis on the universal priesthood.

14. The thesis of the meal-sacrifice and the sacrificial meal ("the communion of the faithful is supposed to belong to the integrity, if not to the essence, of the Mass, the practice of primitive Christianity being invoked to support this; it is forgotten that in fact, even then, on special occasions and in special conditions, Holy Communion was also received outside Mass").

15. Over-emphasis on the liturgy ("I hold, and many share my opinion, that pastoral work went on quite efficiently before an appreciation of the liturgy spread to wider circles").

16. The attempt to make dialogue Mass compulsory ("I shall always regard dialogue Mass merely as a peripheral and temporary phenomenon").

17. The attempt to conciliate the people by introducing the German language even in the Mass (the archbishop considers the adoption of the mother-

B

tongue for the Mass "a loosening of the spiritual bonds with the Church and with Rome itself").

Archbishop Gröber closes his letter with the question, "Can we—the bishops of all Germany—and can Rome remain silent any longer on these matters?"

It would be unjust to criticize this document today in the light of the encyclical on the mystical body, published shortly afterwards in June 1943, in the light of the encyclical on the liturgy, *Mediator Dei* in 1947, or finally from the standpoint of the splendid prospects set before us by Vatican Council II. The document itself was forgotten in the breakdown of the "Third Reich". But it had an effect, which is of great interest here, in connection with the life and work of Karl Rahner. Cardinal Innitzer of Vienna commissioned his pastoral institute to draw up a full refutation: it was in fact composed by Rahner, and went to fifty-three pages. Some of the items from this unpublished Viennese memorandum are reproduced here.

A preliminary observation points out that the Freiburg complaints relate to changes brought about by time which could not have been avoided and should never be delayed. "Just as the Church in earlier times, in her language, in the development of worship, in emphasizing and bringing out particular truths of faith, in her art, in the forms of her organization (so far as these are determined by variable, human, ecclesiastical law), in the concrete practices of the religious life—in all these things—naturally lived by the life of that age, so the Church today also lives into our own age. Since she has the promise of enduring to the end of time, we know she will do this also at all times and everywhere. For all that, this is a task which human beings in the Church at different times accomplish more or less well: they may, indeed, fail completely in this task in particular countries." The danger is clearly indicated of such failure leading to estrangement of the younger generation from the Church. But after that the problem is considered more deeply: "It is only when there is an honest attempt at finding new ways and means that the will to maintain tradition is likely to be effective also in the future."

"There is no reason for being disturbed by the fact that new life is everywhere stirring, or that the problems and tasks of the age are perceived and discussed, and that new ways are opened and tried. Nor need we be disturbed if this initiative is not simply stimulated by orders and directives from above, but comes out spontaneously from below. A leadership which found such a spontaneous initiative of its followers unwelcome and disturbing would thereby betray only its own uncertainty and incapacity to guide and rule a really living Church. Neither dogmatic theology nor Church history provide any evidence that the great vital movements in the Church of God, by which she meets again the needs of each new age, have always to be started by the hierarchy itself." These words closely recall what Pius XII said a few months later about the laity receiving their special charisms in the Church and for the Church.

Rahner then shows how valuable discussions are in the Church. "But in all the heat of debate mutual charity must constantly be maintained. Even when we differ on a particular question, we must still recognize always that the other person's efforts are also inspired by a real love of the Church and genuine concern for her future. Here particularly, unjust generalizations inflict wounds and create bitterness." He raises the question which is still, and indeed must ever remain, urgent in the Church: "If all those who assume that such charges and warnings are addressed to themselves were to withdraw from the

35

Church's life and letters into silence, could this loss be borne?"

He also gives practical advice: "If the complaint is raised that the ordinary parochial clergy scarcely know their way any longer in the confusion of opinions, then we must respond by urging that greater efforts be made to provide for the priest's further training by using lectures, courses, study-days and so on." This, in fact, was done after the war.

The right to appeal to the earlier ages of the Church is similarly asserted, but its limitations are noted. "For in no particular age, taken in isolation, does the Church show forth in her teaching and deeds, without reserve and with equal explicitness, the whole fullness of truth and reality bestowed on her by Christ: so we can always appeal to the Church of an earlier age or to an earlier phase in the history of theology when the very thing that we regard as necessary and useful for the situation in our own time was more clearly manifested than in the immediate past."

Rahner examines closely the state of Catholic theology in Germany at that time. The great names and achievements of historical theology are noted. But: "We are not too richly blessed with great synthetic works making the results of research into the history of dogma available to the average student, which can be turned to account for the real work of dogmatic theology. . . . What is a person to do now if he wants to read a history of dogma? Has he any alternative but to take up Harnack or, better, Seeberg? We have no compendium of biblical theology, we have no history of scholastic theology, we have no history of modern theology, we have no large Catholic history of religion, we have no history of moral theology."

Rahner never ceases to insist that scientific theology

must remain exact: theologians cannot have it handed to them, but must reach their conclusions as a result of persistent hard work. He speaks of the many good text-books in German and Latin, but points out that these provide only a basis for a real study of theology: "These text-books rightly offer the traditional teaching. But theological life with its new questionings, problems, notably in its contact with the whole modern attitude and way of thinking, and living, in Germany does not, as we might perhaps expect, express itself first in the form of strictly scientific studies: mainly and almost exclusively it is expressed in more popular writings directed to wider circles and, therefore, rightly avoiding precise definitions and closely reasoned theological argument (we may mention, for example, Peter Lippert, Romano Guardini, Eugen Walter). For all that, this phenomenon of a theological forward movement outside professional theological circles carries with it an element of danger: first, there is the danger of these hints not being properly appreciated by and embodied in the self-satisfied text-book theology; and so in the long run they will not be sufficiently far-reaching in their effects; . . . then, if the young student of theology is pressed with new questions, he tries to find an answer for himself and others on a plane which more easily permits the provisional, the non-committal, mere 'essays' and the like." He takes a glance across the frontiers: "If we may judge from the number and extent of their learned works, the French clergy appear to be bolder and more industrious in their writing and more ready to make sacrifices in order to buy books."

Even at that time, Rahner was concerned about exegesis and its relation to dogmatic theology.[22] "We perhaps cannot entirely avoid the impression that in some places the courage and confidence to venture into the sphere of exegesis on delicate, but also important and urgent questions of dogmatic theology, is not yet great enough. Severe measures on the part of the Church might indeed prevent blunders, but they could also have the unhappy result of causing these questions to be left untouched through fear of conflict with ecclesiastical authority; exegesis would be applied more or less exclusively to harmless themes, by-passing more pressing problems in this field. . . . In Germany we have no sort of large scholarly commentaries either on the Old or on the New Testament, which might make us at least independent scientifically of Protestant exegesis, . . . no theology of the New Testament, no theological dictionary of the New Testament, no manual concordance."

Afterwards, he deals with a number of individual questions raised by the Freiburg letter.

Kerygmatic theology: This he rejects completely as a science in itself, but "The average student seems unable to discover the way to live preaching from dogmatic theology as it is often taught in the colleges".

Eastern theology: "Eastern theology will always have something fresh to say to the West, as it gave new inspiration to Aquinas, Petavius and Scheeben. The theology of the East on the Resurrection and Transfiguration, on worship, on the unity of asceticism and mysticism, on symbols, and on the transfiguration of the whole cosmos through grace, can even today give a new impulse to our Western theology."

The doctrine of grace and Christ-mysticism: "At a time when man's external social and cultural ties with Christianity and the Church are in practice more or less completely broken, and when an ethical idealism is propagated even by unbelievers, the Christian can in the long run maintain his faith only by living quite consciously on what is at the very heart of Christian existence, namely, his supernatural deifying union through grace with the triune God through the Mediator Jesus Christ."

Liturgical renewal: "Since what is meant by the term 'Catholic Action' even today—and, in fact, to the highest degree—retains its importance, and as the task of the laity which it implies can be fulfilled only if they live by the power of Christ's sacrifice, the greatest possible inward and the clearest possible outward participation of the laity in the sacrifice of Christ in the Church is of fundamental importance."

Summarizing this first part, Rahner concludes that there really is no need for prohibitions and warnings from the highest ecclesiastical authorities, but there are certainly many occasions for positively promoting theological activity. He mentions a renewal of the intellectual formation of theological students, the further training of the clergy in theology, the encouragement of theological students and scholarly work by the bishops and not only by the faculties, literary planning and promotion of greater works by the episcopate. "It is by stimulating forces that one can best direct them. When all the resources are positively and confidently called upon, applied to given tasks with all that is necessary to achieve them, they are most easily directed in an orderly fashion to their goal. Only by seeking boldly a new future ourselves shall we maintain in the long run what is indispensable from the past and gain also a future for it."

Rahner devoted thirty-four pages of the memorandum to this stock-taking and programme-making of theology. The remaining nineteen pages concern philosophy. This cannot be discussed here with the same thoroughness. But one quotation may be permitted. "Modern philosophy also has its series of classical figures (Descartes, Leibniz, Kant, Fichte, Schelling, Hegel, Schopenhauer,

Karl Rahner

Nietzsche, Kierkegaard) whose thought, arising from the
intellectual divisions of modern times, is so original,
vital and deep that a live contact with them is an indispensable requirement for a living Christian philosophy
today. This does not mean any sort of immediate outward
adoption even of a single point, but a vital contact with
these philosophers compels the Christian philosopher
constantly to develop his own system afresh and from its
roots; he must break down again and again every rigid
text-book formula that is merely handed on from the past
and cut out all verbalism: in this way he will always see
afresh the eternally new similarity of problems here and
there and thus learn how to translate the language of
one philosophy into that of the other."

For Rahner's biography, it is interesting that—as this
Viennese memorandum shows—he is not merely a speculative theologian, given to clear analysis, but has practical
ideas and suggestions also. He does not waste time on
individual problems, but keeps in mind the grand
"strategy" of the Church. We need only glance at the
present situation to see how much of his programme has
since been realized. But his suggestions for reforming
theological studies have been too little noticed. I may
therefore be permitted again to quote some of his remarks on this subject:

> *Academic* teaching is teaching with the object of
> making someone, within its special subject, capable,
> in terms of learning and training, of taking his place
> among those who are working to advance that
> subject. It is this goal, and this alone, that distinguishes
> a university from a school for advanced specialists.
> Because of this, there have to be, of course, as many
> specialists in a university as there are lines of advance
> in research, determined by the respective subjects "*in
> themselves*" and differentiated according to subject and

method. Now, the academic teaching in the theological faculties of the universities is going to be done academically in this sense (no matter what modifications and omissions may be imposed by lack of time and the good sense of professors with a personal ideal of education focused on the priesthood). In itself this is an acceptable way to do it. For there has to be theological research, and hence academic training for it. But is it something for the great mass of theological students, who want to be and are to be priests later on, and not the next generation of theological research workers?

The identification between the training of a pastoral priest and of a scholarly theologian must be abolished. . . . The goal to be aimed at in the theology provided for future priests and pastors will have to involve a lightening, a concentration, and a deepening of the course of studies in comparison with what has been in use heretofore.

Lightening: We can spare the theological student a great deal of what is, for him, superfluous ballast of learned material, which he cannot really master nor make any use of later on. Obviously, a man whose abilities are both above average and, as to their quality, of a specifically *scholarly* nature, can make use later on, even in pastoral work, what he has acquired earlier in the course of his learned studies. But the abilities of the majority are not above average, and in still fewer, today, are they specifically scholarly (rational and analytical). . . .

Concentration: The existing mass of special subjects should be pulled together and regrouped from points of view that are priestly and related to pastoral practice; these need to be thought out precisely and radically. It ought to be clear that not everything that a future

41

priest has to learn need necessarily be communicated
to him by formal teaching (an obvious principle, constantly contradicted in practice). . . .

Deepening: If theology keeps its eyes resolutely
fixed on the goal of giving today's priests and pastors
what they need, then it will appear, perhaps very
quickly, that this goal cannot of course be reached by
giving a cut-down version of "scientific" theology as
it has been hitherto. Rather, it will be seen that theology (dogmatic and moral especially) needs in many
respects to be deepened, so that it can be given to
theological students in the way in which they need it.
It is, for instance, or no use (or very little use) for a
future pastor to have acquired merely the formal
framework of concepts, the facts and proofs of the
history of dogma, taught to him out of theological
sources. He cannot, when the time comes, preach that.[23]

Rahner's programme of a training for specialist theologians distinct from that given to the parochial clergy
has never, so far as I know, been adopted, although the
outline was sent with the Viennese memorandum to all
the appropriate authorities.

In summer 1944, his public activity in Vienna was
over. As the Russians advanced nearer to the city, the
terror of the SS increased. Rahner had to leave Vienna.
In July 1944, he came to a small village in Lower Bavaria
and there took over the pastoral care of the local people
and many refugees. After the entry of the Americans, he
was called in August 1945 to the Jesuit college of St
John Berchman in Pullach, near Munich, where the
study of theology had just been resumed. There he taught
dogmatic theology and also did a great deal of work in
the badly bombed city of Munich. In 1946, a year of
hunger and distress, he preached the Lenten sermons in
St Michael's Church on "Need and Blessing in Prayer".

which were published as a book two years later by
Felizian Rauch of Innsbruck. Much as I admire Rahner
as a professional theologian, I feel compelled to describe
this book, together with his small prayerbook, *Words
into Silence*, as the best and most influential part of his
work: for, in the last resort, what is learning by comparison with the realization of God in the heart of the
individual and solitary human being?

In Munich also from 1945 to 1948 he covered five
times the whole range of Catholic dogmatic theology in
courses of lectures for interested adults. In August 1948,
he returned to Innsbruck, where the theological faculty
had been restored, and took over from his predecessor,
F. Mitzka, the latter's dogmatic courses: a three-year
cycle covering creation and original sin, grace, justification, faith, hope and charity, Penance, Anointing of the
Sick and Holy Orders. On June 30, 1949, he was officially
appointed as university professor and soon afterwards
nominated as a member of the philosophical society of
Louvain. He returned to Munich recently, having been
appointed in November 1963 by the Bavarian Ministry of
Culture to take the chair previously occupied by Romano
Guardini: the title is "Philosophy of Religion and
Catholic Weltanschauung" and the course is in the philo-
sophical faculty of the university. Rahner came to live in
Munich in spring 1964 and began his lectures in May.

His career as a publicist began properly with the appointment to Innsbruck in 1949. First of all, there should
be mentioned the duplicated scripts of his three courses
in dogmatic theology: the first, on grace, has been
described above; the second script (likewise, almost a
complete manual), on the doctrine of creation and
original sin, was produced in 1950 (second edition, 1955,
with 298 pages); the third and longest deals with the
history and theology of the sacrament of Penance, first

43

appearing at Pullach as early as 1946 (fourth edition, 785 pages, Innsbruck, 1960). Solid studies on the history and theology of the sacrament of Penance also appeared one after another in *Zeitschrift für katholische Theologie*: on Penance in Irenaeus (1949), in the Didascalia (1950), in Cyprian (1952) and in the "Shepherd" of Hermas (1955); in *Recherches de science religieuse* he wrote on Penance in Origen (1950); to a *Festschrift* for Karl Adam he contributed a study of Penance in Tertullian (if this last work were published, it would provide a survey of the sacrament of Penance in all its aspects).

The many lectures which Rahner has given since the situation in Europe became normal must also be mentioned. It is impossible to enumerate them all, but the fact deserves to be stressed that he spoke at a conference of Catholic and Protestant theologians for the first time in 1948 in Bad Driburg, Westphalia, and that he has been an active member of this body ever since. It meets annually under the patronage of the local evangelical bishop and the archbishop of Paderborn, and is the prototype of the secretariat for promoting the unity of Christians, set up in Rome in 1960, drawing some of its members from the German group. One of the most prominent participants, Hermann Volk, a friend of Rahner, became Bishop of Mainz in 1962. During these years, Rahner has spoken before retreat-givers, superiors of religious orders and abbots, doctors and psychiatrists, youth-chaplains, publicists and sociologists, before teachers and university people of all kinds; he has spoken at pastoral conferences, at family associations and adult educational organizations; he has addressed philosophical societies in Innsbruck and Berne, the German liturgical commission, the study-group of *Lumen Vitae* (Brussels) and has visited for similar purposes Merano, Bolzano, Zürich, Maastricht, the abbey of Mont-César in Louvain, Trent, Basle, Haarlem, Nijmegen, West and East Berlin, Comillas, Granada, Hilversum, Salzburg, Hanover. He has been guest-lecturer at the universities of Würzburg, Bonn, Nijmegen, Heidelberg, at the Pontifical Gregorian University and the Pontifical Biblical Institute in Rome, and in many priests' seminaries. Since 1948 also he has given over a hundred radio addresses on more than a dozen wave-lengths, and has made some appearances on television.

At first, these enterprises, absorbing much time and energy, seemed to have no clear direction. The themes were suggested by the needs of the moment and were freshly prepared on each occasion: any one of them might be a part of the structure of a universal dogmatic theology as it ought to be. They belong to the scope of what I have called in the second part of this little book "the diversity and multiplicity of theological problems". In this sense Rahner has no "life's work" on which he is silently and unremittingly engaged. But for a number of years two groups of themes have been coming to the fore which are outside this field.

Since the Goerres Society set up a branch to deal with the relations between theology and natural science, Rahner has been one of its members and has taken an active part in its annual meetings. His work, for instance, on the question of hominization belongs to this sphere: [24] it is one which has first of all to be discussed between theology and natural science, but which also carries implications for a future confrontation of theology with atheistic materialism. In 1962 the Pauline Society (*Paulus-Gesellschaft*) appeared for the first time in public. It had come into being through the initiative of Dr Erich Kellner and the inspiration of the university professors, Paul Martini in Bonn and Hans Schaefer in Heidelberg. From the beginning Karl Rahner has been the theological partner in this discussion with scholars representing the natural sciences and the arts: they have made Salzburg their centre. The basis here is broader than in the Goerres Society and the problem is to reach an understanding between two ways of thinking and speaking which are more deeply estranged from one another than people in the Church think possible. The esteem in which Rahner is held in this group was shown spontaneously in summer 1962, when 250 German university professors (none of them theologians) gave written expression to their feeling.

The second group of themes may be described as "The relations between Christianity and the non-Christian religions".[25] Here also Rahner envisages a problem which cannot be avoided by the Church of the future.

All this had at least to be mentioned, since it is characteristic of Rahner's open-mindedness towards the world of today. Other items might have been added—for instance, his contacts with Erik von Kühnelt-Leddihn, Walter Dirks, Luise Rinser, Heinrich Böll, or the intense pleasure he takes in ultra-modern art—but this must suffice.

Something further must be said of the work undertaken by Rahner which has now appeared in print. The two first post-war projects required considerable industry and care for detail which had never been properly appreciated. From its twenty-eighth to its thirty-first edition (Herder, Barcelona, 1958), he improved and augmented Denzinger's *Enchiridion Symbolorum*, a collection of texts of the Church's official teaching from the earliest professions of faith to the present time, which is an indispensable source-book for theological studies.[26] Rahner also undertook some of the later editions of what amounted to a German Denzinger, with the documents arranged under subject-headings instead of in chronological order, *Der Glaube der Kirche in den Urkunden der Lehrverkündigung*, first edited by the Jesuits, J. Neuner and H. Roos (sixth edition, 1961, Pustet, Regensburg); this was obviously meant to be of particular use to lay persons studying theology.

After the war, Robert Scherer often turned to Rahner to discuss with him larger theological projects. We can trace back to these discussions two important theological works which Rahner had already suggested in his Viennese memorandum. One is a manual of the history of dogma, planned for five volumes, of which instalments have been appearing since 1951;[27] the other is a learned commentary on the New Testament of which three volumes have appeared since 1953. In addition to these two projects, Herder was anxious to keep up particularly its century-old tradition of theological dictionaries. The *Lexikon für Theologie und Kirche*, which appeared in ten large volumes between 1930-8, is naturally out of date on most points. Discussions about a new edition began in 1955 with Professor Oskar Köhler, the intention at first being to invite Rahner and his followers to contribute a number of longer articles. The draft produced by Rahner of the whole Lexicon (which was not, however, realized in its entirety), was so promising that he was asked to undertake the editorship in collaboration with Monsignor Josef Höfer (Rome). The work began to appear in 1957 under the patronage of the Archbishop of Freiburg and the Bishop of Regensburg. The ten volumes planned (each with about 1340 columns) have now appeared.[28] In more than 30,000 articles all aspects of theology and the Church are covered, together with a great variety of related topics, from Aristotle to symbolic logic, from the Stock Exchange to artificial insemination. Among the 2,400 contributors are cardinals, bishops, abbots and nearly all Catholic scholars of repute; but there are also leading contemporary Protestant and Anglican scholars. A third of the contributors are from outside Germany. We can appreciate something of the labour in which Rahner is involved in the planning and execution of this work (including proof-reading at various stages). The great success of this Lexicon shows it is appreciated for being not only a primary source of information, but also a send-off to the twenty-first century.

While working on this Lexicon, Rahner began to take up the old idea of *Quaestiones Disputatae* and planned with Herder the publication of a series of theological monographs in which themes would be presented for discussion and then left to the theologians to develop. In the preface to the first of these we read:

> Anything that a human being as a Christian might want to clarify in his own mind could find a place in this series, on the sole condition that this clarification is made with that relevance and conceptual exactitude which makes a reflection into a learned study. If we can keep the size of the individual work to reasonable limits, we may perhaps also hope that these studies, without loss to their specialist character, will find a rather wider circle of readers than merely among specialist scholars. If we succeed in helping the priest in his pastoral work to maintain a really vital contact with theology, in certain conditions also help the oft-quoted layman to find the hint of an answer to his frequently really pressing theological problems, then this would be a more pleasing result to us than the tribute of purely theological scholarship.[29]

The co-editor of this series is Heinrich Schlier; since 1957 over twenty-eight titles have appeared, several of which have already been translated into other languages.

In 1953, Dr Oscar Bettschart, director of Benzinger-Verlag in Einsiedeln, urged Karl Rahner to collect together his more important articles, spread about in various reviews, and publish them in a series of volumes. As a result, there appeared from 1954 onwards the *Schriften zur Theologie*, of which there are now six volumes containing over a hundred articles.[30] A similar collection of twenty-four articles, of a more practical and contemporary character, appeared for the first time in 1959, published by Tyrolia, Innsbruck, under the title of *Sendung und Gnade* (*Mission and Grace*). [31]

Rahner recorded for the first time in 1960 meditations on Advent, Christmas, Good Friday and Holy Saturday. These are included in the collection of sermons for the Church's year, published in Germany under the title *Kleines Kirchenjahr*, and in England and America as *The Eternal Year*.[32] Further records are being produced.

In 1961, Karl Rahner and I spent a summer holiday in writing a *Kleines theologisches Wörterbuch* (published in England and America under the title, *A Concise Dictionary of Theology*[33]), wholly, as was natural, from the standpoint of Rahner's theology. Under more than 600 headings we have tried to face and—as far as possible—answer the main problems of dogmatic theology.

In 1962, we edited a six-hundred-page symposium, *Diaconia in Christo*, in which we solicited contributions from an international group of thirty-three writers, on the important question of the revival of the diaconate (more will be said about this in the second part of this book). The work was undertaken expressly in view of the Council and its pastoral aims—for a permanent, married diaconate appears to be the only practical solution to the problems arising from the catastrophic shortage of priests in some parts of the world. At this time Rahner was already very much occupied with preparation for the Council and had written several hundred pages of expert comment on its projects.

"In spare time"—so to speak—he went on with his plans for the future. He prepared the basic outline for a manual of pastoral theology, the first volume of which was published by Herder in 1964. It is the work of a team consisting of Karl Rahner, F. X. Arnold (Tübingen), V. Schurr (Gars and Rome) and L. M. Weber (Solothurn). Considerable progress has also been made on a kerygmatic lexicon, *Sacramentum Mundi*, to be published by Herder. It will appear simultaneously in German (ed. Karl Rahner), French (ed. J. Daniélou), Spanish (ed. J. Alfaro), Italian (ed. C. Colombo), and English[34] (ed. M. O'Connell, S.J. and C. Ernst, O.P.), and perhaps also in Dutch: intended particularly as an aid to the parochial clergy and to preachers, it will be kept free from all unnecessary ballast. Finally, two well-known Swiss theologians, J. Feiner and M. Löhrer, O.S.B., are planning for Benziger-Verlag a manual of theology based on Rahner's outline course of dogma, but including also biblical and moral theology. This will be called *Mysterium Salutis* and will also appear simultaneously in several languages,[35] the contributors including Rahner's students and friends. The first volume is almost ready.

Together with Edward Schillebeeckx, O.P., and other distinguished theologians, Rahner helped to launch the international theological review, *Concilium*, of which the first issue appeared in six languages in January 1965.

This completes the main outline of Rahner's work up to the present time: some of the prospects for the future have been indicated. It is, of course, obvious that so tremendous an achievement with such vast horizons, emerging from so personal a temperament, was bound to rouse strong but justifiable opposition, as well as envious polemics and unreal difficulties. We cannot discuss all this here. But it is certain even now that these criticisms do not seriously affect his work as a whole.

Since 1960 the signs of official recognition by the Church have become more and more apparent. In 1960, Karl Rahner was named consultor to the commission *De Sacramentis*, in preparation for the Second Vatican Council. In 1962, he accompanied Cardinal König of Vienna (a bishop who represents to a rare degree the ideal Pope John had in mind), as theological adviser, to the first session of the Council; there, too, he had the opportunity of explaining his ideas on the preparatory schemes before cardinals and bishops; finally he was chosen by Pope John to join the first group of 195 council experts and so was able to take part in the sessions of the Roman commissions during the first half of 1963. It may be possible at a later date to describe how highly Pope John spoke of Karl Rahner in 1962 in the garden at Castel Gandolfo.

On November 7 and 25, 1963, Rahner had private audiences with Pope Paul VI. The Pope thanked him for his work in theology and at the Council, telling him to continue boldly on the way he had opened; he also said that he had read several of his books and would like to keep in close contact with him. Rahner also attended the subsequent sessions of the Council.

On the occasion of his sixtieth birthday, March 5, 1964, he was given the honorary degree of doctor by the Catholic theological faculties of Münster and Strasbourg. This coincided with the publication of an enormous two-volume *Festschrift*, with contributions and congratulations from cardinals, bishops, theologians, philosophers and other scholars from all parts of the world.[36] Here, too, is further evidence of the importance of Karl Rahner's work for the Church and the world.

2 Basic Questions of Karl Rahner's Theology

The following attempts a brief survey of the theological positions taken up by Karl Rahner. Since this is the first time it has been done, I shall have to repeat—although from a different standpoint—some of what was said in the first part. But in this brief introduction I cannot hope to cover everything.

A preliminary remark may be permitted. Much of Rahner's work is simply an exposition of traditional teaching, particularly when it is a question of his lecture notes or of articles in a lexicon. To crave for originality at any price would be even less fitting in a Catholic theologian than in any other scholar. This is a fact, then, that need not be passed over with embarrassing silence. Here I want to try to show only where Rahner's independence and thus the progress of Catholic theology can be discerned. In all this it is not easy to find a simple and practical principle on which to base and arrange the material. Inevitably, perspectives partly overlap.

1. *The philosophical fermentation of theology*

Karl Rahner is convinced that we must *think* if we are to say anything that matters in theology. He is equally convinced that our thinking must begin from the modern situation, from *modern philosophy*; and that this may be done without preconceived ideas. He is finally convinced that the proper function of theology is not to look back and meditate on its history, but constantly to *renew the effort* of dealing with objective theological questions. Even when the development of dogma has led to the classical formulations of the Church's teaching authority, there remains more to do than simply repeat these classical formulations and explain historically how they came to be established. We may, therefore, understand some of Rahner's theological positions in the light of the basic positions of his philosophy.

We need not overrate the originality of this philosophy. It belongs to that group of essays in philosophy which even now can best be described by linking them with the name of Maréchal. This modern Christian philosophy cannot really any longer be called "neo-scholasticism", since—while holding this tradition in respect and even keeping it alive—it is in fact engaged in direct, unprejudiced and frank discussion with the philosophy of Kant, the German Idealists and contemporary Existentialism.[37] It is not merely the preservation of tradition.

Although they differ considerably among themselves, there is a unity of approach on the part of these philosophers, among whom may be mentioned Siewerth, Max Müller, Hayen, Marc, de Waelhens, Dondeyne, Welte, Lotz and Coreth. To describe their philosophy objectively, in very few words (and somewhat broadly), we might perhaps say this: it deliberately carries further a number of points raised by Aquinas, but understands modern philosophy from within and enters into discussion with it, while conceiving itself as a *transcendental philosophy*. That is to say: it unfolds the *a priori* conditions for the possibility of ontological knowledge and freedom in the subject itself. So it is able from its own resources to develop the themes of contemporary existentialist philosophy. It faces present-day philosophy; it is not merely anxious, on the defensive, but appreciates this "turning to the subject" (properly understood) as an event in the history of the mind, at root inspired by Christianity and its conception of man; so it belongs to

Karl Rahner

the intellectual history of Christianity itself. Because of its anthropocentric, subjective (not "subjectivist") starting point, by contrast with the ancient cosmocentric outlook, this philosophy has an intimate understanding of man's history and of his historical condition. In such themes, embracing history and essence, it sees that a function of the philosophical situation is also imposed upon it ultimately by the Christian conception of existence.

Karl Rahner belongs to this group. His work on the epistemology of Aquinas, as I have already said, is meant to be fundamentally a systematic study and not merely the record of what others have thought in the past. If Rahner sees the human-finite spirit in its transcendental, *a priori* relationship to God, this is a conception which he owes to Maréchal's basic insight and he makes no secret of the fact. Rahner goes further by showing how human sensation emerges from the mind, how this mind can discover itself only by finding expression in symbols; he goes further by providing a transcendental foundation for man's turning to his concrete history—which cannot be explained in terms of any previous condition—as the real point at which the mind can discover its very self as that which is related to the mystery of the infinite.

In his second and last philosophical book, Rahner speaks of man as one who—in virtue of the synthesis of transcendence and history actually realized in him—is necessarily open to a revelation of God which can possibly enter into his history. Perhaps Rahner at that time, when writing *Hörer des Wortes*, did not see as clearly as he later stated it[38] that man's concrete nature, as he experiences it in history and presupposes—even if only implicitly—it in his philosophy, is already conditioned by a "supernatural existential". All of which means that,

54

merely on the basis of a purely natural transcendentality, man can never in fact learn that he is open to a revelation which God may possibly grant; but he is also in his self-reflection already more than mere nature (even if, by simply reflecting on himself, he cannot distinguish what is his natural being and what is in fact an openness through grace to an actual, freely decided divine self-communication). All the same, Rahner's scheme of a philosophy of religion is distinguished from similar attempts in the Catholic field by the fact that he does not artificially construct a merely "natural religion". If this is done, it is all-too-easy to be content with the possession of such a "natural religion": thus a positive revealed religion would be imperilled, for it may then easily come too late to those who are satisfied with the "natural". When Rahner analyses the being to whom a possible revelation is addressed, he does not stick—like the average author of a work on fundamental theology—at a purely formal subject of objective knowledge. He does not establish the possibility of a revelation merely objectively, from the nature of God and his possible deeds. We can easily see what consequences this analysis may have for the preaching of positive revelation to modern man and to the modern world.

Do these basic philosophical views also have an effect on theology itself? For Karl Rahner they certainly have. The point must be raised here, since modern Christian philosophy on the whole has not yet had much influence on theology. In the history of dogma, the influence of the historical method is still too pronounced; systematic theology is often too much inclined to see possibilities of real progress only in peripheral questions and not in the decisive, basic positions of Christianity. Here I would like to point to just a few such influences of this modern philosophy on Rahner's theology.

First of all, there is his *theology of mystery*.[39] For Rahner, the fact that a truth is a mystery (a mystery, that is, of the Christian revelation), does not mean first and last a *negative* qualification of these truths, as if a mystery were always something *still* concealed from us, simply because we are human beings belonging to this world. It shows rather that the creaturely transcendence of the finite spirit is of its very nature related to mystery *as such*. Mystery alone is the true goal of knowing and loving transcendency, so that every quest for understanding arises from the abyss of mystery. And this mystery is man's beatitude. It is not dissolved in the intuitive vision of God, nor does it mean a mere limit to the beatific vision: it means rather that man *is* himself transcendency to mystery as such.

So, for Karl Rahner the three basic mysteries of Christianity—Trinity, Incarnation and Grace, which is completed in glory—are to be understood from this basic nature of man, without thereby losing their character as mystery and without the Incarnation and Grace ceasing to be free dispositions of God himself.

Incarnation and Grace are indeed *the two ways* in which absolute mystery freely and without any obligation communicates itself to man in absolute closeness. In them man's relationship to absolute mystery, the *potentia obedientialis*, is fulfilled.[40] There is here a real self-communication of God to the creature (Rahner defines it more closely as true "quasi-formal causality", as distinct from a created gift). Thus Rahner starts out from the word of revelation, from the "economic" relationship of God to the creature in the twofold "mission", and in this way reaches the necessary diversity in God of the two "processions" which are proper to God in himself. I do not think that any theologian has ever before approached this problem in the same way, namely, that the *divine trinity* in itself has something to do with God's treatment of man in history and vice versa. Rahner, using a theological "telegram style", formulates it thus: the economic trinity (God's triune nature for us) and the immanent trinity (God's triune nature in itself) are in reality the same.[41] But we have to be very cautious in using the concept of "person": it was easier for the theology of the early Church, not confronted as we are today with a notion of person which might lead us to a belief in three gods.

This is a philosophical theology, because Rahner understands man's transcendentality not only as a formal, purely neutral condition for his supernatural destiny and fulfilment, but as a preliminary draft in which these are implicitly contained, even though the order of the Incarnation and of Grace remains beyond all our deserts.

He makes further use of this basic conception to prepare the way for a deeper theological understanding of the mystery of the *hypostatic union* (the unity of God and man in Jesus Christ). It is an approach to be found today otherwise only in the work of B. Welte and F. Malmberg.[42] On this topic also only a brief comment is possible here.

Rahner sees man's nature in its transcendentality in such a way that the hypostatic union—obviously freely chosen by God and in no way due to us—is conceived as the supreme actualization of what man is as spirit. Thus the opposition between a merely static, ontic Christology and a modernistic consciousness-Christology is overcome in a truly ontological Christology.

In this context, Rahner wrestles particularly with the problem of how Jesus is not a God dealing with us in human form, but really God and simultaneously truly man, so that both dogmatic theology and exegesis (with the data obtained from "the quest of the historical Jesus") can therefore be right. To solve the problem, he starts out from the fact that only a *divine* person can possess a freedom really distinct from him as his own, in such wise that it does not cease to be truly free even in regard to the divine person who possesses it and yet qualifies this person himself as its ontological subject. "For we can conceive of no one but God personally constituting a being distinct from himself."[43] From this standpoint, incidentally, we can maintain the Catholic teaching that the human consciousness of Jesus has an immediacy to the divine essence (that is, his human soul had even on earth the *visio immediata*, the intuitive vision of God) and yet respect the biblical accounts of his "learning", "not knowing"—in a word, of his growth as a man.

This philosophy of the transcendentality of the human mind provides Rahner with an opportunity of solving the old controversy between thomists and molinists.[44] Even if the reader is not trained in theology, it is to be hoped that he will read on at this point: for we are concerned with one of Rahner's central themes, from which magnificent prospects emerge.

In the theology of the schools the controversy centres on the question whether a salutary act (a human act raised to a higher mode of being by the supernatural grace of God) needs a proper "formal object", which cannot be attained by a purely natural act.

Here Rahner brings a new factor into the discussion: a *transcendental experience* which cannot be formulated as theme, concept or proposition, in which the formal object is present not in the manner of an object but as an unspecified horizon—and yet is truly present. Thus Rahner strictly maintains—against Molina and against a good many of the post-Tridentine theologians—the thomist doctrine of a proper formal object for every supernatural, salutary act. But he does not stop at the difficulty usually raised against this doctrine: man "perceives" nothing of such a formal object. For according to Rahner the unspecified, *a priori* openness of the natural mind towards being as such and the unspecified *a priori* transcendentality of the mind elevated by supernatural grace are (from the nature of the case) so interlocked with one another that a secondary reflexion cannot necessarily draw one away from the other. And even without direct reflexion, the dynamism directed towards the absolute self-communication of God can therefore be really present in consciousness and have an effect on man's individual and collective mental history. And in this respect we cannot necessarily distinguish it from the unlimited, natural transcendental openness of man.

These considerations lead Rahner to the idea of a *universal and yet supernatural revelation* which is of great importance for the interpretation of redemptive history and of the relationship of Christianity to non-Christians and to non-Christian religions.[45] Rahner takes as his basis the fundamental principles of Catholic theology, the import of which has not yet been measured: God wills the salvation of all men, even though they are in a fallen state. This supernatural will for salvation means for all men at all times—because of Jesus Christ—the offer of supernatural grace (as an interior, really existing factor in the individual and collective history of the human mind), no matter whether this grace is accepted or rejected. These are principles which bind every Catholic theologian.

Rahner argues: Such a communication of grace then means also a change in man's transcendental mental horizon, within which he carries on his history. And there exists also from the very beginning something like a universal history of a transcendental character concerned with a revelation which reaches *all men*. But that is not to say that man is at all times, at every spatial-temporal point of his history, in an objective dialogue with God, formulated and given expression in propositions: in this sense there is not everywhere and at all times an express, thematic, special and official history of revelation. Such a history exists only when God speaks to man also in human words, which can be given conceptual expression, and confirms by signs and wonders the legitimacy of this incarnation of the absolute, divine word in the human. But because of the universality of God's will to save and because of the supernatural grace of Christ in all men, there is nevertheless everywhere already a universal history of revelation: for every free self-communication of God to man may be called revelation, even if it occurs first of all in the transcendental and not yet in the categorial region of human consciousness.

Here lies the pointer to Rahner's doctrine of the "anonymous Christian" and of the "believer in God and Jesus Christ", who in fact thinks that he does not or cannot believe. If what has been said is correct, then there must and can be human beings who have a transcendental, supernatural experience and who by reason of their freedom have accepted this in faith and charity, but who misinterpret it in conceptual terms. That is why such people maintain—in what is always a secondary reflexion—that they are not Christians, perhaps even that they are not theists.

From this starting point we can also recognize in *non-Christian religions* at the historical stage before their real confrontation with Christianity the character of a legitimate religion (in the theological sense, not merely in the sense of a self-evident social toleration).[46] According to the Catholic notion of religion, man can live and necessarily lives only in a religion that is organized socially: it follows that every religion—socially and historically established—that we really meet in a person's historical environment and is, within that environment, the "better", must have in the divine intention of salvation a positive salutary function for that person, and must be "legitimate" for him.

As we see from the Old Testament example, it is not absolutely necessary to the notion of a legitimate religion that in its concrete-historical form there are present only elements positively willed by God. It is not absolutely necessary that an adequate and institutionally established criterion exist to distinguish between divinely willed factors and the phenomena of human degeneration in this religion. It is not absolutely necessary that conceptual reflexion on the religious person's supernatural, transcendental, basic experience of God's grace-giving closeness should always be successful (even if it is never completely lacking and will never be entirely unsuccessful). Finally, it is not absolutely necessary for this historically progressing conceptual reflexion on the basic mystery of religion to be expressed in a form which can be grasped historically and reflexively as given and legitimized by God—as it is in the eschatological situation of Christianity, in which the God-man is present and grasped by faith as the absolute and final synthesis of divine self-giving and its human acceptance.

The metaphysics of the transcendentality of the finite mind—of which we are still speaking here—is applied by Rahner, surprisingly enough, to the doctrine of creation.[47] In this respect he develops and deepens the transcendental philosophy of Maréchal. Absolute being is seen not merely as the goal—static in itself—of the spirit, towards which the latter would move in virtue of

its own dynamism, but as the moving force of this movement itself. The doctrine of final causes begins again to
be taken seriously. Absolute being is the inner force of
the spirit's self-movement, without thereby becoming a
constitutive element of the being of the finite spirit itself.

Rahner then takes this relation of the absolute spirit
to finite being as an instance or example of the becoming
of any being at all: there is a becoming of a created being
when that becoming arises from the creature's active
potency; in principle, this is *self-transcendence*, in which
this being actively seeking fulfilment surpasses itself in
virtue of that absolute being which inwardly belongs to
it, without thereby constituting a part of its nature. From
this conclusion Rahner attempts a synthesis between the
teaching of faith on the one hand—namely, that all finite
being is created and that there are essential differences
between the individual spheres of being—and on the other
the conception of the world as an evolutionary, ascending
process. If it could thus be shown that the notion of
active self-transcendence in virtue of absolute being is
irreducibly original and legitimate, that would be very
important for the future. The traditional theological
notions of the divine conservation of the world and God's
concurrence with creatures could be grasped in a modern
and deeper fashion; at the same time, the world in all its
structures would be left to its own laws (the "secular
world"), without this necessarily involving a profanation.

Finally, the doctrine of the transcendentality of the
finite spirit provides also the background for Karl
Rahner's efforts—which, of course, he shares with other
important theologians of the present time—to establish
the true difference between nature and grace in such a
way as to avoid any "extrinsicism" in the theology of
grace. "Nature" cannot and must not be conceived as in
the concrete complete in itself, rounded off and obvious,

with grace as something granted over and above all this as an unsought and unnecessary gift: rather in the same way that a house with a perfectly habitable first storey might unexpectedly have a second artificially placed above it.[48]

2. *Theology called to preaching*

I would like to emphasize once again what I said already in the first part of this little book: we would misunderstand the work of Karl Rahner if we were to regard his theories as primarily inspired by speculative-philosophical interests. The impulses coming from the present-day state of spiritual distress (which is concealed by our technical, positivist outlook), that is, from pastoral concern—in other words, the kerygmatic and pastoral-theological inspiration—are in principle more decisive for him personally and for his work. Naturally, it is not possible to trace back easily and clearly Rahner's quite definite particular theories, but this inspiration does really penetrate his whole theology. No matter how greatly he appreciates the value of theological-historical work, he refuses for his own part even more decisively to be a scientific theologian for the sake of theological scholarship. We must therefore mention in this context also his less scholarly enterprises: books of sermons, of prayer and devotion, and reviews of gramophone records —all of which might easily ruin a scholar's reputation in Germany. Nor is the composition of a theological pocket dictionary the way to harvest the laurels of scholarship.

As with the plans I mentioned earlier, all this can be understood in one way only: by every means and as well as he possibly can, he seeks to help the priest and the educated layman to preach afresh and to seize in its

original spirit the old Gospel, so that it really reaches
man in his present situation. To Rahner it does not
really matter at all whether or not such an enterprise
appears scholarly. The same mentality can be seen also
in the thick volume of collected essays on pastoral
theology, with its acute analyses of the situation of the
Church and of Christianity today and with its bold programme for the Church's future.[49] Whether he is talking
there about pastoral care of prisoners, parish libraries,
our attitude to modern literature, missions in the railway-
stations or anything else, he is determined to bring
together reflections on theological principles and the
practice of a Christian life.

Two aspects, which are characteristic of this attitude,
deserve special mention. First, there is an emphasis on
the spiritual and social *pluralism* of the modern world,
and the diaspora situation of the Church and the individual Christian which results from this. Rahner explains that this is a redemptive-historical "must" for the
Christian to view and appreciate without prejudice. He is
always insisting that the Christian and the Church today
can exist only if they cease to be anxious and on the
defensive in a Christian and ecclesiastical ghetto (mental,
cultural and ecclesiastico-political); if they are able to
appreciate the worldliness of the world as something
which from the standpoint of Christianity must be something positively willed by God. That is not to render
innocuous this world, its guilt and its peril.

The worldliness of the world corresponds in principle
to the Christian belief in its pure createdness and in the
essential difference between nature and grace : it springs
from this faith. It is therefore a Christian duty and virtue
to endure the persistent and—once again—plural worldliness of the world in patience and sober realism precisely
in its earthly structures, not wanting to bring about by

force the kingdom of God either in an ecclesiastical state
or in a direct consecration of the earthly spheres: for
the Church is still only a beginning, a promise and a
sacrament of the kingdom of God. If the worldliness of
the world is seen as completely legitimate, if it is recognized that its persistent opposition to the Gospel has to
the very end a redemptive-historical function, inevitably
serving the salvation and grace of Christ even in an
"anonymous Christianity", then the prognoses of
"Christianity's chances" may be sober and yet hopeful.[50]
The Christian can be a confessor of the Gospel, a witness
to Christ, without slipping into the rôle of a narrow-
minded sectarian and monomanic ideologist, without
making God's power and God's mercy cease at the point
where he himself or his Church reaches a frontier.

Secondly, the *ecumenical motive* is essential in Karl
Rahner's theology. A theological attitude which recog-
nizes the pluralism of the contemporary world partly as
a necessity springing from the nature of man, partly as a
redemptive-historical "must", cannot overlook the fact
of Christian divisions. It cannot ignore the fact that
Catholic theology can also learn from Evangelical, and
not merely in matters of history and exegesis. Thus we
can always perceive in Rahner's work an effort to learn
from Evangelical theology, using its presentation of
problems to extend the horizon of his own questioning,
and—without falling into a false irenicism—so to formu-
late his own theology and the Church's dogma that these
present to Evangelical Christians and theologians only
those difficulties in understanding which simply cannot
be avoided. Only from this standpoint can a good deal
of what Rahner has said on "the many Masses and the
one sacrifice", on "transubstantiation", indulgences, the
notion of *opus operatum*, and the personal aspect of the
efficacy of the sacraments, be quite justly appreciated.[51]

Karl Rahner

In all this there constantly appears one of Rahner's fundamental preoccupations: even a dogmatically binding and permanently valid formulation must not be regarded as the final stage—never to be surpassed—of a development now brought to its close. It must be seen also as a formulation which—without prejudice to its permanent validity—is open on to the mystery, which never says everything that is true and important from the Christian standpoint, which can create for non-Catholics real difficulties in understanding and therefore likewise constantly imposes on Catholic theology a task to be fulfilled anew. What Rahner had been saying and trying to do for years was confirmed at the highest level by Pope John XXIII in his cheering words at the first session of the Council—a test of the loyalty to the Church of those representatives of a nervous intolerance who otherwise appealed on all occasions to the Pope. Rahner's work is inspired by the thought that the Catholic theologian must always look for the "guilt", for what causes the opposition of other Christians to the theology of his Church, in himself also: for his Catholic theology, too, remains a *theologia viatoris et peccatoris*, a theology of the pilgrim and the sinner.

3. *The diversity and multiplicity of theological problems*

What has to be said in this third section may at first sight create the impression that I have gathered together here simply what I could not bring under the first two headings: in other words, that it is not really a genuine aspect of Karl Rahner's theology. But it is different if we look at the matter more closely. Characteristic of Karl Rahner is the way he adapts himself to the variety of problems brought to him. I want to try to analyse the temporal-historical reason for this.

The period after the first world war meant for the life of the Church and also—involved in this—for theology a definite break and to some extent a new beginning, sharply distinguished from the Church's earlier conservative and defensive attitude. We may recall the movement for liturgical revival, the fact that Catholics were at least in part familiar with the forms of the democratic State (as, for instance, freedom of the press) and undertook political responsibility within the really modern States where Church and politics were kept completely apart. We may recall what was said in the first section about the transformation of philosophy from an essentially restorative neo-scholasticism to a Christian philosophy which is obviously a part of modern intellectual life; we may also mention the emergence of a Catholic literature which no longer confuses comfortable bourgeois sentiment with literary power. We may mention a new Christian art which is no longer neo-gothic, Nazarene or a youthful style; we can look at the new appreciation of the independence, literacy and world-responsibility of the laity, no longer merely objects of the clergy's spiritual ministrations, but active holders of human and Christian functions—and that indeed in the Church's sphere.

When we reflect on this transformation, we can say today in retrospect that the *first generation*, which attained the peak of its social, intellectual and ecclesiastical achievement between the two world wars, brought this new mentality only in a very general way into theology. It was still too early for the new spirit to have an effect on the handling of technical theological problems. In Germany, for instance, theologians like Peter Lippert, Romano Guardini, Erich Przywara and others opened the new period of theology still more or less in a general fashion. They represented the new spirit, but they scarcely entered into the really individual theological problems.

Karl Rahner

The theological text-books, therefore, which certainly go into details, took no notice of these great representatives of the new period. Their names are not to be found in the text-books at all. But there are other reasons for this.

The new movements in the Church arose—and indeed partly arise today—not properly within theology and Christian philosophy at their scientific level. They arose rather out of the life of the Church herself, not from the "official" and, therefore, far too readily conservative circles, but from those which are interested from both the religious and intellectual points of view. The new beginnings in theology, therefore, were seen at first and almost inevitably in the literary form known as *haute vulgarisation*. We must not be too quick to seize on the unpleasant after-taste this word has. We must not think that there can be no genuine and creative achievement in this form of literature. But we can also understand that the themes have to be very general in order to be sure of an immediate interest on the part of this class of reader. Guardini's, Lippert's or even Karl Adam's works are typical in this respect.

Finally, there is one thing that we must not forget. This first generation between the two world wars had experienced the trauma of modernism in their youth when they were studying philosophy and theology and had known that reaction of the Church—perhaps on the whole necessary—which in the intrigues and heresy-hunting of integralism betrayed its all-too-human and indeed repulsive side.[52] It is not surprising that this generation often anxiously avoided tackling or dealing systematically with themes which, they feared, were bound to give rise to conflicts. The tendency at the time was to side-step these dangers from the beginning by choosing both theme and style in such a way that they were without interest to "informers" and "denouncers".

One exegete wrote biblical novels, another plunged into a harmless history of the Vulgate, the third changed sides from exegesis to moral theology—a safe subject at the time. If the dogmatic theologian had no desire or gift for discussion with educated people in the Church or despisers of religion outside her, he simply concentrated on editing texts, the retrospective history of dogma, and left the official theology of the schools as it had hitherto been. This may be seen in the manuals—thorough in their way and respectable—of Bartmann, Diekamp, Pohle, Van Noort and Tanquerey. It was possible in those years to become famous by editing a few medieval manuscripts; in that way, one became sure of a mention later in the theological dictionaries. But one question was never raised: had the earlier theology been so stupid as not to observe what "treasures" were reposing in these manuscripts? or did much remain unprinted two or three hundred years ago because it was not worth printing?

It is from these positions alone that the peculiar character of the *second generation* can be understood. It can no longer be content with proclaiming a new spirit, an open attitude, unprejudiced towards the modern age, its mentality and art. It can no longer be satisfied with the fact that the new spirit exercises an influence solely on the practice of the Christian life. It must face the whole range of individual problems in philosophy, theology and the life of the Church, and here vindicate the new spirit—it must show that this belongs both to the Church and to the present time, not only in general but in the immeasurable complexity of individual problems. Only when this really succeeds, can Christians feel—so far as that is possible in a world of sorrows—the present as an obvious sphere of existence, completely in accordance with Christianity. Only then does it become clear that we have to do more than defend Christianity against

69

a new age: we have to present Christianity as the new, divine response—which today alone is really complete and intelligible—to the question which our historical present and the future advancing upon it impose and are. It cannot be said that the second generation in general is devoting itself to this task with particularly great zeal and success. But there are advantages in this: all the patriotic and nationalist tones are finally vanishing from theology, for this second generation is forced into international co-operation. All the same, we gain the impression that the tempo of the present time provides more tasks than can really be mastered by the theologians.

It is only by reflecting on what has just been said that we can properly understand the unique character of Rahner's theology. We shall see that what I want to say in this third section, in spite of the disparity and diversity of the themes, can nevertheless be appreciated from a unified standpoint. In face of the "diversity and multiplicity" of the problems, I have attempted neither a systematic nor an exhaustive treatment, but sought merely to indicate how a theologian of the second generation attempts for his part to do justice to the tasks outlined here. But the reader must keep in mind both these horizons within which all Rahner's individual works must be considered. Rahner's basic attitude is—by contrast with the ancient cosmocentrism—anthropocentric (and thereby radically theocentric and christocentric); it is transcendental and personalist, it takes man's historicity and his "existence" seriously. And all this theology is intended to serve a kerygmatic function, so that the harmony of Christianity with the mentality of the present time can come into the open.

I begin then with the problem of the *development of*

dogma.[53] In spite of all the difficulties arising from the history of dogma, Rahner insists that we can understand this development rightly and from the Catholic standpoint only if we stick to the principle that the understanding of faith in the Apostolic Church and in the Church today are closely linked with one another even on the conceptual plane and in logical reflexion. The unfolding of dogma cannot be left *merely* to an irrational instinct of faith, beyond rational explanation, or to the *formal* authority of the Church's teaching office *alone*. Naturally, the history of dogma is largely a history of the way in which what had been present implicitly became explicit. Obviously, this implication involves a mental reality in which the elements are not merely concepts. Obviously also, the process of making explicit takes place primarily in the Church's historically developing understanding of faith and not merely in the theologian's study. But Rahner emphatically declares that this process of making explicit must in principle—at least after the event—be capable of being worked out logically (although this does not mean that the certainty of the conclusion rests solely upon the stringency of such a logical-conceptual elaboration). If this were not so, says Rahner, the development of dogma would no longer preserve the revelation which closed with the apostolic preaching, but would be imperceptibly transformed into a new post-apostolic revelation. This campaign for a correctly understood rationality in theology has various consequences.

More clearly than some theologians in fact see it, Rahner explains first of all that if theologians in their work rightly appeal to the Church's understanding of the faith today and to the decisions of the teaching authority today, they can indeed in this way reach a legitimate conclusion of faith. But they are not thereby released from the duty of showing *how* the modern dogma was contained in the apostolic preaching or how it can be proved by a legitimate logical process of being made explicit as really revealed by God himself. When we recall this, we can at once understand the position which Karl Rahner adopts—with many other theologians in the wake of J. R. Geiselmann—in regard to the relation between *Tradition and Scripture*[54] and which he vehemently defended at the second Vatican Council.

If we place the above-mentioned demand before tradition and theology, and consider soberly and objectively how much (or, better, how little) we know historically of this tradition, then a theologian can no longer claim that ancient tradition offers us more by way of really binding, material contents of faith than is also contained in Scripture—apart perhaps from the single instance of our knowledge through faith of the delimitation of the canon of Scripture. At least for us, tradition cannot in practice and in the concrete be placed alongside Scripture as a materially distinct source of the contents of faith : it is, on the contrary, the formal authority which carries Scripture, declares it to be sacred Scripture, that is to say, determines its canon. This means that we must not conceive the authentication of the canon by tradition alone as one example *among others* of how tradition mediates a truth of faith which is found neither explicitly nor implicitly in Scripture. If then we conceive the Tridentine statement on the relation between Scripture and Tradition in this way, we could also come to an understanding with Protestant theology on this problem : for Protestant theology also has gradually learned that Scripture itself is carried by the apostolic oral kerygma of Christ's authorized messengers, that it is the solid substance of this teaching, remains constantly dependent upon it, and can never be understood otherwise than as an instrument of the authoritatively teaching Church (no matter how much this Church precisely in this respect places herself under the word of God in Scripture, interprets this and adds nothing "new" to it).

If we adopt this doctrine, that Scripture is in practice materially sufficient for us, without in any way questioning the importance of the teaching office and of tradition, then we must also have a well thought out idea of the ways in which the later Church can render explicit the apostolic kerygma. And Karl Rahner has a very exact idea of this. He does not restrict these possibilities of the later Church by the sceptical positivism of the exegetes who are no more than that or of the pure historians—of those who, unless their own spirit moves them, make the ancient letter so rigid that its content can no longer be unfolded in history. In a lengthy manuscript already completed before the definition of the bodily assumption of Mary into heaven, Rahner demonstrated his theory of the development of dogma precisely with reference to this most extreme case. He shows there how Mary's assumption into heaven is really contained materially in Scripture and bases the "new" dogma on divine revelation. How ironical that a small mind was able from 1950 onwards to hold up the publication precisely of this work which might have spared the Church so many malicious attacks!

Karl Rahner's doctrine of the *Inspiration of Scripture* also has sometimes been grotesquely misunderstood. It has been asserted that he taught a "collective inspiration".[55] There can be no question of this; but one may well be surprised to see how incapable some theologians are of reading their colleagues' books (and what simplicity of mind is betrayed in book reviews). For Rahner also, it is the actual author of the individual book who is inspired by God and no one else. But, he maintains,

73

this divine inspiration of the individual biblical author takes place directly and formally in order that this work of his should emerge *as* a factor in making the apostolic kerygma objective and as a book of the "primitive Church", believing on account of this apostolic kerygma.

The purpose of inspiration is, therefore, first of all, to ensure that by means of it this primitive Church (because of the apostolic witness) should become and should be the permanent and irrevocable norm of faith for the later Church: it can become and be such by thus being made objective. From this standpoint it is easy for Rahner to understand why the determination of the canon could have a long history: his problem is to establish how the Church's authoritative understanding of the canon may be legitimized. For this purpose, there is no need to appeal—as used to be done—to explicit apostolic testimony to the inspiration of each particular book. Such testimony is neither obvious nor historically plausible. Nor do we need to postulate new, later revelations—which in fact would not be compatible with the Church's teaching that apostolic revelation is closed. Without any new revelation, by reason of her living awareness of faith, the later Church can distinguish the legitimate objectification of the apostolic Church's awareness of faith from other religious testimonies of the first age—and it does not matter when she does this. If we assume that God formally set up the primitive Church's understanding of faith as the enduring norm for the later belief of the Church precisely through the fact of the emergence of the New Testament Scriptures and their becoming through inspiration the word of God in the proper sense of that term, then the determination—possible without new revelation—of how to objectify the faith of the primitive Church by the later Church is of itself and simultaneously also the determination of the canon of the Scriptures, which are the word of God himself.

From the *ecclesiology* of Karl Rahner I shall select here only the more important themes. Rahner attempts to define more precisely the relationship between the *papal primacy and the episcopate*.[56] He wants to render intelligible the doctrine that the bishops—in spite of the pope's universal primacy of jurisdiction, even over the bishops—are not the pope's subalterns, but (in the biblical sense) "pasture" their "flock" in the name of Christ himself and always form together the supreme ruling body in the Church, which itself possesses supreme authority in teaching and legislating in union with the pope but not properly as derived from him (for this would be a contradiction of the very idea of supreme authority).

Rahner insists that while the episcopal college can *never* be conceived as independent of the pope or as an institution with its own competence set up against him, the pope always and everywhere acts *as* the competent head of the episcopal college. Personal primacy of jurisdiction and primacy in teaching belong to the pope because he is personal head of the episcopal college, which acts in him and through him even when he is acting alone. This is clear from the fact that there exists the above-mentioned teaching of faith on the bishops and that the pope is not tied to definite and immutable legal formalities in regard to the rest of the episcopate in order to be able to act as head and representative of the college. If it were maintained that there existed such definite formalities, legal and legally controllable, binding the pope once and for all, then pope and episcopal college would be two distinct juridical subjects, and at any particular time the line of demarcation between their powers would have to be legally determined. But this is just what cannot be done. The pope is not subject to any immutable, legally controllable principles in regard to his concrete relationship to the rest of the episcopate. But he acts always *as* head of the supreme governing body in the Church, which has over itself no higher authority: for that of the pope is certainly higher than that of any individual bishop, but he acts *precisely with* the authority of the personal head of the whole episcopate. The result is that papal rule over the whole Church has always to be finding new ways—historically conditioned as these must be—of maintaining its connection with the universal episcopate, which is never merely a body of men who obediently receive papal instructions, but remains— together with the pope—that supreme holder of authority in the Church which is under the Spirit of God alone. There is no doubt that this doctrine of Rahner's has already had its effect on the form and statements of the Council.

In a further question handled by the Council, it seems as if Rahner has had to revise his attitude. Many years ago he was at pains to study obediently and objectively the encyclical, *Mystici Corporis*, and to justify its teaching on *membership of the Church*.[57] By contrast with this encyclical, under the distinguished leadership of Cardinal Bea, the tendency today is to attribute Church-membership to every baptized person, non-Roman Catholics also. But Rahner's interpretation still has permanent value: he shows that this question always involves a positive-legal decision on terminology. The Church can prescribe a terminology without thereby settling the matter itself, and thus another future variation in terminology is not excluded. Obviously this opens up tremendous prospects, particularly when the Church enters into a dialogue also with non-Christians. Incidentally, Rahner tries in a variety of ways[58] to help the person in the Church who has to admit that the Church is causing him unavoidable suffering and grave disappointment.

Rahner's study of the *Church and the sacraments*[59] brings out new aspects by comparison with the traditional sacramental theology. He understands a sacrament as an act of the Church's total self-realization in regard to the individual human being. The sacraments are thus not merely means of grace in the hands of the Church, but events in which the Church actualizes her own nature. The concept, *opus operatum*, is rendered intelligible from the nature of the Church: there is an *opus operatum* only in the time of the Church considered as eschatological time, in which divine grace is both victorious and tangible; it is not dependent on a purely legal disposition of God. In this way also he is able to show how the seven sacraments of the Catholic Church can be conceived as "instituted" by Jesus Christ himself even if Christ's express words of institution are not preserved for every sacrament—indeed, even if such an express foundation is unlikely. With a deliberate ecumenical aim, Rahner develops a theory of the connection between *word and sacrament* in the Church.[60] The sacramental word, he says, is altogether the most intensive and the perfect example of the effective word in the Church. Thus word and sacrament are not ultimately opposed to one another: the word, too, is the realization of the Church as she is also realized and revealed in the sacraments.

In his little book, *The Many Masses and the One Sacrifice*,[61] Rahner took up a question which is of considerable importance for both ecumenical discussion and the Church's practice. The question is, how often the sacrifice of the Mass ought to be offered, and whether there is a handy norm to decide this which would satisfy both the real dogmatic principles and practical needs. In this connexion, Rahner has never questioned—as has been asserted—or even obscured the fact that every Mass is an act of Christ himself as high priest, since it is willed because of Christ's command to commemorate him, and therefore every Mass takes place in the name of Christ. But, he says, we cannot draw from this a principle to decide how often Mass ought to be celebrated. For the number of Masses does not increase the act of the one earthly and heavenly Christ who carries them all.

Every Mass as an act of Christ has infinite value, but many Masses do not increase the one act of Christ and the honour of God arising out of this in so far as it is realized *precisely* by Christ. Rahner strongly emphasizes that the Mass as a new and multipliable sacrifice is a sacrifice within the dimensions of a cultic sign (sacrament as distinct from *res sacramenti*), but not within the dimensions of reality signified and made present by the Mass—that is, within the dimensions of the unique sacrifice of Christ on the cross. He then brings in the doctrine that formal reverence to God is possible only through genuine moral acts as such (being acts of Christ or of the members of the Church). From all this he argues: the Mass means an increase of honour to God and a growth in grace for those who take part in it, as far and as often as in the Mass and through the grace bestowed in it *ex opere operato* a greater existential, believing and loving participation of those at Mass (priest and people) is practically possible. If this is not to be expected, a further increase in Masses has no meaning. There may then be circumstances in which it is just as good or better for a priest to take part with devotion in another's Mass than to celebrate himself (whether we can speak of concelebration in this connexion, is another question).[62] This conclusion is very important for all those places where Mass is sometimes said hastily, in the midst of disturbing factors, or in one church simultaneously at many altars—as, for example, in monasteries, at congresses, at pilgrimage centres and during retreats.

These considerations also form the basis of Rahner's pastoral-theological reflexions on the *sacrifice of the Mass and an ascesis for youth*.[63] The liturgy must always take such a form that the *opus operatum* is not confused with a magical event. For *opus operatum* never implies a mechanical, impersonal effect, but the absolutely assured divine word of forgiveness: and sanctification becomes effective only to the extent in which it is accepted in a truly existential participation. Therefore, this effective word of God in the liturgy must be so spoken that it is able to call forth this existential realization in the most intensive way possible. This is what must be considered first of all in any reform of the liturgy: not respect for historical, non-divine traditions.

Karl Rahner was one of the first professional theologians to assert forthrightly the need for a genuine *renewal of the diaconate*,[64] even though he deliberately avoids over-estimating the importance of the sacramental and institutional aspects in the Church. He argues in this way: in the Church today there exist in fact those offices which were exercised in the early Church by deacons; and there is no reason why these (mostly married) men should be refused that confirmation and sacramental consecration which has always existed and still exists in the Church, but which today is given to those who have no need at all of it, those who will shortly afterwards be ordained priests. When we produced together *Diaconia in Christo*, we were not concerned merely with suggesting to the Church's official leaders ways in which aid could be provided for the most urgent pastoral needs (that deacons might visit the sick, bring them Holy Communion, take burial services, bless marriages—quite apart from baptizing, preaching and taking services in the absence of the priest, which always belonged to the deacon's office), but also to give a renewed emphasis to the fact that the office of ruling and of sacramental order in the Church are a service. "Your brothers, who serve you as pastors," was the title adopted by the bishops at the beginning of the Council in 1962. Moreover, the existence of married deacons would be a token of appreciation of the Eastern Churches' tradition—and, indeed, of the sacrament of matrimony.

In many studies and articles, Rahner has tried to revive again in the consciousness of the faithful some "forgotten truths" on the *sacrament of Penance*.[65] For this there must be a deeper reflexion on the Scriptural texts about guilt and its forgiveness; but there is also needed a new insight into the nature of "contrition", which "hurts", not because an individual deed is supposed to hurt at the moment, but because the sinner has to break down the system of values he has set up. It must be remembered, above all, that every sin is also a sin against the Church: that "auricular confession" is not a Catholic invention, but a relaxation of the severe penitential practice of the early Church; the sacrament of Penance today, just as in the early Church, shows the sinner placed at a distance, then received again into full communion when the sacrament is realized. Rahner emphasizes the fact that absolution is the assurance of peace with the Church, granted by the Church herself, and that this peace with the Church is the *res et sacramentum* of the reconciliation with God; that the acts of the penitent are an inner, constitutive factor of the penitential liturgy, by which the sinner places himself before the judgment of God's grace, and accepts contritely the divine forgiveness.

In his *theology of priestly existence*,[66] Rahner is concerned with the unity of the cultic and the prophetic elements in the priestly life. The priest sets out from the altar; the primal word that he speaks is the sacramental word, but precisely in virtue of his being empowered to utter that word he has the commission in season or out of season to preach the word of God wherever he is sent by the Church, as commissioned from above, not by reason of his situation in the world (as the layman is commissioned).

In order now to close the account of Rahner's theology of the Church, I would like also to refer to his assertion that the *bishop* has not only a genuinely official mission in regard to his own diocese, but a commission and a responsibility also in regard to the universal Church: for he can rightly be bishop of his particular Church only in so far as he is in addition, by logical priority, a member of the universal episcopate, of the one governing body of the universal Church under and with the pope.[67] The bishop counts as successor of the apostles, not because he is the successor of an individual apostle (which really would be difficult to prove), but because he belongs to the universal episcopate: this as a college is successor to the college of the apostles. Naturally, the bishop's membership of this governing body is realized in the concrete through the pope: this is recognized by the fact that the pope assigns to the bishop a definite territory.

It would be easier to write a book about Rahner's *theology of grace* than to explain it in a few lines to a reader who is not familiar with the text-book theology and therefore cannot very easily observe the differences in Rahner's treatment of the subject.

First of all, we must mention his doctrine of *uncreated grace*. Rahner seeks neither to deny nor obscure the factor of created grace as the effect of uncreated grace.

81

But for him grace is first and foremost uncreated grace, that is, the self-communication of God. "God's self-communication" is perhaps the central idea of Rahner's theology. In explaining it, he seizes on a word coined by medieval theology in an attempt to explain the beatific vision: quasi-formal causality. For Rahner, God's self-communication means that God by a quasi-formal causality communicates his own reality to the spiritual creature, and gives this to the creature as its own. The word, "quasi-formal causality", serves to distinguish this from the creation a reality distinct from God out of nothing. Thus the nature of the entire supernatural order of grace is based on this quasi-formal causality. Every creation of a finite being belongs "in itself" to the natural order. God's self-communication is grace absolutely speaking—obviously it has also "created" consequences in the subject to which God communicates himself.[68]

There are, accordingly, two such self-communications of God: that involved in the very fact of God's becoming man and that of grace, which is fulfilled in final glory. A simple philosophical reflexion suffices to show that this is grace absolutely speaking. Since to every finite being there can be attributed connatural knowledge, namely, the "being-with-itself" of this finite being to the extent of its possession of being, a finite being as such cannot be a mystery properly so-called—but the basic truths of Christianity *are* mysteries. But vice versa, the basic mysteries of Christianity are not arbitrarily chosen (and must not be preached as if they were the result of arbitrary decrees); they have their reason in these two divine self-communications, which are mysteries because they are rooted in God's own incomprehensibility: the reason for both self-communications—as I said already in another connexion in the first part of this book—lies in the immanent Trinity of God, based on the two inner-divine "processions".

At this stage, Rahner introduces a further sequence of thought. Creation is God's free act: God could have created a world in which such a divine self-communication to his creature would not have taken place. And yet the possibility of creating out of nothing is for God ultimately an inner factor of his higher and more comprehensive possibility of expending himself ecstatically on what is not God.[69] Thus Rahner renders intelligible the inner unity of nature and grace (together with and in spite of the ontological differences between them, constituting nature as something "other" which grace itself presupposes as the condition of its possibility), the unity of the theology of grace and Christology, and the possibility of a Christocentrism which embraces the orders of creation and grace.

In the first section of this second part, it was already pointed out that Rahner differs from the usual tradition of the Jesuit school in teaching quite definitely that the "entitative" elevation through grace of the salutary act necessarily involves a supernatural formal object for every such act. In his transcendental philosophy, being and being-with-itself are the same thing: a being, therefore, returns into itself to the extent that it is being and is not itself alienated from being through the real non-being of matter. From which it follows that the supreme existential reality of the conscious spirit—grace—cannot be pure ontic reality beyond the reach of consciousness, but must have an ontological status: this also is in accordance with the teaching of Scripture and Tradition that grace is illumination and inspiration. Grace is therefore also essentially always *experience of grace*.[70] This does not mean that the conscious reality of grace is something appearing within the horizon of consciousness and at that point a proper, definable, objective reality. Consciousness of grace means rather an alteration of man's transcendental horizon itself, which cannot in any way be unambiguously objectified and defined through immediate reflexion. But this does not mean that such an experience of grace is a contradiction of the notion of faith: faith is precisely the acceptance of such a direct self-communication of God and his self-revelation in itself and (where this exists) in its conceptual expression in human words guaranteed by official revelation. I might point out once again how important this teaching is for an "anonymous Christianity" and for a just Christian appreciation of non-Christian religions.

The first Catholic scientific-theoretical reflexions on the meaning of theological anthropology were those of Rahner in the first volume of the *Lexikon für Theologie und Kirche* under the heading, "Anthropology"; in Volume VII of this lexicon he drafted a brief sketch of such a doctrine of man under the title "Man". I cannot and will not simply repeat here these summary presentations. But I may be permitted to draw attention to four special themes of his dogmatic anthropology.

If Rahner—to the surprise of some contemporary professional theologians and informed laymen—has frequently been occupied with the question of devotion to the Sacred Heart, this was not merely in order to give greater depth to a devotion which had been especially fostered in the Society of Jesus, but also with a view to the horizons of his theology. If he analyses more closely "heart" as a primal word and gains in this connexion the notion of *real symbol*, he has thereby seized on an important theme of anthropology inasmuch as man's body is the outward form which both reveals and conceals the essence of the person. From this standpoint, the concept of "real symbol" can also become very important also in Christology, ecclesiology and sacramental theology.[71]

Starting out from a modern metaphysic of personality and liberty, Rahner in one of his earliest articles gave new depth to the notion of *concupiscentia*, using the term *Konkupiszenz* to avoid the misunderstandings which sometimes arise from the more usual German translation, *Begierde* ("desire", "lust").[72] "Concupiscence" is the historical, constantly varying diastasis imposed on man's freedom and never completely brought under control in this world of sinners: it exists between "nature" as the material placed at the disposal of liberty and the realization of the person possessed of freedom, who never completely succeeds in integrating his whole "nature" in good or evil in a completely free decision.

He has produced a short book, for the "Quaestiones Disputatae" series, on the *theology of death* from the standpoint of Christian anthropology.[73] Here Rahner is chiefly concerned to get rid of the idea of death as a mere biological exit. Death corresponds to man's unity in that it is a primal occurrence involving the whole man; it is the absolute deed of man accomplished in absolute suffering, the unity of which stretches throughout the whole life in which dying takes place, and thereby is withdrawn from man himself. Through this existential-ontological interpretation of death, as actively taking up a stand in regard to man's existence—in so far as this is something that comes upon him—Rahner is able to conceive death as the extreme act of despair, as *mortal* sin absolutely speaking, or alternatively as the peak of existence in faith, as dying with Christ. But he tries also in this connexion to expose the defects of the traditional description of death as separation of body and soul. The concept, "separation", is obscure and difficult to reconcile with the Catholic teaching that man's spiritual principle of life (called

85

"soul") is *substantially* one with the body. Since the soul precisely through the body is related to the material unity of the world, the "separation" of the soul from the body cannot mean the absolute cessation of this relationship with the world, so that the soul would only exist as extra-mundane. Rahner shows how the human soul in death enters upon a still greater proximity and a more inward relationship to the material source of the world's unity: from this standpoint he is then able to think out afresh the meaning of the part of the "dead" (saints, purgatory) in the historical determination of the world, in so far as their freely undertaken testimony after death pertains to the spiritual reality of the world.

Out of the many works of Karl Rahner in the whole field of *moral theology*, I shall mention only a few titles here. Long before the Holy Office in Rome had taken notice of a false situation-ethics and mysticism of sin, he had decisively opposed these errors of the time.[74] But he had done something much more important: he had just as clearly and at an equally early date underlined the fact that we must see the individual person possessed of freedom and his history, even in the sphere of "what ought to be", not merely as an instance of a universal idea and thus as a pure realization of a universal moral law. However much each individual human being is subject to and remains bound by the universal law (which Christianity proclaims as natural or positive divine law for all), he is and remains equally unique and unrepeatable and therefore has also a function and an obligation which is his and his alone. In this sense, therefore, within a universally binding essential-ethic there is also an existential-ethic.[75]

This existential-ethic cannot, of course, tell the individual human being precisely what is the material content of the requirement imposed by the divine call on him in particular. But it might and indeed ought to offer a formal logic with the aid of which any individual as such can discover God's will for himself. This is a task which has simply not been noticed by theologians (with the exception of one or two great minds, such as Ignatius of Loyola or Cardinal Newman). For the theory is still widespread that the individual can adequately understand his duty by applying the universal moral principles to the concrete, empirically worked out "case". We may simply note in passing that Rahner's conception of morality is also very biblical. For in our Lord's words about the judgment there is nothing about what sins have been "committed", but he does speak of omissions —disregard for the duty of each as an individual. Rahner has examined the theme in Ignatius of Loyola, but has indicated also the practical consequences for the Church's life : that is, with reference to the "charismatic" element of the individual in the Church which those who hold office in the Church have to respect.[76]

Finally, a word about Rahner's *eschatology*. He has tried to set out dogmatic principles for the interpretation of eschatological statements.[77] Protology—that is, the doctrine of the beginning of the world and of man— speaks of historical events, but it is not an eye-witness account of what happened once, but an "aetiological" statement about the beginning as the necessary reason of that reality which is experienced as our own situation of salvation or damnation. This protology becomes ever richer and brighter as redemptive history advances further. Rahner draws from this his conclusion for eschatology, that is, the theology of the Last Things. Christian eschatology is likewise not an account in anticipation of the phenomena of future events. It is rather the projection of Christian cosmology, anthropology and Christology, which make up and interpret our redemptive-historical present, into man's state of fulfilment. From this standpoint, Rahner goes on to develop a criterion (even though it can never be completely adequate) for distinguishing what is the true, objective meaning in eschatological statements, and what is merely an imaginative presentation. This clearly means that those who preach and teach in the Church must speak about these things more circumspectly and cautiously and maintain better God's sovereignty over the destiny of the world and of mankind. Our Lord's words about heaven and hell were not uttered to satisfy human curiosity, but were a solemn reminder of the real possibilities with which the present moment is endowed for man.

In this very imperfect survey, I have tried to show that Karl Rahner's theology does not consist—as some have maintained—solely of unanswered questions. It really is not his life's plan to create unrest for the sake of unrest. Perhaps it has become clear in the themes collected here that, in theology at any rate, we cannot spare ourselves the effort of thinking. An intensive study of the work of Karl Rahner reveals more answers than questions, particularly in ecumenical discussion and in contemporary society, shaped as this is by the contemporary world-picture. The time for systematizing these suggestions is not yet—nor can we even elucidate them in alphabetical order. At the end of the Flemish edition of this book, I wrote: "The work of Karl Rahner will have a determining influence on Catholic theology even in the twenty-first century." Today there is no reason to revise or even modify this optimistic outlook.

Notes and Bibliography

The notes that begin on this page serve also as a form of bibliography of those works by Karl Rahner which have been translated into English as well as of some that have not been translated. Readers looking for a complete bibliography are referred to the Verzeichnis sämtlicher Schriften 1924-1964, *a complete index of all Karl Rahner's books, published in pamphlet form by Verlag Herder, Freiburg im Breisgau, Germany.*

A separate, alphabetical list of all books by Karl Rahner available in English will be found on page 96.

I

1. "Anthropologie" in *Lexikon für Theologie und Kirche*, I (Freiburg i. Br., 1957), coll. 624-5.

2. *Schriften zur Theologie*, III (Einsiedeln, ²1957), pp. 39 f.

3. *Schriften zur Theologie*, I (Einsiedeln, 1954), pp. 15-16. English translation by Cornelius Ernst, O.P., *Theological Investigations*, I (London: Darton, Longman & Todd, and Baltimore: Helicon, 1961), p. 7.

4. *Sendung und Gnade* (Innsbruck, ³1961), p. 34. English translation by Cecily Hastings, *Mission and Grace*, I (London and New York: Sheed & Ward, 1963), p. 35.

5. An excellent account of the nature and outlook of the youth movement of that time is provided by Oskar Köhler under the title of "Jugendbewegung" in *Lexikon für Theologie und Kirche*, V (Freiburg i. Br., 1960), coll. 1181-2.

6. Luciana Frassati, *Das Leben Pier Giorgio Frassatis*, with an Introduction by Karl Rahner (Freiburg i. Br., 1961), pp. 9-10, 12.

7. We owe the following dates of events in Rahner's life to Dr Robert Scherer (Director of Verlag Herder, Freiburg i. Br.) who was closely associated with him throughout these years.

8. *Zur Erde entschlossen* (Frankfurt, 1948); *Der mächtige Gott* (Frankfurt, 1948); *Kämpfer, Beter, Zeuge* (Berlin, 1955).

9. *Geist in Welt* (Munich, ²1957), p. 407. (An English translation is in preparation with Sheed & Ward, London.)

10. *Ibid.*, pp. 13-14.

11. Rahner makes considerable use of the word *Ursprung* ("source", "origin", but perhaps more literally "primal spring"—*Trans.*), on which Honecker commented, "What then is springing (*was springt denn da*)?"

12. *Geist in Welt*, p. 14.

13. Josef de Vries, *Scholastik*, 15 (1940), pp. 404-9.

14. A retreat, based on the *Exercises*, which he gave in the German college in Rome in 1956, was duplicated—as were the scripts of his lectures—and appeared in a third edition with 208 pages at Innsbruck in 1959.

15. An English translation is in preparation with Sheed & Ward, London and New York.

16. *Hörer des Wortes*, p. 203.

17. *Ibid.*, p. 204.

18. *Ibid.*, p. 209.

19. On the life-work of Hugo Rahner, see H. Vorgrimler, *Den Vätern und dem Vater: Der Theologe und Historiker Hugo Rahner* (Bodenseebuch, 1963), under the patronage of Hermann Hesse and otbers (Kreuzlingen, 1963), pp. 20-30.

20. "A Scheme for a Treatise of Dogmatic Theology" in *Theological Investigations*, I (London: Darton, Longman & Todd, and Baltimore: Helicon, 1961), pp. 19-37.

21. Karl Rudolf, *Aufbau im Widerstand* (Salzburg, 1947), pp. 33, 39, 53, 55, 56, 57, 119.

22. "Exegese und Dogmatik" in *Schriften zur Theologie*, V (Einsiedeln, 1962), pp. 82-111. An English translation of this article appears under the title "Exegesis and Dogmatic Theology" in *Dogmatic versus Biblical Theology*, a collection of important essays edited by Herbert Vorgrimler (London: Burns & Oates, Baltimore: Helicon, and Montreal: Palm Publishers, 1965), pp. 31-66.

23. *Sendung und Gnade*, pp. 345, 352-354. English translation by Cecily Hastings and Richard Strachan, *Mission and Grace*, II (London and New York: Sheed & Ward, 1964), pp. 155-6, 166-8.

24. *Das Problem des Hominisation* (together with P. Overhage), ²1963; "Um des Erscheinungsbild des ersten Menschen" in P. Overhage, *Die Frage nach dem Erscheinungsbild des Menschen* (Freiburg i. Br., 1959), pp. 11-30.

25. Cf. "Das Christentum und die nichtchristlichen Religionen" in *Schriften zur Theologie*, V (Einsiedeln, 1962), pp. 136-158.

26. Latest edition, thoroughly revised by Adolf Schönmetzer, S.J. (Barcelona-Freiburg-Rome-New York, 1965).

27. Two volumes have appeared in English: Burkhard Neunheuser, O.S.B., *Baptism and Confirmation* (London: Herder–

Burns & Oates, Montreal: Palm Publishers, and New York: Herder & Herder, 1965); Bernhard Poschmann, *Penance and the Anointing of the Sick* (London: Herder–Burns & Oates, Montreal: Palm Publishers, and New York: Herder & Herder, 1965).

28. Two supplementary volumes, wholly devoted to the proceedings and the conclusions of Vatican II, will appear as soon as possible.

29. *Über die Schriftinspiration* (Freiburg i. Br., ³1962), p. 9. This general introduction does not appear in the English edition: *Inspiration in the Bible* (London: Herder–Burns & Oates, Montreal: Palm Publishers, and New York: Herder & Herder, ³1965). This essay also appears, in a revised translation, in the volume *Studies in Modern Theology* (London: Herder–Burns & Oates, Montreal: Palm Publishers, and New York: Herder & Herder, 1964).

30. Two of these have appeared in English under the title of *Theological Investigations*. The first, translated by Cornelius Ernst, O.P. (London: Darton, Longman & Todd, and Baltimore: Helicon, 1961); the second translated by Karl-H. Kruger (London: Darton, Longman & Todd, and Baltimore: Helicon, 1963).

31. In English in two volumes, translated by Cecily Hastings: (London and New York: Sheed & Ward; vol. I, 1963; vol. II, 1964); vol. III is in preparation. In America these volumes are published under the title *The Christian Commitment*.

32. London: Burns & Oates, Montreal: Palm Publishers, and Baltimore: Helicon, 1965.

33. Translated by Richard Strachan and edited by Cornelius Ernst, O.P. (London: Herder–Burns & Oates, Montreal: Palm Publishers, and New York: Herder & Herder, 1965).

34. An English translation is in the course of preparation with Herder–Burns & Oates (London), Palm Publishers (Montreal), and Herder & Herder (New York).

35. An English translation is in preparation with Burns & Oates.

36. *Gott in Welt* (Freiburg i. Br., 1964).

II

37. Cf. Gottlieb Söhngen, "Neuscholastik", in *Lexikon für Theologie und Kirche*, VII (Freiburg i. Br., 1962), coll. 923-6.

38. Cf. *Schriften zur Theologie*, I, p. 328; English translation: *Theological Investigations*, I (London and Baltimore, 1961), pp. 311 f.

39. "Über den Begriff des Geheimnisses in der katholischen Theologie" in *Schriften zur Theologie*, IV, ²1962, pp. 51-99.

40. "Zur scholastischen Begrifflichkeit der ungeschaffenen

Notes and Bibliography

Gnade" in *Schriften zur Theologie*, I, pp. 347-75; "Probleme der Christologie von heute", *ibid.*, pp. 169-222; "Natur und Gnade" in *Fragen der Theologie heute*, ed. J. Feiner, J. Trütsch, F. Böckle (Einsiedeln, ³1960), pp. 209-30; "Zur Theologie der Menschwerdung" in *Schriften zur Theologie*, IV, pp. 137-55. The first three of these essays are translated: "Some Implications of the Scholastic Concept of Uncreated Grace" in *Theological Investigations*, I, pp. 319-46; "Current Problems in Christology", *ibid.*, pp. 149-200; *Nature and Grace* (translated by Dinah Wharton), London, 1963, pp. 3-44.

41. "Theos im Neuen Testament" in *Schriften zur Theologie*, I, pp. 91-167 (English translation: "Theos in the New Testament" in *Theological Investigations*, I, pp. 79-148); "Bemerkungen zum dogmatischen Traktat 'De Trinitate' " in *Schriften zur Theologie*, IV, pp. 103-33.

42. "Probleme der Christologie von heute" in *Schriften zur Theologie*, I, pp. 169-222; "Auferstehung des Fleisches" in *Schriften zur Theologie*, II, pp. 211-25 ;"Die ewige Bedeutung der Menschheit Jesu für unser Gottesverhältnis" in *Schriften zur Theologie*, III, pp. 47-60; "Dogmatische Erwägungen über das Wissen und Selbstbewusstsein Christi" in *Schriften zur Theologie*, V, pp. 222-45. The first two of these essays are translated: "Current Problems in Christology" in *Theological Investigations*, I, pp. 149-200; "The Resurrection of the Body" in *Theological Investigations*, II, pp. 203-16.

43. "Hypostatic Union" in *A Concise Theological Dictionary* (London: Herder–Burns & Oates, Montreal: Palm Publishers, and New York: Herder & Herder, 1965).

44. "Zur scholastischen Begrifflicheit der ungeschaffenen Gnade" in *Schriften zur Theologie*, I, pp. 347-75 (in English: "Some Implications of the Scholastic Concept of Uncreated Grace" in *Theological Investigations*, I, pp. 319-46); "Über die Erfahrung der Gnade" in *Schriften zur Theologie*, III, pp. 105-9; "Natur und Gnade" in *Fragen der Theologie heute*, pp. 209-30 (in English: *Nature and Grace* [London and New York: Sheed & Ward, 1964], pp. 3-44.

45. Cf. "Das Christentum und die nichtchristlichen Religionen" in *Schriften zur Theologie*, V, pp. 136-58.

46. *Ibid.*

47. *Das Problem der Hominisation*; "Um das Erscheinungsbild des ersten Menschen" in P. Overhage, *Die Frage nach dem Erscheinungsbild des Menschen*, pp. 11-30; "Erlösungswirklichkeit in der Schöpfungswirklichkeit" in *Sendung und Gnade*, Innsbruck, ³1961, pp. 51-88 (in English: "The Order of Redemption within the Order of Creation" in *Mission and Grace*, I, pp. 59-113).

48. Cf. quotation on pp. 14-15; "Natur und Gnade" in *Fragen der Theologie heute*, pp. 209-30 (in English: *Nature and Grace*, pp. 3-44).

49. *Sendung und Gnade*, Innsbruck, ³1961 (in English: *Mission and Grace* in two volumes (*see* n. 31 above).

50. "Chancen des Christentums heute" in *Das freie Wort in der Kirche* (Einsiedeln, ²1954); "Theologische Deutung der Position des Christens in der modernen Welt" in *Sendung und Gnade*, pp. 13-47 (in English: "A theological Interpretation of the Position of Christians in the modern World" in *Mission and Grace*, I, pp. 3-55); "Würde und Freiheit des Menschen" in *Schriften zur Theologie*, II, pp. 247-77 (in English: "The Dignity and Freedom of Man" in *Theological Investigations*, II, pp. 235-63; "Die Christologie innerhalb einer evolutiven Weltanschauung" in *Schriften zur Theologie*, V, pp. 183-222.

51. *Die vielen Messen und das eine Opfer* (Freiburg, 1951); *Kirche und Sakramente* (Freiburg, ²1961): in English: *The Church and the Sacraments* (London: Herder–Burns & Oates, Montreal: Palm Publishers, and New York: Herder & Herder, ³1964); "Personale und Sakramentale Frommigkeit" in *Schriften zur Theologie*, II, pp. 115-41 (in English: "Personal and Sacramental Piety" in *Theological Investigations*, II, pp. 109-33); "Vergessene Wahrheiten über das Bussakrament", *ibid.*, pp. 143-83 (in English: "Forgotten Truths concerning the Sacrament of Penance" in *Theological Investigations*, II, pp. 135-74); "Bemerkungen zur Theologie des Ablasses", *ibid.*, pp. 185-210 (in English: "Remarks on the Theology of Indulgences" in *Theological Investigations*, II, pp. 175-201); "Die Gegenwart Christi im Sakrament des Herrenmahles" in *Schriften zur Theologie*, IV, pp. 357-97; "Wort und Euchariste", *ibid.*, pp. 313-55.

52. An excellent survey of this period and its intrigues is provided by Oswald von Nell-Breuning in the article, "Integralismus" in *Lexikon für Theologie und Kirche*, V (Freiburg i. Br., 1960), coll. 717 f.

53. "Zur Frage der Dogmenentwicklung" in *Schriften zur Theologie*, I, pp. 49-90 (in English: "The Development of Dogma" in *Theological Investigations*, I, pp. 39-77) and IV, pp. 11-50; "Theologie im Neuen Testament" in *Schriften zur Theologie*, V, pp. 33-53.

54. "Virginitas in Partu" in *Schriften zur Theologie*, IV, pp. 173-205; "Schrift und Tradition" in *Wort und Wahrheit*, 18, 1963, pp. 269-79; also various articles in *Lexikon für Theologie und Kirche*.

55. *Über die Schriftinspiration* (Freiburg, ³1962), in English: *Inspiration in the Bible*; *see* note 29 above.

Notes and Bibliography

56. *Episkopat und Primat*, with J. Ratzinger (Freiburg, 1961): in English: *The Episcopate and the Primacy* (London: Herder–Burns & Oates, Montreal: Palm Publishers, and New York: Herder & Herder, 1962, and reprinted under the same imprints in *Studies in Modern Theology*, 1964); "Zur Theologie des Konzils" in *Schriften zur Theologie*, V, pp. 278-302; "Über den Episkopat" in *Stimmen der Zeit* (1963), pp. 161-95 (in English: *Bishops: Their Status and Function*, London: Burns & Oates, and Baltimore: Helicon, 1964).

57. "Die Gliedschaft in der Kirche nach der Lehre der Enzykika Pius' XII. 'Mystici Corporis' " in *Schriften zur Theologie*, II, pp. 7-94. In English: "Membership of the Church according to the Teaching of Pius XII's Encyclical 'Mystici Corporis Christi' " in *Theological Investigations*, II, pp. 1-88.

58. *Kirche der Sünder* (Vienna, 1947); *Das Freie Wort in der Kirche* (Einsiedeln, ²1954); *Das Dynamische in der Kirche* (Freiburg, ³1960), in English: *The Dynamic Element in the Church* (London: Herder–Burns & Oates, Montreal: Palm Publishers, and New York: Herder & Herder, 1964).

59. *Kirche und Sakramente* (Freiburg, ²1961), in English: *The Church and the Sacraments* (London: Herder–Burns & Oates, Montreal: Palm Publishers, and New York: Herder & Herder, ³1964).

60. "Wort und Eucharistie" in *Schriften zur Theologie*, IV, pp. 313-55.

61. *Die vielen Messen und das eine Opfer* (Freiburg, 1951).

62. "Dogmatische Bemerkungen über die Frage der Konzelebration" in *Münchener Theologische Zeitschrift*, 6, 1955, pp. 81-106.

63. "Messopfer und Jugendaszese" in *Sendung und Gnade*, ³1961, pp. 469-89. In English: "The Sacrifice of the Mass and an Ascesis for Youth" in Mission and Grace, I, pp. 203-54.

64. *Diaconia in Christo: Über die Erneuening des Diakonates*, with H. Vorgrimler (Freiburg, 1962); "Über die Erneuerung des Diakonates" in *Sendung und Gnade*, pp. 275-85 (in English: "Deacons" in *Mission and Grace*, II, pp. 53-67), continued in *Schriften zur Theologie*, V, pp. 303-55.

65. "Vergessene Wahrheiten über das Busssakrament" in *Schriften zur Theologie*, II, pp. 143-83. In English: "Forgotten Truths concerning the Sacrament of Penance" in *Theological Investigations*, II, pp. 135-74.

66. "Priesterliche Existenz" in *Schriften zur Theologie*, III, pp. 285-312.

67. *Episkopat und Primat*, with J. Ratzinger (Freiburg, 1961): in English; *see* note 56 above; "Über den Episkopat" in *Stimmen*

der Zeit, 1963, pp. 161-95: in English, *see* note 56 above; "Über Bischofskonferenzen" in *Stimmen der Zeit*, 1963, pp. 267-83.

68. "Zur scholastischen Begrifflichkeit der ungeschaffenen Gnade" in *Schriften zur Theologie*, I, pp. 347-75; in English: "Some Implications of the Scholastic Concept of Uncreated Grace" in *Theological Investigations*, I, pp. 319-47; "Natur und Gnade" in *Fragen der Theologie heute* (Einsiedeln, 1960), pp. 209-30: in English: *Nature and Grace*, pp. 3-44.

69. "Natur und Gnade" in *Fragen der Theologie heute*, pp. 209-30: in English: *Nature and Grace*, pp. 3-44; "Zur Theologie der Menschwerdung" in *Schriften zur Theologie*, IV, pp. 137-55; "Erlösungswirklichkeit in der Schöpfungswirklichkeit" in *Sendung und Gnade*, pp. 51-88: in English: "The Order of Redemption within the Order of Creation" in *Mission and Grace*, I, 1963, pp. 59-113; "Bemerkungen zum dogmatischen Traktat 'De Trinitate' " in *Schriften zur Theologie*, IV, pp. 103-33.

70. "Über die Erfahrung der Gnade" in *Schriften zur Theologie*, III, pp. 105-9.

71. "Zur Theologie der Herz-Jesu-Verehrung" in *Schriften zur Theologie*, III, pp. 379-415; "Zur Theologie des Symbols", *Schriften zur Theologie*, IV, pp. 275-311.

72. "Zum theologischen Begriff der Konkupiszenz" in *Schriften zur Theologie*, I, pp. 377-414. In English: "The theological Concept of Concupiscentia" in *Theological Investigations*, I, pp. 347-82.

73. *Zur Theologie des Todes* (Freiburg, ³1961): in English: *On the Theology of Death*, revised translation (London: Herder– Burns & Oates, Montreal: Palm Publishers, and New York: Herder & Herder, 1964).

74. *Gefahren im heutigen Katholizismus* (Einsiedeln, ³1953): in English: "Dangers in Catholicism Today" in *Nature and Grace*, pp. 47-131.

75. "Über die Frage einer formalen Existentialethik" in *Schriften zur Theologie*, II, pp. 227-46. In English: "On the Question of a Formal Existential Ethics" in *Theological Investigations*, II, pp. 217-434.

76. *Das Dynamische in der Kirche* (Freiburg, ³1960): in English: *The Dynamic Element in the Church* (London: Herder– Burns & Oates, Montreal: Palm Publishers, and New York: Herder & Herder, 1964); *Löscht den Geist nicht aus* (Innsbruck, 1963).

77. "Theologische Prinzipien der Hermeneutik eschatologischer Aussagen" in *Schriften zur Theologie*, IV, pp. 401-28.

Books by Karl Rahner available in English

(Where bibliographical details have already been supplied in the notes beginning on page 89, the appropriate note is indicated within brackets.)

Bishops: Their Status and Function (56).

The Christian Commitment, American title of *Mission and Grace* (31).

A Concise Theological Dictionary (33).

Encounters with Silence (London: Sands, and Westminster, Md.: Newman Press, 1960).

The Eternal Year (32).

Free Speech in the Church (London and New York: Sheed & Ward, 1959).

Happiness through Prayer (Dublin: Clonmore & Reynolds, 1958).

Mary, Mother of the Lord (London: Herder–Nelson, Montreal: Palm Publishers, and New York: Herder & Herder, 1961).

Mission and Grace, 2 vols. (31).

Nature and Grace (44).

Prayers for Meditation, with Hugo Rahner (London: Herder–Nelson, Montreal: Palm Publishers, and New York: Herder & Herder, 1962).

"Quaestiones Disputatae", a series of books of which seven are by Karl Rahner (London: Herder–Burns & Oates, Montreal: Palm Publishers, and New York: Herder & Herder):

The Church and the Sacraments, 1963

The Dynamic Element in the Church, 1964

Hominisation: The Evolutionary Origin of Man as a Theological Problem, 1965.

Inspiration in the Bible, 1961

On Heresy, 1964

On the Theology of Death, 1961

Visions and Prophecies, 1963.

Theological Investigations, 2 vols. (30).

S0-CMV-368

". . . an invaluable resource book for men and women."

—*Public News*

". . . a fasc. . . market for Today's Woman . . . a must on the reading list of every woman."

—*The Single Parent*

"The book informs women of many not-so-obvious points concerning their employment . . . filled with much useful information."

—*Kirkus Reviews*

". . . hard-core practical book . . . helpful to the male audience also."

—*ETHOS*

". . . researched . . . very useful . . . a convenient, well-written volume."

—*New Jersey Department of Education*

". . . THOROUGH . . . REALISTIC . . . EASY-TO-READ . . . PACKED WITH IMPORTANT DETAILS."

—*Minnesota Daily*

ARE THERE WARNER BOOKS
YOU WANT BUT CANNOT FIND IN YOUR LOCAL STORES?

You can get any Warner Books title in print. Simply
send title and retail price, plus 35¢ to cover mailing
and handling costs for each book desired. New York
State residents add applicable sales tax. Enclose check
or money order only, no cash please, to:

WARNER BOOKS
P.O. BOX 690
NEW YORK, N.Y. 10019

Woman's Work Book

How to Get Your First Job . . . How to Re-enter the Job Market . . . How to Fight for Your Rights in the Work World . . . and More

KARIN ABARBANEL
and
GONNIE McCLUNG SIEGEL

An Information House Book

WARNER BOOKS

A Warner Communications Company

NOTE: *Throughout this book reference is made to women and work—looking for work, finding work, being paid for work.*

For the purposes of this book, work and job, and work and career, have been used interchangeably. We are well aware that women who stay home and care for families also work. In fact, they work very hard.

According to a recent survey by an economic research institute, The Conference Board, a typical housewife spends 57 hours a week caring for family and home; the average work week in industry is 40 hours. And many women meet their responsibilities in housekeeping and child care in addition to the paid work they do outside the home.

WARNER BOOKS EDITION

© 1975 by Information House Books, Inc.
All rights reserved

Library of Congress Catalog Card Number: 74-6723

ISBN 0-446-81353-2

This Warner Books Edition is published by
arrangement with Praeger Publishers, Inc.

Cover design and photograph by Gene Light

Warner Books, Inc., 75 Rockefeller Plaza, New York N.Y. 10019

W A Warner Communications Company

Printed in the United States of America

Not associated with Warner Press, Inc. of Anderson, Indiana

10 9 8 7 6 5 4 3 2 1

Contents

292025
97
650.1
650.1
Allw

Acknowledgments

Karin Abarbanel wishes to thank Ruth Aley, Barbara Boyle, Nancy Comer, Barbara Holt, Janet Jones, Janice LaRouche, Helen Lowe, Kathleen Tappen, Mike Powers, and, finally, Dorothy and Peter.

Gonnie Siegel wishes to thank Jennifer S. MacLeod, Jody Peter, and Mary Tobin.

Information House wishes to thank Art Springer, Pat Fogarty, Joyce Shue, Peggy Bedoya, Anne Columbia, Irit Spierer, Harry Steinberg, Kathi Wakefield, and Kitty Ball Ross.

Introduction

You are a woman and you are looking for a job. Whether you're a recent college graduate seeking an entry-level position or a forty-five-year-old woman re-entering the job market, you'll find some good news and some bad.

The good news is that for the first time since World War II, when women workers were in demand on the production lines, the employment tide is turning in your favor because of your sex. Field after field is opening up to women, from politics to top management, from crane operator to garbage collector. New laws against sex discrimination are obliging employers to recruit, train, hire, and promote women. New attitudes are changing the way society looks at women—their role, their place, their value.

Most important, women themselves are changing. From the narrow perimeters of the past, women are looking beyond to new directions. Frontiers that were closed last week may open up this week, so rapidly are the old definitions disappearing. To accomplish these changes, women are working together. The old myth that women dislike and distrust one another is fading fast. Women as individuals are sharing a sense of pride in the accomplishments of women as a group.

In your search for a job, the greatest untapped resource of all could be the mushrooming network across the country of women in every field, eager to help you succeed. This network, which scarcely existed

9

five years ago, today is vast and growing, and it is touching the lives of all of us. Women are setting up talent banks, placement and career-counseling services, directories, women's centers, and businesses. They are gathering in small groups to lend support to one another. They are writing newsletters and holding employment seminars. They are buttonholing officeholders for passage of equal-rights laws on both the state and national levels and for better enforcement of existing antidiscrimination laws. And they are exerting pressure on small businesses, large corporations, and labor unions to hire, promote, and pay women on an equal basis with men and to make available equal opportunities, such as management-training courses, apprenticeship programs, and union leadership spots.

Whether you live in a small Midwestern town or a large East Coast city, you can take advantage of the new opportunities. But you won't find out about them in the yellow pages. You will find out about them in this book.

And now the bad news.

You are looking for a job in one of the worst economic periods in recent history. And you are looking along with a lot of other people, both men and women. Finding a job today is difficult, and the competition is keen. Some corporations have imposed hiring freezes. Some industries are closing down entirely, turning out hundreds of workers. Unemployment figures continue to rise—and the unemployment rate for women is two percentage points higher than for men.

Nobody knows what will happen to the hard-fought gains women have won in the past five years. Doors just beginning to open could slam shut if the economic situation worsens. Affirmative Action programs established to make equality for women a reality may cease to be enforced aggressively.

Along with doom-and-gloom predictions, you'll hear stories about corporations eager to find "qualified" women to fill $75,000-a-year posts. On closer examination of these room-at-the-top tales you'll generally discover that such jobs disqualify women by demanding the impossible. For example, a great job awaits the woman who has a master's degree in business administration plus fifteen years of top-management experience, is under forty, and became vice-president of a major corporation at twenty-eight. Finding such a woman might not be impossible, but it is about as likely as sighting a flock of bald eagles from your back porch.

First of all, women who might qualify for such a job have had to leap many hurdles. Twenty years ago they were discouraged from taking business courses in college and subjected to a tacit quota in entering MBA programs in graduate school. Next, they were barred from top management except in extremely unusual cases. And if they persevered through all this and succeeded in getting an MBA degree, it was supposed to self-destruct when it came into conflict with a marriage certificate.

Management jobs *are* opening up, but don't expect $75,000-a-year offers. The few such jobs that exist are reserved for the token woman, to be listed on the board of directors, and most corporations already have that position filled. Tokenism, however, is an important first step. Many of those so-called token women aren't just sitting there writing memos about the decor of the reception room. They are asking a very important question: "Why am I the only one?"

So, although in many ways it is a bad time to be looking for a job, don't allow yourself to become discouraged. There never was an economic depression so bad that there wasn't a single job. And all you need is *one* job. Until you find the job you want, make the best of the job you already have, which is *finding* a job. Make it a full-time (if possible), intelligent, dedicated search. Helping you to do this, step by step, is what this book is all about.

Among other things, this book will help you to identify the kind of work you want to do (your goals) and will describe the most effective ways of finding a job. It will tell you where *your* efforts will pay off, where they will be wasted, and how to recognize the right job when you've found it.

At the same time, we hope to give you some psychological support. Looking for a job is an "invitation for rejection," as one psychiatrist put it, and most normal people can't stand much rejection. In the best of times, job seekers get turned down more often than they get job offers. If ten interviews produce one job offer, you are lucky. And if ten interviews produce one *good* job offer, you are extremely lucky.

So when you are feeling low and nothing seems to be going right, at least it should be comforting to know that women all over the country are supporting you, wanting you to succeed, betting on you to win. If *you* believe you can succeed, you can and you will. And when success comes to you, keep a hand outstretched to help the next woman up. Good luck.

I

PLANNING YOUR JOB CAMPAIGN

1

Deciding to Find a Job

Deciding to go out and find a job can be as simple as getting up in the morning or as difficult as parachuting out of a burning plane in a thunderstorm. If you are a bright young woman with a crisp new college degree, finding a job is a natural, logical next step. The same is true for the young woman who ends her formal education with a high school diploma. But what if you are forty-five years old with five kids, have never held a paying job, and your husband just ran away with a fan dancer?

What if you are a factory worker's wife whose kids have the bad habit of eating, and inflation is devouring your husband's paycheck?

What if your kids are grown, your husband is busier than ever, but you're climbing the walls and talking to yourself?

What if your kids are ready for college but your bank account isn't?

What if you are a mother on welfare who hates the system, wants out, and keeps thinking there must be a better way?

What if you are working at a job for which you are underpaid, overqualified, and underappreciated?

What if the only Affirmative Action plan in your company is an Affirmation of No Action?

If you are thinking about going to work, you are not alone. American women are entering the labor force at an unprecedented rate. Nearly 35 million of them (43 percent of all American women) are in the market, making up 39 percent of the entire work force. Of this total, 7.7 million are women who have never married, 19.8 million are married, 2.4 million are widowed, 3.8 million are divorced or separated, 3.7 million are married to men whose incomes are below $5,000 a year, and 3 million more are married to men earning between $5,000 and $7,000 a year. The working women include 13 million mothers with children under the age of eighteen and 4.8 million with children under the age of six.

Of the working women, 6.6 million are the sole support of their fatherless families. Another 2.1 million families are supported by married women whose husbands are either unemployed or unable to work.

Regardless of these facts, the fairy tale that women are not serious about long-term jobs or career planning persists and complicates every working woman's life. For years this myth has been invoked to justify job discrimination against women. Women's jobs are viewed by many employers as brief interludes between school and marriage. Whether they are just out of high school or hold three graduate degrees, women are expected to work only until they get whisked off by a dashing young man who is serious about *his* career.

In reality, as the foregoing statistics show, most women hold jobs for the same reason men do: to support or help support themselves and their families. Survival, not self-fulfillment, is the main goal of most working women. Women work because they *have* to work.

Furthermore, according to the Bureau of Labor Statistics, married women can expect to spend an average of twenty-five years in the labor market, unmarried women forty-six years, and men, married or single, forty-five years. Any way you look at it, twenty-five to forty-six years is not a brief romp. It's ample time for a career path to become well worn. It's high time employers stopped treating women's employment as temporary pin-money excursions before and after marriage and children.

If winter is coming on but the rent is nowhere in sight, the decision to go to work has already been made for you. To work or starve is an easy choice. For most people, however, there are many less dramatic, less clear-cut reasons for the decision.

If you are a young unmarried woman, the decision to look for a job is relatively clear, but the task is not. You are troubled by your lack of sophistication and work experience. Nothing is more frustrating than the impossible demand all young job seekers face: "Come back when you've got experience." Obviously a job must come before experience, but that's your problem, not the employer's. This problem has driven every generation of young job seekers up the wall.

Another shock young job seekers face is the realization that the people out there are not very much interested in what they can do for you. They are interested in finding out what you can do for them. You must convince them you have something they need—not an easy task.

You will be told that hiring anybody for her first job is a gamble in both money and time (which in business terms adds up to money). Will she show up for work on time? Will she lead the stampede at quitting time? Will she ignore a deadline in favor of a date? Will she merely draw a salary and feel no commitment to the company? After a long, expensive training period, will she chuck it all to teach corn planting in Africa, distribute IUDs in India or join a commune in New Hampshire?

The people holding the key to your successful job future probably have a lot of preconceived notions about young people in general. Whether they are right or wrong is not the issue. Recognizing that they have such prejudices will be helpful to you. There is a widespread feeling that young people have been fed caviar with silver spoons for so long that they haven't a clue as to where either came from, much less how much they cost. Remember that you will generally be dealing with an age group that is upward-motivated, money-oriented, and depression-scared. When asking for a job, resist any temptation to tell prospective employers that money isn't everything. In the first place, they might offer you less money just to test your principles; in the second place, they have already discovered this for themselves.

Although by law it isn't supposed to be asked anymore, most prospective employers will find a way to pose the age-old question: "Are you going to hang around the store only until what you really want—marriage—comes along? The moment a likely man appears, won't you punch out your career time clock and depart for a vine-covered cottage in the suburbs, complete with infant? And if not, why not?" You're damned either way. Either you're uncommitted to a career or, if you don't opt for marriage and babies, you're some kind of freak.

Of course these questions are not fair. Men are never asked if or when they plan to become fathers and whether, if they do have babies, they will stay home and take care of them. But who promised you that life would be fair? You need a job, and they have a job to bestow. Face it.

Try to get across some basic principles to your prospective employer. First, that you are serious about long-term job plans; that the only thing you are currently interested in is finding a job, working hard, and getting promoted. You might mention that these aspirations do not exclude marriage, and don't sidestep the next obstacle—children. Respond to the unasked question by indicating that birth-control measures make it possible to plan not only your babies but also your career.

Show an interest in the company to which you are applying for a job. If they make widgets, find out something about widgets. Study the company's last annual report. Know who the chairman of the board is and who the directors are. Find out who started the company, what the earnings were over the past ten years, the company's growth pattern, expansion plans, the number of employees.

Corporations are made up of individuals who have feelings and phobias just like everybody else. Try to tell your interviewer *why* you think his or her company would be a terrific place to work. And if you have any stepping-stone, job-hopping ideas, keep them to yourself. Announcing to Ford that you'd like a little practical experience so you can go on to bigger things at General Motors will get you and your résumé tossed out on the street.

SMALL CHILDREN, BIG DECISIONS

Whether or not to take a job may be a relatively simple decision for a childless woman. But that first baby puts you in another caste altogether. Our culture has a simple, basic rule: mother stays home and brings up *her* children. Mothers whose husbands are unable to work because they are sick or disabled are expected to perform the dual role of breadwinner and home-maker. And many divorced or separated mothers are expected to go to work to support their kids.

This is where the door slams shut—everybody else get back in the kitchen. A married mother stretches that umbilical cord to the office at her own risk. If her kids get in any trouble, she'll be blamed, but the father will be pitied along with the children. If the children get sick, she'd better not be out of town on a business trip.

So if you are the mother of small children and have decided to get a job, prepare yourself by expecting the worst. Expect that centuries of guilt will pour down upon you and the specter of unhappy and perhaps delinquent children will dance in your head. Self-doubts will assail you—not to mention the doubts that will assail your husband. Your parents and in-laws will go around with pinched faces. And the PTA will collectively pout when you send store-bought brownies to the back-to-school program.

The reality of your situation won't change, but your

inner doubts may subside if you thoroughly understand that you are in no way plowing new ground. Every mother of small children who ever went out to work has gone exactly the same difficult route. Swimming against a cultural stream is not easy. A revolutionary new concept may help you to cope with this problem as it has helped many other mothers: no matter what you've been taught to believe, *those children are only 50 percent yours.* It may be a difficult idea to get used to and should be introduced to your husband with the greatest caution and delicacy lest it overwhelm him. If you are very patient, you may someday get help with both children and brownies.

COPING WITH YOUR HUSBAND

Traditional husbands, unless the wolf already is prying open the door, will not be thrilled when the mother, maid, and chauffeur trips off to take a paying job, leaving dust, a dirty oven, and unmade beds behind. Your husband will probably deal with this new threat by racing between logic and illogic. Try to stay calm and separate the two. Among other things, he will probably tell you that if you need more money he will take a second job pumping gas at the local service station; that you'll make no money because he will be shoved into a higher tax bracket; that buying lunches and pantyhose will eat up your entire salary; that you'll be exhausted doing two jobs (which means don't expect any help); that the kids will be psychologically damaged for life by yelling "Mom" to an empty house; that their health will deteriorate on a steady diet of peanut butter and pumpkin seeds; that the dog will die of kidney stones and loneliness; and that the lovely warm house you created will become an empty shell.

Don't believe it, and don't let it worry you. Nothing perks up a depressed husband like an extra paycheck, especially in pinched economic conditions. Many husbands are getting emotional support from other husbands of working wives, and they are happily surprised to find that advantages go along with the disadvantages. Nobody has proved to date that more messed-up kids come from homes where the mother had an outside job than from more traditional arrangements. Furthermore, according to a survey by the Conference Board, a nonprofit economic research institute, only 25 percent of the typical housewife's time is devoted to childcare. Seventy-five percent goes into routine chores.

Children have needs that must be fulfilled, but even Dr. Spock now differentiates between "mother" and "mother figure." The latter can be Uncle Jim, Aunt Jane, Grandma, or Daddy. As most child psychiatrists point out, it helps if the father is the mother figure part of the time. He, along with the mother, must take a share of the blame for messed-up kids.

How to bring up children is something for mothers and fathers to work out together. There is no right or wrong way and no assurances that whatever you do will avoid producing another candidate for another psychiatrist's couch twenty-five years hence.

The current popular theory is that having a mother in the kitchen baking cookies is good for a kid if mother wants to be there, but bad if she doesn't. So if you want to stay, stay. If you don't, do something about it.

THE EMPTY NEST

When the last child has been packed off to college, the army, the marines, an apprenticeship, or the foreign service, objections to mother's working largely disappear. But while the objections at home are falling away, objections out there in the job market are multiplying.

Since you are no longer young, you must cope with a new problem: sex-plus-age discrimination. Many training programs and apprenticeships specify that the applicant be under thirty, or even under twenty-five. Challenging these barriers in the courts will take time, and meanwhile the discrimination goes on. That fifteen-to-twenty-year gap in your résumé glares at you and brings back all the old insecurities to add to the new ones. No matter what you once did, you are probably unsure that you can do it again. If you ever had a field, you are afraid the field has advanced beyond you. Old skills now are rusty. You feel the world has marched on while you have been standing still.

Old friends can drive you wild by asking you what you have done with your life. How can you tell them that you've made 396 trips to the orthodontist and baked four thousand upside-down cakes? And now you're faced with your upside-down life, which may look just peachy to your husband—all that free time in which to "fulfill" yourself. After being the service station for everybody else's needs, many a woman hasn't the foggiest notion of what will fulfill her. She only knows that she feels empty.

Unless you've been living on a distant planet, untouched by human socialization, these feelings are normal and natural. It is perfectly normal not to know what to do after years of being so busy that you couldn't think. The first step in doing anything about a problem is to admit the reality of the situation. You are over forty in a youth culture; you are starting a career at a time when others of your age group are at the peak of theirs; your qualifications look outdated and sketchy. Your looks are fading as fast as your confidence, and you feel nobody wants to have you around, much less pay you to be there. Move over and make way for thousands upon thousands of other women who feel exactly the same way.

WHY WOMEN PUT THEMSELVES DOWN

All the insecurities, doubts, and feelings of worthlessness programmed into women by society come flying out when they look for a job. Selling a product is an assertive art. Looking for a job means you are selling yourself. And women are taught to do the exact opposite. From the nursery to the grave, women are supposed to be supportive, passive, reticent. Films taken of people with newborn babies show the difference in the treatment of boys and girls. Girls are treated more gently and told they are "beautiful." Boys are spoken to in louder, more aggressive tones, told how strong they are, and mentioned frequently for the presidency. A little girl never gets off this programming track. She is given the tools of her ordained occupation—dolls, dishes, pots and pans, a telephone, a make-up kit. Boys are given action toys—footballs, trucks, erector sets, building blocks. Later, girls are directed into jobs that are supportive—nurses, secretaries, administrative assistants.

Along the way, guidance counselors remind girls in a thousand subtle and not-so-subtle ways that civil engineering, medicine, and nuclear physics are not for them. And when they finally go out to look for jobs, their life-long training inhibits them from pursuing high-paying occupations, demanding salaries equal to men's, or being able even to recognize and capitalize on their strengths. Most women are timid, ready to settle for things they will later resent: too little money, dead-end jobs, yeoman duty with the credit going elsewhere.

Mary Tobin, regional director of the Women's Bureau, U.S. Department of Labor, says: "Too many women are quick to take any job that is offered to them. Often women are so insecure about finding a job that they will take the first thing that comes along instead of carefully investigating all job possibilities." Employers know that your bargaining position undergoes considerable erosion the moment you accept a job. It is vital therefore to plan a thorough campaign, matching your talents to the best job possibilities. Care enough about yourself to put some work into the planning. Even though jobs are hard to come by, especially in depressed times, avoid jumping at the first opportunity. It's a rare employer who won't give you a few days to think things over. Use those days to investigate carefully. Careful sleuthing may reveal that the last person holding that job was a man whose salary was three thousand dollars more than that offered you.

MYTHS AND REALITY

To help combat some age-old prejudices about women, the Women's Bureau has published a pamphlet entitled "The Myth and the Reality." Here are some widely held misconceptions about women workers:

MYTH: Women aren't serious about working; they work only for pocket money.

REALITY: Nearly 35 million women are in the labor force. Half are working because of urgent economic need. They are either single, widowed, divorced, or separated or have husbands whose incomes are insufficient to support their families.

MYTH: Women are out sick more than male workers; they cost the company more.

REALITY: A recent Public Health study shows little difference in the absentee rates of males and females due to illness or injury: 5.6 days a year for women, 5.2 for men.

MYTH: Women don't want responsibility on the job; they don't want promotions or job changes that add to their load.

REALITY: Relatively few women have been offered positions of responsibility. But when given these opportunities, women do cope with an increased work load in addition to their personal or family responsibilities. In 1973, 4.7 million women held professional and technical jobs, another 1.6 million worked as nonfarm managers and administrators, and many others held supervisory jobs at all levels in offices and factories.

MYTH: The employment of mothers leads to juvenile delinquency.

REALITY: Studies show that there are many determining factors for juvenile delinquency. Whether or not a mother is employed outside the home does not appear to be one of them. These studies indicate that it is the quality of a mother's care (also true for a father's) rather than the time consumed in such care that is of major significance.

MYTH: Men don't like to work for women supervisors.

REALITY: Most men who complain about women supervisors have never worked for a woman. In one study where at least three-fourths of both the male and female respondents (all executives) had worked with women managers, their evaluation of women in management was generally favorable. Those who reacted unfavorably to women as managers showed the traditional cultural bias against women in positions of authority. In another survey, 41 percent of the reporting firms indicated that they hired women executives, and none rated the women's performance as unsatisfactory; 50 percent rated their performance adequate, 42 percent rated it as good as that of their male predecessor, and 8 percent rated it as better than the males'.

MYTH: A woman's place is in the home.

REALITY: Homemaking in itself is no longer a full-time job for most women. Goods and services formerly produced in the home are now commercially available; labor-saving devices have lightened or eliminated much work around the house. Today more than half of all women between eighteen and sixty-four years of age are in the labor force, where they are making a substantial contribution to the nation's economy. Studies show that nine out of ten women will work outside the home at some time in their lives.

DON'T JUST SIT THERE—DO SOMETHING

Okay, so you were promised a rose garden but delivered into a thicket of thorns. Your castle is leaking and every prince you kiss turns into a toad. Don't just sit there licking your wounds. Get out and do something about it—not next week, not tomorrow. NOW!

There is one good thing about being at the bottom of the heap: there's only one way to go, and that way is up.

If your particular needs—no matter what they are—will be filled by finding a job, plunge on. This book is for you. Remember, no matter how hard it may seem, there never was a better time to be a woman. And although this book discusses long-range career planning in much greater depth than short-term jobs, the techniques for finding both are the same.

It's great to discover talents you thought were buried forever or didn't know were there in the first place. It's terrific to be well paid for a job well done. It's rewarding to do work you enjoy and spend time with co-workers you like and respect. It's satisfying to be motivated by a job and rewarded by success. It's delightful to feel self-supporting instead of dependent. It's even rewarding to be exhausted after performing a particularly difficult task.

And it is exhilarating to learn you have well-wishers all over the country—even the world—whom you never knew you had. Women everywhere are counting on you to succeed. Your psychological chains are still there, but with one vastly important difference: they are no longer locked. Whether or not to step free is your choice.

2

The Job Market

No matter what you have to sell or how good it looks to you, you must find somebody who is willing to buy it. You may have a closetful of diamonds, but if nobody is buying diamonds this week, you're out of luck. Learning the demands of the job market and fitting your skills to it are the first steps in your job campaign.

If you haven't decided precisely the kind of work you want to do, don't worry about it—you might be in a better position because of your flexibility. According to current projections, new areas of employment will be opening up for women during the next five or ten years. The job market is moving from a production to a service orientation. While the total number of workers needed is expected to increase 20 percent by 1980, the number needed will vary by occupation. The greatest percentage of women will be hired in areas where the fewest number of women are now employed. (Before you get your hopes high, remember that a company employing 30,000 men and one woman can increase the percentage of women employed 100 percent by hiring only one more woman.)

NEW OPPORTUNITIES FOR WOMEN

You want a challenging job at a good salary with a chance for advancement. Where should you look?

27

For the most part, forget the traditional "women's jobs" (unless you are already in one, in which case concentrate on advancement) and move into a new market—one that didn't exist for women five years ago. Bank management, carpentry, police work, engineering, law, medicine, college administration, garbage collecting—these used to be all-male occupations. Women were (and still are) concentrated in education, social services, and the health fields, where many of the jobs are low-paying and dead-end. The few women who defied custom and entered business chose, or were directed toward, the "soft" industries—advertising, publishing, broadcasting, fashion, public relations—the glamour fields where turnover is high and salaries for women are generally low.

Salaries in female-dominated industries have always been lower than in male-dominated fields. For example, in 1974 telephone switchboard operators earned an average of $126 a week while linemen earned an average of $228. Is a lineman's work worth twice that of an operator? Is twice as much skill required? Now that women are becoming "linepersons" and men are becoming operators, it will be interesting to watch what happens to the salary differentials.

An accurate rule of thumb has been: the more women in any occupation, the lower the pay and the lower the status. For example, at a time when bank tellers were mostly men, the job was considered well-paying and moderately high in status. Now that most tellers are women, the status of the job has dropped and so has the pay.

The days of "women's work" are numbered. Women are moving into all fields, demanding equal pay and getting it. As a result of the feminist movement, new laws against sex discrimination, Affirmative Action plans, and their new self-awareness, women are making inroads into male-dominated industries. Employers in many major industries are actively seeking women for jobs in managerial positions, in the skilled trades, and in other jobs formerly closed to them. Women MBAs, engineers, lawyers, scientists, bricklayers, telephone installers, and automobile mechanics are being recruited, as pressures continue to open up the job market.

How can you turn these new job opportunities into job openings for you? Begin by exploring the fields you never thought of entering—those traditionally closed to women. You'll find more advancement potential and better pay in these male-dominated areas than in the old-fashioned supportive-type jobs women have always held. The best bets for women will be the fields which now employ the fewest women. For example, since 39 percent of the country's work force is female but only 1 percent of all engineers are women, a lot of women engineers will have to be hired before things even start to even up. Make these numbers work for you.

When you choose a field, give careful consideration to its growth potential as well as to the number of women already in it. Keeping up with the changing job market is like trying to catch a shooting star. First you see it, then it disappears. At best, predictions are educated guesses based on current conditions. But they can be useful guides. For example, there was a great demand for teachers only a short time ago. Anyone with a teaching certificate was snapped up for part-time or full-time work. Now the market has collapsed, with seven trained teachers for every four available jobs. (This fact has apparently been slow to reach students in teacher-training schools; no corresponding drop in enrollments has occurred.) The sad fact is that many women (and men as well) are preparing for jobs that don't exist.

According to a booklet put out by the Women's Bureau of the U.S. Department of Labor, "Women must change their career aspirations. Since openings in the usual 'women's' occupations will not be sufficient to supply jobs for all women seeking work, they must choose alternatives in nontraditional occupations." This grim-sounding prediction has a silver lining, however, for the booklet goes on to point out: "Many of these nontraditional jobs pay higher wages and offer greater opportunities for promotion."

To give you some idea of present predictions for

the remainder of the 1970s and the beginning of the 1980s, here is a partial survey of the new opportunities opening up to women in the professions, in technical pursuits, in business management, the skilled trades, the armed services, and government work, as well as in traditional jobs and part-time work.

THE PROFESSIONS

The women who are reaping the first benefits of the equal-opportunity climate are those who entered and stayed in male-dominated fields regardless of hardships, cultural conditioning, and the ubiquitous pressure to settle for traditional women's jobs. They are the engineers, scientists, accountants, architects, doctors, lawyers, and other professionals who make up the tiny percentage of women in these male-dominated fields. There aren't many of them—for example, only 7 percent of all chemists are women, 4 percent of all architects, 7 percent of all doctors, and 1 percent of all engineers—but those who stuck it out have a one-way ticket to the top.

Since equal opportunity in employment is a farce without equal educational opportunities, the push is on to open up to women not only law schools but medical schools and other graduate and professional schools where quotas have long existed.

College-bound girls should explore nontraditional professions where few women are now employed. A Department of Labor career-planning booklet for high school girls suggests that accounting, engineering, business, and scientific fields are good prospects. Traditional guidance counselors have discouraged girls from going into these fields and directed them instead toward teaching, nursing, library work, social work, and home economics—fields that currently employ two-thirds of all women professionals. With the exception of the health field, all have limited growth potential. Table 1 is a list of estimated openings in a number of professional fields, published by the Department of Labor as a career guide for women in the 1970s.

Before making up your mind what career you will try for, give some careful thought to the following fields:

LAW

Although the scarcity of women professionals will continue for many years, the enormous gap *is* narrowing. Nowhere is this more apparent than in the legal profession. In 1973 the total enrollment of women in law schools was nine times that in 1963, and in the past two years alone it has increased by one-third. Women now comprise 15.6 percent of law-school students, which means that over the next four years the number of women attorneys will double.

TABLE 1
PROFESSIONAL-JOB PROJECTIONS

	Total Employees, 1970	Women in Field, 1970	Annual Openings to 1980 (est.)
Accountant	491,000	20%	31,200
Architect	33,000	4	2,700
Chemist	137,000	7	9,400
Dentist	103,000	2	5,400
Dietitian	30,000	90	2,300
Economist	33,000	10	2,300
Electrical engineer	*	**	12,200
Employment counselor	8,000	50	1,100
Life scientist	180,000	10	9,900
Mathematician	75,000	10	4,600
Market research worker	23,000	*	2,600
Occupational therapist	7,500	90	1,150
Personnel worker	160,000	25	9,100
Physical therapist	15,000	66	1,600
Physician	305,000	7	22,000
Physicist	48,000	4	3,500
Programmer	200,000	**	34,700
Psychologist	40,000	25	3,700

31

Public relations			
worker	75,000	25	4,400
Recreation worker	13,500	50	1,700
Registered nurse	700,000	99	69,000
Rehabilitation			
counselor	13,000	30	1,600
Speech pathologist			
and audiologist	22,000	75	2,200
Statistician	24,000	33	1,400
Systems analyst	100,000	**	22,700
Urban planner	8,000	**	750

*Majority are men.
**Data are not available.
SOURCE: Women's Bureau, Employment Standards Administration, U.S. Department of Labor.

SCIENCE

Long-range prospects for women scientists are excellent. The recent slowdown in the growth rate of scientific research has affected the short-term demand for scientists in some fields; however, by 1980 the demand is projected to outstrip the supply again. At that time, the demand for chemists is expected to reach 200,000—about a 55 percent increase over actual employment in 1968—largely as a result of increased production of high-energy and nuclear fuels, new fertilizers, fibers, drugs, and plastics. The demand for physicists will also increase—75,000 by 1980, a 64 percent jump over 1968 employment. Since only 7 percent of chemists and 4 percent of physicists are women, these fields offer prime possibilities.

In other scientific fields, such as geology and geophysics, demand is also high and supplies are low. By 1980 the demand for geologists is expected to increase 19 percent over 1968 employment and 26 percent for geophysicists.

Demand for ecologists similarly is expected to grow as environmental problems demand solutions.

No matter what branch of science you choose, the

number of women in the field is low, making it a good prospect for women of the future.

MEDICINE

There is a riddle that goes: "A boy and his father were injured in an automobile accident and were rushed to a hospital. The examining surgeon, upon uncovering the boy's face, gasped, 'I cannot operate—he's my own son.' What is the relationship of the surgeon to the boy?" This amazingly simple riddle has stumped many people. That the boy's *mother* was a doctor never entered their minds.

And that's the way it's been with this, the highest paid (on a per capita basis) profession. Women make up about 7 percent of all doctors—a figure that has remained the same for so long as to make one suspicious. Medical schools and associations will deny it, but the number of women entering medical schools has been limited according to a strict quota system. Women's applications have traditionally been set aside for comparison with the applications of other women, instead of considering both male and female applications on the same basis.

Girls have been discouraged from taking the necessary prerequisite courses—chemistry, higher math, physics—and told flatly by many counselors to stay out of medicine or prepare for a life of spinsterhood since training requires long and dedicated study.

At the same time, girls were told that although they were suited for work requiring manual dexterity (typing, sewing, chopping onions), the skill wasn't transferable to brain surgery; that although women are naturally more gentle, kind, and humanistic, they are not suited to be physicians. "Be a nurse or social worker" was the usual, albeit illogical, advice to young women who would be healers.

Becoming a doctor is difficult for anybody. Education stretches nine years or more beyond high school; the cost is high, and scholarships are available, at this time, only for full-time students. (The Health Pro-

33

fessions Educational Assistance Act of 1963 makes loans and scholarships available to medical students.)

The demand for doctors, however, is very high and is expected to outstrip the supply by more than 10,000 by 1980. The image of the starving intern remains essentially intact, but at the end of the road, perhaps no other profession guarantees so much financial success as medicine. It would be a rare experience to find a doctor in an unemployment line.

DENTISTRY

Dentistry is another profession traditionally closed to women, also for suspect reasons. Less than 3 percent of all dentists in this country are women, whereas in Greece half the dentists are women, and in Finland and the U.S.S.R. the figure rises to eight out of ten.

The traditional arguments used to keep women out of other professions obviously never applied in dentistry, a profession with working hours and locations that can be adapted to individual needs more easily than most. Offices can be at home, part-time clinic or group practice is readily available because of the shortage of dentists, and maternity leave can be arranged with minimal disruption.

Nevertheless, dentistry in the United States remains a male profession. The myths are that women are to weak to pull teeth, too emotional to respond to emergencies, unable to stand on their feet for long hours, and, the ultimate presumption, that patients "expect" dentists to be men. So women have become dental assistants, hygienists, and laboratory workers, leaving the lucrative practice of dentistry to men.

By 1980 the demand for dentists, like that for doctors, will outstrip the supply by more than 10,000, making this a prime occupation for women to enter. A dental education requires six to seven years of training after high school and is expensive. Often, however, loans are available to qualified students through HPEAA for the final four years.

As one satisfied dentist put it, "I earn as much

money as most medical doctors with none of the house calls. Plus I take off four days a week during the summer." If you are a young woman thinking about a long-term career in the health field, how about becoming a dentist? There never was a better time.

ENGINEERING

In terms of percentages, there are fewer women in engineering than in any other profession—less than 1 percent. The supply of engineers is declining (the number of male college graduates with engineering degrees is down about 10 percent from 1968), which makes it a wide-open field for women. The only way to go is up.

The prediction is that there will be more engineering jobs during the next decade, despite the present unemployment in some specialties such as aerospace. Environmental pollution, urban deterioration, and depletion of natural resources all require engineering-based solutions. Automation is becoming ever more complex, creating jobs for engineers.

If you are a woman with an analytical mind, an ability to visualize form and function, and an aptitude for math and science, think of engineering. Men have no monopoly on engineering aptitude.

If you want to become an engineer, you can choose from among dozens of specialties. There are engineers who work on construction sites, do research in laboratories, probe the ocean depths, and direct trips into outer space. In 1970 women college graduates with engineering degrees were offered beginning salaries in excess of $10,000 a year. Whether you choose industrial, civil, mechanical, electrical, or any other type of engineering, there are more than 250 schools in the country offering training—and loans, grants, and work-study programs are available in many of them.

A woman with an engineering degree is likely to be a hot commodity in the marketplace during the next ten years.

TECHNICIANS

"You are all but guaranteed work," states a booklet promoting technical careers, produced through the efforts of the U.S. Office of Education, the Conference Board, and the Manpower Institute. What's most impressive about this pamphlet is that its publication was paid for by thirty-eight corporations, among them AT&T, Ford, General Electric, IBM, ITT, Standard Oil, and Xerox. Who can better determine the need than the buyer? These corporations are prime employers of technicians.

Not only is the demand for existing technical jobs increasing, but new technical jobs are being created. The scientific and technological revolution is developing new opportunities, thousands of them. The demand for people with technical skills is growing twice as fast as for any other job category. For example, who ever heard of an inhalation therapist a few years ago? Now there are 10,000, with a projected demand for 2,100 more by 1980. Table 2 shows projections for various other technical jobs, furnished by the U.S. Department of Labor.

Technicians require a combination of basic scientific or technical knowledge and manual skills, which can be learned through specialized education or on-the-job training. Technicians assist various professionals such as scientists, physicians, and mathematicians.

While most technical jobs have been held by men,

TABLE 2
TECHNICAL-JOB PROJECTIONS

	Total Employees, 1970	Women in Field, 1970	Annual Openings to 1980 (est.)
Draftsman	310,000	4%	16,300
Engineering and science technician	650,000	11	33,000

Food-processing technician	3,400	*	150
Dental assistant	91,000	**	9,200
Dental hygienist	16,000	**	3,100
Electrocardiographic (EKG) technician	9,500	**	1,600
Electroencephalographic (EEG) technician	3,000	**	950
Inhalation therapist	10,000	*	2,100
Medical assistant	175,000	80	20,000
Medical laboratory workers	110,000	80 to 90	13,500
Occupational therapy assistant	6,000	**	1,300
Optometric assistant	5,000	**	300
Physical therapy assistant	10,000	50	2,200
Radiology technician	80,000	66	7,700
Surgical technician	25,000	**	2,600

*Data are not available.
**Majority are women.
SOURCE: Women's Bureau, Employment Standards Administration, U.S. Department of Labor.

women in record numbers are breaking into the technology field, partly because of the demand for equal job rights.

If you are re-entering the job market or thinking about changing jobs, a technical job might be exactly what you are looking for: the training entails less challenge than a professional school, and the job would certainly be more interesting than working in the local dime store.

You can qualify for some technical jobs with one to two years of study after high school. Other jobs require an A.A.S. degree (Associate in Applied Science). While a high school education is a basic requirement, some schools will help drop-outs complete their high school studies.

There are three kinds of training schools for technicians.

37

Technical institutes offer two- to three-year concentrated training programs in scientific theory and mathematics.

Junior and community colleges generally offer some theoretical courses similar to those given at technical institutes. The training program is usually two years. If you decide on more education at a later date, you can transfer credits to a four-year college. (This is also true of technical institutes.)

Technical vocational schools offer one- or two-year programs and often combine technical courses with high school–level courses. They tend to have liberal admissions requirements.

Although scholarship aid is limited for technical training, there are many student-loan programs. And many technical schools can arrange part-time work to help you through your training. If you are a high school or college student interested in becoming a technician, ask your student counselor or placement officer for a listing of technical schools and possible scholarships or loans.

There are even some technical jobs you can prepare for through home study. For details, contact

> The National Home Study Council
> 1601 18th Street, N.W.
> Washington, D.C. 20009.

Technical careers that you can train for in two years or less, according to the U.S. Office of Education, are in the following fields: aeronautics and aerospace, air conditioning and refrigeration, agriculture, architecture and construction, automotive industry, chemistry, civil engineering, commercial aviation, electrical work, electronics, electromechanics, electronic data processing, fire protection, forestry, health services, industrial production, instrumentation, library and information science, marine life and ocean fishing, mechanical design, metallurgy, nuclear physics and radiology, oceanography, office-management specialists, police science, and sanitation and environmental control.

BUSINESS ADMINISTRATION

The hottest item on the business market today, according to the president of a well-known corporation, is an MBA with a woman attached to it. If she's black, Spanish, Chinese, or Indian, so much the better. This man has hired three female MBAs during the past two years—two from Harvard and one from Stanford—and considers himself lucky to have attracted that many.

There is no doubt that the scramble is on to find female executive talent. Colleges are beefing up their business programs to help supply the new demand, executive search firms are being hired to ferret out talent, and personnel directors are combing their files for women to promote.

Career paths for women, once unheard of, are now routine in most larger corporations and in many smaller ones. A career path is a carefully charted series of steps leading from an entry-level job to a higher position. It's like a road map. It tells you which turns lead to what jobs and where the road ends.

While much of the search is real—women *are* being promoted to middle- and top-management positions—some of it is strictly "show and tell" for the benefit of the federal government. Firms holding government contracts are required to file Affirmative Action plans stating what they are doing to recruit, hire, train, and promote women. Some employers, while claiming to look under every pebble for "qualified" women, are motivated to fail. Many an applicant has been told in an interview that no jobs are available, only to read in the newspaper next day that the very same company is beating the bushes for "qualified" women. It's better to know at the outset that some of these serious men in black kneesocks tend to speak with forked tongue.

The number of women classified as managers and administrators by the Bureau of the Census rose 22 percent in the decade from 1960 to 1970, as against a 37 percent increase of all women workers during those years. What these figures show is that women

39

have generally been locked out of top- and middle-management jobs. At the present time only 2 percent of all managers are women. And most managers (male or female) are only in first- or second-level management.

Progress *is* being made, however. A survey by Frank S. Endicott of Northwestern University of 190 private companies revealed that these companies expected to hire 35 percent more women college graduates from the class of 1973 than they had hired from the class of 1972. In 1972, these companies had anticipated only a 15 percent increase over 1971.

The Women's Bureau sponsors many employment conferences attended by business and industry representatives. "Difficulty of finding qualified women" is reason most often cited to account for the fact that more women aren't hired by business.

"One obvious answer is the need to inform young women and girls about the situation," states a Women's Bureau publication. "It is generally acknowledged that few women have been encouraged to prepare for business careers, because of traditional views about women's place. Repeated emphasis on women's interests in and qualifications for the 'nurturing and helping activities' has propelled the large majority of college-educated women into teaching, nursing, social work and library professions."

SKILLED TRADES

There are more jobs in skilled trades than there are workers to fill them, according to the Bureau of Labor Statistics. With the increasing demand in many industries for skilled workers, women are breaking into "men's jobs" at a rapid rate. Even age-old superstitions preventing women from entering such sacrosanct male compounds as coal mines and construction sites are collapsing. Women are becoming carpenters, metal workers, bakers, printers, and plumbers.

There are today some 11 million skilled workers in nearly 400 trades, but as of 1970 only 60 of these trades had ever admitted women to apprenticeships. Those trades that did admit women were female-typed, such as cosmetology and cooking. Only 4 percent of all craftworkers in 1973 were women.

Nowhere is there more opportunity for women seeking new fields than in skilled trades. A 20 percent overall increase in the number of skilled jobs is projected for the next decade. Since few women are now employed in skilled trades, a lot of opportunity exists.

APPRENTICESHIPS

Apprenticeships are programs through which workers learn a recognized trade by combining formal instruction with on-the-job training. The Bureau of Apprenticeship of the U.S. Department of Labor has set the following criteria for the registration of new apprenticeship programs:

- A clearly identified trade that can be learned in a practical way through work and on-the-job training
- A job involving manual, mechanical, or technical skills and knowledge requiring a minimum of two thousand hours of work and training
- A job requiring on-the-job training with related instruction that can be given in a classroom, through correspondence courses, self-study, or other approved means of instruction
- A job that does not fall into selling, managerial, clerical, or professional categories

Apprenticeships have long been the route by which young unskilled men have entered skilled, well-paying jobs. The length of training varies generally from one to four years, with about 144 hours of classroom instruction.

Except in a handful of female-typed trades, women, when not blatantly excluded, have been discouraged from entering apprenticeship programs. Women themselves have played their part: they have shied away from interesting, well-paying jobs in the trades to accept low-paying office work. But the attitudes of employers, unions, and the educational system have been the most formidable barriers. Schools have traditionally channeled non-college-bound boys into vocational training and girls into home economics or business courses.

Government manpower-training programs, including the Job Corps, Jobs Optional, the Labor Education Advancement Program, and the Work Incentive Program, have also been guilty of sex stereotyping. Even the state and federal agencies tend to shunt girls into unskilled clerical, food-service, or institutional jobs rather than encourage them to enter apprenticeships.

In April 1974 the Manpower Administration expanded its apprenticeship programs to include new opportunities for women. The program places emphasis on recruiting, counseling, and tutoring young women to enter *all* apprenticeships. Pilot projects are being conducted by the National Urban League in Atlanta, Chicago, and Los Angeles; the Mexican-American Foundation in Los Angeles; and the Recruitment and Training Program in Boston, Cleveland, and New York.

Although resistance to opening up the trades to women remains high, apprenticeship programs in the more than 300 trades that traditionally kept women out will be prime job targets. The Bureau of Apprenticeship and Training of the U.S. Department of Labor requires all trades, including those in construction, to establish equal-opportunity standards for recruitment, selection, and employment of apprentices.

Here are a few examples of apprenticeships that are predicted to have a high demand for workers in the next ten years:

Welders. Welders are needed in almost all industries, from automobile and airplane manufacturing to building houses and furniture. There are about 22,000 openings each year. Often it is possible to take a high school or vocational course in welding methods before applying for an apprenticeship.

The building trades. These include such skilled workers as carpenters, construction electricians, and plumber-pipefitters. Women who like working with their hands might be well suited to these trades. Although the construction industry has been in a serious slump for the past two years, high labor demands are predicted for the future. The federal government predicts annual openings for 40,000 carpenters, 12,000 construction electricians, and 20,000 plumber-pipefitters. Apprenticeship programs consist of on-the-job training.

Appliance services. Women who have been repairing their own toasters and television sets may be able to turn this skill into a good job. The employment outlook is excellent. Training can be obtained through vocational courses, federal job-training programs, or on-the-job training.

Automobile mechanics. About 23,000 openings a year are expected. The requirements are dexterity in handling tools and equipment plus mechanical aptitude —both of which many women have. Getting dirty is also part of the job—and women can do this too. Apprentice programs and on-the-job training are available.

Think carefully about an apprenticeship, especially if you are a high school student who doesn't intend to go on to college. Recognize the psychological conditioning that prompts you to think "a lady can't be a plumber." Maybe a lady can't be a plumber, but a woman can.

According to the Department of Labor, a rapid employment increase is expected in a number of skilled occupations. Table 3 lists some of these fields.

THE NEW MILITARY

The thirty-year-old slogan "Be a WAC, be a WAVE, be a nurse—release a soldier for active duty" has been scuttled as an effective way of recruiting the women's army of the future. Equal opportunity is creeping up on the military, but one women brigadier general does not an open army make.

Changes have taken place, and more are in the offing.

TABLE 3
EMPLOYMENT IN VARIOUS SKILLED OCCUPATIONS

	Total Employed, 1970	Annual Openings to 1980 (est.)
Air conditioning, refrigeration, and heating mechanic	115,000	7,900
Aircraft mechanic	140,000	6,000
Appliance serviceman	220,000	11,000
Automobile mechanic	610,000	23,300
Business machine serviceman	80,000	6,000
Electrician (construction)	190,000	12,000
Industrial machinery repairman	180,000	9,000
Instrument maker—mechanical	8,000	400
Instrument repairman	95,000	5,900
Operating engineer (construction machinery operator)	310,000	15,000
Plumber and pipefitter	350,000	20,000
Television and radio service technician	132,000	4,500
Truck and bus mechanic	115,000	5,200

SOURCE: Women's Bureau, Employment Standards Administration, U.S. Department of Labor.

These may include you, if you are thinking of joining the army.

The most frequently heard argument against approving the Equal Rights Amendment is that women will be forced into combat. But even during wartime, combat troops make up a tiny percentage of military forces. In war or peace there are benefits to be derived from a military career—pensions, free medical care, educational advantages, career-training programs, and retirement after twenty years—which for many men

44

has meant a second career beginning at the age of thirty-eight.

The military has been the quickest way out of poverty for underprivileged young men. Many professional men today would never have been able to go to college had it not been for the G.I. Bill of Rights. Since World War II more than 17 million persons have been educated in programs administered by the Veterans Administration, but only 1.8 percent have been women. This is an obvious injustice to women, and one that is currently receiving a great deal of attention.

The National Citizens' Advisory Council on the Status of Women in 1973 reported to the President that "the career options of many young women are being limited by lack of knowledge of the splendid opportunities in the military." While the council praised the military services for their progress in increasing the employment of women and eliminating discriminatory practices, it recommended that the services move rapidly toward total elimination of discriminatory practices; that the same standards for enlistment and commissioning be applied to both men and women; that high schools invite career military women and members of the Defense Advisory Committee on Women in the Service to help acquaint young women with opportunities in the military; and that women's organizations and PTAs be asked to help educate young women as to military-service opportunities.

Regulations that treat women and men differently

TABLE 4
WOMEN IN THE ARMED SERVICES

	1970	1973	Target for 1978
Army	16,724	20,935	51,988
Air Force	13,787	19,863	48,399
Navy	8,254	12,289	19,774
Marines	2,418	2,288	3,100

SOURCE: *U. S. News & World Report*, December 10, 1973.

in the military are being reassessed. As a result, jobs are opening up, and they are *not* in the typing pool. Women are now serving in such areas as flight training, ship duty, and space exploration. Few combat jobs remain closed to women.

Table 4 shows the number of women in the services in 1970 and 1973 and the target number for 1978.

GOVERNMENT WORK

Government at all levels, federal, state, and local, is a major employer of both men and women. Like other employers, the government has reflected society's work pyramid: the top jobs are held almost exclusively by men, with women clustered in clerical-type jobs at the bottom.

This situation makes the government vulnerable in a special way. It is glaringly inconsistent for the government to hound the private sector to institute Affirmative Action programs while the government itself continues discriminatory practices.

Pressure to change the government's practices is mounting on many fronts—not the least of which are women government employees. Five women's organizations recently filed a lawsuit charging the government with failing to enforce its own laws against sex discrimination.

You might be able to turn the government's problems to advantage if you show up at the right time in the right place with the right qualifications. For the first time in history, you are of the right sex to qualify for a really *good* government job.

Since the various levels of government employ such a huge number of people across the country, government is a prime source of both traditional and nontraditional jobs for women. Virtually every occupation in private industry is found in government, from zoology to archeology, from aeronautics to accounting. Federal salaries, and many state and local salaries as well, are competitive with private industry at the entry and middle-management levels. It is only at the top that private-industry salaries leave the government far behind.

Each year thousands of young women apply for civil service jobs. If you are one, be sure to investigate the expanding opportunities. The Women's Bureau of the Department of Labor can give you much help. For if the branch of government you choose is guilty of discrimination, the Women's Bureau will point out your job rights and advancement possibilities. The lid is off. The sky's the limit for women in government. Don't settle for less than you're worth.

TRADITIONAL JOBS

Besides the nontraditional jobs described in this chapter, projections for some traditional women's jobs remain high. About 69,000 openings a year are projected for registered nurses, 74,000 for bookkeepers, 23,500 for receptionists, 247,000 for stenographers and secretaries, and 61,000 for typists.

Women may also find jobs in traditional sales and service-type jobs. Table 5 lists a few projections in these areas by the Department of Labor.

Despite the continuing high demand in some traditional women's fields, such as nursing, women as a

TABLE 5
SALES- AND SERVICE-JOB PROJECTIONS

	Total Employees, 1970	Annual Openings to 1980 (est.)
Clerical		
Cashier	847,000	64,000
Claims adjuster	114,000	4,500
Library technician	76,000	7,200
Traffic agent and clerk (civil aviation)	45,000	4,800
Service		
Cosmetologist	484,000	43,000

Hospital attendant	830,000	111,000
Licensed practical nurse	370,000	58,000
State police officer	41,000	2,900
Stewardess	35,600	*
Sales		
Insurance agent and broker	350,000	19,000
Manufacturer's salesman	510,000	25,000
Real estate salesman and broker	226,000	14,800
Securities salesman	200,000	11,800
Wholesale trade sales worker	539,000	27,700

*Not available.

SOURCE: Women's Bureau, Employment Standards Administration, U.S. Department of Labor.

group must look outside the traditional job categories or end up standing in unemployment lines. To push forward into new careers is no longer a choice—it is a necessity.

PART-TIME WORK

Many women have found interesting, well-paid part-time jobs that have allowed them to combine home and work. Part-time work has solved the dilemma of many mothers, caught between their children's needs and their own financial or career needs. And some fields, such as writing and teaching, are especially suited to this dual role for women.

Although child-care methods are expected to change somewhat, it is still true that virtually all young children today are cared for by their mothers. The traditional business world has endorsed this arrangement, but has done very little to make part-time careers possible for women.

Catalyst, a national nonprofit organization dedicated to expanding part-time employment opportunities for college-educated women, reports some success in moving the business world toward more part-time employment. Catalyst points out many advantages for employers, such as the lower turnover of part-time women, their greater productivity, and the larger recruitment pool they supply.

Perhaps future technology will make obsolete the eight-hour-a-day, five-day-a-week job as past technology has done to the twelve-hour day and six-day work week. Perhaps the time will come when mothers and fathers will share child care, both working part time. Perhaps the future will bring first-rate child-care centers run by professionals that are good for parents and for children. And perhaps the world of business will change drastically from today's rigid demands.

But none of this has happened yet. And you as a woman looking for a job are faced with today's realities. The business world is competitive. It takes time and dedication to succeed. Competing on a part-time basis with others who work full time is a handicap for even the most superior person.

It isn't impossible to succeed in a job by working part time, but your chances of doing so are less than if you work full time. Part-time work may be right for you, or it may be your only alternative. If you decide to pursue it, however, you should be forewarned about the business world's general attitude about part-time work.

Business runs on its schedule, not yours. Part-time employees are not part of the problem-solving staff from which round-the-clock efforts are sometimes demanded. You will be relegated to a "helper" role and paid accordingly.

Your career will not be taken seriously. If your boss is a firm believer in women's keeping the home fires burning, he will not promote you to a position of responsibility with corresponding pay even if he is pleased with your work.

If you do fantastically well in your job, you'll probably be offered as a reward a full-time job—not a promotion in your part-time position.

Your fringe benefits, unless you do some fancy bargaining, will be nil.

You will be the first to be fired or laid off. Part-time employees frequently are considered "buffers" for full-time employees in bad times. But part-time employees are owed nothing.

Other staff people may resent you or consider you a threat to their jobs. This will be especially true if you do in four hours what they do in eight. Tact is required in order to do your best and yet avoid creating mutiny.

Employers want employees to be dependent on their jobs. This creates an atmosphere of competition in which, it is believed, workers make their best efforts. The entire business structure is founded upon dependency, hard work, and rewards (promotions). As a part-time employee, you are outside this circle.

Business functions are interrelated and coordinated. As a part-time employee you break this chain, forcing others to plan their work around you—which is sure to be a sore point.

The best scapegoat in the world is a part-time employee. No matter what comes up, you can be blamed if you aren't around to defend yourself.

ANTIDISCRIMINATION LAWS

Affirmative Action, EEOC, Executive Order 11246, NLRB, the Equal Pay Act of 1963, Executive Order 11478, OFCC, Revised Order No. 4, Title VII, Title IX. What does it all mean? What has this alphabet soup to do with you and your getting a job?

The answer is everything. You need not memorize each acronym, but in a general way you'd better know what this whole collection has done for you and can do for you in the future. It is vital to your job search, especially if you're looking in nontraditional areas. It does not mean that discrimination has ended. It means that for the first time in the history of our country, refusing to hire you or to promote you because you are a woman is against the law.

During the original congressional debate over passage of the Civil Rights Act of 1964, Title VII was amended to prohibit sex discrimination along with discrimination based on race, religion, or national origin. The amendment was proposed in an attempt to defeat the entire act: sex discrimination seemed so natural and desirable that if it were included, the whole bill, it was felt, would appear ridiculous.

The ploy backfired, and Title VII became law, effective July 2, 1965. Some legislators chuckled publicly about the prospect of male Playboy bunnies.

The joke spread throughout the country, but so did the women's movement. Title VII worked. It worked so well that in the first year of its operation one-third of the total number of cases filed cited sex discrimination.

The Equal Employment Opportunity Commission (EEOC), which is composed of five members appointed by the President, administers Title VII. Specifically, the commission

- Investigates and settles complaints and tries to correct discriminatory practices permanently
- May assist people who file claims and may refer cases with a pattern of discrimination to the U.S. Attorney General for legal action
- Issues guidelines to help employers better understand the law
- Offers technical assistance on request and encourages employers to take affirmative action
- Promotes better understanding of the mandates of Title VII and funds antidiscrimination projects operated by state and local fair-employment-practices agencies
- Holds public hearings to examine the employment practices of major firms and labor organizations and seeks to remedy any discriminatory practices found
- Requires reports on minority and female employees to determine compliance with the law and to compile analyses of employment patterns
- Compiles research studies, which so far have shown that women are concentrated in the lowest-paying and least-skilled classifications and are severely underutilized as officials, managers, professionals, and skilled craftspeople

51

Because of the years of discrimination against women, the EEOC has ordered that employers in some cases take remedial action. When this action is taken it becomes Affirmation Action. The EEOC requires the filing of written goals and timetables for Affirmative Action in the recruiting, hiring, training, and promotion of women. Any organization receiving federal funds or any company doing business with the federal government is in danger of losing that funding or business unless Affirmative Action requirements are met. This is a very powerful threat even though it is seldom exercised.

A number of executive orders and amendments to the Civil Rights Act of 1964 have extended sex-discrimination coverage and enforcement, the most recent addition covering teachers and administrators in educational institutions.

An executive order administered by the Office of Federal Contract Compliance (OFCC) prohibits federal contractors or subcontractors from working on projects where discrimination exists. Revised Order No. 4, issued by OFCC, requires contractors with fifty employees or more and contracts totaling $50,000 or more to take Affirmative Action and submit written goals and timetables for eliminating discrimination.

An executive order extends enforcement powers to the Civil Service Commission to ensure equal opportunity in the federal government, and the National Labor Relations Board has jurisdiction over labor unions.

Further, the Protection Against Age Discrimination in Employment Act prohibits employment agencies, employers, and labor unions from discriminating in hiring, firing, and promotions on the basis of age against any person between the ages of forty and sixty-five.

With this battery of laws and executive orders, why have five women's organizations filed suit against the Department of Labor and the Department of Health, Education, and Welfare? They have done so because laws are only as effective as their enforcement and/or court interpretation. They are charging the government with lethargy in enforcing its own laws against sex discrimination.

The suit seeks to direct the government to withhold millions of dollars in federal funds from colleges and universities that allegedly discriminate against women and to enforce the Public Health Service antibias law with regard to medical and nursing schools. The group claims that the Department of Health, Education and Welfare has failed to resolve more than 550 complaints of discrimination under 1969 and 1972 executive orders. If the outcome of the suit is favorable, the equal employment of women will take a giant step forward. Furthermore, a national Equal Rights Amendment will make it unnecessary to press for case-by-case legislation, as must be done now.

You don't have to become a lawyer to learn your job rights (described in detail on pages 333–347) and how to use them. But a little knowledge will better qualify you to make decisions about prospective employers and how to weigh one company's offer against another's—assuming that you have two offers.

Employers are on the line as never before. Bright women everywhere will want to work for those whose Affirmative Action plans are real instead of make-believe. The other companies will have to settle for second-best—which is exactly what they deserve.

KEEPING UP WITH THE MARKET

So now, with thoughts of becoming a flagpole sitter or jackhammer operator dancing in your head, do a little reading. You don't have to become a market analyst, but it helps to know a few things about the economy and business in general. If nothing else, this will keep you from mailing a résumé to a company that has just laid off two thousand workers or nodding enthusiastically when a representative of a company known for discrimination describes their Affirmative Action plan in glowing terms.

Financial magazines such as *Forbes, Fortune,* and

Business Week can give you much information. Syndicated newspaper columns like Sylvia Porter's are informative and written in language that the average reader can understand. Reading *The Wall Street Journal* daily will give you more information than you can get from any other business publication.

In addition to these national publications, there are many specialized publications about individual industries. Some of these are listed in the directory section of this book. Do a little research at the local library and apply what you learn to *your* job problems and *your* job possibilities.

Every scrap of information you gather now may be useful to you someday. At the very least it will give you something to talk about in your first interview.

At any rate, stay loose and confident, and start shedding those psychological blinders. Nobody is limiting you anymore except possibly yourself.

3

Choosing Your Field

A career army officer, a few months from retirement, remarked that he had never really liked his job, hated the regimentation of army life, disliked giving orders, and was delighted to retire from his chosen career.

"If you so dislike what you are doing," a logical questioner asked, "why did you choose it?"

"Choose it!" exploded the commander. "I didn't choose it. Some stupid eighteen-year-old, day-dreaming dummy chose it. Not me."

We all change. As an eighteen-year-old boy, the commander wanted to join the army and see the world. He believed the romantic recruiting posters of far-away places and South Sea island maidens. As the years passed, however, the reality of his day-to-day job replaced the unrealistic dreams of his youth. To some degree, this happens to everybody.

You can't buy insurance against making wrong decisions about your career, but you can employ some simple safeguards. If you don't like to read, don't go to work for a publisher; if you can't sit still for three seconds, don't drive a bus; if whales terrify you, don't become a marine biologist; and if you get claustrophobia in an elevator, scratch any plans for becoming the first woman in space.

People live out their lives in the wrong job because of a lack of planning or failure to face up to hard decisions. Some are so fearful about making wrong choices that they make none at all. Some find it easier to allow others to make decisions for them, eschewing responsibility. Regardless of what fits you, an important fact remains: something is going to happen to the rest of your life beginning now. You can trust to fate and the whims of others, or you can stiffen your backbone and start directing your own life.

According to one traditional guidance counselor, women approach the choice of a career very differently from men. Women, he says, are more interested in personal issues such as "Will I be happy?" "Will I like my boss?" "Can I do the job?" "Will I get along with other staff members?" Concern about these issues, he says, reveals insecurity and short-term goals. Men stress their abilities and weigh the possibilities for advancement. They are interested in title and position. Personal satisfaction, while important to men, is seldom a major consideration as it is with women. Men are interested in long-term goals.

A feminist counselor, specializing in helping older women return to work, disagrees with this analysis. "When I talk to women about jobs I listen with a third ear," she says. Sometimes, she explains, when a woman wonders if she will be happy in a job, she is actually wondering if her husband and children will be happy about her working and if she can juggle the responsibilities of home and career. "Besides," this counselor continued, "why on earth should anybody expect women to react like men when their entire life experiences have been different? It's like expecting birds with clipped wing feathers to fly south with the flock as if nothing had ever happened."

Sad but true, our culture retains the age-old assumption that if a girl is attractive enough she won't ever have to dirty her hands except to dust her diamonds. Unfortunately, this is only a slight exaggeration of the kind of nonsense many girls are still being fed from cradle to college. Parents and guidance counselors should care enough about these young women to level with them and prepare them for reality, namely:

- Even if she marries, a girl can expect to work outside her home for an average of twenty-five years;

if she remains single, it will be about forty-six years.
- One out of ten families is headed by a female wage earner.
- One out of three marriages (in California it is one out of two) ends in divorce.
- Women make up the single largest poverty group in the country.

It is reasonable to expect, then, that you too will be employed at some time in your life. It is wise to plan for that likelihood. Common sense will tell you that choosing a field and planning your life's work is not a luxury—it is a necessity.

DEFINING YOUR JOB GOALS

Exactly what do *you* want from a job? Exactly what do *you* expect? Wishes and expectations often differ. You may want to be President but expect to be a dishwasher (a fine excuse for doing nothing). Should you do what you want, or should you want what you do? Get out of this vicious circle and make up your mind. You don't have to plan the next twenty-five years of your life in order to plan one step.

First you must decide whether your job goals are going to be short-range or long-range. If your goals are short-range, your job assessments will be simple and to the point: what is the salary and what are the working conditions? But if your career goals are long-range, you will need much more information about any company you approach. Among other things, you will want to know about its training programs, career paths, your title, advancement possibilities, travel expectations, Affirmative Action plans, the percentage of women already in the company management, the attitude of the company about hiring and promoting women, pension plans, and other company benefits.

You also will need this information if your career goals change. If you are a housewife who wants to work for a couple of years to help put a child through

57

college and intends to quit once the financial crisis is over, you will look for a job with maximum salary benefits and pleasant working conditions and forget the pension plan. But if after working a few months you change your mind and decide your job goals have changed, the list then becomes important to you. Even if you are a woman of forty-five, remember that you too can have a twenty-year retirement plan fulfilled by the time you are sixty-five. In long-term plans, always consider your next job or promotion. There is a vast difference between a job hopper and a careful planner: both may change jobs, but for different reasons.

In defining your goals think of your needs, interests, and skills in relation to what you have learned about the job market. Everyone has at least a few interests and special abilities that can be translated into job-market terms: working well with children, the aged, or people in general, raising funds for special projects or causes, organizing people or events, public speaking, artistic talent, keeping accounts, selling.

If you've never been employed before or had only temporary jobs, you'll be selling "potential," not experience. You will have to identify marketable skills based on nonpaid activities and special interests. If you've been out of the job market for several years or want to change fields, you'll be looking for transferable skills to bridge the time gap.

When toting up your assets and interests, keep potential employers in mind. Instead of waiting for somebody else to fit you in, figure out for yourself how you could fit into a particular company or organization. Many a new job has come from an applicant's convincing a prospective employer that he or she can build a better mousetrap. An employer's mind is always on the profit-and-loss sheet. Find a way to increase profits and you're in. Your new look at somebody's old business may be just the spark you both need.

IDENTIFYING YOUR SKILLS

Women often put down their very real talents because

those talents are either unpaid or underpaid. But a skill is not a trade requiring advanced study and specialized training. Basically a skill is merely the ability to do something well, with ease and efficiency, in an office or at home, under pressure or in a relaxed atmosphere. Anything from organizing a car pool to managing an office demonstrates a special skill. As simple as it sounds, preparing a breakfast of juice, eggs, bacon, toast, and coffee and getting everything to the table piping hot requires enormous skill. Skills required for a job are valued more than skills used in a hobby or in homemaking, though they may actually be the same skills.

Skill never exists in isolation. Any one skill involves a whole series of related skills and transferable abilities, mental and manual. Take typing, for example (setting aside for the moment the debate over whether this skill is an asset or a liability to a working woman). Typing with speed and accuracy involves manual dexterity; good hand-eye coordination; concentration—the ability to focus line by line on copy or shorthand notes; planning—the ability to visualize how much will fit on a page, including corrections, footnotes, etc.; proofreading—the ability to recognize and correct errors smoothly.

Now look at an extracurricular activity such as editing a high school or college newspaper. The skills required include:

Determining editorial content
Supervising other students
Designing layout and preparing paste-ups
Interviewing teachers, administrators, professional
    speakers, community leaders
Recruiting new staff members
Writing feature stories and news items
Coordinating editing, proofing, and printing, from
    layout to press
Distributing issues
Selling ads, budgeting

Or take the following situation:

Perhaps you were a counselor at a summer camp. One of the children in your group had trouble reading the simplest book. So in your spare time you began reading aloud to her, helping the child spell out each word. Before a week had ended, the child was able to read one story, pronouncing each word correctly, and was asking you for more to read.

What were you doing? You thought you were giving a child you liked a little help. But you actually were taking a problem, analyzing it, breaking it down into parts, and designing an individualized solution for it.

The problem: inability to read well, poor concentration.

The reason: wrong technique, low morale, and poor motivation.

The solution: morale building, supervised practice, heightened interest.

Almost anything you have done can be broken down into a series of steps and analyzed in terms of function and skills. The skills used in the solution of one problem can be transferred to the solution of others. A new set of skills is not needed for each problem—far from it.

Analyze your hobbies and interests, as well as your educational strong points and extracurricular activities, with a view to the transferable skills they entail. One housewife who had never held a job before was able to turn the skills acquired in twenty-years of running a large, complicated household to performing a first-rate job as executive assistant to a famous, harassed, and somewhat disorganized person. Another woman, who loved to entertain friends and did so with great warmth, and who had a remarkable talent for considering details, landed a job with a large public relations firm planning and arranging fund-raising dinners for political and other clients.

Do you like to do needlepoint? Sing in a church choir? Play tennis? Bake cakes? Make model airplanes? Any or all of these pursuits involve skills you can use on a paying job—*some* paying job.

YOUR INFORMAL WORK INVENTORY

It is difficult for people to see themselves as others see them. You are too close to yourself to be objective. Getting some answers down on paper helps you put your goals in perspective and see what you are really interested in doing.

There are no right or wrong answers. These questions are intended to help you collect your thoughts, clear your head, and generate a few ideas.

Job Needs
Which of the following factors are most important to you as you look for work (rate them in order of importance)?

Salary	_____
Responsibility or job title	_____
The training or experience you would gain would gain	_____
The skills you would develop	_____
Advancement opportunities	_____
Company benefits	_____

Financial Needs

	Yes	No
Do you have enough money to support your job search for three months?	_____	_____
For six months?	_____	_____
Could you afford to work only part time while you looked for a full-time job?	_____	_____
If you're working now, have you saved enough money to tide you over if you should leave your job today?	_____	_____

Job Preferences
Do you work more effectively with:
    people_____information_____or ideas_____?
Would you rather:

perform a service_____or produce a product_____?

Would you like to work in a large organization where your responsibilities would be well defined_____or in a smaller company where the lines aren't so clearly defined?_____?

Do you want to step into a well-established, efficiently run work situation_____or are you more attuned to moment-by-moment decision making and flexible chaos where you can invent your own way of doing things_____?

Would you prefer to work with energetic, dynamic individuals_____or with more low-key, quiet types_____?

Do you prefer a work situation in which you are constantly called upon to produce new ideas on your own_____or one in which you are involved with others in designing and planning new projects_____?

Work-related Assets

	Yes	*No*
Do you find that careful listening allows you to gather and remember information?	_____	_____
Are you a visual person? Do you learn best by reading or seeing?	_____	_____
Are you able to manage your time well and to set priorities for completing your work?	_____	_____
Even under deadline pressure?	_____	_____
Do you need reassurance about your work from the people you work with?	_____	_____
Do you have your own standards for measuring what you accomplish in your job?	_____	_____

Special Interests and Talents

Have you ever been involved in planning a project (extra-curricular, academic, or job-related) that you especially enjoyed?

If so, what projects?_____

At what stage of the project did you contribute the most?

The planning stage—designing materials, getting ideas, writing proposals. _____

Keeping track of the various people or groups involved in the work. _____

Maintaining the project once it was put into action. _____

Planning the budget. _____

Following through to get the results desired. _____

If you're working now, in what aspects of your job do you perform best (rate in order of your ability)?

Following a consistent plan or pattern of work. _____

Reorganizing systems to make them run more smoothly. _____

Directing the work of others. _____

Handling follow-through details after a project or program has been pulled together. _____

What job skills do you have that you could transfer into another field or job?

Administration	_____	Research and	
Budgeting	_____	analysis	_____
Interviewing	_____	Supervising	_____
Marketing	_____	Training	_____
Organizing	_____	Writing	_____
Program		Others	_____
planning	_____		

Are there any specific fields or types of jobs that you want to investigate?

Fields _____ Job types _____

_____ _____

Are these fields or jobs related to:

Your extracurricular interests? _____

Your previous work experience? _____

Your education? _____

Long-Range Work Goals

	Yes	No
Do you expect to be working one year from now?	_____	_____
Five years from now?	_____	_____

Are you willing to relocate if your job or career makes it necessary to do so? _____ _____

Are you prepared to move from one job to another or one field to another in order to advance? _____ _____

Or are you more interested in salary and job security than in advancement? _____ _____

Are you career-oriented? Do you accept the long-range commitments of time and energy a career demands? _____ _____

Would changes in your life-style or needs, such as marriage, children, or an opportunity to return to school, make you decide to stop working? _____ _____

USING YOUR WORK-INVENTORY RESULTS

Answering the work-inventory questions should have helped to clarify your immediate work preferences. You should have a better idea of where you would like to fit in, what you would like to try for in a job. In narrowing your possibilities further, suppose you decide you want to work in a small operation where you're more in control—big-fish-in-little-pond theory. You feel you have good ideas, you can work well under pressure and can organize your activities without constant supervision. You are highly motivated to succeed, you are a quick learner, and you want a job that will sharpen your skills and give you experience.

You have defined a goal. You know something of the general type of job and responsibility you want, the atmosphere and scope of the operation. You are ready to begin fitting together your skills and your goals.

Draw up a list of three or four fields you think you might want to investigate further. If, for example, you want a writing or research job, you might choose closely related fields such as publishing, advertising, house-organs, public relations.

But how can you narrow your choice to one field when your interests seem as different as night and day? Suppose you think that photography, ecology, teaching, and broadcasting are all appealing? In this case, focus on the availability of jobs in each field. This should narrow your choice, as you will probably find that certain fields are already overpopulated. Statistically, for example, teaching is not going to be a good bet since there will be many more teachers than jobs over the next few years. Ecology, however, is up-and-coming. Pollution seems to be here to stay and will need a lot of problem solvers.

INVESTIGATING A FIELD

Once you're down to three or four occupational areas, you're ready for some in-depth investigation. Begin by finding out the answers to these questions about each field:

What kinds of entry-level jobs are available?
What salary can I expect to make at first? After five years?
What skills and education will I need to get a job?
What is the demand for workers?
What are the advancement opportunities?
What are the Affirmative Action plans?

With these questions in mind, you'll be able to check out a particular field using library research and "people research."

Library Research
Library research is especially valuable in giving you a wide view of any field you choose. It should be done before your people research. Always learn as much as you can about a field from printed sources before going out on interviews. You'll appear much more intelligent about the subject, and you'll also be able to spot contradictions between what's been written about a field

and what's actually practiced. The two are seldom exactly the same.

Here's a brief rundown of some of the sources available to help you research a field:

Professional women's organizations, such as the Society for Women Engineers. Almost every profession has one.

Trade associations can provide you with basic data such as salary levels, job opportunities, and names of useful contacts.

Trade magazines contain a wealth of information on specific fields. You can probably find in the library current and back issues of the trade magazine that covers your area of interest.

Want ads in both national and local publications will give a rough idea of the education and experience required for the field that interests you.

Occupational guides such as government pamphlets, particularly the ones published by the Women's Bureau in the series

"Why Not Be an Engineer?" ". . . an Urban Planner?" ". . . an Optometrist?" etc.

The "Job-Finding and Career-Building Directory" at the end of this book tells where to write for information on a wide variety of fields. Chapters 4 and 5, on the hidden job market, also suggest organizations to contact for help.

People Research
From the outside looking in, organization wheels may appear to be running to perfection. From the inside, the people who turn the wheels know what a miracle it is each day that those wheels don't come to a grinding halt.

People research will give you a view you can't get sitting in a library and will clear your head of any notion that the most qualified person always gets the job or that business functions the way it's supposed to function.

Don't let the insiders discourage you, because people

tend to talk more about problems than solutions. And the higher up the corporate ladder you get, the more unsolved problems there are. That's why the chairman of the board is paid all that money, but that's also why he has very little job security—one big wrong decision and he's out.

Don't leave a stone unturned to find people who have first-hand knowledge in the field you have chosen. Friends, members of trade associations, retired workers, current employees all can help you, and most will be willing to do so even if they don't know you.

There's an added advantage to people research. While you are exploring job opportunities, you are also laying important groundwork for your job campaign and meeting people who may be helpful to you later.

Here is the way one management consultant suggests you do your people research.

Set up information interviews, not just job interviews. Most companies will be willing to supply you with information even if they have no job openings. You can either call up the personnel department or, in the case of a huge corporation, the head of the specific department in which you are interested. Be patient; your call is likely to get transferred from one department to another. But it's not too important where you begin—it's important where you end up. If your calls produce endless circles, call the president's office and ask that someone assist you.

When you finally get an interview, don't feel that you are wasting the person's time. Most people are happy to talk about themselves and their work, and also willing to help others along the way. They remember when they were in your position.

During the interview indicate that you're aware the company has no job openings and then do as little talking and as much listening as possible. Don't waste your own time and theirs by talking about things you already know. Direct the conversation into areas you need to learn about.

Take notes. It's flattering to the man or woman you are talking to and also serves another purpose: when people see that the things they say are being written down, they tend to give you straight answers rather than guesses. Ask about the business in general, growth possibilities, planned mergers, relocation of people, whether the person to whom you are talking would choose to enter the same occupation today. Are related fields pulling ahead? Is there a related field with more growth possibilities? Ask about the competition—who, where, what? Ask about entry requirements. People who work in a company know what the *real* prerequisites are.

Also ask about the company's Affirmative Action plans. What percentage of the management is women? What is the attitude about hiring and promoting women? If you get evasive answers, restrain your annoyance. Be polite and calm. Remember that you are there for information, not for a job, and the information you're collecting may include the fact that you don't want to work there.

Back home, be sure you write letters of thanks to all the people you interviewed as well as the ones who referred you to them. Include a résumé with your letter in the event of a future job opening. Then compare all the material you have gathered and all the facts you've assessed. Are you on the right track? Are things falling into place? Is nothing falling into place? If not, why?

A SAMPLE FIELD: BANKING

Here's how a selected field, banking, can be traced through these investigating steps:

Occupational Organizations

Using the "Occupational Organizations" section at the back of this book, you would find a listing for the National Association of Bank Women and the name of the journal this group publishes.

To find out more about banking and other professional associations you might consult the *Encyclopedia of Associations*. Under "Banking" you'll find descriptions of all trade associations, professional clubs, and directories in the field, such as the American Bankers Association and the Independent Bankers Association of America.

Each entry lists the association's address, the name of the director or president, a description of the organization, and membership data.

Write to these associations for information on job opportunities and salary levels, copies of newsletters or other publications, and the names of local chapter directors whom you can contact for other data.

Directories
In the *Guide to American Directories*, under "Banking and Investments," you'll find *American Bank Directory* and *Banker's Almanac and Year Book*. These directories give you the names and addresses of banks in your locale, along with the names and titles of bank officers and directors.

Trade Magazines
Trade magazines give the basics on job types, current trends, new branches opening, and names of people you might contact.

To find the names and addresses of these trade publications, use the *Standard Periodical Directory*. Under "Banking and Finance" you'll find dozens of magazines, including *Banker's Magazine, Banker's Monthly*, and *Journal of the American Bankers Association*.

Each entry also gives the circulation data and price. You might find recent issues at your library, or get them through a contact in the banking field or by writing for a sample issue.

Want Ads
Looking through banking help-wanted ads in newspapers, business magazines, and newsletters will suggest job types available, salaries offered, and experience required.

Occupational Guides
The "Banking Industry" section of the *Occupational Outlook Handbook* gives a description of job types, job prospects, and the background required.

Catalyst, a national women's organization specializing in part-time jobs for college-educated women, prints a "Career Opportunities Series" of eighty occupational guides, including one on banking.

Contacts
Whenever you write to anyone in the banking field, keep the person's name, address, and other data. If you come across a promising contact name in a newspaper or magazine article, keep it.

You might also begin to build a list of banking professionals, male and female, whom you could contact for your people research.

II

THE HIDDEN
JOB MARKET

4

Nontraditional Job Sources

When a French high-wire artist, in search of bookings, danced a jig a quarter of a mile above Manhattan's pavement last year, he added a new wrinkle to an old idea. The old idea was the hidden job market. The new wrinkle (in this case, of dubious value to anybody else) was an innovative way of finding a job.

When you say to a friend, "I'm looking for a job—let me know if you or any of your friends or their friends can turn up anything," you are setting up a network of possible job leads and using the hidden job market.

Job-placement experts estimate that more than 60 percent (some claim up to 90 percent) of all jobs are found through personal contacts. This method is as old as civilization and as varied as the collective ingenuity that produces it.

The hidden job market remains hidden primarily because it is vast, fragmented, and different for each person. It incorporates all the search methods people use to find jobs, from the traditional to the bizarre.

The effectiveness of the hidden job market depends upon the individual using it. The extent of your own hidden job market will depend upon your ability to ferret out leads, your creativity in devising new ones, and your perseverance in following up possibilities which at times may resemble needles in haystacks.

THE OLD AND THE NEW

In the past, the hidden job market has been used much more effectively by men than by women. Take the example of a national corporation looking to replace a retiring vice-president of marketing. The search continued for months. An executive search agency combed the country for just the right candidate.

Thirty applicants were turned down—all of them perfectly qualified to do the job. The chief executive had found something wrong with each—his prerogative of course. Another search firm was warming up in the bull pen.

In the midst of all this, the chief made an announcement that surprised no one since it happens so often. He had found the perfect candidate and hired him— all in a day's golfing at the local country club. The "old boy" system had struck again. And the "old boy" system has been part of the hidden job market for years, serving not only male executives but men in all professions and trades. (One union posted job openings in the men's room—a difficult system for women to penetrate.)

The women's movement is today uniting women into a powerful nationwide force akin to the male old-boy system. It is different in that it is open to all (each male system is limited to one group or business), but it is similar in the support its members lend to one another.

For years an unspoken assumption has been that a Harvard MBA carries with him the advantages of influential friends from his school days—not illogical since one in twelve chief executives of the "Fortune 500" companies attended Harvard. Although Harvard's women MBAs may one day be admitted to this exclusive club, "we hope they keep their feet on the ground and join our movement instead of the old guard," said a feminist leader.

A new spirit of cooperation is growing among

women. Today there is help and understanding and shared pride in the accomplishments of all women. Each time a woman breaks another all-male barrier, it becomes a victory for all women.

From this feeling of group identification has grown a national network of women providing various kinds of help for other women. This is a new and exciting hidden job market that can be a valuable resource in your job search. Women all over the country are eager to help you succeed. Your success is their success.

"I was in the stands the evening Billie Jean King beat Bobby Riggs," one woman reported. "It was the most electric moment of my life and I kept repeating to myself that I shouldn't get so hung up over silly things. But that tennis match was not just another tennis match. It had become a symbol for all of us, and that's why it was so important to me."

"It's an amazing thing," said a young car-wash attendant in Miami. "So many women stop by just to wish me good luck. I guess they know how tough it is being the only girl here—all the kidding I get about women's lib."

A female college graduate looking for a job in banking interviewed a Human Rights Commission employee (also female) who told the job seeker that she was not allowed to give out privileged material about different banks' Affirmative Action records, whether good or bad. "But," she added, "name some banks. I get a terrible tic in my right eye when you mention the bad ones."

A public relations consultant, setting up a schedule of television interviews to publicize a national seminar, was phoned by a Boston television producer who wanted to schedule an appearance by one of the six congressmen attending the seminar. Having more requests from the media than people to fill them, the consultant firmly refused until she heard the magic words: "This program is written, directed, produced, and staffed entirely by women." Her answer changed from an abrupt no to an enthusiastic "When do you want the interview, and which of the six would you like?"

Members of many chapters of the National Organization for Women regularly exchange information about job openings. In one chapter a member explained, "We have a dual purpose," citing the example of another NOW member who had gotten a copywriting job at a local radio station. "The station's offensive sexist commercials immediately stopped. Six months of picketing wouldn't have produced such results," she said. "Our member benefitted by getting a job, and we all benefitted from her work."

But before you get the idea that all the women in the world are ready and eager to help you, be forewarned that you may occasionally run into a queen bee. There aren't many, but some are still buzzing around, especially in executive suites. Don't allow such a woman to discourage you. Keep in mind that she represents the old, not the new.

Not only does the queen bee fail to acknowledge that other women's efforts helped her to the top, but she wants to pull up the ladder and use it as a club to keep her sisters down. Her idea of a perfect Affirmative Action program is herself and three hundred secretaries. She is quick to put down women and eager to build herself up. She will lend herself to any form of subtle discrimination against women and delights in being "one of the boys." Stay away from her. She will be as much help to you as Tokyo Rose was to the Allied troops in World War II.

YOUR JOB CONTACT LIST

Begin compiling your own hidden job sources by listing the name, address, and phone number of every person you can think of who has the remotest chance of helping you find a job. Put each name on a separate sheet of paper or an index card. This gives you space to write down useful information about each contact, and you can later file the names in alphabetical order.

Don't overlook the obvious, such as your mother, father, aunts, uncles, friends, teachers, and clergy. Also include your neighbors and the people you do business with—bankers, lawyers, doctors, nurses, store owners, accountants, even the service-station manager. You'd be surprised how often somebody knows somebody who is looking for somebody just like you. And if each of the people on your list gives you the names of another ten, you can begin to get an idea of how fast your contact lists can grow.

Be sure you determine the relationship of your contacts to their contacts. Is it casual or close, business or personal? Were they high school classmates, or did they meet for the first time on the train last week? This can be important information that will keep you from tripping up. Some prominent people in highly visible positions become so familiar to the general public that they seem like old friends. So if somebody says to you, "Call up the governor, he's an old buddy of mine," let your friend know you intend to relay this information to the governor.

The personal contact you make with the people on your list will probably be the most important single resource in your job search, so be sure to take careful notes. It may seem unlikely at the time, but after five phone calls and twenty names you could mix them up and unmatch them and sometimes attribute entire conversations to the wrong people. Concise notes will enable you to recall conversations accurately when you need them—and you will need them.

Follow up each phone call or personal contact with a copy of your résumé. It's "just for information" unless they request additional copies. Often your résumé, plus a personal letter of recommendation from a friend who knows your interviewer, is twice as effective as a direct approach. It gives your friends the opportunity to tell a lot more about you and your accomplishments than you could possibly say about yourself without appearing boastful.

Keep careful notes on where and to whom you have sent résumés. Duplications make you look careless and sloppy—not an undeserved assumption about anyone who fails to keep track of what she is doing.

Keep your army of contacts up to date about your job progress—remember, they won't know if you found a job ten minutes after you talked to them. Explain that you expect your job campaign to take a while, since you are not merely looking for a job—you are looking for the right job. (You can compromise later when the wolf is growling at your door.)

People like to help other people, but they don't like to waste their efforts when they are no longer needed. So when you find a job, don't fail to let all your contacts know, not just the ones who were successful in helping you. Thank them—and keep your list. Even if you think you've found the ideal job, you might need it again.

WOMEN'S JOB NETWORK

A full-page ad showing an empty executive's chair appeared in a New York State NOW publication. A caption over the chair read, "Yours?" and under it, "It Can Be at Xerox." Five years ago the publication didn't exist. Five years ago Xerox wasn't running ads like that.

Eleven women in Princeton, New Jersey, began a national professional society (the Association of Feminist Consultants) to provide assistance to employers attempting to bring their employment practices in line with legal requirements and to prevent wholesale rip-offs by management firms that themselves discriminate while posing as Affirmative Action experts. Five years ago there was nothing to rip off. Five years ago management had never heard of a feminist consultant.

In San Francisco, a carpenter's daughter who wanted to be a carpenter learned about Advocates for Women. Through this organization she got pre-apprenticeship training, counseling, and help in getting into an apprenticeship program. She also got strong emotional support in her attempt to break into a field traditionally taboo for women. Without this help she might never have become a carpenter. (Advocates got some help too. At its opening as the country's first economic development center for women, Gloria Steinem and

Betty Harris, founders of *Ms.* magazine, responded to the call for help by attending the ceremony.)

A pilot project, Women in Wisconsin Apprenticeship, began in 1970 with modest government funding. Three years later it powerfully documented the barriers women face in breaking into the skilled trades. In identifying and analyzing the existing discrimination and publicizing the results in a film, Norma Briggs, director of the project, opened up the way for thousands of women to enter trades and crafts.

FEJOP, Female Job Placement Program, began in 1971 in Chattanooga, Tennessee, to increase the job options and pay of poor women who are heads of households in the Model Cities neighborhoods.

NAWIC, the National Association of Women in Construction, offers scholarships to girls (and boys) who plan to enter a construction-related field of study.

The Lady Carpenter Institute of Building and Home Improvement, Inc., in New York City offers women training and placement in carpentry and cabinetmaking.

Project Repair in San Diego, California, began a pilot program in 1973 to develop skills in home repair and related fields for young women fourteen to eighteen years of age.

The American Association of Women Truck Drivers, Charter Oak, California, was organized to help women become truck drivers.

Coast-to-coast projects, newsletters, counseling services, employment agencies, magazines, books, women's centers, talent banks, seminars, special studies, career-development courses, caucuses, consortiums, task forces, and coalitions are springing up like mushrooms after a spring rain. It's all happening faster than the *Women's Rights Almanac* can get it together. Never before in history have women banded together on such a wide scale for the common good of their half of the human race.

Women have always helped other disadvantaged groups. They helped blacks escape slavery. They helped black men get the vote fifty years before they themselves got it. They have helped elect men to every political position from dogcatcher to President. They have helped the poor, the helpless, the depressed, the diseased, and the dying. Now they are helping themselves. This is history in the making.

The following listing is merely the tip of the iceberg of this enormous movement. To list each service in the entire country would produce a fifty-pound book that still wouldn't be complete. New sources spring up each day.

Some of these sources will provide actual job leads for you. Certain newsletters, for example, run help-wanted ads. Some will provide you with the names of job-preparation services, such as special courses, training programs, counseling. All will provide you with psychological support. The tougher the field you choose, the greater the support you will find. The women setting up these new services all have been in your shoes.

TALENT BANKS AND ROSTERS

It is becoming increasingly dangerous for an unenlightened employer to proclaim the old dodge "Show me a qualified woman and I'll hire her" unless he's willing to put his company's money (and legal staff) where his mouth is.

There always were qualified women in virtually every field. There are now new ways of locating them—some by the flick of a computer switch.

Suppose that you'll soon be a graduating physicist and are wondering where in that haystack to start looking for a job. So you half-heartedly list your name with the American Physical Society, a professional society you don't expect much from in the way of special help for women.

And suppose that on the very same day an employer somewhere in middle America remarks to an alert friend that his firm has an entry-level job for a physicist and that he'd like to find a woman to fill it, but, you know, "Women physicists are scarcer than hen's teeth."

"Not so," says his friend. The employer should contact the Committee on the Status of Women in Physics, which is working actively within the American Physical Society to supply people like him with people like you. The committee has the names of 1,500 qualified women on its roster.

In virtually every profession similar committees are hard at work finding opportunities for women. The Registry Committee of the Federation of Organizations for Professional Women reports that of fifty-two surveyed professions, twenty-three had rosters listing from 60 to 10,000 women, for a combined total of 38,000 names. Everything from women theologians to engineers, scientists, medical and paramedical specialists. Plus those professions without rosters are working on setting them up.

In a project on the status and education of women, the Association of American Colleges publishes a list of rosters as recruiting aids. An employment registry of women is available to educational institutions from the Cooperative College Registry in Washington, D.C.

Many colleges and women's centers also keep talent banks and rosters where you can list your name without charge.

You'll find talent banks in places like the YWCA and job listings on the bulletin boards of women's groups. Anywhere the activity for women's rights goes on, you're likely to find a talent bank to go with it. Ask, and sign up.

WOMEN'S CENTERS

It might be a tiny hole in the wall, barely big enough for three women to meet, or a sprawling old house. Regardless of size, places exist where women can meet, collect, and have access to central materials and receive sympathetic attention for their problems. They are called women's centers, and if your area doesn't have one yet, help start one—after you've found a job.

Women's centers vary in scope and funding. Some centers have developed in conjunction with women's studies courses in colleges and universities, the personnel from these departments helping to establish the centers. Examples are the continuing education center at the University of Michigan and the Radcliffe Institute in Cambridge, Massachusetts.

Many women's centers are operated exclusively through the volunteer efforts of feminist coalitions, while others are funded by the federal government for "disadvantaged" women—a term some feminists believe should apply to all women because of their second-class citizenship. (The government's definition of "disadvantaged" applies only to low-income women.)

A mere trickle of federal money, mostly from Manpower Administration funds, has gone into women's centers. Most Manpower funds, as the title indicates, have gone into man-training programs instead of woman-training ones. This has been true despite the fact that young women, not young men, constitute the largest group of unemployed in ghetto areas. (In 1973, 26.9 percent of minority teen-age boys were unemployed as compared to 34.5 percent of minority teen-age girls.) And some of these centers, set up to aid unemployed women, are still funneling women into typing courses instead of pointing out apprenticeship and other nontraditional job possibilities. Don't be surprised if you run into a Manpower Administration director who still thinks the best way to help "girls" is to introduce them to marriageable men and in the meantime teach them to type sixty words a minute. It happens all the time. But if it happens to you, kick up a fuss or at least ask about other jobs.

The women's centers, established, directed, and staffed by women, can be of great aid and comfort to you. A good way to test which kind of women's center you're in is to announce you're looking for a job as a jackhammer operator. If there's no applause, you're in the wrong one.

The new women's centers offer a wide variety of services ranging from day-care programs for working mothers to referral services for legal problems. They are also a fertile source of information on employment for women. Here's a list of services a women's center might offer:

- Posting news of current job openings
- Organizing employment workshops and seminars
- Providing information and a talent bank for prospective employers
- Providing information on employment agencies and counseling services in the area—fees, methods of operation, ones to avoid, etc.
- Providing information on nontraditional job possibilities and apprenticeship programs
- Conducting courses in a variety of trades and crafts, such as auto mechanics, carpentry
- Posting calendars of events for the area—seminars, lectures, programs of interest to women—and information about other women's groups
- Providing a referral service for legal problems
- Giving information on continuing education courses, financial grants, scholarships, and government aid

For a list of such centers see pages 288–314.

UNION COALITIONS

Blue-collar unions have long been reluctant to join what they perceived to be an upper-crust movement for college-educated women. They are reticent no more. In fact, they are forming their own women's movement.

More than three thousand women belonging to fifty-eight unions met in Chicago in 1974 and set up the Coalition of Labor Union Women. This new coalition intends to bring an estimated 30 million working women into unions and to expand the influence of women within the unions. A major goal is to bring about better access to high-level jobs for women in their own unions. No longer are women willing to sit by while openings are posted in men's rooms.

Women workers who belong to unions earn up to 70 to 80 percent more than their nonunion counterparts, according to a four-year government survey. But women union members have long been treated as second-class citizens in their own unions, the top union

83

offices and best job opportunities going to men. Through their new coalition, women fully intend to penetrate the high-skill, high-paying jobs within their own unions.

If the field you choose is covered by a union, check it out as a valuable source of inside information. Unions that were previously closed to women are now opening up, and through their new coalition women will be able to maximize their strengths.

A number of union women's groups publish information of interest to their members. If you are interested in apprenticeship programs, consult the relevant publications. There may be a good job lead there for you. Check the directories at the end of this book for addresses.

NEWSLETTERS, NEWSPAPERS, MAGAZINES

Historians a thousand years from now may wonder what happened at the close of the 1960s to turn every third woman into a writer. Never before in history have so many words been written by women for women. It's almost as if a vow of silence had been lifted from 53 percent of the population, providing fresh subject matter and fresh impetus for both beginning and seasoned writers. Some of these writings are calm in tone and helpful, others enraged and inaccurate, and some enraged and accurate.

This deluge of printed materials ranges from tiny quarterly newsletters typed by the president of a feminist group and hand-delivered by members, to the enormously successful *Ms.* magazine. In between there are hundreds of newspapers, pamphlets, and bulletins. In almost every town there is somebody in a basement mimeographing something with valuable information in it for you.

There are monthly and weekly newspapers crammed full of information about employment: where jobs are; the names of women's businesses, committees, and task forces and what they are doing to open up jobs for women; Affirmative Action suits and settlements;

which corporations are setting up training programs for women and which are still ignoring women.

If you need counseling, you'll find ads in these newspapers and newsletters. If you think you'd like to go back to school, you'll find announcements by colleges and universities listing schedules and study programs for women. You'll find ads for seminars and one-day conferences on everything from high school dropouts to grandmothers on the march.

Added to this you will find help-wanted ads. Employers who take the time and trouble to find these publications and place ads in them aren't trying to fool anybody. Their Affirmative Action programs are set up to work.

Just about every specialized profession has its own newsletter with specific information about that profession. Law, medicine, engineering, science, advertising—you name it; the women in those professions have started their own newsletters.

Watch the news stories carefully in these printed sources. If there's a story about a telephone-repair woman, it means the local telephone company may have other nontraditional jobs opening up. If it's a story about a women's group that is filing a class action against a major employer, it may mean many jobs will begin to open up in that particular industry, especially if the suit is won or settled out of court.

National magazines such as *Ms.* and *Woman Sports* are excellent sources for an overall view of what women throughout the country are doing and for occasional advice on employment. Even the traditional magazines, with their out-of-date names—*Good Housekeeping, Glamour, Ladies' Home Journal, Woman's Day*—occasionally run excellent employment articles. For a list of these sources, see pages 315–323.

PLACEMENT SERVICES, CAREER COUNSELING, CONTINUING EDUCATION

"What are you going to be, Mommy, when you grow

up?" is a question a number of women don't find very funny. It hits a sore spot.

Led to believe that growing up confers responsibility and authority, many women linger in perpetual childhood, never feeling that they have quite made it to adulthood. And because of these vaguely disquieting feelings, they may be more comfortable spending their lives in preparation (passivity) than they are getting a job (action). When to go to school, when to go to work, how to tell the difference between preparation and avoidance—these are questions that women often require counseling to answer.

Sometimes returning to school is the very best thing you can do. If you need six hours of math to finish a degree that you need to get a job, then going back to school is sensible for you. If your undergraduate degree in chemistry produces turndowns in favor of M.A.s or Ph.D.s, graduate school may be the right choice.

But if you are forty years old, have only a high school diploma, and have never held a paying job, should you go to school or try to find a job?

Or maybe you are forty years old with a bachelor's degree, and you see in the Sunday paper that a nearby college is offering business courses for women like you. Should you leap for the phone or think it over?

There are hundreds of situations where counseling can help you, as it has helped other women in your shoes. It can clear your thinking and help you identify and overcome obstacles you may never have thought about.

Dozens of new counseling services for women have been set up in the past few years, and traditional counseling services are beefing up their staffs to take care of the growing demand. Colleges and universities provide counseling. Business and industry are hiring counselors not only for their women employees but also for their male supervisors—in both instances to cope with new responsibilities for women. Women managers are going to counseling services for advice on how to be more effective in their jobs and how to cope with their unenlightened male superiors.

Many of these new counseling services are excellent, supportive to women, understanding of women's problems, and lower in cost than traditional ones. But tucked in among both traditional and nontraditional counseling and placement services are rip-offs promising jobs that don't exist.

You as the buyer must beware. Anybody promising you a $25,000 job selling encyclopedias in return for a week's training is not going to produce. The size of the organization or its appearance of prosperity is no guarantee of integrity. Some organizations are extraordinarily talented at raising money to keep themselves in business. And keeping *their* jobs comes before their avowed purpose, which is finding you a job.

Nonprofit organizations are among the best sources for finding out about profit-making ones. Call up a chapter of NOW (National Organization for Women), WEAL (Women's Equity Action League), or the Women's Political Caucus and ask them for referrals to counseling services that match your interests and budget. Keep in mind that traditional counseling services generally have counselors to match the old, not the new, attitudes. You may find yourself being led down the garden path back to your kitchen door or routed into some female-typed, low-paying, low-aspiration job.

If you investigate carefully, you're likely to find some free counseling help in your area along with excellent low-cost services. Check to see if perhaps some nearby college or YWCA is conducting group counseling sessions on employment. The Career-Counseling section of the directory (pp. 232–255) will help.

Whatever you do, don't plunk down a single dime or sign any contract until you investigate thoroughly. Any training course should target the training to actual jobs—not mythical ones tied to a fantasized future. Don't allow yourself to be trained for a job which doesn't or won't exist. Ask exactly what the service is supposed to do for *you*, how long it will take, how much it will cost, and the names of others helped. Be specific in your questions and get specific answers. Ask for the names and telephone numbers of the success stories and call them up. If any service that seeks to take your money cannot tell you how many jobs for women it has found in the past, do not expect too much for the future.

Don't go the blind route of trusting all women just because they are women. That's as shortsighted as refusing to trust any man because he is male. Some women, just like some men, will rip you off. Most will not—especially not the ones working so hard for women's rights. But it's up to you to investigate carefully any counseling, placement, or training service before committing yourself.

Don't allow yourself to be run through some magical-sounding computer mill that resembles a broken soda machine. The slot where the money goes in is kept in apple-pie order, but nothing comes out the other end.

FEMINIST ORGANIZATIONS

From the Women's Political Caucus to the senior citizens' group Gray Panthers, from the network of NOW chapters to Older Women's Liberation, there are feminist organizations dotting the country. A few years ago there was a mere handful.

Only five years ago the annual national convention of NOW was attended by fewer members than regularly attend a regional conference today, so much has the membership grown. The same is true for the many specialized groups of feminists. Nobody can accurately estimate the number of feminists in the country today, but everybody knows they exist in impressive numbers, far exceeding the early feminists' fondest hopes.

It's a sheltered person today who doesn't know a feminist—or several. In fact, many feminists are men. (A feminist is nothing more—or less—than a person who believes in and works for equal rights of women.)

Feminists are everywhere. They work in large corporations, small businesses, in all the professions, in all the trades, in television, radio, newspapers. They are mothers, wives, and something else—they are people intent upon ensuring that the women who come after them will not be defined and limited by the prejudices of the past.

Many a woman who never in her wildest dreams thought of herself as a feminist has become one after looking for a job and being asked—for the tenth time in one day—to take a typing test.

In almost every town there is at least one feminist organization or consciousness-raising group. The women in these groups are generally extremely well informed about employment possibilities. They will know where you should look for a job and what you should steer clear of.

If the organization has an employment chairperson, talk to him/her (yes, sometimes it is a him). Although this may not produce any specific job leads, the information will be helpful generally. Often such organizations plan seminars or special programs on employment.

Employment is a key issue in the women's movement. Economic survival is generally the most serious of all problems for women. Feminists promote equal job opportunities for women in conjunction with equal training and education. One without the other doesn't work. It is dishonest to tell a woman she can become a doctor but continue an admissions quota system that keeps her out of medical school.

You are likely to discover that any time a feminist can help a woman find a job, he or she will be delighted to do so.

TASK FORCES

On December 14, 1961, President Kennedy signed into existence the President's Commission on the Status of Women. Soon thereafter government task forces on the status of women were formed in many states, joining a host of others already in operation. For example, the National Organization for Women has task forces on everything from the image of women to Affirmative Action compliance.

By its existence the President's Commission on the Status of Women recognized the institutionalized sex discrimination in our culture and committed the nation to the basic principle of women's rights. So entrenched is this discrimination, however, that the first employment committee set up by the commission included nine men and only four women.

From the dozens of working task forces investigating discrimination in every conceivable area have come thousands of words advocating action. But all their recommendations will be meaningless unless existing laws are enforced and the Equal Rights Amendment, awaiting ratification by a few remaining states, is passed. The message from the task forces is always the same: the weak link in the existing chain of laws is ambiguity in enforcement, which ERA would clean up once and for all.

Information provided by these task forces has contributed greatly to opening up job possibilities for women and getting on the books new laws and executive orders benefiting women. Find out if your city, county, or state has a commission on the status of women and contact it for any material that may have been published about job opportunities in your area.

WOMEN'S DIRECTORIES

The *Woman's Rights Almanac* is unique; it contains 620 concise pages of information *about* women *for* women and *by* women. The *Almanac* lists the names of women elected to office in each state and gives other pertinent information—some relating to employment, such as how many women are employed in each state and the fields in which most of them work. It keeps tabs on elected officials and how they voted on women's issues such as the Equal Rights Amendment, as well as on child-care, abortion, credit, and social security laws.

In addition to the *Woman's Rights Almanac* there are dozens of local directories—anywhere from two pages to book length—listing women's professions, women's businesses, doctors sympathetic to women's problems, attorneys or groups to turn to for legal help, local organizations set up to help women, women's centers, and so on. To learn what exists in your area, call up any feminist organization.

AFFIRMATIVE ACTION, EEO DEPARTMENTS

Equal Employment Opportunity and Affirmative Action departments in business, industry, and educational institutions have been in existence since early in the civil rights movement. What's new about these departments set up to deal with minorities is that now they must include women in their Affirmative Action plans. Virtually every law prohibiting race discrimination has been extended to prohibit sex discrimination.

These various departments—from those in medium-size colleges and companies to those in the nation's corporate giants—are generally only as effective as the intentions behind them. Sometimes the job is performed aggressively. Sometimes it is window dressing.

Most of these departments can provide you with valuable information about a company's or college's commitment to equal opportunity for women. Read between the lines. Evasive answers to specific questions like "How many women do you have in management positions?" or "How many full professors are women?" mean "Very few if any." When a company has fed its computers everything imaginable, including the color of its employees' eyes, and if its spokespeople still claim to have no information about women, you can bet something is being held back. In this case you no longer need the answer. You have it.

Among these ineffective Affirmative Action departments, however, there are some real jewels—women (sometimes men) who take their jobs seriously and will be of enormous help to you.

Keep in mind that all companies and educational institutions are nervous about their Affirmative Action programs, because they are all guilty of *some* discrimination against women. The degree of guilt is the only issue to be determined. And they will all be in trouble if the government takes action to enforce the laws and its own executive orders.

EEO departments, good ones or bad ones, are good starting places for you to get information about the company. And if nontraditional jobs are available, these departments will know about them.

In the Job-Finding and Career-Building Directory, Part V of this book, you will find listings of the resources mentioned in this chapter and addresses to write for specific information. The purpose of all this information is to give you some assistance in compiling your *own* list of job resources. Only you can do that effectively; only you can decide what is useful to you and what isn't. Be selective, take what you need, file the rest away for future reference, and get on with your goal—finding the right job for you.

5

Traditional Job Sources

By this time you have developed into a seasoned job seeker. Now add a dash of evangelist's fervor. You'll begin to discover hidden job possibilities blinking at you on all sides, because if nontraditional hidden job sources number in the thousands, traditional ones number in the tens of thousands. They are all around you—everywhere you go—and most of them have been around much longer than you have.

Too often people go about the serious business of finding a job with the casual approach of a Rip Van Winkle wearing a WIN button. Others behave as if looking for a job were a social disease, apparently believing that a job seeker must be a real loser or else the job would seek her. Don't buy that kind of attitude. Tell the world you are looking for a job.

Look for job possibilities in all those traditional sources you pass unnoticed each day of your life: your local newspaper, the telephone book, churches, sororities, house organs, business publications, women's organizations that have been around as long as the DAR. There's the YMCA and YWCA, the Girl Scouts, the Boy Scouts, business and professional women's clubs, bulletin boards in bus stations, posters in the post office. Even the corner druggist, who might hand out job tips along with prescriptions. Wherever jobs exist, job possibilities also exist.

And don't overlook such obvious sources as political officeholders, from the town supervisor or mayor to state and federal bureaucrats. In terms of numbers of employees, government—on all levels—makes General Motors look like a Ma and Pa establishment. Even if you aren't interested in working in government, it is still a first-rate source for all kinds of employment publications and information.

The following examples will give you a basic idea of traditional job sources. But it is a generalized list. Your own list is the one that counts. So stay alert and keep your thinking cap on. Something in this chapter should trigger something in your mind that links up with something in your locality and tells you where your special opportunity may be hiding.

LOCAL AND BUSINESS NEWSPAPERS

When you see in your local newspaper that a corporation is moving to town and you get your application in before the building goes up, you are effectively using the traditional hidden job market. If you wait until the corporation's recruiting brochures and newspaper want ads are published, chances are there will be five people lining up for every job and your likelihood of success will dwindle proportionately.

Newspapers contain a wealth of information about jobs, and not just in the classified sections. Reading newspapers carefully can tell you a great deal about job possibilities and the general employment picture in your locality. Check to see if your area has a specialized newspaper for business and industry. If so, it will give you many good job leads.

Business publications will tell you who is hiring and who is laying off, which company is moving into town and which is moving out, the number of jobs gained or lost by the town, the tax revenues gained or lost, and the effect on the real estate market of executives' buying or selling houses.

During your job search it is a good idea to subscribe to business publications or pick them up regularly at the newsstands. If you miss an issue, you can usually find it, plus back issues, at your local library.

Often it is possible to walk in and talk to the editor or one of the reporters on a small business publication. And a reporter covering business every day has a lot of information that doesn't get into print. (Plus the fact that reporters are generally happy to be helpful. Just be thoughtful and check deadlines. A reporter who takes time to be nice to anybody ten minutes before a deadline won't be a reporter long. Make sure you're not the one who costs his/her job.)

The more business publications you read, the better informed you will become. If journalism happens to be your field, there's even a possibility (a remote one) that you may find a job with one of the publications themselves.

Read the *Wall Street Journal, Business Week, Barron's,* and the business section of the *New York Times* as well as your area's local business newspapers. New products, changes in personnel, expansion—movement of any kind in an industry means job opportunities. For information about a specific business or field check the *Guide to Business Periodicals*, which contains field-by-field breakdowns of all current business articles.

TRADITIONAL WOMEN'S MAGAZINES

Many traditional women's magazines, once devoted almost exclusively to advice on cooking, decorating, and fashion, are now publishing articles on job opportunities. Employment has become a prime interest of women, and magazines follow their readers' interests or suffer the consequences. Naturally, some are ahead of others, but they are all changing.

For example, *Mademoiselle*, a magazine directed at college women, has a regular feature on careers and job opportunities. The magazine also publishes articles on careers for women, both traditional and nontraditional, ranging from "agents (literary, theatrical, art gallery)" to book publishing, crafts, ecology, food, law, mental health, midwifery, oceanography, retailing, and television. For a free complete list of reprints write to

Mademoiselle
Box 3389
Grand Central Station
New York, N.Y. 10017

TRADE MAGAZINES

Whether you want to know about working in a supermarket or practicing faith healing, you'll find information in trade publications covering virtually every field.

In the health field alone there are more than seventy-five trade magazines. Some reach medical professionals, others are directed at medical suppliers, still others at technicians and researchers. There's even a magazine for doctors' wives—as though some doctors don't have husbands.

Generally published on a weekly or monthly basis, these specialized publications often carry help-wanted sections and always provide data on industrial trends and new businesses in the field. They can give you a general picture of conditions in the field they cover. You can find them by checking the following directories at your library:

Standard Rate & Data, Business and Consumer Edition

> Contains the name of every publication in the United States, indexed alphabetically by industry, plus detailed help-wanted ads and instructions for placing your own ad in the publication.

Standard Periodical Directory

> Lists over 62,000 different publications, from directories to newsletters, in over 200 fields of interest: children, hospitals, radio and TV, ecology, etc. The directory gives the name and address of each publication, descriptions of content, circulation, and price.

Directory of National Trade and Professional Associations of the United States

> Contains a complete listing of all trade and professional associations, personnel.

GENERAL BUSINESS INFORMATION

Almost every scrap of information you might want about a company is available. The trick, of course, is finding the source.

The company itself is the best place to begin—get its annual reports, brochures, recruiting pamphlets, books underwritten by the company. Then move on to critical material if you can unearth it—newspaper stories, magazine articles. It's always helpful to know the unpleasant details.

Check up on any recent changes in personnel or in the financial standing of the company. Some of this general information will be available in your local library, but some sources are available only in large city libraries or in the libraries of major universities and colleges. In this case it may become necessary for you to travel to the city nearest you for a day's research.

Large corporations often have good business libraries. They're not open to the general public, but if you have a friend who works for the company it may be possible to get a special pass. Or try calling up the corporation's librarian, pleading your "desperate" need to use their reference materials. It might work.

Three aids of exceptional value in researching an industry or a specific company are the *Guide to Business Periodicals*, the *Wall Street Journal Index*, and the *New York Times Index*.

The periodicals guide lists articles from a wide range of business and trade publications, while the other two index only their own material. All can direct you to very valuable information on whatever you're trying to learn about a specific company or industry, whether it's analyses of long-term profitability or inside information about which executive was fired by whom and for what reason.

Other References
Dun and Bradstreet Reference Dictionary

National and International Employment Handbook
    for Specialized Personnel
(Angel's) National Directory of Personnel Managers
The Macmillan Job Guide to American Corporations
Poor's Register of Directors and Executives
Thomas Register of Manufacturers

DIRECTORIES AND PROFESSIONAL JOURNALS

Directories give basic statistics of industries, organizations, and services. Professional journals, like trade magazines, contain a little more. There is a directory for everything—even a directory for directories—and every profession has its specialized journal.

Both directories and professional journals are available in public and college libraries, professional-association offices, and business libraries. They can provide you with names and titles of people in specific companies, but make sure you have an up-to-date copy. If not, double-check the information by phone.

Some directories that might be helpful to you are:

Directory of National Trade and Professional As-
    sociations of the United States
Guide to American Directories
Standard Periodical Directory
The Encyclopedia Directory (of professional
    organizations)
The Foundation Directory
College Placement Manual
Federal Career Directory

TRADE ASSOCIATIONS

Just as every field has its own trade magazines, so each special-interest group and industry has its own trade or professional association. Often the national headquarters is in Washington, D.C., so that members can keep track of current legislation affecting their field. These associations act as public relations offices for their industry and usually publish state directories giving the names and addresses of local members. Whatever field you want to enter, these trade-association directories are an invaluable source of contacts.

Encyclopedia of Associations
Lists thousands of different associations, organized by broad fields of interest. Contains data on each organization's purpose, publications, and chief officers.
Directory of National Trade and Professional Associations of the United States

HOUSE ORGANS

Individual companies and organizations frequently publish house-organ pamphlets and newsletters. These usually contain up-to-date information on industrial employment trends, government projects in the field, employee benefits, and management-trainee programs. As equal opportunity pressures increase through Affirmative Action programs, more company newsletters include information on women.

Gebbie House Magazine Directory
Lists the major house magazines by company name and gives data on internal house organs.
Standard Directory of Newsletters
Lists newsletters by broad subject areas, such as accounting, advertising, health.

RELIGIOUS AND SOCIAL SERVICE ORGANIZATIONS

These groups have traditionally offered services often overlooked by job seekers. Free counseling and vocational guidance services are sometimes available, and these organizations are also good sources for information on part-time jobs.

Many religious organizations conduct practical career workshops for adults of all ages and backgrounds. Frequently these groups are affiliated with nonprofit or private social service organizations, which may provide an additional source of job leads and references. Some religious centers have valuable vocational libraries and publish employment newsletters for general circulation. Here are a few examples:

Commission on the Status and Role of Women
United Methodist Church
2121 N. Sheridan Road
Evanston, Ill. 60201

Women's Division
United Methodist Church
475 Riverside Drive
New York, N.Y. 10027

Women in Leadership
United Presbyterian Church
730 Witherspoon Building
Philadelphia, Pa. 19107

Check your phone directory for religious and social service organizations in your area.

COLLEGE PLACEMENT OFFICES

If you're a college student, check your college placement office. The newest annual edition of the *College Placement Annual* ($5) lists over 1,500 corporations and government agencies that usually hire college students. Check your college or public library for this publication or write to the publishers:

The College Placement Council
P.O. Box 2263
Bethlehem, Pa. 18001

Also, contact your college placement office for information about on-campus interviews with corporate recruiters.

Changing Times magazine publishes in February of each year a survey of entry-level job opportunities in management. The survey gives company names and skill requirements for almost one hundred businesses. Write to:

> *Changing Times* Educational Service
> Annual College Survey
> 1729 H Street N.W.
> Washington, D.C. 20006

GOVERNMENT SERVICES

Government can either be useful to you or give you a supersize headache. Although the government does provide excellent, vital services performed by dedicated people, it also employs an army of drones who push papers from one desk corner to the other, stopping only to join the stampede at quitting time. Try to find someone in the first category. If the people you talk to offer the bureaucratic evasion "It's not my department" or can't answer your questions, bypass this department or ask for a supervisor.

Here's a rundown of some of the services that may be useful to you:

Federal Job Information Centers provide information on job opportunities in the federal government; data on job types, requirements, and civil service ratings; limited counseling.

State Employment Services provide counseling and information on job opportunities in your state.

State Civil Service Centers provide data on state jobs and civil service requirements.

City Civil Service Commissions furnish information on employment within local government.

The Women's Bureau (U.S. Dept. of Labor) provides publications, statistics, and other data on employment for women.

The Federal Women's Program, though geared to women already holding government jobs, furnishes data on employment rights, advancement, job options, and training programs. Monitors federal Affirmative Action programs.

State Departments of Labor publish data on state fair-employment laws and current and projected labor trends.

State or Municipal Departments of Human Resources and *Departments of Industry or Commerce* publish employment data for local and state areas.

The Women's Bureau

The Department of Labor may be traditional, but there's some extremely nontraditional information coming out of the Women's Bureau in the department's ten regional offices across the country. The bureau offers down-to-earth job advice, employment projections, and statistics that dispel long-established myths about women in general and women workers in particular. No soft-pedaling here, and no attempts to route women into female-typed jobs.

In fact, the reverse is true. Because of projections showing that many traditional women's jobs are on the decline, the Women's Bureau is advocating that women break out of female-typed jobs and get into nontraditional areas.

The Women's Bureau publishes an excellent series of career pamphlets on fields previously closed to women, entitled *"Why Not Be an Engineer?" "Why Not Be an Optometrist?" "Why Not Be an Apprentice?"* and so on. In addition to these and other publications on specific occupations, the Women's Bureau publishes booklets on continuing education, child care, job rights, and the lag in women's wages in all fields.

The bureau sponsors employment conferences for employers and employees and will send representatives to speak to business, industry, and community groups. On many women's rights task forces you'll find a member of the Women's Bureau.

The Women's Bureau is an excellent place to start investigating any field. It can save you years of training for jobs that may no longer exist and give you sound job tips for the future.

But, like the rest of society, the bureau has problems with its own structure, set up by men many years ago. For example, each Women's Bureau regional director reports to an assistant regional director of the Employment Standards Administration, who in turn reports to an assistant secretary of labor. With one exception, all these jobs are held by men. Job requirements set up long ago effectively dead-end most Women's Bureau regional directors.

Nevertheless, the Women's Bureau, in its long years of service to women, has amply disproved the public declaration of the senator who said, "No woman is worth more than $2,000 a year," a figure used to establish the beginning salaries of the bureau's staff fifty years ago. The Women's Bureau is alive and well. The senator is long gone.

To add your name to the mailing list of future publications, write to:

> Women's Bureau
> Employment Standards Administration
> U.S. Department of Labor
> Washington, D.C. 20210

Be sure to state the specific subject in which you are interested along with your name and mailing address.

In the directory section of this book you'll find the locations of Women's Bureau regional offices plus a list of publications you can order. Check it over carefully. There's lots of vital material for your job search.

The Federal Women's Program
This program operates within the federal government and is the government's equivalent to Affirmative Action programs found in private industry. Under the Equal Opportunity Employment Act, each federal agency must appoint a Federal Women's Program coordinator or chairperson of an FWP committee (similar

to the Equal Opportunity or Affirmative Action director in a private company).

The agency coordinator is responsible for establishing hiring priorities and overseeing plans for advancing the status of women in the federal government. Agency coordinators also act as advisers to the head of each agency on equal employment for women.

The stated aims of the Federal Women's Program are

- Recruitment and hiring of more women in high-level jobs
- Opening up of dead-end jobs and advancement opportunities
- Counseling of women in the federal government
- Expansion of part-time work
- Continued education and training for women

Although the agency coordinators have begun to make strides in opening doors to women in the federal government, the government is no more enlightened an employer than many private companies.

The Federal Women's Program publishes information on employment opportunities in the civil service and independent federal agencies. For information in this area contact

Federal Women's Program
U.S. Civil Service Commission
1900 E Street, N.W.
Room 7540
Washington, D.C. 20415

Several professional women's organizations have also been active in publicizing the rights, training, and advancement options for federally employed women. Washington Opportunities for Women (WOW), a professional women's group, has published a book, *Washington Opportunities for Women: A Guide to Part-time Work and Study for the Educated Woman.* To order, write to

Federally Employed Women (FEW)
621 National Press Building
Washington, D.C. 20004

Government Employment Services

Government employment offices, both federal and state, are as efficient as the people who operate them. Some are good, and some are a waste of valuable time. It's up to you to find out which kind yours is.

Most are still funneling women into the same old female-typed jobs, with their sexist D.O.T. classifications. The D.O.T. is the two-volume *Dictionary of Occupational Titles*, which lists 36,000 job titles in 22,000 occupations covering 230 industries. Last updating was 1965, with revisions promised for 1975 and long overdue.

D.O.T. evaluates jobs on the basis of their complexity and the responsibility and training required. A cluster of women's jobs are at the bottom of the classification heap, meaning that these jobs are so simple they can be done by the slowest, dullest worker.

Examples of these low-rated jobs are: Foster mother, Childcare attendant, Home health aide, Nursemaid, Nursery-school teacher, and Homemaker (cross-referenced to Maid, general). In contrast, the following male-typed jobs got higher D.O.T. ratings: Delivery boy, Hotel clerk, Short-order cook, and Chauffeur. Nursery-school teacher (generally female) is rated lower than Dog trainer (generally male). (Unfortunately, the job of D.O.T. classifier was not rated.)

The D.O.T. costs $10, for each of the two volumes, so if you need any information from it, use the library.

It's possible to get worthwhile job leads from government employment agencies—a source you should not overlook—but it's wise to save yourself frustration by not expecting too much. Use these agencies in connection with your other job sources, but don't spend a lot of time beyond the initial visit. Write your questions down in advance, and if it looks as if the department maze is too thick, get to the supervisor quickly or give up.

Here's a rundown of how things are supposed to work. How they actually function is sometimes a different can of bureaucratic worms, especially for women seeking nontraditional jobs.

State Employment Offices

The Computer Bank Program (also called the Job Matching System or the Job Bank and Screening System) began several years ago. The program is now offered in Utah, Wisconsin, New York, California, Texas, Nevada, Pennsylvania, Vermont, and Connecticut.

This system goes several steps beyond the "Job Bank" listings found in all state employment offices.

Each Job Bank in the program has computer listings of all job openings listed with the state employment service. A job seeker entering the programs is interviewed, tested, and "matched up" with jobs banked in the computer system. Each applicant is given twenty-six "job variables," including desired location, salary, type of industry, and job type. Once these specifications are ranked and screened, they are coded according to the *Dictionary of Occupational Titles*.

The job codes can be broad or specific as you choose. There is a "soft search system" for job seekers who don't know the exact type of job they want. In this kind of search, aptitudes, outside interests, and experience are fed into a computer to determine broad employment fields.

Whatever your job specifications, once they are fed into the computer you are supposed to be given data on five job openings "matched" to your skills and work history. The next steps are contacting the listed employers and arranging interviews.

For further information on the Job Bank Program, contact your local state employment office or write to

U.S. Department of Labor
Manpower Administration
Washington, D.C. 20210

Federal Job Information Centers
Almost all types of occupations found in private industry are also available in the federal civil service system. Appointments in the civil service are competitive, and in order to be eligible for a civil service position you must be rated through a complex examination system. Salaries are competitive with private industry and often higher for middle-level jobs.

Most jobs in the legislative and executive branches of the government or with agencies having independent hiring powers (the TVA, the Foreign Service, the Postal Service, for instance) do not fall within the civil service system.

Sixty-five federal job-information centers are located throughout the country. These centers have information on job openings, requirements, salaries, examination dates, and application procedures. A toll-free telephone information service is also available for job seekers interested in civil service openings.

Specialized counseling services are also provided through these centers, but again, the help you receive will vary with the efficiency of the local center.

Civil service information may also be found in local post offices, state employment offices, national and state personnel offices of government agencies, and college placement offices. Division heads of independent agencies and government officials are also good sources of civil service and other job information (see "Government Publications and Services" in directories).

Skilled Trades
If you are interested in becoming a skilled craftswoman, your best source of information is probably the National Apprenticeship Program. While the program has been geared mainly to young male workers with limited education, it is supposed to provide help for women who want to enter apprenticeships. But be prepared to be persistent.

Apprenticeship agencies recognized by the U.S. Department of Labor operate in twenty-nine states as part of the National Apprenticeship Program, and each state has a Bureau of Apprenticeship and Training. These bureaus work with employers and labor unions in establishing guidelines for local apprenticeship programs, monitoring contracts between employer and employees, and promoting the general idea of apprenticeships. The bureaus are mainly clearinghouses: they do not recruit or place applicants in apprenticeship programs.

If you want to enter a trade, you can apply directly to a local employer or labor union, or consult your local state employment service. For further information on skilled trades and apprenticeship locations, see "Government Publications and Services" in the directory.

III

LAUNCHING YOUR JOB CAMPAIGN

6

Planning Your Job-Finding Strategy

Plan your job-finding strategy with the care of a diamond cutter, but go about it with the expectations of a pearl diver. Each oyster you pry open—each job lead you trace down—may produce results.

Keeping this in mind, launch your job campaign on these five points:

1. Enlist the help of *personal contacts*—friends, neighbors, relatives, former business associates—and all the other leads mentioned in Chapter 5, "Traditional Job Sources."
2. Use the *new resources* available to women, as described in Chapter 4, "Nontraditional Job Sources."
3. Approach as many *key employers* as possible in the field you want to enter.
4. Answer *want ads* in newspapers, trade magazines, and newsletters (see Chapter 8).
5. Register with two or three carefully selected *employment agencies* (see Chapter 9).

YOUR JOB-SEARCH TOOLS

Ideally, when you begin to look for a job you should have a stable base of operations, enough money to see you through for three to six months, and no other major worries cluttering up your brain, such as planned surgery. And ideally, you should look for a job when you don't need a job and can jest about salary, which you intend to donate to charity.

But life plays nasty tricks on most of us. People are always looking for jobs six hours away from a soup kitchen or after they have packed up and moved lock, stock, and barrel to a strange city in the dead of winter. Of course they shouldn't do it that way, and neither should you. But if you've already done it, dig in and make the most of digging your way out.

Try to have as many of the following items as possible, or make up your own list to suit your particular case.

A stable base. It is mentally and physically tiring to worry about where you are going to sleep each night, where to tell a prospective employer to reach you, and where to keep your working materials. Have your own mailing address and your own phone if possible.

A concise, well-written résumé (see Chapter 7), along with covering letters you can adapt to each job you apply for.

Contact lists of all the people who might be able to help you (see Chapters 4 and 5).

Prospective employer lists (see Chapters 4 and 5).

Necessary supplies for writing letters, clipping newspapers, pasting up ads, taking notes: stamps, stationery, glue or tape, pen, pencils, scissors, stapler, paperclips, paste-on labels, file cards, filing box. Make a list and buy all this at once—not in dribs and drabs.

Enough money to buy you the time you will need to wage a successful and selective job campaign. A sense of urgency about getting a job is good; a sense of panic is not.

A week-by-week timetable for researching your field,

completing your résumé, writing letters, and, in general, going about your job search in an organized and intelligent way. Your schedule must remain flexible but not so flexible that you frequently put off the search for such things as a trip to the beach.

A STEADY SOURCE OF INCOME

The most crucial item on the list, and the one you're likely to have the most trouble checking off, is a steady source of income. In the best of times, job seekers take an average of two weeks to find a job, but you should be prepared to support yourself for three to six months or even longer in economically depressed times.

Sure, this seems like forever. But diligent searching now could save you from spending ten years in the wrong job. Even if you're forty-five or fifty, six months isn't so long in terms of the rest of your life.

If you are working now but have decided to change jobs, resist the temptation to tell your boss clever things he or she can do with your present position as you flounce out the door. No matter how much you hate your work or your boss, looking for a new job from the base of an old job is much better than from an unemployment line. Being employed gives you self-assurance and space in which to maneuver. Having a job also saves you from the question—even if unasked: "Did you get fired from your last job and, if so, why?" Having a job tells a prospective employer that you're looking for a better opportunity and are unwilling to settle for less than you already have.

Being a recent graduate also puts you in this class of not having to explain why you're looking for a job—unless you remain in this class too long. If mountain climbing in Asia has occupied you between the date of your graduation and your job search, be prepared to explain not only the time lag but also the interest lag. Do it even if the question is unasked, because your explanation will be better than the employer's assumptions.

113

If your funds are hitting bottom and your collect calls home are being refused, you might begin to think seriously about accepting one of those typing or filing offers you probably are getting. When the well runs dry, you have no choice. You won't need a computer to tell you when this time has arrived. Your checkbook will do. But even at this critical period, hold out for part-time or free-lance work if possible. This will enable you to survive while you continue your job search.

Watch out, however, for those so-called part-time jobs that sneak up on you and become full-time. A casual two more hours here, another day there—and you wake up one morning with all the responsibilities of a full-time employee minus any of the benefits. This may be a good deal for the employer, but it is a bad one for you. Don't get hooked into doing it, no matter how good it sounds. If it's good enough to get hooked on, it should be good enough to be full-time with full benefits.

SETTING UP YOUR TIMETABLE

If you are unemployed or working only part time, take advantage of your open-ended time by setting up a schedule for yourself. Decide on the number of hours each day you can realistically spend on your job campaign, then plan your activities accordingly.

If you are working full time, job hunting will have to take place during lunch hours, after work, and a very occasional "personal leave time" day off. You'll have to be prepared to spend weekends and nights on your campaign.

But if you can spend full time on your job search, do it as if it were a regular job. Establish a starting hour and stick to it. If you must break the schedule, do so by quitting later than you planned. And unless you're threatened with a nervous breakdown, don't take days off or weekends in between. You'll lose continuity, and drifting may dissipate your momentum.

As your own temporary employer, be tough with

114

yourself—tougher than any prospective employer would think of being. Since you're working for yourself, work hard. The harder you work, the sooner you will see results.

To help you budget your time and organize your priorities, here's a four-week sample plan for a full-time job search. Naturally, you will need to adapt it to your own needs and problems, but it will give you a rough idea of the schedule you should follow.

Week 1

Write résumé. Check final draft carefully before typing.

Make arrangements to have résumé printed (allow 1 to 5 days).

Begin compiling contact lists of traditional and non-traditional sources.

Begin research into chosen field. Collect all material possible from print sources.

Make phone calls to people in field; set up information interviews.

Draft covering letter for résumé.

Begin reading want ads.

Week 2

Mail sample résumés to each of your best contacts, attaching note to jog memories that you are looking for a job!

Locate and list names of 20 to 30 prospective employers in your field.

Divide employer list into the "top ten," with the rest forming a "number 2" list.

Type covering letters for résumés and mail to the "top ten."

Read want ads for leads and to familiarize yourself with the best agencies.

Week 3

Continue answering want ads.

Visit employment agencies and register with two or three.

Draft covering letter for "number 2" employer prospects. Mail letter and résumé, keeping careful records of mailing dates.

Follow up your top-ten contact letters with phone calls to set up interviews.

Set up interviews generated from answering want ads or by employment agencies.

Follow up leads generated by contacts.

Week 4

Four or five days after mailing letters to "number 2" employers, telephone for interviews.

Follow up new job leads from interviews.

Follow up any interviews set by employment agencies, contacts, etc.

Continue answering want ads.

Continue following up leads given you by contacts, organizations, etc.

PROSPECTIVE-EMPLOYER LISTS

Now you know exactly the type of company or organization you want to work for. You've done your basic research and you've come up with the following:

- Names and titles of people in each organization you want to contact
- A history of the company dating back to its founding
- Some idea of the company's competitors, products, problems, and prospects for growth
- The company's present employment picture— whether it is hiring or has imposed a hiring freeze
- The company's past record in relation to hiring women and present Affirmative Action plans
- A friend of a friend who is employed by the company and who has given you some inside information

- A general view of the department in which you'd like to work, plus the approximate salary you'll shoot for if you're offered a job
- A conception of your own value to the company—where you will fit in, what you can do for them, and why they need *you*.

So you have a fistful of information and you need a place to put it. What do you do at this point?

Sit down with your information and your résumé and work out a covering letter that is positive in tone and specific in detail. In one page you must condense all your information and come up with the following:

- Why do you want to work for that specific company (reveals you've done your homework—you're not flying blind)
- Why you are looking for a job (you're not a nut who gets tossed out of every job)
- Why your qualifications are uniquely suited for the job you want
- What you can do for the company—which should be modest and understated, never overstated or inflated.

Even if you've written what you think is the perfect letter, don't rush for the mailbox. Look at it again the following day. A little distance between you and your writing efforts permits more objectivity on your part. Ask a friend to read it—a business associate, somebody in the field. Chances are you won't come up with the perfect letter without a lot of effort. It can be harder to write a concise letter than a fifty-page report, which is the reason there are so many bad reports but so few good letters.

Once you are satisfied with your covering letter, mail it with your résumé to both the department head (name spelled correctly, title checked) and the personnel manager of the company. It might also be helpful to send copies to the employee to whom you spoke, especially if there's a chance he or she will put in a good word for you where it counts.

Wait a few days—three or four—and follow up your résumé and letter with a phone call to the department head you wrote to, not the personnel manager. (You might be referred to personnel anyway, but it's better to get as near the job you want as possible.) If you don't get through on the first call—a reasonable assumption—try again and again. You may have to call four or five times, but do it graciously. Be calm, reasonable, cheerful, but persistent. When you get through, keep the conversation short but don't settle for "We'll call you." Try to set up a meeting even if you are told no jobs are available. If the department head cannot see you, ask him or her to assign somebody else to talk to you. Explain that you are in no hurry (no matter how much of a hurry you are actually in) and that you think a job in this particular company, in this specific department, is worth waiting for.

Be persistent, but not a nuisance. Know when to take no for an answer and when to try again another day. It may take you a few slammed phones to get the hang of it, but the delicate balance will manifest itself.

Remember that it is flattering to any employer to have his or her company singled out as a terrific place to work, one in which you would like to spend the rest of your working life. The employer is thinking about all the problems with current employees—complainers, freeloaders, and ingrates by the dozens—and here you are, willing and eager. It's the kind of attitude that can get you in from the cold.

TIMING YOUR RÉSUMÉ

It is tricky to attempt to outguess the U.S. Postal Service, but try. It does make a difference when your résumé reaches prospective employers.

One placement professional has suggested mailing résumés to local addresses on Sunday so that they will arrive midweek, when the stack of beginning-of-the-week mail has diminished. Friday is the day to avoid mailing your résumé, since it may get buried in the Monday shuffle.

If you are sending résumés out of town, don't waste energy trying to outguess the mails. Just allow plenty of time for them to arrive before you place any long-distance telephone calls to follow up.

It is rarely helpful to send résumés by air mail, special delivery, or registered mail, even if you are wealthy enough to bear the expense. The moment your important-looking envelope is opened, it may produce results opposite to the ones you want. Your résumé is important to you, but generally not important to the recipient.

The same goes for clever tricks designed to set you above the crowd of job seekers, like hiring a carrier pigeon or a balloonist. For every gimmick that works, there are a thousand that backfire.

There are some notable exceptions to this rule. Remember the high-wire artist back in Chapter 4? He *did* get a job. In fact, he got more offers than he could accept. So if you want to work for a circus or be a press agent, think up your own gimmick and good luck. Just don't try it on a conservative corporation—and most corporations *are* conservative.

ARRANGING THE INTERVIEW

It may sound elementary, but when you arrange an interview be sure to write down the interviewer's name, the time, the date, and the address. Then repeat it carefully—every last word—to the person setting up the appointment. According to one personnel manager of a large corporation, elementary details constantly trip up job seekers. "They show up on the wrong day, at the wrong hour, with the wrong name in the wrong place. Right away, they get a demerit that's hard to erase."

Not only must you be perfectly clear in your own mind as to exact time and place, but you must make sure there is agreement between you and the other person. No matter which of you makes the error, it will be charged to you.

Showing up even ten minutes late is another mark against you, and a deserved one. You don't have to sit in the parking lot waiting for the sun to come up and the doors to open, but you must do your homework about how to get there and how much time it will take. It's better not to show up at all and say a catastrophe occurred when you reschedule the appointment, than to arrive late.

You may get to your appointment at the correct time only to be obliged to cool your heels in an outer office for the next hour, but that's different. Being on time is the job seeker's burden, not the employer's. Your prospective employer has no reason to impress you, and some employers, like some employees, are chronically late. But you can't count on it. Go to each appointment with the assumption that your interviewer works like a precision clock, and that exactly at the appointed hour you will be whisked into his or her presence.

Being late says many things about you, none of them good. A person who is always late presumes by this action that his/her time is more valuable than the time of the person waiting at the other end. No matter who does it, it is inconsiderate and rude.

THE UPS AND DOWNS OF JOB HUNTING

By carefully concentrating your job-hunting efforts, you will avoid frantically ferreting out want ads, blindly mailing out dozens of résumés, registering with twenty employment agencies, and then collapsing for a week.

If you have spurts of energy and efficiency followed by down periods and unproductivity, you don't need a clinical diagnosis. You are merely being human. Recognize this and make it work for you instead of against you.

When you're feeling down, get busy and get organized. If you're going to feel lousy anyway, make as much out of a bad situation as possible. Do all things that must be done—such as making contact lists, filing, clipping, pasting, and reading background material.

But when you're feeling up, arrange appointments, follow up leads by phone, and try to pry open those difficult doors that seemed permanently closed during your down periods. Your attitude is important. Salespeople don't get pep talks, psychological "up" films, and promises of trips to Hawaii for nothing. These things work. You'll have to provide your own pep talks, since you are a salesperson with a product to sell—yourself. Whether or not you believe in your product and what it can do makes all the difference in the world. But it's only natural to believe in yourself a lot more on some days than on others.

Of course, if you make an appointment on an "up" day but have to show up on a "down" day, that's fate. Take a deep breath and plunge in. Who knows, this may be your oyster day of all days. And nothing chases the blues away like finding that pearl of a job amid the rubble.

7

Writing a Successful Resume

A résumé is your *entire* life condensed onto two sheets of paper in such an interesting way that it makes somebody who has never heard of you want to meet you. It works a little like a blind date—enough advance publicity to work up an interest but not so much that your date is disappointed when you show up.

There's a rule of thumb among employers: the longer the résumé, the less important the person. Two pages for your résumé is tops—a page and a half is better—and use adjectives as sparingly as Mexican hot sauce. You'll be amazed how much terse, to-the-point information you can get into a limited space. And the discipline of restricting yourself to two pages forces you to list only your solid accomplishments, saving you from verbosity, braggadocio, and other long-winded sins of the inexperienced résumé writer. As proud as you may be of your ninth-grade oratory award, avoid the temptation to mention it in your résumé—unless you've lived an exceedingly sheltered life in the interim.

Perhaps the ultimate sin in résumé writing is pomposity—explaining a job emptying wastebaskets as "accountable for conception and implementation of sanitary logistics." Don't laugh—this can happen to the best of us when we're fondly remembering how important we wish we had been in our last job or when we are anxious to impress the person who has the power to give us the next job.

Every résumé is ultimately aimed at one person—

the person who makes a final yes-or-no decision on your qualifications. Unfortunately, it's impractical to produce a specific résumé for each interview, tailored to the particular interests of every one of the varied personalities you'll be talking to through a lengthy job hunt.

It is possible, though, to tailor a résumé to a specific job or field or industry. You can do this by examining your own strengths and experience, stressing those that are most relevant to the job you're trying to get, and using language familiar to your interviewer. "Direct sales experience" can also be stated as "experience in meeting many types of people, determining their interests and feelings, and persuading them to buy products and services."

Never forget that a résumé has one purpose: to make the reader want to meet and talk to you. If it gets you inside the door, it's done its job.

You may have twenty years' experience, but unless you communicate it in a positive, interesting way and convey an image of yourself as an achiever, your résumé is likely to end up in the wastebasket. By the same token, you might be just out of college with a work history that could be stuffed into a thimble but win an interview for a good job if you present yourself effectively on paper—if you manage to make your accomplishments seem interesting and worthwhile and create an image of yourself as a special kind of person.

A concisely written résumé incorporating a sense of your personality carries the reader's imagination beyond the printed pages and produces a desire to meet the individual behind the words.

CONVENTIONAL VERSUS FUNCTIONAL RÉSUMÉS

Basically, there are two approaches to a résumé. If you have fairly extensive experience in a series of well-defined, clearly understood jobs—such as designing bridge abutments or managing used-car sales agencies or writing advertising—the conventional résumé is generally the approach to use. It's straightforward, lends itself to concise writing, and if done properly, comes across as strong, believable, and persuasive. An example of a conventional résumé is Frances T.'s on pages 124–126.

The alternative approach is the so-called functional résumé, which stresses the kinds of strengths and accomplishments you have to offer rather than presenting your job history in chronological sequence. It's called a functional résumé because work experience is organized under the headings of skills or functions rather than in time blocks or by company.

If you do not have a long, consistent job history or a demonstrable record of accomplishment in a clearly defined series of positions, the functional résumé is especially effective. If you are entering the job market for the first time, have been out of it for a number of years, are interested in changing fields, or are open to the idea of working in one of several different fields, the functional résumé is probably best for you.

[A CONVENTIONAL RÉSUMÉ]

FRANCES T.
60 State Street
Washington, D.C. 20009
(203) 123-4567

Background in both commercial and nonprofit areas, including professional associations, trade-magazine publishing, social welfare organizations, and government.

I want to utilize my diverse experience in the social welfare, publishing, and personnel fields as Executive Director of Public Relations in a large professional association.

EXECUTIVE ADMINISTRATOR
People, Personnel & Placement Publications
1972 to 1975

Developed and implemented more than 30 projects, from assignment through manuscript and final publication stages.

Supervised the collection and analysis of information and interviews on 15 topics, ranging from
business law and health care to retirement insurance and corporate group benefits. These data
were used as the basis for determining marketing
goals and employee benefits for a trade magazine
with a circulation of 500,000.

Supervised editing and printing of 12 periodicals
in the personnel, insurance, and health-care fields.

PROJECT DIRECTOR
Social Welfare Services Department,
City of Boston
1970 to 1972

Directed an evaluation study of employee benefits
for the Social Welfare Services Department of
Boston. The two-year project included:
—data analysis and field observation of two
other major cities: Atlanta and Philadelphia
—evaluation of the professional background,
on-the-job training, and employee benefits
of the 150-person staff of the Social Welfare
Services Department
—preparation of a special three-day orientation
program for executive-level personnel

As a result of this study, I was asked to
report on my findings before the Massachusetts
Committee on Public Employees. On the basis of
the report, I was engaged to organize and conduct
a state-wide convention on employee benefits
for the Trade Union Association of America.

ASSOCIATE EDITOR
Executive Personnel magazine
1968 to 1970

Wrote and edited more than 20 reports on employee
benefits and personnel relations for a magazine
targeted to personnel directors.

Prepared promotional materials including
brochures, letters, and flyers for management
and business publications.

COMMUNITY SERVICE ACTIVITIES
I managed the re-election campaign of the town
commissioner and four local officials in
Lexington, Mass. During this campaign, I raised

and dispersed a budget of over $20,000 and
arranged over 100 public appearances. When the
Commissioner's Public Relations Manager became ill
two months before Election Day, I assumed responsibility for the design and distribution of over
30,000 pieces of campaign literature.

EDUCATION: M.A., Public Administration, Temple
               University
               B.A., Georgetown University,
               psychology major

PERSONAL DATA: Date of Birth: 2/26/39
               Health: Excellent
               Willing to travel
               Single

Suppose you're looking for a job as a department
manager in a retail store, but you last did this kind
of work ten years ago and have been completely out
of the job market for seven or eight years. The skill
headings for your résumé might be:

> Buying and Inventory Control
> Hiring and Managing Employees
> Financial Control

These words focus on what you did and the kinds
of responsibilities you held, rather than on where you
worked and when. Each word is designed to conjure
up an image of a range of work activities.

There are a number of basic rules for résumé writing
that apply whether you are using the conventional or
the functional approach. But before getting into specifics, let's look at how Sarah A. put her résumé
together.

Sarah had been out of college for two years. At
first she was able to get only part-time work. Then she
landed a job as a secretary with a magazine. But she
was bright and energetic, and as she became more
comfortable in her job, she began taking on more and
more duties. She started handling correspondence, then
advanced to writing short pieces for the magazine's
section on consumerism and shopping. Soon she was
editing and rewriting articles by other authors. Although
she was promoted to editorial assistant, she felt she

was ready for more responsibility and more challenging work. She decided to look for a spot elsewhere as a copy editor.

Sarah knew she'd need a résumé, so without giving it much thought she sat down and wrote a draft of a simple conventional résumé:

1973   <u>Front</u> magazine: assistant editor: handled all correspondence for the American edition, edited letters, contacted doctors and psychologists for information, wrote news items for magazine on regular basis.

1972   Cooper Museum: helped organize research files for the museum's vast collection of prints and news clippings in preparation for opening of the museum in New York.

1969-70 Green Museum: organized catalogues, catalogued photographs of museum collection, routed information about the museum to the public through correspondence.

Trouble was, when the basics were on paper Sarah realized the résumé wasn't exactly the kind of thing that was likely to motivate a potential employer into grabbing a phone and asking her for an interview. She recognized that her real ability and experience weren't coming through. Her résumé just didn't convey the experience she'd gained in her jobs—she'd emphasized *where* she had worked a lot more than *what* she'd done.

This time, she decided to put together a functional résumé. The first thing was to learn all she could about what a prospective employer might expect of a copy editor: the skills, experience, and knowledge she had to bring to the new job and also had to feature in her résumé.

She read a lot of want ads for various editorial positions to get a general idea of what an employer would expect of a job applicant. She talked to copy editors on her own magazine and an editor she knew who worked for a book publisher. She also found some useful material on job opportunities in publishing at the local library.

Then she compiled an inventory of the things she'd done, as contrasted to the specific job titles she'd held.

127

She came up with four headings to cover her range of skills that correspond to the work a copy editor does:

> Copy editing
> Writing
> Manuscript screening and selection
> Research

She thought through carefully and objectively the things she'd done and learned in her current job, in previous jobs, and in school that would fit under these headings—experience and skills that would make her a desirable addition to a publisher's staff. She wrote an introductory paragraph that summed up her job experience and stated the kind of job she was seeking. Then she completed the following résumé:

[A FUNCTIONAL RÉSUMÉ]

SARAH A.
117 North Street
New York, N.Y. 10017
(212) 123-4567

CAREER SUMMARY
Two years' experience in publishing, including writing articles and columns; copy editing; screening and selecting manuscripts for the American editions of Front and View magazine. Job objective: copy editor's position.

COPY EDITING
As copy editor for View magazine (circulation 700,000) was responsible for editing contents pages and writing brief summaries of all major articles. Edited major articles submitted by free-lance and staff writers. Supervised layout and production of feature pages.

As assistant editor of Front magazine (circulation 500,000) did all preliminary screening and selection of manuscripts for possible publication. This magazine is based largely on material sent by professional correspondents, and I selected, edited, and prepared for publication the contents of two major sections of the book—about half its monthly contents. Researched and wrote replies to reader correspondence and developed news briefs on medical news and legislation.

WRITING
Wrote major article on medical research for _Front_ magazine, and short articles and items for _View_ on consumerism and medical legislation. Free-lanced several articles for Tunes-In Records, including a biography of a major recording star based on newsclips and press releases. Currently writing an article on fashion trends on assignment from _Fashion World._

MANUSCRIPT SCREENING AND SELECTION
Reviewed all incoming correspondence from stringers and from physicians for possible use in _Front_ magazine. Did initial reading of unsolicited fiction for _View_. Responsible for maintaining contact with literary agents and writers to help ensure a flow of copy for both _View_ and _Front_ magazines.

RESEARCH
At Green Museum, set up research files for photographs of museum collection. Researched and wrote letters in reply to inquiries from the public. Set up research files at Cooper Museum, including selection and organization of a large collection of news clippings and monographs.

JOB CHRONOLOGY
    1974 — _View_ magazine, copy editor
    1973 — _Front_ magazine, assistant editor
    1972 — Cooper Museum, researcher
    1971 — Green Museum, research assistant

EDUCATION
B.A. in English, 1971, Eastwest University, New York City. Earned 20 credit hours toward M.A. in Journalism from City University.

REFERENCES
Tim Jones, Associate Editor, _Fashion World_
John Smith, Executive Editor, _View_ magazine
Jane Parker, Associate Editor, _Front_ magazine

PERSONAL BACKGROUND
Born December 26, 1951; single, excellent health; own automobile, free to relocate; have long-range career plans.

The result was a stronger résumé, allowing Sarah to highlight what she had done rather than where she had done it.

In putting together any résumé, you have no need to sell your former employers, to focus on them in any way, except to help sell you. Don't forget your product —yourself—whatever type of résumé you write.

Patricia D.'s before-and-after résumés offer additional examples of how a conventional résumé can be made into a more effective functional presentation.

The samples in this chapter should give you a rough idea of the format and contents your own résumé should have. Before you begin to structure your own promotion piece, read the following pages for suggested format basic guidelines.

[RÉSUMÉ—BEFORE]

PATRICIA D.
11 Deer Park Drive
Philadelphia, Pa. 19124
(215) 123-4567
Personal Data:
Birth date: December 25, 1953
Marital status: Single

Education:
B.A.: 1975, University of Pennsylvania
Major: Political Science
Minor: History, Public Administration
    Special emphasis on international relations,
    American and Asian history

Scholastic Awards:
    Undergraduate: Honors three semesters. Grades good
    to excellent in major; average in others.
    Graduate: Graduate Assistantship awarded for six
    terms. Limited college-level teaching experience.
    Grades excellent in all subjects. 3.8 cumulative
    average. Awarded Ph.D. candidacy.

Employment Experience:
    Earned approximately 40% of college
    expenses during summers. Worked during summers
    as a counselor for underprivileged children

(Children's Aid Society of New York). Also earned
college expenses as a researcher for a stock
brokerage house.

Background:
Active in Political Science Graduate Student
Association. Have traveled extensively throughout
southwestern part of United States. Active in
athletics—cycling, swimming, tennis.

References will be furnished upon request.

[RÉSUMÉ—AFTER]

PATRICIA D.
11 Deer Park Drive
Philadelphia, Pa. 19124
(215) 123-4567

Experience in education and administration including college-level teaching, writing, and academic
research. Field of specialization: East Asian
history and political affairs.

PROFESSIONAL EXPERIENCE: College-level teaching in an
experimental introductory political science
program for undergraduate students. As one of six
department majors participating in this program, I
prepared lectures, led weekly discussions, and
advised 30 to 40 students over a one-year period.
Selected for this special course on the basis
of a written questionnaire and three-day interview.
Invited at the conclusion of program to contribute
to the departmental evaluation report and to
conduct a summer mini-session. (Political Science
Department, University of Pennsylvania)

RESEARCH & ANALYSIS:
Extensive experience in all phases of academic
research and writing, with emphasis on political
science and Far Eastern affairs. Special projects
included research reports written for a forth-
coming book by a specialist in political history
of Japan. Independent, intensive research and
writing project in fields ranging from modern
American foreign policy to East Asian international
relations and history. Experience in the use of
research materials including statistical data,
primary documents, reference and periodical
sources.

COMMUNICATIONS SKILLS & ADMINISTRATION:
Provided scheduled academic assistance and
consultation for an average of 15 to 20 undergraduate students for more than four semesters.
Problems ranged from academic scheduling problems
to the design of individual study programs for
several foreign students. In one case, I worked
intensively for six months with two Japanese
students whose political science grades had fallen
below the D level. At the end of this period, their
grades rose to B and B+ respectively.

EDUCATIONAL BACKGROUND:
B.A., University of Pennsylvania, 1975
Major: Political Science; Minor: History,
    Public Administration
Magna cum laude; Special Honors in Political
    Science

PERSONAL DATA:
Financed 40% of college tuition through part-time
    work.
Date of birth: December 25, 1953
Unmarried
Excellent health
Willing to travel and relocate

[RÉSUMÉ—BEFORE]

Cathy L.
Pillsbury Road
Milwaukee, Wisc.

EDUCATION:
Maryville College, Maryville, Tenn., 1971-72.
Transferred to Wisconsin State University for
greater course selection. Will complete
requirements for B.A. in English, June 1975

Milwaukee High School, class of 1971
Milwaukee Junior High School, class of 1967

EXPERIENCE:
Summer jobs have included a job as a waitress
at the Greenway Country Club, typist at Ellan
Insurance Agency, and helper at the Long Library
in Milwaukee.

I have also held a number of Christmas part-time
jobs including Fry's Department Store, selling
toys; and Elkhart Crafts and Fabrics, helping

out in a number of tasks including selling and
stacking bolts of fabric.

ACTIVITIES:
Member National Honor Society in high school and
elected president of my senior class. Member of
a creative writing club and poetry class.

REFERENCES:
Dr. Edward Calhoun, Chairman, English Department,
Wisconsin State University
Prof. Henry Underwood, Psychology Department,
Wisconsin State University
Rev. Arthur James, First Universal Church,
Milwaukee
Ms. Mabel Egan, Manager, Elkhart Crafts and
Fabrics, Milwaukee

BACKGROUND: .
I was born in Milwaukee 10/13/54.
I have lived all my life in Milwaukee and I want
to remain here.

[RÉSUMÉ—AFTER]

CATHY L.
Pillsbury Road
Milwaukee, Wisc.
Birth Date: 10/13/54
(765-251-4327)

SPECIAL SKILLS: writing, editing and research

As a university undergraduate, my areas of study
have been unusually diverse: English, sociology,
psychology, anthropology, and history. These
disciplines have given me wider perspective in my
field of writing.

WORK EXPERIENCE:
As reporter on university newspaper, wrote feature
stories, covered student elections, researched and
wrote four articles about part-time jobs for
students.

Edited newspaper on regular basis for one
semester.

Summer jobs included: waitress at local country
club, typist at an insurance firm and research
assistant in local library.

Christmas jobs included: selling children's toys in large department store; assistant in fabric department of local crafts store.

EDUCATION:
Maryville College, Maryville, Tenn. (1971-72) Transferred to Wisconsin State University for greater course selection.
Will complete requirements for B.A. in English, June 1975 (grade average 3.5 out of possible 4.0).

SPECIAL ACTIVITIES:
Member of the National Student Honor Society in high school; president of senior class; member of creative writing club; wrote poem used as dedication in annual yearbook.

REFERENCES:
Dr. Edward Calhoun, Chairman, English Department, Wisconsin State University
Prof. Henry Underwood, Phychology Department, Wisconsin State University
Rev. Arthur James, First Universal Church, Milwaukee
Ms. Mabel Egan, Manager, Elkhart Crafts and Fabrics, Milwaukee

FORMAT

Your résumé should contain the following essentials: Name, address, telephone number

Job objective: the exact title of the job you want, if you know it.

Scope paragraph: a two- or three-sentence capsule of your career—your skills and experience.

Work experience: your job history, set up into skill categories with specific examples of the results you produced.

Company names and dates of employment, complete and in detail.

Education: high school or college, degree, year of graduation and/or attendance. Any honors.

References (optional): If they are very impressive, include them. Otherwise indicate that "references are available on request" or save them for the interview.

Personal data (optional): marital status, age, willingness to relocate.

BASIC GUIDELINES

Be concise. Select those work experiences or activities that are directly related to the job you want. If you don't have a specific position in mind, create a composite picture of your skills and interests. *If a detail doesn't fit, leave it out.*

Use active language. Every word in a résumé should be chosen for impact. Stress *results* by giving concrete examples of what you did. Give the name of government programs, sponsoring organizations, funding sources, company affiliations if it helps highlight your results.

Avoid self-serving words such as "invaluable," "crucial," "well-qualified," "proven ability." Let the reader decide.

Don't put yourself in the role of a helper. If you had less than total responsibility for a task or project, describe it in some positive way. "I assisted in designing" or "I helped plan" dilutes the impact of your work.

Say you took responsibility for a task or project: planned it, designed it, coordinated it. Separate your part out and describe it in *action* words.

Before you begin writing, think through all the information you have at your disposal.

1. First set up a job history. List all the places you've worked, beginning with your most recent job and working back in time. Take each job, paid or unpaid, full- or part-time, and list it on a separate index card or sheet of paper. Write down the basic information about the job—your title and department, the length of time you held it, your salary and any promotions you received.

2. Then write a concise paragraph describing the skills you used in the job. (If you're working now, you might try keeping a brief diary for a week. Every time you do a different task, jot it down.)

3. The next step is to select four or five different

skill headings from your job descriptions which also are relevant to the job you're looking for. If you're looking for a personnel job, for example, your work might fall under these headings: Recruiting; Interviewing; Hiring and Training; Office Administration.

4. Take each of your on-the-job accomplishments and place it under the appropriate skill heading. Begin each sentence with an action verb describing what you did. If you were a production assistant on a local radio program, your résumé might include

Planned a radio program for preschool children.
Selected guests for weekly interviews.
Introduced a ten-minute "read aloud" segment.
Produced a "special" on day care.

Use the same action-verb-plus-description formula for each separate job or accomplishment. Avoid weak verbs or phrases.

Active Verbs
planned, sold, selected, supervised, analyzed, budgeted, screened, managed, designed, developed, edited, introduced, established, directed, conducted

Weak Verbs
was given responsibility for, was involved in, helped, assisted, arranged, worked under, was subordinate to

Give your reader some way to measure the range of your responsibilities and achievements by stating where you started from and where you've arrived. For example:

Planned programs for preschool children, from arts and crafts to reading classes.
Directed a newspaper subscription campaign, from the design of a questionnaire to the selection of the population sample to be polled.

If your job experience is substantial, you may want to show a progression in responsibility and title by showing the level at which you began work and where your skills took you. Time range, title range, project range—all these help your reader to see your potential for growth and problem solving.

5. The next step is problem-solving examples: Take each accomplishment and function and ask yourself, "What problem made this work necessary in the first place?" Then describe the skills you used to solve the problem. For instance:

- Did you do any writing: letter drafts, reports, research outlines?
- Did you recommend or bring about any changes in procedure: reorganizing a filing system or setting up a form letter to streamline communications? What were the results?
- Did your work cross over into different departments? Did you provide for feedback to your department?
- Did you train new people for your department, program, or activity? Did you interview or hire?
- Did you supervise anyone? If so, what work did he or she do?
- Did you design or write any promotional or educational material? Any handbooks, pamphlets, flyers?
- Did you maintain contact with or coordinate other organizations? Which ones and why?

6. Then give the results that your work produced. Results can be measured in several ways:

Numbers: increasing the number of members in a club, increasing sales in a business, increasing circulation in a newspaper.

Time saved: how quickly you solved a problem and how much time you saved to devote to the next challenge.

Effects: the long- and short-term effects of your problem solving.

Durability: how long a suggestion, idea, or solution of yours has been in active use.

Expansion: whether your idea was used in another department or became part of another project.

7. List your employment history at the end of the résumé. For example:

1972–75, Raytheon Cor., Sales Manager
1970–72, Chemplex, Assistant Sales Manager

8. List your academic background with the most advanced degree first. For instance:

M.A., University of Pennsylvania, 1973
B.A., Oberlin College, 1971

9. If you like (remember it's optional), list references and any relevant personal data: age; marital status; willingness to relocate, if it is a factor; extra-curricular activities, honors, memberships.

Congratulations. You've written your résumé.

BRIDGING THE TIME GAP

Although young women looking for entry-level jobs are frustrated by a lack of practical experience and the repeated "come back when you've got some" turn-down, the older woman returning to the job market often finds it difficult even to write a résumé. A recent college or high school graduate has had plenty of experience putting things on paper. But what if you're forty-three years old, you quit college or high school to get married, and you've done nothing since except change diapers and clean bathrooms—neither of which you are interested in doing on the open market. You feel you won't have a bit of trouble keeping your résumé to two pages, because a paragraph is all you need.

True, your work has been unpaid. And it is also true that on the open market unpaid activities are considered less valuable. In a money culture like ours it's hard to get past the dollar signs. Many a woman has found new respect even from her own husband and children by going back to the same field she quit to wait on them. But to have driven a child to the emergency room in time to avoid a catastrophe is more

138

important than all those papers office workers are pushing—and you did it without pay. If you changed this into business language you would have been "responding to an emergency," "able to remain cool under pressure," "capable of leadership," "able to help and direct others"—valuable assets that can be translated into cold hard cash.

Refusing to recognize the contributions of women because they are unpaid has been a way of discriminating against them. Are they unpaid because they are worthless, or worthless because they are unpaid? This circle is being broken. Many employers are paying more attention to what you did instead of how much somebody paid you to do it.

One way you can combat the prejudice against the housewife is by writing your résumé as if this prejudice doesn't exist. You have control of what goes on those résumé pages. Your ability—what you have done and can do—is what is important.

Suppose, for example, that you've been an active member of League of Women Voters for the past twenty years. That has been unpaid work, sometimes forty hours a week of it. The League has provided women with continuing educations and practical experience for more than half a century. Suppose you were in a League government workshop that had studied the pros and cons of a city-manager form of government for your town. Then suppose you later became the workshop chairperson and finally the chapter president or vice-president. You have had management experience, and don't let anybody tell you that you haven't. You have paced the floor worrying about real—not make-believe—problems. You have accomplished a lot on a limited budget. You have juggled and set priorities, and you have chaired countless board meetings while babies crawled under the table.

In short, you have worked under circumstances as trying as those faced by the corporation president. Put your experience up front on your résumé, not down in the extracurricular activities with your hobbies.

The same goes for other kinds of volunteer or unpaid activities: hospital work, sewing, cooking, entertaining, library, school, PTA, Girl Scouts, Boy Scouts, flower arranging, car pooling, budgeting, bookkeeping, child care, and so on. Just be sure, in arranging these tasks on your résumé, that you highlight the ones that fit the job you're seeking. If you're trying to land a job in government, flower arranging is obviously of secondary relevance. But if you are applying for a job in a florist shop, it's not.

So make your hobbies, your interests, your experience pay off for you. Many women have turned hobbies into good jobs or businesses of their own. And don't get hung up on your age—you've gained a lot of experience in those years, and someone will be willing to pay for it.

If you are an efficient, well-organized housewife who has run a household and cared for a family for many years, you have plenty of experience for many jobs. You are not a beginner. And keep in mind there are laws against discriminating against you because of either your age or your sex. So begin looking at yourself with an analytical eye. View yourself in terms of your skills and how they can be related to jobs: planning, budgeting, coordinating, directing—you've done these things. It's not always necessary to run back to college or enroll in a training course. Sometimes this is a good idea, but sometimes it is a way of avoiding looking for a job.

So you're forty-three. You have plenty to offer an employer: experience, stability, life experience, an accumulation of knowledge, and twenty-two good years before retirement at sixty-five. If an employer thinks all this is worthless, maybe you should try for his job. It's apparent that he's not doing it very well.

Sue C.'s before-and-after résumé and the covering letter she wrote in answer to a newspaper want ad will give you an idea of how a housewife's experience can be presented in such a way to attract a potential employer.

[RÉSUMÉ—BEFORE]

SUE C.
1007 East Street
Dallas, Texas

EXPERIENCE:
  Jones Art Supplies (1946–summer job)
  Dallas Crafts (1960–part-time at Xmas)

EDUCATION:
  North Dallas High School, 1948

BACKGROUND:
  Born January 1, 1930, Dallas, Texas.
  Married, four children. Husband permanently
    located in Dallas.

COMMUNITY ACTIVITIES:
  Den mother Cub Scouts, leader Girl Scouts;
  PTA past vice-president; active in church affairs;
  worked with children in Menlo Children's Home
  and designed symbol for the Home; member
  League of Women Voters; worked as volunteer
  at local hospital.

HOBBIES:
  Cooking, sewing, gardening, reading

REFERENCES:
  Ms. Frances Cisco, Director, Menlo Children's Home,
    211 Second Street, Dallas, Texas
  Rev. John Gulligan, First Baptist Church,
    Dallas, Texas
  Mrs. Helen Thomas, President,
    Texas League of Women Voters,
    30 Forester Street, Dallas, Texas

[RÉSUMÉ—AFTER]

SUE C.
1007 East Street
Dallas, Texas
(214) 123-4567

FUND-RAISING DIRECTOR
  My objective is a full-time job in which I can
  utilize the skills and abilities I have developed
  over the past 20 years as a fund-raiser.

EXPERIENCE:
  Directed volunteer program involving 50 people

at Menlo Children's Home for retarded children,
for the past 10 years.

Coordinated and helped manage a special fund-
raising program which has raised $150,000 for
Menlo in the past 5 years.

Designed symbol for Menlo—Helping Hands—
used in posters, pamphlets, and stationery
for the home.

As co-chairperson of volunteer group, raised
funds to build a new children's playroom at
a local hospital.

Active in PTA and League of Women Voters for
past 20 years, holding offices in both.
My League work was instrumental in getting
more state and federal funds allocated for
child-care centers.

REFERENCES:
Ms. Frances Cisco, Director, Menlo Children's Home,
   211 Second Street, Dallas, Texas
Rev. John Gulligan, First Baptist Church,
   Dallas, Texas
Mrs. Helen Thomas, President,
   Texas League of Women Voters,
   30 Forester Street, Dallas, Texas

PERSONAL BACKGROUND:
Born Jan. 1, 1930, Dallas, Texas.
Married, four teen-age children.

EDUCATION:
North Dallas High School, 1948. Attended adult
study courses at North Dallas High School and
extension courses at Dallas State College in
art, history, and philosophy.

Sue C. wrote the following letter in reply to this ad:

DIRECTOR WANTED:
Dynamic, take-charge person to direct
fund-raising program for foundation.
ONLY EXPERIENCED PEOPLE WITH
PROVEN RESULTS NEED APPLY!
Ability to direct others, some travel,
salary open. College graduate preferred. Reply: National Health Foundation, Dallas, Tex.

142

Ms. Linda Myers, Executive Director
The National Health Foundation
417 Second Avenue
Dallas, Texas

Dear Ms. Myers,

In response to your ad in the Sunday *Times,* I am
enclosing my résumé. It shows, I believe, the kind
of proven results you are seeking in a fund-raising
director.

I have managed and directed successful fund-raising
programs for the past 20 years. I have worked with
both volunteers and professionals in the field
and am thoroughly familiar with the personnel
problems such coordination requires.

Having coordinated a fund-raising program for the
Menlo Children's Home several years ago, which
indirectly involved the National Health Foundation,
I am familiar with your programs and the excellent
work of your foundation in general.

Although my work in fund raising has been unpaid,
it has been both professional and dedicated. Please
feel free to check my references, particularly the
director of the Menlo Children's Home.

I will telephone your office in a few days in the
hope of setting up an interview appointment.

Sincerely,

SUE C.

THE FINISHED PRODUCT

So now you have a résumé—two pages on your desk
and four hundred in your wastebasket. That's par for
the course. Whoever said "easy writing makes hard
reading" could have been talking about résumés. Unless
you suffered a little, there must be something wrong.

You will need a perfectly typed copy of your résumé,
ready to be printed and mailed to prospective employers
and contacts. The visual layout of the résumé is important. Leave plenty of white space. Don't cram all
your information onto one page. If you need two pages
—even three on rare occasions—use them. (If you
think you need three, read the résumé carefully to see
if something can be left out.)

Before the final typing, have several people check your résumé for conciseness and clarity of language. What you thought was absolutely clear and to the point may seem confused or unimportant to a detached critic. It is important that your critics level with you too. You don't need their praise, you need their help. Make sure they understand the difference.

If you're not a good typist, have a professional typist or a typing service prepare your final copy. In medium-size and large cities you will find these services listed in the yellow pages under "Résumé Service."

Proofread the final version carefully for spelling and punctuation errors. These leap out at a prospective employer and cast a cloud of doubt about your thoroughness.

If possible, have the résumé duplicated by photo-offset rather than mimeographed or Xeroxed. This way you can have a large number of copies printed relatively inexpensively and you'll have a range of paper weights and textures to choose from. A high-quality, heavy bond, although a little more expensive, is worth the difference. But this is as far as you should go. Don't let anybody sell you fancy type or gold trim. It will be a detriment.

Have 100 to 200 copies printed (the difference between 100 and 200 in cost is generally minimal). You may find, as you go for more interviews, that your résumé will need to be revised. If necessary, do so. Stifle the urge to write in the corrections so as to save money. This may cost you a job.

When you have your printed résumés in hand, buy all the supplies you will need for your job campaign—appointment calendar, envelopes, notebook, a roll of stamps—everything you will need to be quick off the mark.

COVERING LETTERS

A copy of your résumé and an individually tailored covering letter, preferably addressed to a specific person and title, should be sent to each potential employer.

Writing "personal and confidential" on the envelope may or may not get it past secretaries and into the intended hands. Usually, even if the ploy works, a secretary gets it right back and passes it on to the person assigned to do preliminary screening of résumés. It is probably a good idea only if you really know the addressee or if the person is in a very small department of a large company.

Learning to write a good covering letter requires some practice. Here are some guidelines:

- It should be crisp and to the point, and it should stand on its own, independent of your résumé.
- Each letter should be carefully adapted for each employer, demonstrating that you understand the needs of this particular company.
- The letter should contain examples of results you've produced and problems you've solved.
- It should not be more than one page long.

When you are giving examples of problems you have solved, they should be immediately relevant to the prospective employer. You can select one or two achievements from your résumé for particular emphasis as you write each letter.

End your letter by saying, "I will call you in a few days to arrange an appointment," thus sparing yourself the "don't call us, we'll call you" syndrome. Try to stay in control of setting up the appointment. Even if you get the old "don't call us" brush-off, call back anyway and try to set up a specific appointment. If not this week, how about next week? Nobody's calendar is filled through two Christmases. The person you're speaking to will finally have to level with you, which is better than an indefinite brush-off.

Below are sample covering letters and résumés. Marion H. and Rachel F. are college graduates with a good deal of work experience; Cathy L. is a soon-to-be-graduated college student with very little paid work experience.

[COVERING LETTER]

201 North Shore Drive
Detroit, Michigan
April 12, 1975

Vice-President of Marketing
Astral Vision, Inc.
Central Station
Cincinnati, Ohio 45203

Dear Sir:

Since you are seeking a Marketing Manager with
knowledge of the audiovisual field, you may find my
background in marketing, sales and distribution of
interest:

By marketing a film lease "package" to college
students, designing a high school film guide and
expanding into three suburban areas, I increased
the sales of 16mm film equipment over 30% in
one year.

Result: $500,000 in additional revenue was gen-
erated for the Finest Film Company.

As Sales Manager for a small photographic supply
firm, I initiated a five-week workshop series to
improve customer relations and increase telephone
solicitation sales.

Result: The 20-person sales force under my supervision increased its direct contributions to
overhead and profits from $500,000 to $2 million
in two years.

A "portable photolab" marketing program I designed,
including a two-minute film, promotional brochure
and direct mail campaign, resulted in over 10,000
new orders, the strongest response to a new
product in the history of Fast Foto, Inc.

I will call you in several days to discuss your
need for a Marketing Manager with an extensive
experience in audiovisual equipment. My résumé is
enclosed.

Sincerely,
MARION H.

[RÉSUMÉ]

MARION H.
204 North Shore Drive
Detroit, Michigan 48210
313/751-0204

Ten years' experience in marketing sales and
distribution for two major companies in the photographic and audiovisual fields. Seeking a position
as Marketing Manager for a Midwest corporation
specializing in audiovisual equipment.

MARKETING

Established the marketing goals and policies for a
corporation with $2,000,000+ in annual revenue.

Directed the advertising and marketing efforts as a
support to the sales efforts of a major film
corporation. Annual promotional budget: $200,000.

Directed the mail-order and cash-sales business of
the company for a six-month period. During that
time I designed a program with the Sales Department
which resulted in over $500,000 in new orders.

Solicited new clients and increased distribution
base to include several untapped suburban areas.
Result: sales increased by more than 30% in
one year.

—Finest Film Company

SALES MANAGEMENT

Handled the sales and distribution of 25 brands
of photographic equipment to every major retailer
in the Chicago metropolitan area.

Sales increased by more than $2,000,000 while I
supervised the sales efforts of a 20-person sales
force.

Negotiated the purchase of $12,000,000 worth of
merchandise, which we distributed to the retail
trade.

—Fast Foto, Inc.

DISTRIBUTION

Controlled distribution of photographic equipment
for the Tri-City area of Minnesota. Managed key
national accounts including Matrix Corporation,
Photos Unlimited and Snapshot, Inc., representing
aggregate revenue of $3,000,000.

Succeeded in increasing distribution by more than
10,000 items for one product line two years in a
row. As a result, received the company's "Saleswoman
of the Year" Award for 1973.

One of a three-person team representing the Distri-
bution Department at monthly marketing meetings.
My suggestions for a new portable photolab campaign
are currently being implemented by the company.
Projected sales: $1,000,000 for the first year.
—Fast Foto, Inc.

WRITING AND RESEARCH
Recently completed a feature article for the
Summer 1975 issue of Industrial Marketing Magazine
on development of the education market.

EDUCATION
M.B.A., University of Chicago
B.A., Forrester College
Attended seminars in Effective Sales Training,
Marketing & Public Response, Audiovisual Retailing

[COVERING LETTER]

Ms. Georgia Reed
Director of Budget & Finance
Unlimited Oil Corporation
New York, N.Y. 10013

Dear Ms. Reed:

If you are looking for a Financial Manager with
more than ten years' successful experience in
budgeting, finance and cost-controls planning, you
may find my qualifications of interest.

I designed a cost-controls system for an international oil corporation which resulted in a
20% reduction in operating expenses and a savings
of $4,000,000 per year. (Anchor Oil)

When a financial crisis threatened employee pension
benefits, I developed a program for staggering
company contributions over a ten-year period
which was unanimously accepted by 100 senior
employees. I also established innovative cost-
accounting procedures and conducted orientation
programs for new accounting personnel.
(Cosmic Cosmetics)

148

A Financial Management Handbook, which I wrote for
Anchor Oil personnel, has been distributed to
more than 500 employees and executive staff
members.

I will contact you in the near future to set up an
interview. My résumé is enclosed.

Thank you for your consideration.

                              Sincerely,

                              RACHEL F.

[RÉSUMÉ]

RACHEL F.
201 Park Place
New York, N.Y.

   Background in financial management and planning
   includes the design of cost-efficiency programs
   and accounting systems for three major
   corporations.

FINANCIAL MANAGEMENT
   Established new data-processing methods and new
   automated electronic cost-analysis system to
   streamline the financial operations of an insurance
   firm with branches in twenty states and Canada.

   Designed a cost-controls systems for the main
   headquarters of an international oil company
   resulting in annual savings of more than
   $4,000,000. This represented a 20% reduction in
   production-line operating expenses.

   Created a cost-efficiency program which reduced
   payroll and production-line man-hours by almost
   25% in one year.

   When the research efforts for a new line of
   cosmetic products proved unsuccessful, I co-
   developed a proposal for an emergency bank loan.
   As a result of these efforts, a transfer of
   $800,000 was negotiated. This cash inflow allowed
   the company to weather a serious financial
   downturn and to emerge in the black a year later.

ADMINISTRATIVE EXPERIENCE
   Developed and implemented a cost-effectiveness

checklist and handbook on company policy for the 200 employees. After four years and minor changes, the handbook is still in use.

Initiated a personal expense-account program for the top management of a major oil company. The program increased the efficiency of the Accounting Department and allowed a 30% staff reduction.

As a member of the Executive Committee, I recommended a special pension-benefit plan to improve management relations with employees. The plan was approved and now operates in five other branch offices.

OFFICE SUPERVISOR
When our corporation negotiated a merger, I organized and supervised the Cost Accounting Department for the new corporate headquarters.

Wrote and put into effect a Financial Management Booklet covering cost-effectiveness procedures for improving the output of six different departments, from Accounting to Public Relations.

Set up orientation program for over 50 employees and handled the recruitment of all personnel up to a salary level of $25,000.

EMPLOYMENT HISTORY
1973-75, Instant Insurance Co.
1970-73, Anchor Oil Corp.
1965-70, Cosmic Cosmetics

ACADEMIC BACKGROUND
C.P.A., Dayton School of Accounting
B.A., Boston College
I am at present completing an evening M.B.A. program at Parker University. Degree expected in 1977.
Born Jan. 1, 1947; married, one child.

[COVERING LETTER]

Mr. John Fox, Personnel Director
Clarified Chemical Company
Milwaukee, Wisc.

Dear Mr. Fox,

Although you may have more résumés from graduating college students than you will ever need, I believe that you will find the enclosed résumés of special interest.

I can demonstrate an outstanding record in writing and editing and am an excellent researcher. Since your company has recently expanded, you may need to add to your staff in order to prepare essential materials for this new marketing area. If so, or if you have an opening in publicity, internal communications or market research, I would welcome an opportunity to meet with you to discuss my qualifications.

Thanks very much for taking the time to read this letter and my resume. I'll phone your office in a few days to set up an appointment.

Cordially,

CATHY L.

See pages 132–134 for Cathy L.'s résumé.

8

Answering Want Ads

```
┌─────────────────────┐
│     EXCITING        │
│     CAREERS         │
│     IN THE          │
│     WORLD           │
│     OF              │
│     MOTION PIX      │
│     NEED            │
│     GAL FRIDAY      │
└─────────────────────┘
```

The "exciting career" awaiting this "Gal Friday" involves answering telephones, filing, typing, checking equipment orders, and sweeping up cuttings from the screening-room floor—and all for slavery wages. She will be no closer to Paul Newman or Robert Redford than her neighborhood theater, and about as close to breaking into the movies as a stray tom is to replacing Morris as a TV commercial star.

Who puts the "want" into the want ads? Who writes these little three-line dramas designed to appeal to your need for money, happiness, popularity, and sex after death?

Writing want ads is a job—like other jobs—that can be either long or short on integrity. Some ads are truthful, and written in simple, straightforward English. They are designed to bring people and jobs together. Others are designed to trick you, to flatter you the better to hoodwink you.

152

Being unable to separate the honest ones from the others will waste your job-looking time and leave you angry and confused. The first rule in reading want ads is: beware of any ad that promises too much. An ad that implies you can earn "big" money for "small" tasks will produce only disappointment. If such a job exists, the boss's daughter (or son) already has it. The reason these ads continue to run every day in hundreds of newspapers is because they produce what they are designed to produce: gullible people who can be persuaded to take unrewarding jobs by promises of fringe benefits written only on the wind. Television, radio, newspapers, movies, and related fields like advertising have all been guilty of hiring typists by selling the dubious promise of "rubbing elbows" with "celebrities." If you are interested in such benefits there's a better way. Become a masseuse. It pays better and you get a lot closer.

WANT AD SOURCES

Want ads are placed by employers seeking to fill a particular job or by employment agencies looking for prospective clients to fill specific openings or to add to their applicant pool. The last is what you want to avoid.

Many companies and employment agencies do not write their own want ads but hire advertising agencies to handle their recruitment advertising. This explains why the exciting jobs you read about are sometimes a far cry from the reality of the job. If there's little resemblance between the two, you'll know that either the ad writer had faulty information about the job or the ad was intended to confuse. Within the advertising agency, specialists are generally responsible for different fields, such as medical, chemical, educational. Usually the company gives the advertising agency a list of job specifications—job title, duties, educational requirements, previous experience, and salary (often omitted in the actual ad). This skeleton description is turned over to the ad writer, who does the embellishment and sends it on to the classified-advertising department of the newspaper or magazine in which the want ad will appear.

TYPES OF ADS

Want ads fall into several categories, including laundry lists (a long string of short ads covering a range of job fields), glamour ads (those promising you everything from plush carpeting to a room with a view), solid agency ads (those that state clearly defined requirements), and company ads with the name of the company (open ads) or without it (blind ads).

It doesn't take long to spot which type of ad you are reading. The first two categories, laundry lists and glamour ads, are the ones you need to guard against. They are strictly "come-on" concoctions designed to look like a silk purse. Dig under all those adjectives and you'll generally find a sow's ear.

Want-ad writers estimate that more than half the jobs advertised by employment agencies never existed in the first place or were already filled before the type was set for the classified pages of the newspaper. They are designed strictly to pull you into the employment agency's offices and add your name to their applicant lists. This talent pool, in turn, is used as bait for prospective employers. It is a never-ending circle of setting and baiting traps—for the applicant and the employer.

The ads written to draw you to an agency's door must use some potent language to accomplish this purpose; otherwise you won't show up. You can spot "come-on" ads, designed to appeal to a broad range of skilled and unskilled job seekers, by their vague descriptions. Airlines, for example, are well known for using come-on ads to recruit clerical help.

To help you learn to distinguish legitimate ads from come-on types, here are a few samples:

Laundry-List Ads
When you turn to the help-wanted section of any large newspaper, you'll find row after row of agency ads

listing job after job in a wide variety of fields. These laundry-list ads are virtually always come-ons. Agencies often receive generous discounts from newspapers for buying this ad space on a regular basis. Pass them by.

Glamour Ads

Coll Grad Fee Paid **CAREER GALS** Top Flite Corp seeks men & women with NO EXP to enter manage. trng. program. Great future with terrif raises. Future Agency	Coll Grad Never a Fee **FASHION WORLD** Asst dir of this fab firm. Promote cosmetics to chic NJ stores. Jones Personnel
Gal/Guy Friday Fee Pd **SKY'S THE LIMIT!** Bubbly personality & desire for public contact along w/good typing is needed for this glamorous spot. Moxie Agency	Gal/Man Friday **STAGE STRUCK!** Movie exec needs brite person to serve as secretary and admin asst. Must be resourceful, responsible, attractive appearance. Typing, skills. Starting salary depends on exp. Canning Agency

These ads are easy to spot. Count the number of glowing adjectives used to describe the job. Notice the lack of specific information about salary and skills. Their language is designed to appeal to your vanity: "attractive," "brite," "bubbly personality." Skip these ads unless you're looking for low-paid clerical or secretarial work.

Solid Agency Ads

TEACHER Editor Trnee—Sm College work in elem math req'd. Tchng grade 1, 2, 3 & ability to write well nec. Relocate. Resume first. Marvel Agency	EDITOR—Requires in-depth knwl of advanced curriculum. Education Admin exp helpful. Will edit elem math texts. Novice Agency
TEACHER—f/pd. English major + 2 yrs H.S. lit teaching exp. College-level tchng a plus. Teach grades 9-12, N.J. high school. Superior Agency	Personnel/Fee Paid **WORK ANALYST** Detail indiv needed w/min 2 yrs exp by a major corp to handle work analysis. Write job descriptions, conduct surveys & assist in personnel screening. Personnel Agency

These agency ads are written for actual job openings and clearly specify the experience and education the company requires. After running this type of ad, agencies are generally swamped with applicants. Use these ads to identify the agencies that specialize in the field that interests you and the ones you want to register with. (See Chapter 9, "Using Employment Agencies.")

Blind or Open Company Ads

Biology
LAB TECHNICIANS
Seeking indivs with either a M.S. or B.S. Degree and some experience in tissue culture and sterile tech. Should be able to work without close supervision. We can offer you good salary and benefits. If you meet our requirements, call:
Research Institute
XY5-1234

ADV—RESEARCH ASST
Major Midtn Co. seeks recent college grad. Project & client contract responsibilities. Some typing. Send resume to:
X2346 Times

MARKET RESCH MGR F/PD
Medium-sized R.I. Insurance Co. needs 2-3 yrs market rsch exp. Supervise staff of 6.
XX123 Times

Banking
FINANCE TRAINEE
Large Manhattan bank offers hard work, long hrs & oppty to learn finance w/ a young, dynamic inst that is a leader in its field. If you are personable, energetic & ready for oppty, send resume.
Home Trust Co.

Whether blind or open, a company ad for a specific job opening can offer good job possibilities. A well-written résumé and covering letter could get you an interview.

TRANSLATING WANT ADS

Translating help-wanted ads is a minor art, requiring practice and patience. There are three stages to comprehending them: decoding the language, deromancing the benefits, and defining the job requirements. Once you break an ad down in this way, you can then frame an effective covering letter targeted at the job it offers.

Decoding Ads
Want ads are riddled with abbreviations and trade jargon. The best method of translating this special language is to check through surrounding ads or ask professionals in the field. There are also many vague-sounding phrases in the ads that actually have very specific meanings. Here are a few you may have run into:

June grad = high school, not college, graduate.

Great earning potential = poor base salary but a reasonable commission on sales work.

Good with figures = the back room, little contact with people.

Skills required = typing and sometimes shorthand.

Will train, no experience necessary = clerical work.

Experience preferred = the employer may consider hiring an applicant lacking the specific experience but who is otherwise well qualified.

Send résumé = the job is above secretarial level, at least in title.

Deromancing Benefits

Want ads are designed to appeal to both present and future job applicants without promising benefits the employer has no intention of delivering. Therefore, most want ads stress one of two selling points:

1. If the salary, company benefits, vacation time, and advancement opportunities are equal to or better than those offered by the company's competitors, then these job advantages will be highlighted. You'll see specific salary figures or phrases like "exceptional pay" or "outstanding benefits."

2. If the salary, benefits, and advancement potential are average or less than average, the ad will present an emotional appeal. You'll find phrases like "opportunity to work in a dynamic new company," while such specifics as salary and job requirements are not mentioned.

Once you've looked through a few want ads you'll find it easy to decide which category an ad falls into. Try crossing out all the adjectives in a company ad and see what you're left with. If all the specifics disappear with a red pencil, go on to the next ad.

Defining the Job

A well-written classified ad or display ad (ads you'll find in the business or education section of your newspaper) should give you these specifics:

Job title
Job functions or responsibilities

157

Education and skill required/preferred
Benefits
Salary (often omitted or given as "salary open" or
   "salary commensurate with experience")
Advancement potential
Relocation or travel requirements
Method of reply

If you find an ad that fits your experience, skills, and
job needs, cut it out and paste it on a card or sheet of
paper. Set up two headings—benefits and requirements—and jot down all the information from the ad.
   If the ad is well written, it should provide enough
information on job requirements to permit you to tailor
a covering letter for the employer. Check the phrasing
to see how open-ended the requirements are. "Experience preferred" doesn't screen you out if you can highlight related skill or parallel experience in another field.
Here are some ads that give you all you need to frame
a good reply:

Management
INVENTORY
OPPORTUNITY
Head manager of expanding co.
seeks assistant to coordinate
production planning, scheduling,
inventory control, and more. Excellent oppty to move into management w/expansion program.
Any related experience qualifies.
Benefit package. JOB Agency.

ADMIN ASST
Educational organization needs
organized, intelligent person with
typing & good communicative
skills to coordinate production
and planning of public presentations & seminars in education
area. Office procedure & some
admin exp. necessary. Send resume to ZZ2Z Times.

LINE INSPECTORS
Need trainees to learn assembly-
line inspection. Field, office, cal-
culating & supervisory work. No
exp nec. Rapd advancement possible. Write XXXX Times.

EDITOR
Tenafly Knitting Co. has opening for individual capable of as-
sisting in planning and production of needlework and craft publications. Must have aptitude for
technical writing. English major,
editorial exp helpful. Top salary,
benefits. Call XY8-1122.

Management Trainee
BUSINESS-MINDED
Large investment firm seeks
bright business-minded person
to handle client liaison with light
secy responsibilities. Write XXZZ
Times.

EDITORIAL/RESEARCH
Responsible, bright person to
edit serious trade publications.
Research-minded to write summaries of federal regulations.
Writing / business experience
helpful. CLASS Agency.

As a further example, take this ad for a copy editing
director:

> EXPERIENCED COPY EDITOR with in-
> terest in children's books. Must be
> flexible, decisive & capable of over-
> seeing copy editing & proofreading of
> 80+ titles per year. Handle traffic and
> scheduling for several departments,
> prepare progress reports for produc-
> tion dept. 2 years of copy editing exp.

The ad clearly spells out the functions of a copy
editing director:

—Oversee copy editing and proofreading.
—Handle scheduling and traffic.
—Prepare progress reports for production
   department.

It also tells you that if you want to apply for this job
you should have two years' copy editing experience,
preferably in children's books.

This is all you need to know to tailor a résumé and
covering letter for this job. From the ad you could
set up the following functional headings for your
résumé:

Copy editing and Proofreading
Department Supervision
Traffic and Scheduling
Research and Writing

This is another advantage of careful want-ad reading—it can help you to research the available job types
in almost any field and to select appropriate skill
headings for your résumé.

WHICH WANT ADS SHOULD YOU READ?

The key to finding good job leads in the want-ad
columns of newspapers or magazines is to look under
more than one category. Don't bypass a section be-

cause it isn't specifically your field—ads are often mis-classified, lumped together in broad categories, or hidden away. For example, if you're interested in writing, you may find an ad for a chemical-company house-organ writer in the chemical section—no science degree required. Other writing jobs would be listed under the editorial, publishing, public relations, advertising, and copywriting headings.

The size of the ad is no indication of the potential the job may offer. A small ad written in concise language might not immediately attract your eye, but don't neglect it. It may be a better job for you than one touted in a lavish display. Some small companies with good jobs but small advertising budgets write their own ads and phone them in to the newspaper.

IDENTIFYING SEXIST ADS

Although it is now against the law for newspapers to separate help-wanted ads into male/female categories, many ads are still designed to recruit either males or females. The Gal/Guy Friday ads don't fool anybody.

The law forbidding categorization has been enormously beneficial to women job seekers, and it has made even the most blatantly sexist employer or employment agency cautious. Many an employer who once routinely listed a "chemist" opening under Male/Help Wanted has been made to change his ways. The law has also put the shoe on the other foot as far as job applicants are concerned. A woman who applies for a traditionally male job is no longer called upon to explain why she is doing so. The burden is on the employment agency or employer to explain why she doesn't qualify. The law is a powerful ally to have on your side—even if it doesn't work perfectly.

College Grad, Gal/Guy Friday, Gal/Guy Anything ads are come-ons for basic clerical and secretarial work. Don't even bother with them unless you like poor wages, low-level office work, and exploitation. Even if you want a clerical job, it's better to look under the proper category—clerical, secretarial, office work—and to restrict your attention to ads that are specific about job type, salary, and experience required.

Here are more translations for your list. All the terms are to be eyed with suspicion.

Guy/Gal Friday: usually means low pay, long hours, scullery maid's duties, no chance for advancement. Instead, look for ads for management trainee or junior executive.

Administrative assistant: generally means secretarial work with a title in lieu of salary. Your duties will be what your boss thinks up, including making coffee and buying his wife's birthday and Christmas gifts. Before you decide to take this job, find out what you will administer.

Glamour job: unless a glamorous salary goes with the clerical job, forget it.

College grad: the employer generally wants typing done by a college graduate in the belief that he or she can spell better than a mere high school grad. Stay away, even if you can spell.

Female-typed ads often give themselves away by listing *weekly* salary, as opposed to male-typed ads, which generally specify *annual* earnings. Female-typed ads tend to use phrases like "bubbly personality" or "chance to meet people." Male-typed ads are generally phrased in broad career terms such as banking, engineering, while female-typed ones describe specific jobs —e.g., legal secretary, secretary to the president.

Sexist categorizing still occurs, so include every possible field in your search through the want ads. Look through the business section of your local newspaper or the Sunday edition of a large national paper. Check the ads for management positions, research openings, bank training programs. Some employers, spurred by Affirmative Action, are using outside recruiting agencies to locate women for traditionally male-typed jobs. Many of these agencies are now more open to applications from women who have less immediate work experience.

Read the professional display ads, which you'll find

in the special sections of the Sunday paper. Most large-city newspapers run such ads keyed to educational, financial, health, and other professional fields.

Many employers run ads for the same job in both the classified and the special display sections of the newspaper. An employer who does this is usually looking for a large number of applicants to screen for a job. If you find an opening duplicated in this way, you may have a chance for the job even if you're not as highly qualified as another applicant. Send a good covering letter with your résumé.

OTHER WANT-AD SOURCES

The classified and display sections of your newspaper aren't the only sources of want-ad job leads. Here are several others women often overlook:

Trade magazines and newsletters in every field usually print want ads. While the positions offered generally require specific skills and experience, some have open-ended requirements.

Women's newsletters are published in almost every field—communications, medicine, management—and many run ads for job openings placed by companies recruiting women.

Local business newspapers are another fertile field for the job hunter. Often these papers include articles on business and industry expansion programs in the area. Want ads for employees to go with the new projects may appear concurrently or within the next few issues.

ANSWERING COMPANY ADS

Most company ads request that you send a résumé and sometimes a "salary history" to a box number. Suppose you've found several ads of this type that you'd like to answer. Should you send your résumé or write an interview-generating letter, omitting the résumé? This question provokes different answers from different career counselors. Some experts advise against sending a résumé, even when it's requested. The theory is that once you've sent in your full job background, you've closed the interviewer's door before it's been opened, because all he or she needs to know has been supplied by your résumé. This school advises another tactic: instead of sending a complete résumé, send a letter keyed to the job requirements of the ad, giving concrete examples of your accomplishments and ability.

While this may be effective if you've had a long job history or great responsibility, it probably will not go over well at the entry level. Your best approach is to send a strong covering letter adapted to the job advertised, *and* your résumé.

Once you've identified the job requirements in a given ad, you should be able to pull out of your résumé all the pertinent work you've done in the past and indicate it in a covering letter outlining your ability to meet the job's needs. The more responses an employer receives from a company ad, the more likely he or she is to review only those applications which satisfy at a glance all the job requirements included in the ad. That's why it's important to spend time on your covering letters, even if you answer only three or four ads a day.

So in taking the want-ad route, answer only the ads for jobs you think you want, and answer them fully. And remember, company ads are the best want-ad leads. Most agencies' ads are designed to lure you into their offices; company ads mean business.

Answering Blind Ads

Less than 2 percent of the want ads placed in newspapers and magazines give the names of the employers running the ads. When you write to a box number, your letter usually arrives at the newspaper that carried the ad and then is forwarded to the employer who placed it. If you answer this kind of ad, called a "blind ad," don't expect a reply for at least a week. A blind ad may generate anywhere from twenty-five to several hundred responses, depending upon how specific its requirements are. It takes time to forward responses to the company, and it may take the company four or five days to screen the résumés and select applicants for interviews.

Do most companies read the résumés they receive? The answer is a qualified yes—most applications are screened; which ones get selected for interviews depends on who is doing the screening and on the type of experience, skill, and responsibility the job requires. Again, the more responses an employer receives, the more a well-targeted covering letter and résumé stand out.

Once you've gotten the hang of it, answering want ads becomes a routine but important part of your daily job campaign. You'll just naturally read newspapers each day and clip the ads worth answering. And answer them promptly; good jobs don't go begging.

Chances are, if you are like almost everybody else, you've been reading want ads for years—fantasizing about that very special job opportunity that will leap out of its neat black-bordered box and knock on your door. It could happen, so keep your eyes peeled.

9

Using Employment Agencies

Signing a contract with an employment agency is like entering into a short-term marriage. And it makes people almost as nervous—with good cause.

Unless you are careful, you could end up paying the agency fees for a job you didn't want at a salary that barely covers the train and bus fares it costs to get you there each day. There are agencies that will send you to Spain in the rain if they can collect a fee from you. They will promise you anything, string you along, shove you into the first opening they find, and then get you back for a second fee when the first job doesn't work out. The only thing it takes to make a contract like this work is a meek applicant with masochistic tendencies.

Everybody has heard scare stories about employment-agency rip-offs. Allowing for embellishment, some of these are true, as reputable agencies are painfully aware. As somebody once said, "When the meek inherit the earth, it won't take a week for the greedy to grab it back from them." Certainly not all agencies are in that category, but look out for the ones that are.

Employment agencies can play a valuable role in your job search. What you need to know is what they can do *for* you and what they can't do *to* you. Once you understand contract obligations, how the fee system works, and how agents work, you'll be ready to look for the good agencies that will work for you.

Keep in mind, however, that only 4 percent of all

entry-level jobs and 15 percent of all other jobs are filled through private employment agencies. This source occupies only a small corner of the total job market, so keep it in perspective.

WHAT AGENCIES CAN DO FOR YOU

If you're new to the job market or are re-entering after a long absence, registering with a few reputable agencies can provide you with certain advantages. A good agency can give you background information on kinds of jobs, salary range, the general employment picture, and specific information about specific companies. Employment is the agency's business, and the good ones know their business.

Corporations and industries, like people, build patterns of employment behavior. An agent who has worked with a specific company for many years will know a lot more than just its job requirements and salary levels. He or she will have an educated guess as to how well you will work out there. Employees and companies need to match for maximum benefit to both. Agents are often good matchmakers.

If you're scared by the thought of interviewing for jobs, an agent can give you valuable pointers about prospective employers, such as "Smoking drives him up the wall," "He said not to send another perfume factory," or "Her hobby is collecting racing cars." These seem like small things, but attention to small things often can tilt a delicate balance in your favor.

An agent can also tell you if your résumé hits the mark and how to beef up your covering letter for a specific employer. If the agency charges for this advice, run—do not walk—for the door.

A good agent may call you up a year or two after your job search ends to ask if you're interested in changing jobs. An agency's success depends on job turnover, and an innovative agent keeps complete files on his or her former clients.

An agent can tell you when your demands are unrealistic—too high or too low—and how to bring them in line with the actuality of the job market.

SELECTING AN AGENCY

Talking to experts in the employment field to get inside advice on how to choose an agency is a terrific idea—so long as the conversation is general. When you get down to specifics, however, the advice begins to sound like "Buy yourself a Ouija board." The unmistakable conclusion is that there is no foolproof way of selecting an agency. Like choosing a surgeon, it's hard to tell what the results will be until it's too late.

Each state has different regulations for licensing agencies, but few are of much help to the consumer. As one expert said, "certification generally means that one person—the owner—needs a license to open an agency; then he or she can hire counselors from off the street."

The only sure guide is "Let the buyer beware." Beware you should, but despair you shouldn't. There are ways of identifying the bad agencies. For example, check off in your Sunday paper all the agencies that run list after list of come-on ads reading "Coll grad," "Gal Friday," "Gaze upon celebrities," or "Run barefoot through our thick carpeting." Right away that gives you a sizable list of rejects. Don't go near them.

Here are some of the other things employment experts recommend that you keep in mind when choosing an agency:

Look for small agencies specializing in the field you want to enter. They will generally serve you better than the large impersonal agencies claiming to be all things to all job seekers.

Ask friends and business associates, especially people who frequently work with employment agencies, for recommendations. Ask if they can recommend specific agents within the suggested agencies.

Women's professional groups, counseling services, and feminist organizations often know which agencies are blatantly sexist (many still are) and which ones are trying to mend their ways. They will also know which new women's recruiting agencies are real and which are rip-offs.

If you are interested in working for a specific company, try to find out whether the company uses an agency, and if so, which agency. (Some companies fill their top jobs through agencies and lower-level openings through their own personnel department.) If you can't learn any other way, call up the company personnel department and ask.

If you phone an agency about a job just advertised and they tell you, "That job's been filled," and then try to sell you something else, you probably should pass them by. Compare several agencies in this manner.

Beware of agencies that make a job selling vacuum cleaners door to door sound like a once-in-a-lifetime opportunity. What you need is an agency that will give you a realistic assessment of a job's potential and your possibilities of getting it. You are in no need of a con job.

For a woman, evaluating an agency is especially important. Despite all the laws to the contrary, sex discrimination is still widely practiced by employment agencies. Most still accept "male preferred" job orders, passing the responsibility on to employers, "What the client wants the client gets" is the prevalent attitude. Often the employer need not mention his preference— it is understood.

Some employment agencies have separate "job books" for male and female applicants or "women's desks," which handle only "women's work"—clerical, secretarial, receptionist jobs. Often these desks are staffed by agents who view women only in terms of traditional positions and direct them down the same old paths.

There are two current schools of thought about women's taking clerical jobs to gain access to better-paying jobs later. One recommends that you get your foot in the door by any method possible—take anything from typing to bootblacking, just so you are available when and if better jobs open up.

The other school just as vehemently claims that the

foot-in-the-door approach is no longer valid. Instead, women are urged to get into training programs, management-career paths, and apprenticeship programs. "Once a mailgirl, always a mailgirl" is the theory.

Regardless of which viewpoint you accept, unless you are *looking for* clerical work, steer clear of gal-friday-type agencies. But if you have decided on a "glamour" job at any cost, don't balk at typing. Just try to determine how many hours a day you'll spend typing and whether there's any chance of advancing past the keyboard. Then, when you take the job, spend all the energy you can muster trying to move up. Do anything from taking night courses to working Sundays and Christmas. Determination and hard work will generally get you up and out of anything—given enough time.

At the same time, recognize that new equal-opportunity laws may work to your benefit, especially if you register with the new type of employment agency, specializing in recruiting women. More and more employers are turning to such agencies to locate qualified women. And more and more women applicants are registering there—but find a real one, not a rip-off.

You should also equip yourself with a general knowledge of the laws governing employment agencies—what they can and cannot do (pp. 176–177). If an agency knows you know its legal obligations, it might hesitate before taking advantage of you.

LOCATING SPECIALIZED AGENCIES

In your newspaper, keep track of the agencies advertising in your job category and you'll soon have a list of three or four names to check out.

Trade magazines in every field run columns of "positions open" at specific companies. Agencies often advertise their services in the same columns.

Trade directories give the location, field, and services of private agencies. For instance, the National Employment Association (the placement industry's trade organization) publishes an annual directory of agencies with 2,500 state-by-state listings. For a copy, write to

Employment Agency Directory
National Employment Association
2000 K Street, N.W.
Washington, D.C. 20006

Classified-ad departments of large metropolitan newspapers often publish directories of local agencies as a promotional service to companies and job seekers. The *New York Times*, for example, prints a "Time Saving Guide" listing the specialties of their agency advertisers. For further information, contact the classified-ad department of the large metropolitan daily papers in your area.

THE AGENCY INTERVIEW

A visit to an agency office will generally dispel all doubts about what kind of organization it is. It's easy to spot a hard-sell, glad-hand, sign-here approach as well as to identify a which-rock-did-you-crawl-out-from-under attitude. Try for something a little less extreme.

The tempo and personality of the office should be apparent as soon as you walk in the door. The agency's attitude toward you as a job seeker will be reflected everywhere: in the office decor, in the receptionist who hands you an application form, and in the other job applicants you'll see coming in and going out.

The average agency is small. Most of the nine thousand licensed agencies have four or five agents plus a switchboard operator/receptionist. You will be handed an application form to complete (these used to be color-coded by sex, but now that this is illegal, some employ more subtle devices). On the back of the form you may find the agency contract, or it may be printed separately.

Most agencies handling jobs in the $10,000–$12,000 salary bracket will expect you to sign a combination application form/contract as a matter of course. You'll be interviewed by a counselor only if you register with the agency. Since you pay a fee only to the agency that finds you a job, you can sign up with as many agencies as you like. But be certain to ask the agent to explain your fee obligations. Listen carefully, ask specific questions, and take notes.

Treat an agency visit as if it were a formal interview. Dress as you would if you were being screened by a potential employer, and bring your résumé. If you work with an agent, he or she is going to have to present you to an employer in the best possible light, emphasizing your skills, dependability, and personality. So remember, appearance is important. Agents respond to neatness, accuracy, openness, honesty, and punctuality—like everybody else—and they sometimes resent casual, off-hand behavior by applicants.

At the end of your interview at the agency, ask for a copy of the contract to take home with you. All agencies using contracts are legally required to give registrants a copy, but sometimes you must ask.

THE AGENCY CONTRACT AND FEE STRUCTURE

"Agency Application," "Agency Agreement," whatever title floats above the fine print, you are signing a legal document outlining your obligation to the agency and its responsibility to you. Be absolutely sure you know what you're signing.

An employment agency contract should always be *in writing*. Never make an oral agreement with an agency about the amount of fees, delayed payment, reference checks, and the like without having that agreement included in your written contract.

The contract must spell out your *fee liability* as a client—the cases in which you must pay either all or part of the agency fee.

It must state the agency's obligation for a *fee return* if you leave a job within a set period of time or if your job is ended by an employer through no fault of your own.

171

LAWRENCE EMPLOYMENT AGENCY, INC.
9 West 42nd St., N.Y., N.Y. 10036

Offers its services to you on the following terms and conditions:

For any employment you accept through our direct referral our service charge to you, based upon New York State Law, will be as follows:

1) CONDITIONS ON FEE PAID POSITION: In the event that I accept employment where the employer has agreed to pay the fee, I understand that such payment is contingent on my reporting to work as agreed and my continuing such employment. In the event, however, that I do not report to work as agreed or I am terminated for cause or leave of my own accord, then and in any such event, I am obligated to pay said fee in accordance with paragraph #4 of this contract, provided, however, that the employer is not obligated to pay the fee or has not paid the fee.

2) REGULAR EMPLOYMENT: 25% of the total amount of the first full month's agreed salary or wages if less than $225.00; 35% of at least $225.00 but less than $270.00; 40% if $270.00; but less than $300.00; 45% if $300.00 but less than $330.00; 50% if $330.00 but less than $365.00; 55% if $365.00 but less than $400.00; 60% if $400.00 or more.

EXAMPLES

Weekly Salary:	$ 85.00	$ 90.00	$ 95	$100	$110	$125	$140	$150
Fee:	$202.58	$214.50	$247	$260	$286	$325	$364	$390

employment means to assure an employer that you will report for work on the terms he has offered you. B) If the employment is terminated without your fault your fee will be figured at the rate of 10% of your gross earnings but shall not exceed the maximum fee outlined in Clause (2). C) If it is terminated under any other circumstances, the fee shall be 50% of your gross earnings but shall not exceed the maximum fee outlined in Clause (2).

5) PAYABLE: Our fee is fully earned and due when you accept such offer of employment made by or on behalf of the employer but if such employment is within the Continental United States same may be paid in equal installments either on your first 3 pay days, or during the first 6 weeks, whichever period is shorter.

6) CONFIDENTIAL: All information you receive from us is solely for your use and benefit. It must not be divulged to any person. Further, it is understood that you have voluntarily submitted your application to us for our service.

YOUR ACCEPTANCE: I have read and hereby accept the terms and conditions outlined above. I agree to immediately notify this agency of the results of the interview with the employer to which it directs me. I hereby acknowledge that I have received a copy of this agreement indicating the fee I am to pay for your service and a copy of the required sections 185 and 186 of the General Business Law.
I further authorize your completing any reference check necessary and/or required by law.

3) **TEMPORARY EMPLOYMENT:** Where all parties to the employment contract agree and understand at the time the employment contract is entered into that it shall be for a period shorter than 4 months the gross fee shall not exceed fifty per cent of the fee as outlined in Clause #2 or ten per cent of the wages or salary actually received, whichever is less.

4) **MODIFICATION:** A) If after you accept the employment you subsequently decide not to comply therewith and do not report for work, our fee shall be one-quarter (¼) of that outlined in Clause (2), unless you remain with your same employer, in which case, our fee shall be (½) of that outlined in Clause (2): Accept

Signed **X** ....

.... (applicant)

SIGNED AGENCY SIG. **LAWRENCE EMPLOYMENT AGENCY, INC.**

Dated New York, ...19..... Social Security #.....

Does anything prevent you from making payments on date due?
....

The New York Human Rights Law prohibits discrimination be-cause of age or sex.

References:— Non Business	Can You Be Bonded?	In reference to your Husband or Wife or	DO NOT WRITE IN THIS SPACE
1.		Parent, give Name	
2.		Employed at—	
Name And Address of Credit Reference or Bank		Co. Address	

DATE	COMPANY (DO NOT WRITE BELOW)	DATE	COMPANY (DO NOT WRITE BELOW)

It must include a *fee schedule* that enables you to compute the agency fee.

And it must have a clearly stated *payment arrangement*—one lump sum or installments.

On pages 172 and 173 is a sample agency contract for you to look over. While some of the details might vary, this should give you an idea of the kind of language and clauses to expect.

Once you sign an employment-agency contract, you have agreed to pay the agency's fee in the method specified if the agency finds you a job that you accept. Many job seekers make mistakes here that they later regret. Whatever pressure you're under, financial or otherwise, make sure your eagerness to find a job doesn't create still another burden for you—an agency fee you can't afford to pay. To give you an idea of the types of fee arrangements you may come across, several fee schedules are outlined below.

Applicant-paid Fee

Under this arrangement you pay the entire agency fee if you accept a job located by the agency. Usually the fee is based on a percentage of your starting salary. The agency receives a portion of either your monthly or yearly earnings; a sliding scale of fees is set up and the percentage you pay depends upon the size of your annual salary.

If you get a high-paying job, the agency fee can be anywhere from 5 to 15 percent of your annual salary. If you accept an entry-level job somewhere in the $6,000 to $10,000 range, the agency will probably charge a percentage of your first month's salary. Since the agency's fees are competitive in most states and have no ceiling, you can be charged whatever the market will bear—at least 25 percent of your first month's earnings, and in some cases as much as twice that amount.

You will have to pay the fee either in a lump sum within a specified period after you begin working or in monthly or weekly installments. Sometimes you can use a credit card to pay the fee. Always find out about payment plans before you register or sign anything.

"Fee-paid" Jobs

If a job is listed with an agency as "fee paid" or if you are told by an agency that the job is "fee paid," this means the employer pays the entire fee. You pay the agency nothing if you fulfill your part of the contract. "If you fulfill your part of the contract" is the catch here, so be careful. If you accept a fee-paid job and don't show up for work, if you are fired by your employer for any reason, or if you begin work and then leave the job, *you* may have to pay the entire agency fee yourself. Agencies usually have "guarantee" arrangements with employers to cover fly-away applicants who fail to appear for a job or leave suddenly. Usually, the agency returns its fee to the employer and then turns to the applicant for reimbursement.

There may also be other problems with fee-paid openings. You may specify that you will accept only a fee-paid job and assume that the agency is setting up interviews with only fee-paid employers. But once you accept a position, you may learn that there is another fee arrangement altogether. Protect yourself by establishing *who pays* before, during, and after *each* interview.

Or an agency may direct you to a company that interviews you for a fee-paid opening but then offers a different job. If you accept it, you may end up footing the agency bill. You can avoid these hazards by checking with each company interviewer to make sure that he or she *is* discussing a fee-paid job.

"Fee-refunded" or "Fee-reimbursed" Jobs

Under this arrangement, you pay the agency if you accept one of its jobs. If you continue working after a probationary period, usually three months, your employer will reimburse you for the agency fee. But if you leave your job during that trial period, you will not receive your fee back from the employer. An employment agent may not know that a particular employer is willing to return your fee, so don't depend on the agent for this information. Always ask a prospective employer if he or she will make this type of arrangement with you—and the length of time you have to work before you'll be reimbursed.

"Fee-split" Jobs

Under this plan, you and your new employer each pay a mutually agreed-upon portion of the agency fee within a set period of time.

Now that you know the types of fee plans you'll come across in agency contracts, be sure the following information is included in any contract you sign:

- Do you have to pay the agency fee all at once, or can you pay in installments? If so, how many payments are there and when are they due?
- If you specify that you'll take only a fee-paid job, will the agency agree to send you only to fee-paid employers?
- What happens if you accept a job through an agency and then a better job comes up—are you required to pay all or part of the agency fee if you don't appear for the first job?
- If you accept a job and shortly afterward your new employer fires you, do you have to pay the entire agency fee? Will part of the fee be returned to you if you've paid it already?
- If you accept a job and then decide to leave it, are you still liable for the fee?

LAWS GOVERNING EMPLOYMENT AGENCIES

According to federal law (Title VII of the Civil Rights Act of 1964), most state laws, and some municipal codes, it is illegal for an employment agency to

- Discriminate against any job seeker because of

race, religion, age, sex, national origin, or (in some states) physical handicaps.

- Classify applicants according to race, religion, age, or sex, except when these factors can be proved to relate to a specific type of job.
- Accept applicants of only one sex unless sex is a *bona fide* occupational qualification for the jobs the agency offers.
- Set up separate fee schedules or coded applications for male and female job seekers applying for the same opening with the same qualifications.
- Accept job orders from an employer who specifically requests only male or female candidates or applicants of a certain race or age (with *bona fide* occupational exceptions and there aren't many).
- Specify an age requirement in either ads or interviews. However, minimum age requirements established by state law ("not under 18" or "not under 21") are legal for some jobs.
- Verify a reference or credit rating without permission from the applicant.

Although the laws governing sex discrimination are strong, enforcement by individual government agencies has been lax. Several recent surveys reveal that job discrimination is still actively practiced by many employment agencies throughout the country.

Some Better Business Bureaus publish brochures outlining the laws governing employment agencies and the fee schedules in local areas. Other sources of information on employment-agency regulations are your local Department of Consumer Affairs, Human Rights Commission, the state Division of Human Rights, and local chapters of national feminist groups or of the American Civil Liberties Union. Or you might write to your secretary of state and ask for laws governing employment agencies.

Charges of discrimination on the basis of sex, race, national origin, or age, brought against either an employer or an employment agency, are handled by the Equal Employment Opportunity Commission (EEOC).

For information on how to bring such charges, see pages 336–340.

DON'T BE BULLIED BY THE AGENCY

In your short-term marriage with an employment agency, be an equal partner. Realize that your finding a good job will benefit both partners.

Before you sign any agency agreement, make sure you fully understand the terms—then live up to your part of the agreement. A good job is well worth paying for, and a good agent's time and advice are valuable.

But don't feel obligated to interview for a job you don't want or settle for a job that you have reservations about. Know your own mind, communicate clearly and honestly, but resist pressure to jump at the first offer.

Don't worry about wasting the time of the employment agent. No one knows better than you do what is productive use of *your* time. And no agency ever went out of business because the agents were too timid to toss out a few chronic fence-sitters. But a lot of people have been shoved into jobs they shouldn't have taken. Don't allow this to happen to you.

IV

LANDING
THE JOB

10

Going for Interviews

The word "interview" makes some people jumpy. It conjures up visions of a cat and mouse, the powerful and the powerless. Often the job seeker feels stripped and vulnerable, small and unimportant.

People react to the interview situation in various ways. Some otherwise quiet and unassuming people babble on like a gushing waterfall. Women who are usually articulate stumble over their own names. Some reveal intimate details that would make their doctors blush. Others remain as inanimate as a plastic plant, conceding only name, rank, and serial number.

It's natural to feel insecure about being interviewed—especially if you have little interviewing experience. It's natural to feel uptight about your performance—which is what it is. But even though your performance is being watched and measured, an actor is the last thing in the world you want to appear to be.

You need to project as much self-assurance and openness as you feel comfortable with—but no more. If you are nervous, don't waste your energy trying to conceal it, and don't make a big deal out of it. Sitting on your shaky hands will only make you look silly. Using up fifteen minutes of the interviewer's time explaining how nervous you feel will do the same thing. Accept the fact that you feel nervous and move on to subjects over which you have some control. You can't control the way you feel. You can control what you do about it. And there are many things you can do to prepare for an interview.

CREATING AN IMPRESSION

An interviewer's first impression of you—his or her gut reaction—is often the deciding factor in whether you get the job. It isn't fair. It isn't professional. It isn't rational. But it is human. It's been said that there are two reasons for most decisions, a good one and the real one.

Nobody has figured out the intricacies of human chemistry—why you click with some people and fall flat with others—but it's a real factor to be reckoned with in preparing for an interview.

An interviewer's initial reaction to you is based upon a number of seemingly trivial and unimportant details. These include:

Your physical appearance. Just by walking into a room, you create a reaction. If you're wearing red velvet toreador pants with silver buckles on your purple suede shoes, you've said a lot—probably enough to get you tossed out. Are your eyelids deep blue? Are there black circles penciled around your eyes? Could initials be carved in your pancake? Will your perfume remain after you go? Is half a can of spray cementing your hair in place? Or did your grooming consist of throwing on a pair of tie-dyed jeans, dashing a little cold water on your face, slipping on your sneakers, and running your fingers through your hair in the waiting room?

Your voice. Is your voice rasping, grating, loud, soft, child-like, sultry, clear, garbled, whining, soothing? Does it sound strange to you? Are you enunciating each word so distinctly that you sound like either an elocution teacher or a drunk? Are you faking a British or finishing-school accent even though you come from Brooklyn? Would you talk this way if awakened in the middle of the night?

Your hands. Did you offer to shake hands? Is your handshake firm or limp? Are your fingernails three

182

inches long and painted? Are they cracked and dirty? Do your hands shake?

Your first actions. Did you remain standing until invited to sit, or did you flop down and kick off your shoes? Are you too friendly or not friendly enough?

Your personality. Are you frozen in ramrod position, barely talking—or are you bouncing up and down like a Yo-Yo? Is your fixed stare focused on the ceiling or on your shoelaces? Do you give barely audible "yes" and "no" answers or are you interrupting the interviewer's questions?

Any of these details can trigger a series of associations in your interviewer's mind. Sometimes a tiny factor that has nothing to do with your ability to do the job will hit the interviewer, prey on his or her mind, and poison the water for you. It can be as subtle as a whiff of perfume or as obvious as a wart on the end of your nose.

Exactly this happened when an interviewer for a large, very conservative corporation was screening applicants to send to his boss. "Out of about a hundred and fifty résumés from an ad in the *Wall Street Journal*, I had invited six people for interviews," he said. "One looked especially good on paper—his age, education, experience, salary were about what we had in mind. When he showed up he was neat, nice-looking and wearing a dark-blue suit, white shirt and conservative tie. His shoes were shined. Then it hit me. I couldn't believe my eyes because it looked like the old joke— the guy was wearing white socks! During the entire interview my eyes kept darting back to his shoes. I couldn't concentrate on what he was saying because I was trying to decide whether to ask him bluntly why he did it—maybe he had an allergy or something.

"He didn't mention the white socks and neither did I. But I figured that since his judgment on choosing a pair of socks wasn't too hot, maybe his business judgment wouldn't be any better. I still wonder what made him do it."

Of course, a psychiatrist might figure out that the man in the white socks was revealing deeper feelings— maybe he didn't want the job in the first place. Or he may have been a rugged individualist who liked white socks. But the results were the same—he didn't get the job.

As this interviewer said, "Only authentic geniuses with rare specialities are absolved from these petty considerations. If you're one of those whose work may make a billion-dollar corporation out of a million-dollar one, you can name your own terms. You can patter barefoot into the president's office wearing feathers, beads and faded denims. You can sprout an Afro requiring a special door and get it built. But you'd better be a genius. For us lesser mortals, other rules apply."

Here are a few do's and dont's for lesser mortals.

- Dress neatly in an unobtrusive dress or pants suit—not an unmatched pair of pants and shirt. (Even the conservative business world has accepted pants suits as proper attire.) Avoid loud colors, far-out styles, too-short skirts, and revealing necklines.
- Apply make-up so sparingly (or deftly) that nobody can tell whether you're wearing any.
- Be friendly but businesslike. Don't linger after the interview.
- Take to an interview only those things you need—two copies of your résumé, references, important work samples, a pen and pad—which will all fit in your purse or a large envelope. Don't take packages, wet raincoats, or pets. And don't bring friends with you for "moral support." (It frequently happens.) If they are so necessary to your mental health, at least be sure nobody sees them—even if you have to lock them in the trunk.
- Act natural. Nobody likes a phony, not even another phony.
- Don't smoke unless your interviewer smokes. In any case, ask permission to smoke.
- Avoid attention-getters such as heavy, clinking jewelry or a low-cut blouse.

AN AGE-OLD ACCUSATION

Throughout history women have been accused of using sex to get a job or anything else they want. The merest suggestion of seductiveness is all that is required to slap you into this category. So it is especially important to keep this in mind as you dress for an interview. Don't wear tight-fitting clothes or skirts slit to your thighs—no miniskirts or see-through tops.

Avoiding every suggestion of sex in your job search will probably not be possible. Most women get at least a few job offers with hints of dubious fringe benefits. Just make sure that you're not doing anything to invite such offers by transmitting subtle messages. And if you are faced with a leer, don't over-react. Be businesslike and firm but cut the interview short if the suggestions persist.

EVALUATING YOUR INTERVIEWER

There are times when you will sense a communications gap between you and your interviewer. What is behind that feeling you have as you walk out the door frustrated and confused, knowing that you haven't come across well?

"Anyone going out on a job interview faces an invisible hazard," according to one placement specialist. "Seventy percent of the people interviewing are incompetent to evaluate an applicant. You go in feeling you should shine and come out feeling that something was wrong, something was missing. There's no guarantee that the person interviewing you is superior—or even competent—in any way."

Most of the people you'll talk to are not professionals when it comes to interviewing. They are not trained to ask the questions that will put you at ease or allow you to highlight your strengths and skills. Some interviewers may be more nervous than you are. Others may be preoccupied with problems that have nothing to do with you.

Inexperienced interviewers often adopt a negative approach in screening applicants, using the interviewing process itself as a tool to define both the job and the person to fill the job instead of establishing their own criteria. Their theory goes that if they screen enough unsatisfactory applicants, they will be able to identify the proper person by the process of elimination, which doesn't work unless the interviewer knows what to eliminate. So they end up counting daisy petals. If you're the last one interviewed you're likely to get the job.

Some interviewers, with sadistic tendencies, may put you through a "stress" interview, guaranteed to give you an ulcer if you take it seriously. So don't take it seriously. If you look at it the way it deserves to be scrutinized, you'll laugh at it.

The "stress" interviewer will bombard you with questions like "why were you fired from your last job?" Since this type of interviewer is supposed to gauge the way you react under pressure, be sure to stay calm. Sometimes these interviewers work in pairs: one to beat you up verbally and the other to supply sympathy. If you run into this type (there aren't many—it's already out of vogue), don't let it upset you. People with nothing to hide have nothing to fear from any kind of question.

The opposite of the stress interview is the one that is so low-key you have to check to make sure your interviewer hasn't fallen asleep. You may get a few easy questions and a lot of false assurances from this type. If this happens, wake up the interviewer and ask yourself the questions. Make sure you get across the points you came to make.

Often you have no control over the time of your interview, but if you can arrange it, try not to be the last interview of the day. Morning is generally best because your interviewer will be more alert. Interviewing is a tedious, wearing task, and after seeing four or five applicants for the same job the interviewer may be groggy. If yours is the last interview of the day—or of the week—your interviewer could be thinking about getting home through the traffic, an early date, a dinner party, making a plane, or getting to the nearest bar. You, as the obstacle to this, may be given short shrift.

ANSWERING THE UNASKED QUESTIONS

Affirmative Action laws preventing employers from asking women about marriage and children are like a judge instructing a jury to disregard certain damaging evidence. It sounds good, but it doesn't work.

It's good to have the laws. They are valuable in forcing employers to rethink their discriminatory employment practices, but when you get down to the wire in an interview, you must either clear up what's in the interviewer's mind or suffer the consequences. If you don't, you're likely to get some vague-sounding "We'll call you" dismissal.

Occupying a prominent place in the interviewer's mind are these questions:

- If you are single, will future marriage mean the end of your career?
- If you're now married and childless, will children later mean the end of your career?
- If you have children, will your home duties interfere with your job responsibilities? Have you made child-care arrangements so that you will not have to stay home every time a child has the sniffles?
- Will you refuse to travel because of your husband or children?
- Are you as good a bet in which to invest time, training, and money as a man would be?
- Will you be as dedicated to your job as a man would be?

Sometimes in answering these questions, a woman runs into a "Catch 22" situation where the interviewer's true feelings are concerned. The interviewer may feel that women should stay home, take care of children, and travel only with their families. Other men feel uncomfortable with competent women (generally the least competent men), and there are also a few women interviewers who will hand you bigoted generalities about women by the dozens.

Sometimes an interviewer literally will try to talk you out of a job. He (this is almost always a man) will reel off a list of problems: you'll be on the road half the time, men in the department won't respond favorably to a woman in the job, your husband or boyfriend won't like the late hours you'll have to work, traveling home at night isn't safe for a woman, the job is too tough for a woman, the pay is too low, the boss is a tyrant, and the elevators in the office building don't work.

Be alert to this kind of sexist ploy and answer all negative assumptions with positive statements: the road doesn't frighten you, people generally respond favorably to you, your personal life is well in hand, life itself is a risk, you've successfully performed tough jobs before, you're used to dealing with demanding bosses, and exercise is better for you than elevators.

Work out straightforward, concise answers to the following questions in advance of the interview. Write them down if you need to, and do a little role-playing with a friend to practice answering them with ease. A little pre-interview rehearsal may be helpful, giving you a greater sense of control when you walk through the interviewer's door.

- How long do you plan to work?
- What job do you want?
- Why are you more qualified than someone else?
- What are your career goals?
- What do you see yourself doing in five years?
- Would you be willing to travel?

UNCONSCIOUS SEXISM

A feminist consultant who conducts awareness programs for employers says that many managers (both men and women) are unaware of their own deeply rooted negative attitudes about women.

"Their surface attitudes—those they recognize—are simple to deal with compared with the ones they don't even know they have," she said. "And the worst kind are employers who explain how free of prejudice they are ('Some of my best friends are women')—that they would be more than willing to hire a woman if only a 'qualified' one could be found. Trying to uncover this type of prejudice is like flailing away at a dense fog with a tennis racquet. Scratch the surface and you'll find a Neanderthal who believes in the biological and psychological supremacy of men."

In a survey conducted and published by the *Harvard Business Review,* 1,500 participating managers responded to a questionnaire designed to sample executive decision making concerning women. Form number 1 in the survey set forth a list of problem circumstances involving a male employee; form number 2, the same circumstances involving a female employee. Half the participants were given form 1 and the other half form 2. In addition, they were given a series of memos, letters, reports, and other communications. The participants were asked to assume the role of an important official in a hypothetical organization.

The result of the survey showed the following:

- Managers expect male employees to give top priority to their jobs when career demands and family obligations conflict. They expect female employees to sacrifice their careers to family responsibilities.
- If personal conduct threatens an employee's job, managers make greater efforts to retain a valuable male employee than an equally valuable female.
- In hiring, promotion, and career-development decisions, managers are biased in favor of males.

A further conclusion was that "beneath these patterns of discrimination there is an underlying assumption that is not at first apparent from the survey

189

findings: it would seem to be the women who are expected to change to satisfy the organization's expectations. For example, written comments from participating managers often suggest that women must become more assertive and independent before they can succeed in some of the case examples in the survey. These managers do not see the organization as having any obligation to alter its attitudes toward women."

Even with all the laws and the many people working to change such attitudes, these biases will remain with us for many years. Recognize what you are up against, but push ahead. Out there among the others you'll find some terrific employers—both men and women—who will evaluate you fairly, treat you equally, and pay you what you're worth.

INTERVIEW TIPS

From many placement experts, career counselors, and employers who do their own interviewing, here are some interview tips that may be helpful to you:

Enthusiasm, flexibility, ease of communication, a willingness to take on more than the duties in a job description—these are qualities you should try to project during your interview.

If you know of a new product being marketed by the company or a new service being performed, ask about the latest developments. If you've seen an ad on TV or read something in a trade magazine that might affect your potential employer, bring it up.

When you meet someone who clearly isn't used to interviewing, the burden is on *you* to make the interview informative and relaxed. If the interviewer has your résumé, ask what in it interested him or her most. Ask about the company or organization. Find a way to shift your interviewer into the role of information giver—someone with knowledge and expertise. Many people find it easier to give answers than to ask questions. Allow your interviewer to tell you what he or she wants, what the company's problems are.

Don't be windy—but don't give one-syllable answers

to questions; one-liners are conversation stoppers. Always elaborate briefly on your experience, your skills, and your background—this gives the interviewer a chance to frame another question as well as to relax and listen to what you have to say.

Don't wait to be asked about what job you might want or where you might fit in. Again, the burden is on *you*, not the interviewer, to decide what contribution you can make and what skills you can bring to a job or field—to know what you want.

Don't *ever* talk about a former employer unless you have something positive to say. One counselor told a story about a man who spent fifteen minutes running his old supervisor into the ground. The interviewer waited, let him finish, and then told him quietly that his former supervisor had just been made vice-president of the company!

Never disclose confidential information about a former company, supervisor, or co-worker. Don't volunteer information on the financial status of the company or the private habits of your boss. If he's been chasing you around the office, say you're looking for a different work environment; if you've been refused a raise or denied credit for work you've accomplished, say you want to develop new skills in a new field.

Try to avoid the appearance of opportunism. If you view the job you're interviewing for as a stepping stone, don't step on it during the interview. If you come on too strong for advancement, an employer may think you're not interested in staying very long.

If you interview for a specific opening, remember: that's the job the interviewer wants to talk about. Don't steer the conversation to other job possibilities; let the interviewer bring them up if it's appropriate.

Don't lie to an interviewer. As one counselor put it, you can't lose just *part* of your credibility: put a pin in the balloon and *all* the air goes out. You don't have to embroider. Present yourself as you are. One counselor tells of a woman who applied for a job and thought she might be overqualified, so she told her interviewer that she'd finished only three years of college. It took a simple phone call to reveal that she had graduated with a B.A., and the job was lost.

As a rule, you're better off being accurate about your degree, date of graduation, last salary. It's one thing to nudge the truth slightly and another to lie about things that can be checked out. This goes for business references too, so be sure yours will be positive about you and accurate about your work background.

Have specific questions you want your interviewer to answer, but be careful about the order in which you bring them up. Don't ask about salary and fringe benefits first or about advancement or hiring practices for women. Let your questions take a natural course. Begin by asking about the job itself: What your responsibilities would be (your hidden question: what do I have to do?). Where your responsibilities will take you if you perform well (what will I be allowed to do?). Who your co-workers will be (how closely will I be supervised?). Information on salary, raises, and company benefits is usually volunteered by the interviewer. If these subjects are brought up, it probably means you're a strong contender for the job.

Ask how many people have had the job before you and why the last person left. Ask to talk to the previous job holder if he or she is still with the company. Try to meet and talk to the people with whom you'd be working. These are legitimate requests. As one counselor put it, the president of a company she works for goes through people like Coca-Cola—so don't be the next bottle!

You can indicate in an interview that you're eager to continue your education or training. Ask about tuition-reimbursement or sharing programs—this type of concern can enhance your potential contribution in an employer's mind.

If your interviewer asks how you've been supporting yourself while you're looking for work, there are several ways to answer. If you've just graduated from college, you can say your family is helping you out until you locate the job you want and that they consider this financial support an investment. Or you can say you planned ahead for your job campaign by setting up your own job-search fund during the school year. This shows that you're organized, career-oriented, and have planned ahead. Don't tell the interviewer that you're waitressing or typing part-time to make ends meet. Once you're identified with this type of work, a potential employer may have a hard time seeing you in a more responsible position.

Always be courteous. If you've enjoyed speaking with your interviewer, say so, and let him or her know *why* you've found the interview helpful or informative. If you want the job you've been discussing or you'd like to work for the person you've been speaking to, say so.

Whatever your plans are when you leave the interview, write a brief note of thanks to the person you talked to. If you have thought of a new idea or point you didn't bring up on the interview, mention it briefly in your note. And if someone has helped you on the way or arranged the interview for you, drop them a line also. If you take the job, let them know how it's working out; if you are still looking, say so.

KEEP A POSITIVE SELF-IMAGE

By the end of the first two weeks of your concentrated job campaign, you should be getting some replies from potential employers. If your no-thank-you stack is ten times higher than your come-see-me pile, don't despair. You have just proved a statistic: for every thirty letters you send out, you can expect to get back at most three positive replies.

Keep up your courage and remember that a positive self-image communicates itself instantly to others. Feel sympathy for those twenty-seven prospective employers who wrote you off. If they make more poor decisions like that one, there may soon be twenty-seven new job seekers in the market, and *they* will be reading this book.

11

Taking the Job

Your pavement pounding has paid off. Your job campaign has produced results. One of your interviews has turned into a job offer. In that sea of rejection, you found somebody who wants you.

Congratulations. If the job that chose you is the job you would have chosen, take yourself out to dinner, buy a bottle of wine, and celebrate. It will be good for you and good for the economy.

But if your first job offer happens early in your job campaign, or if it is not the job you really want, or if you have more than one offer, hold off on the celebration. You still have a problem, even though it's a nice problem to have. You must sort out many variables and find a solution. And unless you believe in fortune-tellers or divining rods, the decision you must make will be at best an educated guess.

The gut reaction of most job seekers is to take the first job offered and run, because accepting a job ends the painful process of looking for a job. And in a severely depressed job market, this may be an intelligent decision. What you want must always be measured against what you can get. But even in a full-scale depression, give yourself time to tote up your own personal balance sheet—the advantages and disadvantages of taking any one job.

It's a rare employer who would refuse an applicant a day or two to think over a job offer. Take the time and use it wisely. You could be making the most important decision of your life. Every successful person has made a decision at a crossroad. And many a business failure can recall a bypassed route to the land of might-have-been.

THE FIRST JOB OFFER

Suppose you have just begun your job campaign, but before you even buy a paste pot you get a call. The friend of a friend wants to talk to you about a job.

You go for the interview, and within ten minutes you're offered the job. It's not exactly the job you've been dreaming about, but it *is* a job. The salary isn't what you had hoped, but it's close. The hours are long but not impossible, and the work isn't in your field but it's related. And your prospective employer is sitting there wearing an expectant look, waiting for you to speak. What do you do?

A situation like this presents more questions than answers. If one employer is hooked, can others be far behind? Or will your first offer be your last offer? Has one offer caused you to inflate your worth? If you take the job, will you be underselling yourself? If you take the job, will you be sorry? If you don't take the job, will you be sorry?

All these questions can be answered with one word: maybe. The best you can do is carefully size up the situation, weigh your options in the light of as much information as you can put together quickly, and leap one way or the other. Whatever decision you make doesn't have to be forever. Just do the best you can with the information you have. Any energy for later recriminations can be better used in finding your next job.

Whether such an offer comes early or late in your campaign, your reaction should be the same. Be enthusiastic, say you are 90 percent sure you want it, give a "qualified" yes—but don't accept without a little time to think it over. Unless you have previously decided that this is exactly the right job for you.

If you are pressed for an immediate yes-or-no answer, press back. Sometimes this is an attempt to stampede you into taking something you would refuse if you had time to think it over. Even if you intend to accept the job at 9 A.M. the following morning, at the very least say you always sleep on big decisions.

LISTEN TO YOUR INNER VOICE

With whatever time you have to think over a job offer, do as thorough a research job as possible. Then, in the light of your research, take the job market into consideration. Is the news filled with layoffs? Do more economists predict gloom than growth? Is the stock market up or down?

After these basics are considered, pay attention to your own feelings. Do you really want the job, or are you settling for less than you'd be likely to get later? Are you glad you have a job offer, but sorry it's this one? Is a nagging doubt in the back of your mind trying to get out? Are you in internal conflict—your head telling you one thing, your heart another? Sometimes your heart makes better decisions than your head.

One woman recently went through this kind of psychological push-pull about a job offer. She was offered a very good job in another city—not a problem, she thought, because it was a city she had lived in at one time and liked. She got two weeks to think over the job offer, then a two-week extension. She felt complimented because the employer wanted her enough to make all kinds of concessions concerning moving and living expenses, but after three weeks she still was saying yes one day and no the next.

"I knew what a terrific opportunity the job was for me, but a nagging doubt remained each time I thought about packing up and going," she said. "Finally, I got angry with myself and made a definite decision to take the job. That same day I bought new plants for my apartment and talked to the superintendent about some permanent improvements. Then it hit me. I wanted the job, but I didn't want to uproot the kids and myself. Moving mattered more than I originally thought. Now I'm back looking for a job closer to home, with more understanding of myself. I won't waste my time interviewing for jobs out of town."

What's left out of this story is the fact that although the woman isn't wealthy, she comes from a family very willing and able to help her through several months of job searching, if necessary. It does make a big difference in the final decision. Without such backing, she might have been on the first plane out of town.

TALK OVER TERMS

If you fail to settle all the terms of a job before accepting the job, you can end up squarely behind the eight ball. Prospective employers are not above the "fuzz it up" approach. Many know exactly what they are doing. When they fuzz it up, you'd better clear things up or be prepared to live with costly consequences.

You cease to be a free agent the moment you accept a job. To accept a job first and *then* discuss salary, duties, and benefits puts the cart before the horse. What can you do if you don't like something? Threaten to quit and demand severance pay?

When a prospective employer wants you for a particular job, you are in a bargaining position. How strong a position depends upon how much you are wanted. It is a precarious balance; don't push your luck. Talk specifics, not generalities. Be persistent and, if possible, imply that you are weighing more than one offer. While you shouldn't lie, comparison shopping does set up an advantageous situation for you if prospective employers become bidders. But do it carefully or it will backfire.

Bargaining and bidding apply to women and men alike, but women should be extra careful to be specific about salary, duties, and chain of command. Women generally have been paid less than men for the same work. Although this practice is now against the law, it still continues in many places—it has merely gone underground. Where employers once openly paid women less for the same job, many now use deceptive titles and job descriptions to accomplish the same thing. They get away with it as long as nobody complains.

You need to know the following before you accept a job:

Salary. Is there an organizational chart with starting salary specified for each job? Was the salary for your job arrived at with you specifically in mind? If so, exactly how? Who held the job before you? What was his or her salary? (If your predecessor was a man, be sure your beginning salary is at least the same as his was.)

Advancement. Are you boxed in before you begin, or do you have room to move up? Ask the employer to chart your possible moves up the organizational pyramid, assuming you do a first-rate job.

Line of command. To whom will you report, and to whom does that person report? You can tell how far down you are in the pecking order by seeing how far your boss is from the top of the chart. Don't let anybody tell you it doesn't matter to whom you report. Buck passing begins at this point, unless the chain of responsibility is clearly established.

Job duties. Have these made as explicit as possible. It could later save you from being dumped on with duties other employees are trying to avoid. Be suspicious of any employer who reassures you, "We'll find plenty for you to do—don't worry your pretty head." Worry your pretty head.

Salary raises. Are they based on evaluation? On whatever the employer decides? Given regularly? Minimum or maximum percentage? What difference will performance make?

Where you work. Unfortunately it matters. Your office says something about how you rank in the corporation: size of office, number of windows, thickness of carpeting, the furniture, embossed stationery, and how close to the chairman of the board or the president of the company your office is located. You won't be able to change these things, but you will get an idea of how important you are.

Title. This also matters. Sometimes tiny prepositions count. "Director of marketing" often is more important than "marketing director." Discuss the structure set up by the company and where you fit into it.

Company rules. In many companies you will be given a booklet that explains company policies, rules, and benefits. If not, ask for one, or if there is none, a verbal explanation.

Benefits. Vacations, pension plans, holidays, retirement programs, medical and dental plans, sick leave, and so on. You generally can't alter them, but understand what they are before you take the job.

ORAL AGREEMENTS

Naturally, you can't get answers to all your questions in writing. And if you insist, you'll probably get tossed out. Many agreements will be oral. Make mental notes about the important ones and later write them down.

Without written notes, even you won't remember what was said at the time of your job offer. And you can bet your prospective employer won't remember as much as you do. This memory lapse doesn't have to be deliberate. It generally isn't. Memories do fade, and with them promises. Keep a careful record of exactly what you were promised, date it, and file it away to refresh both your mind and your employer's when necessary. Your word against your employer's isn't enough (though neither is your memo enough if he or she chooses not to recall any such promises).

DISCUSSING MONEY

The greatest stumbling block for most women is to overcome their feelings of worthlessness about themselves and talk about money realistically. If you have trouble doing this, you're not alone. Asking for a raise or discussing a beginning salary makes many women uncomfortable. They are far too willing to accept society's expectations that men are supposed to earn money and women to marry it. Therefore, a young man is expected to be more interested in high pay than a woman is. Even if a man is single, he is assumed to be preparing to support somebody other than himself some day. His financial ambitions, no matter how great, are taken seriously.

The opposite is true for women. If a woman is married, her salary needs are discounted; it is assumed that the family doesn't need her pay. A man whose wife works, on the other hand, is rarely—if ever— penalized by having his salary lowered on the ground that his earnings are nonessential. If a working woman is single, her financial needs are assumed to be less than a man's because she is expected to support only herself.

One woman deals with this sexism effectively by letting it be "known" that her mother (who is in fact alive and well and living in a distant city) is an invalid living in an expensive sanitarium. As a result the woman's spared the joking about her salary needs that afflicts many other women. "I can't swear to it," she said, "but I believe that over the years I have increased my salary measurably because of my invention. Maybe this is dishonest, but so is the false assumption about women's needs for money."

Try to think about money in a logical way. In the job world the amount of money you earn is a measure of your worth, your value to a company. Generally speaking, the less you are paid the less you are valued, and the more you are paid the more you are valued. When a prospective employer offers you less than you think you are worth, tell him the offer is not acceptable and negotiate the figure upward. Don't allow yourself to be put on the block and marked down. If you're shy about bargaining for yourself—a problem many women have—pretend to yourself you're speaking in behalf of a friend.

Prospective employers will try every trick in the book too. They will give you sob stories about their financial problems—then offer you $5,000 a year less than the job should pay. Play the game right back. Be sympathetic, but let them know your needs. Some employers will promise you a raise in six weeks but not deliver one for six years. Don't be put off by promises. Your beginning salary is the base you will work from as long as you are in the job market. Beginning at rock bottom leaves a wide gap to overcome later, not to mention your next prospective employer, who will take one look at your low salary and assume you're being paid all you're worth. Why else did you accept it?

12

After You Take the Job

Beginning a new job is an exciting adventure—or should be. Your enthusiasm and motivation are high. Your energy and creativity are at a peak. You want to succeed, to be appreciated, and to be rewarded.

With all success indicators pointing to go, why do some people bog down while others forge ahead? What invisible tides propel you forward or keep you back in a job?

Many villains are available who can be blamed for failure: bad luck, "the system," your age, your color, your sex. These factors are often stumbling blocks. Women have been, and will continue to be, denied jobs or promotions because of age, color, or sex in an unfair system that has kept our sex down.

But solutions to these and any other problems come through changing what can be changed, living with what can't, and learning to tell the difference between the two. You can't change your color, your age, or, for all practical purposes, your sex. And while the system *is* in many aspects unfair, neither you nor anybody else will change it overnight. Learning where to concentrate your energies will maximize your possibilities for success. Nothing comes of butting your head against a stone wall except a feeling of relief when you stop. If you find yourself constantly doing this, it may be constructive to ask yourself why you always find the wall but never the gate.

Take a hard, objective look at yourself. What makes

you angry, sad, glad, bad? What makes you comfortable or uncomfortable? What motivates you or demotivates you? What are your limitations, and what is limiting you?

Understanding yourself and learning to change are a far cry from compromise. Perhaps you will find that you have been compromising too much—or perhaps not enough or not about the right issues. Today, with the growing insistence on equality for women, some women feel that they are compromising their principles if they don't come on strong. While these feelings are understandable, the actions they sometimes lead to are not. For example, if you are refused a promotion on the basis of sex or race, it is much more intelligent to calmly ask your boss for an explanation than to slam out the door. Often, in the attempt to make discrimination seem justifiable and logical, employers have come to realize that it isn't. And even if you're dealing with a diehard racist or sexist, it is much more useful to gather information that might later be used in filing a discrimination action than to leave the fray. Many otherwise valid legal actions are thrown out of court because of a lack of carefully documented evidence. So in any situation, no matter how difficult, try to think ahead to future courses of alternative action rather than settle for the rage of the moment.

In the past, women have generally been willing to settle for less than they are worth and to take a back seat in office politics. These patterns are hard to break. One woman, given a promotion but not the accompanying raise her predecessor got, stewed for a week before summoning the courage to ask why. By the time she got to her boss's office, her pent-up rage exploded, providing the boss with a convenient excuse—her behavior. It also probably gave him some support for his personal prejudices about women's unsuitability for executive positions because of their emotionalism. Always keep your goals in mind in situations like this. If any explosions occur, let it be the boss who uses rage to evade logical, pointed, and persistent questions about his or her actions.

BUILDING YOUR OWN CAREER PATH

Building your own career path means looking at a job as a beginning, not an end—looking forward to new possibilities instead of digging your own rut. Naturally, this must be done gradually, and it requires planning. Nobody goes from clerk to president except in carefully constructed steps. When you construct those steps, you are building a career path.

Thinking in terms of a career path is important for your self-image. It keeps you on track, constantly assessing yourself and evaluating your own work. Although evaluation by others is helpful, your evaluation of yourself can be more valuable. Sometimes it tells you when you've "topped out" in a certain company and should move on to another. Sometimes it tells you that the price of a bigger job is too much to pay in terms of time, travel, and work you may not enjoy. Sometimes it tells you that you are in the wrong field. Nobody else can determine these things for you. You must direct your own life and career.

The first step in building a career path is to do a first-rate job in your present position. Be a problem-solver and assume responsibility in areas that count. If this is your first job, make sure the old "previous experience" monster never again rears its ugly head. Create jobs for yourself. Look for more efficient ways of doing your work. Look beyond your small corner to the problems your boss or his/her boss must handle. Understanding the problems of others can give you insight into the reasons for their actions. If, in reply to "Good morning," your boss snaps, "What's good about it?" chances are you are not the target of the anger, so don't be ready to assume the sacrificial goat position. In fact, don't waste time worrying about what you may have done wrong. If you've done anything wrong you can be sure somebody will tell you.

Never duck responsibility by taking the line of least resistance. And never fall into the trap of doing the easy tasks first, putting off the big ones. Do the reverse. Many successful executives say it helps to make a list of tasks to be performed at the beginning of each day. Then begin with number one, no matter how much you would prefer to work on number ten. This way the big problems—the things you have a tendency to put off—get tackled first. Things left undone by the end of the day probably didn't matter very much anyway.

At the end of each day, consider what you have done from the perspective of defining your job to a prospective employer. Step by step, go through the entire day. You may be shocked to realize you wrote six make-work letters, telephoned ten unimportant people, helped somebody with a task that didn't require two people, went to lunch with somebody who didn't need or deserve more than a few minutes of your time, drank ten cups of coffee, and refilled your paper-clip container. Some people keep themselves so busy doing trivia that they never get anything important accomplished. How hard you appear to be working is not important. What you accomplish is important. Keeping a chair warm doesn't count.

In building your career path, look carefully at your present job and figure out what is the next step up that path for you. Don't wait for your superiors to figure this out for you. It's true that you may get offered a job you never thought about, but chances are you'll be offered a promotion into a job you have been preparing for. Don't be modest about wanting to be promoted. If somebody calls you an aggressive woman, tell him or her that you are *assertive*. And there's nothing wrong with being assertive.

If you learn you need more education to qualify for a promotion, find out if the company has a training program or will pay for your advancement training before you race out to night school. Many companies will do this, but you must speak up.

In any job, never expect the boss to be a mind reader. You must speak your aspirations clearly. Thousands of women have failed to get promotions because the boss "assumed" they weren't interested in being promoted. Employers make decisions for their em-

205

ployees all the time, particularly for women. Many a boss has rejected a promotion for a woman employee on the ground that "she wouldn't want to travel," "she wouldn't like the work," "she's happy where she is," or "what would I do without her?" The only way you can successfully foil these decisions—made for you—is to make your job expectations crystal clear, both orally and *in writing*. A single memo is worth a thousand oral requests, especially now, because of Affirmative Action programs. Employers see such memos as potentially damaging evidence—which, of course, they can be.

KEEPING YOUR RÉSUMÉ UP TO DATE

No matter how content you are in your present job, it is important to keep your résumé up to date. This can help you focus on doing important tasks that advance your career, and can clarify your work experience in terms of accomplishment. It can help you define what is important and what is trivial in your day-to-day job. And it can alert you to the need to take advantage of opportunities to extend your knowledge to new areas.

Each time you take on a new responsibility or help make an important decision, keep a record for use in updating your résumé. Important records have a habit of eluding you when you need them most. So does memory. It's not easy for most people to reconstruct events of last week, much less six months or a year ago.

Keep a folder within easy reach containing your résumé and notes about your job accomplishments. Make it a habit to jot down descriptions of any new responsibilities. Make sure your notes are dated.

Keeping your résumé up to date can also result in a startling self-appraisal. At the end of six months or a year, if you haven't a single item to add to your résumé, you'd better take a look at yourself. You're doing something wrong.

THE JOB HONEYMOON

In every new job there's a period of adjustment in which a new employee is allowed to make mistakes while learning the job, finding out the rules, and fitting into the pecking order. You can use this period to good advantage or squander it foolishly.

Being given special privileges and treated gently during the learning process doesn't mean that you are invisible. Far from it. You are being scrutinized more carefully than the casual treatment you seem to be getting suggests. This fact needn't make you nervous, but it should make you aware of possible advantages and disadvantages.

One advantage is that in a large organization with layers of management, you will probably have more direct contact with your immediate superior during this first month than ever again. Naturally, this close contact can also be a disadvantage, depending upon you.

An executive has only so much time to allocate among all the squeaky wheels trying to get his or her attention. Getting in to see him or her can become a real problem for employees who must get approval before their work can begin or progress. The executive's priorities won't always include your needs, and a very accessible executive has either a very small staff or a very busy assistant.

It's generally true that the boss is more available to a new employee than to old ones. But at this point it is a good thing to remember that corporations and companies are at best benevolent dictatorships. Executives often promote people because of proximity and personal feelings about them. Being in the right place at the right time and making the most of it, can send you up the corporate ladder. If you make a good impression those first few weeks, the extra personal contact can serve you well for years to come. Use your honeymoon to learn as much as possible about the company, the business, your boss, and his/her boss.

207

Make sure you work hard. You can relax later—never during those first few weeks and months. Like all honeymoons, this one ends quickly, and you'll find yourself settled into a routine with no more access to the boss than others have.

ENJOY YOUR WORK

You will spend too much of your lifetime working to put up with a job you don't enjoy. Eight hours a day, five days a week can stretch to eternity unless you look forward to doing your work.

You owe your employer loyalty, honesty, and first-rate performance, but you owe yourself more—to enjoy your life and be fulfilled in your work. You can have the greatest job on earth but still feel miserable if you don't feel satisfaction in doing it. And you can strain so hard for the brass ring that your personal relationships crumble, making it impossible to enjoy the fruits of your labor.

Success obsessions are self-defeating, because success in the final analysis must come from within. People obsessed with succeeding to the exclusion of everything else almost never feel that they have succeeded. Many an executive has collapsed into depression upon finding that the top spot did not bring the expected fulfillment.

Your work is an important part of your life, but it is only a part. Working women, used to dividing their attention, have always understood this better than success-obsessed men. A more realistic approach for both men and women in sharing their lives—home, children, and work—is already replacing the rigid stereotypes of the past. Fathers are discovering their children, and mothers are discovering the world. Both are exciting discoveries. With a little judicious bending and good luck, your working life and your private life can fit together beautifully.

There's a phrase that has become a slogan among today's new women who are helping one another as individuals and sharing a sense of pride in the accomplishments of women as a group. It is "Pass it on," and it means that if another woman has helped you along the way, show your concern for the progress of all women by passing that help along to somebody else.

If this book has helped you clear your head, focus your thoughts, think deeper about your life, feel better about yourself, and feel excited about the new world opening up to women—pass it on.

V

JOB-FINDING AND CAREER-BUILDING DIRECTORY

This directory of employment resources is divided into seven sections:

A. Occupational organizations
B. Career-counseling services
C. Educational opportunities
D. Government publications and services
E. Women's centers
F. Newsletters and magazines
G. Books

The sources you'll find listed in these sections complement one another. To take full advantage of the directory, be sure to look through every section and note *all* the organizations, publications, and services that can supplement your work search. Also remember that large national organizations can provide information by mail or direct you to local chapters.

Again, be resourceful in your approach. For instance, if there is no listing for a facility near you in the "Career-Counseling Services" section, check through the "Women's Centers" section; women in such centers may be able to refer you to a good counseling service in your locality.

Many of the entries listed here can provide you with ready-made contacts, whatever your field or employment needs. Women who have never met you are ready and willing to help you get your job search off the ground.

HOW TO USE THE DIRECTORY

To help you locate the organizations and services most relevant to your particular job-finding needs, we've set up a letter-coding system for the first three sections. The code pinpoints the specific employment services offered by each organization in the directory. Here's the code key:

CC = Career Counseling: Offers vocational guidance, career-planning aid and/or advice on entering specific fields.

CL = Career Library: Maintains a library of books, pamphlets, newsletters, etc. related to women and work, legal rights, and specific careers.

EmR = Employment Referral: Refers women looking for work to specific job-finding or career-counseling services.

ICH = Information Clearing House: Provides general rather than specific employment information and/or referrals.

JP = Job Placement: Locates actual job openings. May specialize in particular fields.

LC = Legal Counseling: Provides legal advice on sex discrimination, Affirmative Action, and other legal issues.

TB = Talent Banks: (also called résumé banks or rosters). Résumé files or lists of women, set up by professional groups to help employers locate qualified women in their field.

VT = Vocational Training: Provides vocational training in specific job fields.

Many of the organizations are listed in more than one section of the directory with slightly different information in each, so cross-check all listings.

Note: The following listings were provided by the *Women's Almanac:* Women in Education; Women in Real Estate; National Black Feminist Organization; Boston Women's Collective; Hartford College Counseling; Merlin D. Bishop Center; Chicago Women's Liberation; Center for Women's & Family Education; Career Clinic for Mature Women; Women in Community Service.

A

Occupational Organizations

Women in every field and type of work have begun organizing into caucuses and committees. These women's groups provide a wide range of valuable services to women inside and outside their fields. They publish lists of current job openinges and news on equal employment laws. Often they provide job counseling and contacts through informal résumé and job-finding seminars. In addition, many women's groups publish newsletters, directories, and pamphlets that give an insider's view of a field, whether you're looking for a job in construction or astrophysics.

To help you locate the organizations in your field of interest, the entries here are listed *alphabetically by occupational area or profession.* If there isn't a specific women's group in your field, you can always turn to the traditional trade associations to help you in your job search. Check the *Encyclopedia of Associations* for field-by-field listings.

Whatever your job or career goal, these groups are among your richest resources. Don't hesitate to take advantage of their experience and advice.

AMERICAN SOCIETY OF
  WOMEN ACCOUNTANTS
327 S. LaSalle St.
Chicago, Ill. 60604
312   427-1989
CC   ICH
Publication:
  The Woman CPA

ADVERTISING WOMEN OF
  NEW YORK
153 E. 57th St.
New York, N.Y. 10022
CC

202 659-1000
CC ICH
Publication: *Exchange and Washington Report*

AMERICAN ADVERTISING FEDERATION WOMEN'S DIVISION
1225 Connecticut Ave., N.W.
Room 200
Washington, D.C. 20036

AMERICAN STUDIES ASSOCIATION COMMITTEE ON WOMEN
c/o Joanna S. Zangrando
National Coordinator
501 Mineola Ave.
Akron, Ohio 44320

AMERICAN ANTHROPOLOGICAL ASSOCIATION
COMMITTEE ON THE STATUS OF WOMEN IN ANTHROPOLOGY
c/o Carol Vance and Lucie W. Saunders
Dept. of Anthropology
Lehman College
Bronx, N.Y. 10467

ALLIANCE OF WOMEN IN ARCHITECTURE
18 E. 13th St.
New York, N.Y. 10003
212 989-8414
ICH
Publication: Newsletter

ASSOCIATION OF WOMEN IN ARCHITECTURE
c/o Dorothy G. Harrison
2115 Pine Crest Dr.
Altadena, Cal. 91001
ICH TB

ORGANIZATION OF WOMEN ARCHITECTS
1079 Broadway
San Francisco, Calif. 94133
415 771-7770

WOMEN ARCHITECTS, LANDSCAPE ARCHITECTS, AND PLANNERS
c/o Boston Architectural Center
320 Newbury St.
Boston, Mass. 02115

SOCIETY OF AMERICAN ARCHIVISTS
AD HOC COMMITTEE ON STATUS OF WOMEN
Mabel Deutrich, Director
Military Archives Div.
National Archives & Records Service
Washington, D.C. 20408

COLLEGE ART ASSOCIATION
COMMISSION ON THE STATUS OF WOMEN IN ART AND WOMEN'S CAUCUS
c/o Ann Harris
560 Riverside Dr., #17P
New York, N.Y. 10027

CC = Career Counseling	JP = Job Placement
CL = Career Library	LC = Legal Counseling
EmR = Employment Referral	TB = Talent Banks
ICH = Information Clearing House	VT = Vocational Training

DISTRICT OF COLUMBIA
REGISTRY OF WOMEN
ARTISTS
1023 Independence Ave., S.E.
Washington, D.C. 20003
202   543-1635
TB   ICH

NATIONAL ASSOCIATION OF
WOMEN ARTISTS
156 Fifth Ave.
New York, N.Y. 10010
Offers no career-guidance
information.

ASSOCIATION OF ASIAN
STUDIES
COMMITTEE ON THE STATUS
OF WOMEN
c/o Joyce K. Kaligren
Center for Chinese Studies
2168 Shattuck Ave.
Berkeley, Calif. 94705

AMERICAN ASTRONOMICAL
SOCIETY
WORKING GROUP ON THE
STATUS OF WOMEN IN
ASTRONOMY
c/o Anne P Cowley
Research Associate
Astronomy Dept.
University of Michigan
Ann Arbor, Mich. 48103

UNITED AUTO WORKERS
WOMEN'S DEPARTMENT
8000 E. Jefferson
Detroit, Mich. 48226

NATIONAL ASSOCIATION OF
BANK WOMEN
Ms. Sharon Pierce
111 E. Wacker Dr.
Chicago, Ill. 60601

312   644-6610
Publication: *National
Association of Bank
Women Journal*

AMERICAN SOCIETY OF
BIOLOGICAL CHEMISTS
SUBCOMMITTEE ON THE
STATUS OF WOMEN
c/o Loretta Leive
Bldg. 4, Rm. 111
National Institute of Health
Bethesda, Md. 20014

SOCIETY FOR CELL BIOLOGY
WOMEN IN CELL BIOLOGY
c/o Virginia Walbot
Dept. of Biochemistry
University of Georgia
Athens, Ga. 30601

SOCIETY FOR DEVELOP-
MENTAL BIOLOGY
WOMEN'S CAUCUS
c/o W. Sue Badman
P.O. Box 502
Kalamazoo, Mich. 49005

BIOPHYSICAL SOCIETY
PROFESSIONAL OPPORTUNI-
TIES FOR WOMEN OF THE
BIOPHYSICAL SOCIETY—
CAUCUS OF WOMEN
BIOPHYSICISTS
c/o Daphne Hare
School of Medicine, SUNY
Buffalo, N.Y. 14215

AMERICAN BUSINESS
WOMEN'S ASSOCIATION
9100 Ward Pkwy.
Kansas City, Mo. 64114
816   361-6621
Publication: *Women in
Business*

PHI CHI THETA
(Society for Business and
Economics)
718 Judah St.
San Francisco, Calif. 94122
See "Educational Opportunities—National"

BUSINESS AND PROFESSIONAL
WOMEN'S FOUNDATION
2012 Massachusetts Ave.,
N.W.
Washington, D.C. 20036
202   293-1200

NATIONAL FEDERATION OF
BUSINESS AND PROFESSIONAL WOMEN'S CLUBS
2012 Massachusetts Ave.,
N.W.
Washington, D.C. 20036
202   293-1100
Publication: *National
Business Woman*

AMERICAN WOMEN BUYERS
ASSOCIATION
450 Seventh Ave.
New York, N.Y. 10001
212   524-3665
CC   ICH

CENTRAL INTELLIGENCE
AGENCY
FEDERAL WOMEN'S PROGRAM
Rm. 2E24
Headquarters Bldg.

Washington, D.C. 20505
202   351-5504
CC

AMERICAN CHEMICAL
SOCIETY
WOMEN CHEMISTS
COMMITTEE
c/o Susan Collier
Research Laboratory
Eastman Kodak Co.
Rochester, N.Y. 14650

CHURCH EMPLOYED WOMEN
c/o Mildred G. Lehr
The Westminster Press
900 Witherspoon Bldg.
Philadelphia, Pa. 19107

UNITED PRESBYTERIAN
CHURCH IN THE U.S.A.
TASK FORCE ON WOMEN
Board of Christian Education
United Presbyterian Church
Witherspoon Bldg.
Philadelphia, Pa. 19107

ASSOCIATION OF COLLEGE
UNIONS
INTERNATIONAL COMMISSION
ON THE STATUS OF WOMEN
c/o Adele McMillan
Erb Memorial
University of Oregon
Eugene, Oreg. 97403

ASSOCIATION OF AMERICAN
COLLEGES

CC = Career Counseling	JP = Job Placement
CL = Career Library	LC = Legal Counseling
EmR = Employment Referral	TB = Talent Banks
	VT = Vocational Training
ICH = Information Clearing House	

PROJECT ON THE STATUS AND
EDUCATION OF WOMEN
1818 R. St., N.W.
Washington, D.C. 20009
202 387-1300
ICH
See "Educational Oppor-
tunities—National"

NATIONAL ASSOCIATION OF
COLLEGE WOMEN
1501 11th St., N.W.
Washington, D.C. 20001

COMMUNICATIONS WORKERS
OF AMERICA
Women's Activities Dept.
1925 K. St., N.W.
Washington, D.C. 20006

WOMEN IN COMMUNICA-
TIONS, INC.
c/o Mrs. Mary Utting
8305-A Shoal Creek Blvd.
Austin, Tex. 78758
512 452-0119
CC CL ICH—only for
members
See "Career Counseling—
National"

NATIONAL ASSOCIATION OF
WOMEN IN CONSTRUCTION
Executive Office:
2800 W. Lancaster Ave.
Fort Worth, Tex. 76107
817 332-7635

JOB PLACEMENT PLAN
1340 Kenwood Rd.
West Palm Beach, Fla. 33401
305 833-0391
See "Career Counseling—
National"

ASSOCIATION OF FEMINIST
CONSULTANTS

4 Canoe Brook Dr.
Princeton Junction, N.J.
08550
609 799-0378
See "Career Counseling—
National"

NATIONAL ASSOCIATION FOR
WOMEN DEANS, ADMINIS-
TRATORS AND COUNSELORS
Ms. Joan McCall
1028 Connecticut Ave., N.W.
Suite 922
Washington, D.C. 20036
CC JP

ASSOCIATION OF AMERICAN
WOMEN DENTISTS
938 Kenilworth Lane
Glenview, Ill. 60025
CC ICH
Publications: Newsletter,
Membership Directory

AMERICAN ECONOMIC
ASSOCIATION
COMMITTEE ON THE STATUS
OF WOMEN IN THE
ECONOMICS PROFESSION
c/o Carolyn S. Bell
Wellesley College
Wellesley, Mass. 02181
CC JP ICH TB
See "Career Counseling—
National"

ADULT EDUCATION
ASSOCIATION
COMMISSION ON THE STATUS
OF WOMEN IN ADULT
EDUCATION
c/o Margaret B. Nevin
Director, Adult Advisement
Center
Div. of Continuing Education
3 Allenhurst St.

217

Buffalo, N.Y. 14214
CC EmR ICH

ADULT EDUCATION
ASSOCIATION
CONTINUING EDUCATION FOR
WOMEN SECTION
810 18th St., N.W.
Washington, D.C. 20006
CC CL ICH
See "Educational Oppor-
tunities—National"

AMERICAN COUNCIL ON
EDUCATION
1 Dupont Circle, Suite 800
Washington, D.C. 20036

AMERICAN EDUCATIONAL
RESEARCH ASSOCIATION
COMMITTEE ON WOMEN IN
EDUCATIONAL RESEARCH
c/o Carol Kittle
City University of New York
1411 Broadway
New York, N.Y. 10018
    or
Patricia Steiger
AERA
1126 16th St., N.W.
Washington, D.C. 20036
CC EmR ICH TB

ASSOCIATION FOR CON-
TINUING HIGHER
EDUCATION
1700 Asp Ave.
Norman, Okla. 73069
405 325-1021

Publications: Newsletter,
$7.50 per year; other
relevant materials

NATIONAL ASSOCIATION OF
EDUCATIONAL
BROADCASTERS
1346 Connecticut Ave., N.W.
Washington, D.C. 20036
202 785-1100
CC ICH JP
See "Career Counseling—
National"

NATIONAL ASSOCIATION FOR
PUBLIC CONTINUING AND
ADULT EDUCATION
(NAPCAE)
1201 16th St., N.W.
Washington, D.C. 20036
202 833-5486
Publications: comprehensive

NATIONAL COUNCIL OF
ADMINISTRATIVE WOMEN
IN EDUCATION
c/o Ms. Fern Ritter
1815 E. Fort Myer Dr.
N. Arlington, Va. 22209
703 528-6111
CC JP
See "Career Counseling—
National"

NATIONAL EDUCATION
ASSOCIATION
WOMEN'S CAUCUS
1201 16th St., N.W.
Washington, D.C. 20036

CC = Career Counseling	JP = Job Placement
CL = Career Library	LC = Legal Counseling
EmR = Employment	TB = Talent Banks
Referral	VT = Vocational Training
ICH = Information	
Clearing House	

218

202   833-5412
CC   EmR   LC
See "Educational Oppor-
    tunities—National"

PHILOSOPHY OF EDUCATION
    SOCIETY
WOMEN'S CAUCUS AND
    COMMITTEE ON THE
    STATUS OF WOMEN
c/o Elizabeth S. Maccia
Dept. of History and
    Philosophy of Education
Indiana University
Bloomington, Ind. 47401

WISCONSIN COORDINATING
    COUNCIL FOR WOMEN IN
    HIGHER EDUCATION
University of Wisconsin
Stevens Pt., Wis. 55481
ICH   LC
See "Educational Oppor-
    tunities—Midwest"

WOMEN IN EDUCATION
Ms. Carol Wacker
District #7 office
Stern School
Hedge and Unity Streets
Philadelphia, Pa. 19124
215   535-0414

WOMEN EDUCATORS (WE)
c/o Mary Craik
Psychology Dept.
St. Cloud State College
St. Cloud, Minn. 56301
CC   ICH
See "Career Counseling—
    National"

INTERNATIONAL UNION OF
    ELECTRICAL, RADIO AND
    MACHINE WORKERS
AFL-CIO-CLC

Education and Women's
    Activities
1126 16th St., N.W.
Washington, D.C. 20036

SOCIETY OF WOMEN
    ENGINEERS
c/o Winfred D. White
345 E. 47th St., Rm. 305
New York, N.Y. 10017
212   752-6800
CC   EmR   ICH   JP   TB
See "Career Counseling—
    East"

NATIONAL ASSOCIATION FOR
    FEMALE EXECUTIVES
10 E. 40th St.
New York, N.Y. 10016
212   889-2260

NATIONAL COUNCIL ON
    FAMILY RELATIONS
TASK FORCE ON WOMEN'S
    RIGHTS AND
    RESPONSIBILITIES
c/o Rose Somerville
Sociology Dept.
California State College
San Diego, Calif. 92115

AMERICAN FARM BUREAU
    FEDERATION
WOMEN'S COMMITTEE
225 Touhy Ave.
Park Ridge, Ill. 60068
Publication: *Farm Bureau
    News*

SOCIETY OF WOMEN
    GEOGRAPHERS
1619 New Hampshire Ave.
Washington, D.C. 20009
CC   ICH
Publication: *Bulletin*

ASSOCIATION OF AMERICAN GEOGRAPHERS
COMMITTEE ON WOMEN IN GEOGRAPHY
c/o Ann Larrimore
Dept. of Geography
University of Michigan
Ann Arbor, Mich. 48104

AMERICAN GEOLOGICAL INSTITUTE
COMMITTEE ON WOMEN IN GEOSCIENCE
c/o Theresa F. Schwarzer
ESSO Production Research Co.
P.O. Box 2189
Houston, Tex. 77001

AMERICAN ASSOCIATION FOR HEALTH & PHYSICAL EDUCATION

COMMITTEE ON WOMEN
c/o Ione G. Shadduck
Drake University
Des Moines, Iowa 50311

AMERICAN PUBLIC HEALTH ASSOCIATION
WOMEN'S CAUCUS
c/o Mary Plaska
A.P.H.A. Women's Caucus
1015 16th St., N.W.
Washington, D.C. 20036

AMERICAN HISTORICAL ASSOCIATION
COMMITTEE ON WOMEN HISTORIANS

400 A St., S.E.
Washington, D.C. 20004
CC TB
See "Career Counseling—National"

AMERICAN HISTORICAL ASSOCIATION
COORDINATING COMMITTEE ON WOMEN IN THE HISTORICAL PROFESSION
c/o Sandi Cooper
Richmond College, C.U.N.Y.
Staten Island, N.Y. 10301

NATIONAL COMMITTEE ON HOUSEHOLD EMPLOYMENT
1625 I St., N.W.
Washington, D.C. 20006

AMERICAN ASSOCIATION OF IMMUNOLOGISTS
COMMITTEE ON THE STATUS OF WOMEN
c/o Helene C. Rauch
Dept. of Medical Microbiology
Stanford University
School of Medicine
Stanford, Calif. 94305

NATIONAL ASSOCIATION OF INSURANCE WOMEN
(International)
1847 E. 15th St.
Tulsa, Okla. 74104
918 932-5195
CC ICH VT
Publication: *Today's Insurance Woman*

CC = Career Counseling
CL = Career Library
EmR = Employment Referral
ICH = Information Clearing House
JP = Job Placement
LC = Legal Counseling
TB = Talent Banks
VT = Vocational Training

INSURANCE EMPLOYEES FOR
EQUAL RIGHTS
593 Market St., Rm. 223
San Francisco, Calif. 94105
415 495-0923
LC ICH
See "Knowing Your Job
Rights"

NATIONAL ASSOCIATION OF
LIFE UNDERWRITERS
WOMEN LEADERS ROUND
TABLE
1922 F St., N.W.
Washington, D.C. 20006
202 638-3122
CC ICH VT
Publications: *Life Association
News,* Membership
Directory

INTERSTATE ASSOCIATION OF
COMMISSIONS ON THE
STATUS OF WOMEN
Suite 1249, National Press
Bldg.
Washington, D.C. 20006
202 347-8726
CC

JOURNALISTS FOR
PROFESSIONAL EQUALITY
c/o Eileen Shanahan
New York Times
1920 L. St., N.W.
Washington, D.C. 20036
202 293-3100
Membership open to
journalists.

THETA SIGMA PHI
(National Society for Jour-
nalism/Communications)
c/o Fran Harris
WWJ Stations
Detroit, Mich. 48231

MODERN LANGUAGE
ASSOCIATION
COMMISSION ON THE STATUS
OF WOMEN
c/o Cynthia Secor
Dept. of English
University of Pennsylvania
Philadelphia, Pa. 19104
or
Joan Hartmen
Staten Island Community
College
CUNY Staten Island
Staten Island, N.Y. 10301

MODERN LANGUAGE
ASSOCIATION
WOMEN'S CAUCUS
c/o Helen Batchelor
University of Wisconsin at
Milwaukee
Milwaukee, Wis. 53201

LATIN AMERICAN STUDIES
ASSOCIATION
WOMEN'S COALITION OF
LATIN AMERICANISTS
c/o Elsa M. Chaney
Dept. of Political Science
Fordham University
Bronx, N.Y. 10458
or
Asuncion Lavrin
8501 Manchester Rd.
Silver Springs, Md. 20901

LATIN AMERICAN STUDIES
ASSOCIATION
WOMEN'S COMMITTEE
c/o Nancie L. Gonzalez
Dept. of Anthropology
Boston University
Boston, Mass. 02215

AMERICAN ASSOCIATION OF
LAW SCHOOLS

WOMEN IN THE LEGAL
PROFESSION
c/o Fredricka Lombard
School of Law
Wayne State University
Detroit, Mich. 48202

ASSOCIATION OF AMERICAN
LAW SCHOOLS
COMMITTEE ON WOMEN IN
THE LEGAL PROFESSION
c/o Mary M. Wenig
St. Johns University
School of Law
Jamaica, N.Y. 11439
or
Shirley R. Bysiewicz
University of Connecticut
School of Law
1800 Asylum Ave.
West Hartford, Conn. 06117

INTERNATIONAL FEDERATION
OF WOMEN LAWYERS
150 Nassau St.
New York, N.Y. 10038
212 227-8339
LC

LAW WOMEN'S CAUCUS
Condon Hall
University of Washington
Seattle, Wash. 98105
206 525-6106
LC

NATIONAL ASSOCIATION OF
WOMEN LAWYERS

1155 E. 16th St.
Chicago, Ill. 60637
Publication: *Women Lawyers
Journal*

AMERICAN LIBRARY
ASSOCIATION
SOCIAL RESPONSIBILITIES
ROUND TABLE—TASK
FORCE ON THE STATUS
OF WOMEN
c/o Lynne Rhodes,
Chairperson
4004 Whitman North
Seattle, Wash. 98103
CC ICH EmR TB
See "Career Counseling—
National"

LINGUISTIC SOCIETY OF
AMERICA
WOMEN'S CAUCUS
c/o Lynette Hirschman or
Georgette Loup
162 W. Hansberry
Philadelphia, Pa. 19144

ACADEMY OF MANAGEMENT
COMMITTEE ON THE STATUS
OF WOMEN IN THE
MANAGEMENT PROFESSION
c/o Kathryn M. Bartol
Dept. of Management
School of Business
Administration
University of Massachusetts
Amhurst, Mass. 01002

CC = Career Counseling	JP = Job Placement
CL = Career Library	LC = Legal Counseling
EmR = Employment Referral	TB = Talent Banks
ICH = Information Clearing House	VT = Vocational Training

AMERICAN MATHEMATICAL
SOCIETY
321 S. Main St.
P.O. Box 6248
Providence, R.I. 02904
401 272-9500
EmR

ASSOCIATION FOR WOMEN IN
MATHEMATICS (Indepen-
dent Group)
c/o Mary Gray
Dept. of Mathematics
American University
Washington, D.C. 20016

AMERICAN MEDICAL
WOMEN'S ASSOCIATION,
INC.
1740 Broadway
New York, N.Y. 10019
TB
Membership open to women
M.D.s in good professional
standing.
Publication: *Journal of
American Medical Women's
Association*

CENTER FOR WOMEN IN
MEDICINE
Medical College of
Pennsylvania
3300 Henry Ave.
Philadelphia, Pa. 19129
CC JP

AMERICAN SOCIETY FOR
MICROBIOLOGY
COMMITTEE ON THE STATUS
OF WOMEN MICRO-
BIOLOGISTS
c/o Mary L. Robbins
School of Medicine and

Health Sciences
George Washington
University
2300 I St., N.W.
Washington, D.C. 20037

INTERNATIONAL ASSOCIATION
OF WOMEN MINISTERS
1464 W. 101st St.
Cleveland, Ohio 44102
416 623-5713
Publication: *Women's Pulpit*

WOMEN OF THE MOTION
PICTURE INDUSTRY,
INTERNATIONAL
c/o HOWCO, International
P.O. Box 1805
Charlotte, N.C. 28201
CC ICH
Publication: Newsletter

COLLEGE MUSIC SOCIETY
WOMEN'S CAUCUS
c/o Carolyn Raney
Peabody Conservatory of
Music
Baltimore, Md. 21202
or
Adrienne F. Block
Dept. of Performing &
Creative Arts
Staten Island Community
College
Staten Island, N.Y. 10301

NATIONAL ORGANIZATION
FOR WOMEN (NOW)
5 S. Wabash
Chicago, Ill. 60603
312 332-1954
Membership open to women
and men.
Dues: $10–$1,000.
Local chapters.

Publications: Newsletter, *Do It Now*; pamphlets on various women's issues

NATIONAL ASSOCIATION OF NEGRO BUSINESS AND PROFESSIONAL WOMEN'S CLUBS
2861 Urban Ave.
Columbus, Ga. 31907

AMERICAN NEWSPAPER WOMEN'S CLUB
607 22nd St., N.W.
Washington, D.C. 20008
202   332-6770
CC   ICH
Publications: *Shop Talk*, Membership Directory

NATIONAL FEDERATION OF PRESS WOMEN
5529 C. Roxbury Terrace
Indianapolis, Ind. 46226
CC   ICH
Publications: *The Press Woman,* Membership Directory

AMERICAN ASSOCIATION OF INDUSTRIAL NURSES
79 Madison Ave.
New York, N.Y. 10016

AMERICAN NURSES' ASSOCIATION, INC.
2420 Pershing Rd.

Kansas City, Mo. 64108
816   474-5720
Membership open to R.N.s in all areas of practice

MIDWEST CONTINUING PROFESSIONAL EDUCATION FOR NURSES
1401 S. Grand Blvd.
St. Louis, Mo. 63104

NATIONAL LEAGUE FOR NURSING
10 Columbus Circle
New York, N.Y. 10019

NATIONAL LEAGUE OF AMERICAN PEN WOMEN
1300 17th St., N.W.
Washington, D.C. 20036
Members: Writers, composers, artists.
Publication: *The Pen Woman*

AMERICAN COLLEGE PERSONNEL ASSOCIATION WOMEN'S TASK FORCE
c/o Mary Howard
Federal City College
425 2nd St., N.W.
Washington, D.C. 20001

AMERICAN PERSONNEL AND GUIDANCE ASSOCIATION
1607 New Hampshire Ave., N.W.
Washington, D.C. 20009

CC = Career Counseling	JP = Job Placement
CL = Career Library	LC = Legal Counseling
EmR = Employment Referral	TB = Talent Banks
ICH = Information Clearing House	VT = Vocational Training

202 483-4633
CC
See "Career Counseling—
National"

AMERICAN PERSONNEL AND
GUIDANCE ASSOCIATION
WOMEN'S CAUCUS
c/o Helen Roehlke
Counseling Center
University of Missouri
Columbia, Mo. 65201

COLLEGE AND UNIVERSITY
PERSONNEL ASSOCIATION
1 Dupont Circle, Suite 650
Washington, D.C. 20036
202 833-9080
CC EmR ICH
See "Career Counseling"

INTERNATIONAL ASSOCIATION
OF PERSONNEL WOMEN
Ropes & Gray
225 Franklin St.
Boston, Mass. 02110
617 423-6100
CC EmR ICH
See "Career Counseling"

NATIONAL ASSOCIATION OF
STUDENT PERSONNEL
ADMINISTRATORS
TASK FORCE ON WOMEN
c/o E. Susan Petering
Asst. Dean of Students
Framingham State College
Framingham, Mass. 01701

AMERICAN PHILOLOGICAL
ASSOCIATION
WOMEN'S CAUCUS
c/o Sarah B. Pomeroy
Hunter College
Box 1264, 695 Park Ave.
New York, N.Y. 10021

AMERICAN PHILOLOGICAL
ASSOCIATION
COMMITTEE ON THE STATUS
OF WOMEN
c/o Mary R. Lefkowitz
Dept. of Greek and Latin
Wellesley College
Wellesley, Mass. 02181

AMERICAN PHILOSOPHICAL
ASSOCIATION
WOMEN'S CAUCUS
c/o Mary Motherskill,
Chairperson
Dept. of Philosophy
Barnard College
New York, N.Y. 10027
CC EmR ICH JP
See "Career Counseling"

SOCIETY FOR WOMEN IN
PHILOSOPHY
c/o Connie C. Price
Dept. of Philosophy
Tuskegee Institute
Tuskegee, Ala. 36088

AMERICAN PHYSICAL SOCIETY
COMMITTEE ON WOMEN IN
PHYSICS
c/o Mildred Widgoff
Physics Department
P.O. Box 1843
Brown University
Providence, R.I. 02912

AMERICAN PHYSIOLOGICAL
ASSOCIATION
TASK FORCE ON WOMEN
c/o Elizabeth Tidball
Dept. of Physiology
George Washington
University
Medical Center
2300 I St., N.W.
Washington, D.C. 20037

AMERICAN INSTITUTE OF
PLANNERS
WOMEN'S RIGHTS
COMMITTEE
c/o Diana C. Donald
1776 Massachusetts Ave.,
N.W.
Washington, D.C. 20036

AMERICAN WOMEN PLAY-
WRIGHTS ASSOCIATION
Box A
Old Chelsea Station
New York, N.Y. 10011
212   477-5744

POLICEWOMAN'S INFORMA-
TION CENTER
11 First Field Rd.
Gaithersburg, Md. 20760
301   948-0922, ext. 295
CL   ICH

INTERNATIONAL ASSOCIATION
OF WOMEN POLICE
6655 North Avondale Ave.
Chicago, Ill. 60631
CC   ICH
Publications: Newsletter,
    Membership Directory

AMERICAN POLITICAL
SCIENCE ASSOCIATION
COMMITTEE ON THE STATUS
OF WOMEN IN THE
PROFESSION
c/o Carole Parsons

2400 Virginia Ave., N.W.
#1102
Washington, D.C. 20037

NATIONAL BLACK WOMEN'S
POLITICAL LEADERSHIP
CAUCUS
111 Cadillac Sq. No. 10A
Detroit, Mich. 48226
517   965-2169

AMERICAN POLITICAL
SCIENCE ASSOCIATION
WOMEN'S CAUCUS FOR
POLITICAL SCIENCE
Mount Vernon College
2100 Foxhall Rd., N.W.
Washington, D.C. 20007

FEDERATION OF
ORGANIZATIONS FOR
PROFESSIONAL WOMEN
1346 Connecticut Ave., N.W.
Rm. 1122
Washington, D.C. 20034
202   833-1998
CC   EmR   ICH   TB
See "Career Counseling"

ORGANIZATION OF WOMEN
PROFESSIONALS
c/o Avriel Goldberger
Hofstra University
Hempstead, N.Y. 11550

POPULATION ASSOCIATION OF
AMERICA
WOMEN'S CAUCUS

CC = Career Counseling	JP = Job Placement
CL = Career Library	LC = Legal Counseling
EmR = Employment Referral	TB = Talent Banks
ICH = Information Clearing House	VT = Vocational Training

c/o Nancy E. Williamson
Brown University
Providence, R.I. 02912

PROFESSIONAL WOMEN'S
  CAUCUS
P.O. Box 1057,
Radio City Sta.
New York, N.Y. 10019
       or
Sue Kaplan, President
Professional Women's Caucus
743 Fifth Ave.
New York, N.Y. 10022

PROFESSIONS TASK FORCE
c/o Yale Sells
95 Circle Dr.
Hastings-on-Hudson,
  N.Y. 10706
ICH

AMERICAN PSYCHIATRIC
  ASSOCIATION
TASK FORCE ON WOMEN
c/o Nancy Roeske, M.D.
1700 18th St., N.W.
Washington, D.C. 20009

AMERICAN PSYCHOLOGICAL
  ASSOCIATION
AD HOC COMMITTEE ON
  WOMEN IN PSYCHOLOGY
1200 17th St., N.W.
Washington, D.C. 20036

AMERICAN PSYCHOLOGICAL
  ASSOCIATION
AD HOC COMMITTEE ON
  WOMEN IN THE
  PROFESSION
c/o Brenda Gurel
1200 17th St., N.W.
Washington, D.C. 20036
or Martha Mednick

Dept. of Psychology
Howard University
Washington, D.C. 20001
ICH   TB
Publication: *Roster of Feminist Therapists* is available from KNOW, Inc., P.O. Box 86031, Pittsburgh, Pa. 15221

AMERICAN SOCIETY FOR
  PUBLIC ADMINISTRATION
STANDING COMMITTEE ON
  WOMEN IN PUBLIC
  ADMINISTRATION
c/o June Martin, Chairperson
State Leg. Bldg., Rm. 830
Albany, N.Y. 12224
CC   EmR   TB
See "Career Counseling"

PUBLIC RELATIONS SOCIETY
  OF AMERICA
COMMITTEE ON WOMEN IN
  PUBLIC RELATIONS
c/o Joan Gaines
Director of Public Relations
Music Educators National
  Conference
1201 16th St., N.W.
Washington, D.C. 20036

CHICAGO WOMEN IN
  PUBLISHING
P.O. Box 392
Morton Grove, Ill. 60053
CC

WOMEN'S NATIONAL BOOK
  ASSOCIATION
Bro Dart Industries
124 Church St.
New Brunswick, N.J. 08901
212   689-8920
Publications: *The Book*

Woman, Membership Directory

AMERICAN WOMEN IN RADIO AND TELEVISION
1321 Connecticut Ave., N.W.
Washington, D.C. 20036
202 296-0009
Publication: *Careers for Women in Broadcasting*

MEDIA WOMEN
c/o Susan Protter
320 Central Park West
New York, N.Y. 10025
Publication: *Women's Guide to the Media*

NATIONAL ASSOCIATION OF RAILROAD WOMEN
c/o Ann Armistad
Norfolk & Western Railway Co.
8 N. Jefferson St.
Roanoke, Va. 24011
CC ICH
Publication: Bulletin

WOMEN IN REAL ESTATE
5702 N. Western
Chicago, Ill.
312 561-9883

NATIONAL ASSOCIATION OF REALTORS
WOMEN'S COMMITTEE
155 E. Superior St.
Chicago, Ill. 60611
Publication: *Real Estate Today*

AMERICAN ACADEMY OF RELIGION
TASK FORCE ON THE STATUS OF WOMEN—THE ACADEMIC STUDY OF RELIGION
c/o Mary K. Wakeman
Dept. of Religious Studies
University of North Carolina
Greensboro, N.C. 27412
or
Margaret M. Early
Dept. of Religious Studies
Alverno College
Milwaukee, Wis. 53215

WOMEN'S CAUCUS
RELIGIOUS STUDIES
GRADUATE THEOLOGICAL UNION
2465 Le Conte Ave.
Berkeley, Calif. 94650
EmR ICH—for theologists

WOMEN'S THEOLOGICAL COALITION
WOMEN'S DOCTORAL PLACEMENT SERVICE
Boston Theological Institute
210 Herrick Rd.
Newton Center, Mass. 02159
617 696-2946
EmR ICH JP TB

CC = Career Counseling
CL = Career Library
EmR = Employment Referral
ICH = Information Clearing House
JP = Job Placement
LC = Legal Counseling
TB = Talent Banks
VT = Vocational Training

228

AMERICAN ASSOCIATION FOR
  THE ADVANCEMENT OF
  SCIENCE
WOMEN'S CAUCUS OF
  THE AAAS
c/o Virginia Walbot
Dept. of Biochemistry
University of Georgia
Athens, Ga. 30601

ASSOCIATION OF WOMEN
  IN SCIENCE
1346 Connecticut Ave., N.W.
Washington, D.C. 20036
202   833-1998

GRADUATE WOMEN IN
  SCIENCE
(Sigma Delta Epsilon)
c/o Hope Hopps
1762 Overlook Dr.
Silver Springs, Md. 20903

NATIONAL SECRETARIES
  ASSOCIATION
  (International)
2440 Pershing Rd.,
  Suite G-10
Kansas City, Mo. 64108
CL
Membership open to secre-
taries and teachers of business education. Dues: $10
per year.
Publications: Magazine and
an on-the-job human-rela-
tions book. Slide presentations also available.

NATIONAL COUNCIL FOR
  THE SOCIAL STUDIES
COMMITTEE ON SOCIAL
  INJUSTICE FOR WOMEN
c/o Dell Felder

University of Houston
Houston, Tex. 77004

NATIONAL ASSOCIATION OF
  SOCIAL WORKERS
2 Park Ave.
New York, N.Y. 10016
212   686-7128
CC
See "Career Counseling"

AMERICAN SOCIOLOGICAL
  ASSOCIATION
AD HOC COMMITTEE ON THE
  STATUS OF WOMEN IN
  SOCIOLOGY
c/o Cora B. Marrett
Dept. of Sociology
Western Michigan University
Kalamazoo, Mich. 49001

SOCIOLOGISTS FOR WOMEN
  IN SOCIETY
c/o Joan Huber
Dept. of Sociology
University of Illinois at
  Urbana-Champagne
Urbana, Ill. 61801
217   352-5144
CC   ICH   JP
See "Career Counseling"

SPEECH COMMUNICATION
  ASSOCIATION
COMMISSION FOR WOMEN
c/o Bonnie R. Patton
County Office Bldg.
Rockville, Md. 20850

AMERICAN SPEECH AND
  HEARING ASSOCIATION
SUBCOMMITTEE ON THE
  STATUS OF WOMEN
c/o Dorothy K. Marge
8011 Longbrook Rd.
Springfield, Va. 22152

AMERICAN STATISTICAL
  ASSOCIATION
CAUCUS FOR WOMEN IN
  STATISTICS
c/o Marie Wann
Statistical Policy Division
OMB, Washington, D.C.
  20503

AMERICAN STATISTICAL
  ASSOCIATION
COMMITTEE OF WOMEN IN
  STATISTICS
c/o Jean D. Gibbons
College of Commerce and
  Business Administration
University of Alabama
University, Ala. 35486

STEWARDESSES FOR
  WOMEN'S RIGHTS
1 Rockefeller Plaza,
  Rm. 1076
New York, N.Y. 10020
212   586-7804

STOCKHOLDERS' ACTION
  PROGRAM
P.O. Box 1267
San Francisco, Calif. 94101
CC
See "Career Counseling"

AMERICAN FEDERATION
  OF TEACHERS
WOMEN'S RIGHTS
  COMMITTEE

1012 14th St., N.W.
Washington, D.C. 20004

NATIONAL COUNCIL OF
  TEACHERS OF ENGLISH
WOMEN'S COMMITTEE
c/o Johanna S. Stefano
20 Ramseyer Hall
Ohio State University
Columbus, Ohio 43210

TOIL (TEACHING OPPOR-
  TUNITIES INFORMATION
  LISTING)
CSR Executive Office
Wilfred Laurier University
Waterloo, Ont.
Canada N2L3C5
CC EmR ICH JP
See "Career Counseling"

AMERICAN SOCIETY FOR
  TRAINING AND
  DEVELOPMENT
WOMEN'S CAUCUS
c/o Katherine Kirkham
1718 P St., N.W.
#404
Washington, D.C. 20036
See "Educational Oppor-
  tunities—National"
CL ICH JP TB

UNION W.A.G.E. (UNION
  WOMEN'S ALLIANCE TO
  GAIN EQUALITY)
P.O. Box 462

CC = Career Counseling	JP = Job Placement
CL = Career Library	LC = Legal Counseling
EmR = Employment Referral	TB = Talent Banks
	VT = Vocational Training
ICH = Information Clearing House	

Berkeley, Calif. 94701
415   444-8757
Publication: Newspaper

AMERICAN ASSOCIATION OF
UNIVERSITY PROFESSORS
COMMITTEE ON THE STATUS
OF WOMEN IN THE
PROFESSION
1 Dupont Circle
Washington, D.C. 20036
202   466-8050
EmR   ICH   LC

AMERICAN ASSOCIATION OF
UNIVERSITY WOMEN
2401 Virginia Ave., N.W.
Washington, D.C. 20037
202   785-7700
EmR   ICH

NATIONAL UNIVERSITY
EXTENSION ASSOCIATION

DIVISION OF WOMEN'S
EDUCATION
c/o Betty Siegel
Dean of Continuing
Education
University of Florida
Gainesville, Fla. 32611

NATIONAL VOCATIONAL
GUIDANCE ASSOCIATION
COMMISSION ON THE
OCCUPATIONAL STATUS
OF WOMEN
c/o Thelma C. Lennon
Director, Pupil Personnel
Services
Dept. of Public Instruction
Raleigh, N.C. 27602

AMERICAN VOCATIONAL
ASSOCIATION
1510 H St., N.W.
Washington, D.C. 20005
202   737-3722

231

B

Career-Counseling Services

The career-counseling resources listed here vary in the range of services they provide, in fees they charge, and in the counseling techniques they use. Some of these groups and services offer intensive vocational testing and individualized career-planning programs. Others run career workshops designed to help small groups of women assess their skills, prepare résumés, and carry on their own job search.

Fees for individual counseling programs or workshops may range from twenty-five dollars to several hundred dollars. There are no hard-and-fast rules for selecting the best services, but beware of services purportedly geared to women's needs that charge exorbitant fees and promise to enable you to find a $20,000-a-year job in three weeks.

Many colleges operate career-counseling services. College services are listed here only when they are available to nongraduates as well as graduates. If your college is not listed, you should write directly to its placement office for information.

While your own needs, finances, and time should be your guides in choosing a career-counseling service, here are a few points to keep in mind:

- Determine your own employment requirements as specifically as you can *before* you consult a service. If you need professional help in choosing a field, then look into services emphasizing vocational testing and guidance. If you need specific information on the marketplace or help in polishing up a rusty résumé or writing one from scratch, a workshop program may be better suited to your needs.

● Shop around. Use the services listed here as a starting point, but also contact women's centers and professional women's groups for additional names. And don't forget the word-of-mouth approach: ask friends, relatives, or even vocational counselors at a nearby college for recommendations.

● Once you have the names of a few services, ask if they have brochures or flyers describing their programs. Some counselors give free or low-cost demonstration sessions in which they outline their goals, methods, and fees. Compare fees and techniques.

● Check the background of the counselors or services you're considering working with. Ask about previous clients, business background, knowledge of a specific field, and experience in the employment field.

NATIONAL

ADULT EDUCATION
  ASSOCIATION
COMMISSION ON THE STATUS
  OF WOMEN AEA/USA
810 18th St., N.W.
Washington, D.C. 20036
CC EmR ICH

Membership limited to dues-paying members of the AEA. Job openings listed in the AEA Newsletter. Announcements of jobs in higher education sent to interested persons.

ADULT EDUCATION
  ASSOCIATION
CONTINUING EDUCATION FOR
  WOMEN SECTION
810 18th St., N.W.
Washington, D.C. 20006
CL ICH

ALUMNAE ADVISORY
  CENTER, INC.
541 Madison Ave.
New York, N.Y. 10022
212 758-2153
CC CL EmR ICH
Membership: 47 Colleges and individual women graduates.
Fee: $15 for member-college alumnae; $35 for others.
Publications: Job fact sheets, booklets, cassette tapes, guides, bibliographies.
Write for publications list.

AMERICAN ASSOCIATION OF
  UNIVERSITY PROFESSORS
COMMITTEE ON THE STATUS
  OF WOMEN IN THE
  PROFESSION
1 Dupont Circle
Washington, D.C. 20036
202 466-8050
EmR ICH LC JP

233

AMERICAN ASSOCIATION OF
UNIVERSITY WOMEN
2401 Virginia Ave., N.W.
Washington, D.C. 20037
202   785-7700
EmR   ICH
Membership is open to any
woman who has a bacca-
laureate degree from an accredited four-year college or
university.
Local chapters in all states.
Concerned with equal opportunities for women in education and work. Sponsors
fellowship program for graduate study or post-doctoral
research.
Dues: $6.50 per year.
Publications: *AAUW Jour-
nal,* newspapers, reports on
higher-education issues.

AMERICAN ECONOMIC
ASSOCIATION
COMMITTEE ON THE STATUS
OF WOMEN IN THE
PROFESSION
c/o Carolyn S. Bell
Wellesley College
Wellesley, Mass. 02181
CC   ICH   JP   TB
Membership open only to
economists.
Publications: American Eco-
nomic Association Newsletter,
Committee Newsletter; free

for members and nonmem-
bers. The newsletter contains
a listing of job openings.

AMERICAN EDUCATIONAL
RESEARCH ASSOCIATION
WOMEN'S CAUCUS
c/o Noele Krenkel,
Chairperson
San Francisco Unified School
District
135 Van Ness
San Francisco, Calif. 94102
EmR   ICH   TB

AMERICAN HISTORICAL
ASSOCIATION
COMMITTEE ON WOMEN
400 A St., S.E.
Washington, D.C. 20003
202   544-2422
TB—AHA Women's Roster
Membership open to any
woman interested in history.
Does not do job placement,
but circulates résumés of
women meeting requirements
for available positions, mainly
in college and university
teaching and administration.
"Women's Roster" contains
brief vitae of about 2,000
women historians.
Publication: *Employment Information Bulletin*, $7 per
year, available to nonmem-
bers, lists academic openings
for historians.

CC = Career Counseling
CL = Career Library
EmR = Employment
        Referral
ICH = Information
        Clearing House

JP = Job Placement
LC = Legal Counseling
TB = Talent Banks
VT = Vocational Training

234

AMERICAN LIBRARY
  ASSOCIATION
SOCIAL RESPONSIBILITIES
  ROUND TABLE—TASK
  FORCE ON THE STATUS
  OF WOMEN
c/o Lynne Rhodes,
  Chairperson
4004 Whitman North
Seattle, Wash. 98103
EmR ICH JP TB
Membership open to women
with a degree in library re-
search.
Works on Affirmative Action
and discrimination.
Publication: Newsletter

AMERICAN MATHEMATICAL
  SOCIETY
321 S. Main St.
P.O. Box 6248
Providence, R.I. 02904
401   272-9500
EmR TB
International professional organization devoted to scholarship and research in mathematics.
Publications: *Directory of
Women Mathematicians* —
listing women Ph.D candi-
dates who expect to receive
degrees in year of publication,
$6, $4.50 for members; *Employment Information for
Mathematicians*, six or more
times yearly, $20 for indi-
viduals.

AMERICAN PERSONNEL
  GUIDANCE ASSOCIATION
1607 New Hampshire, Ave.,
  N.W.
Washington, D.C. 20009

202   483-4633
CL ICH JP
Membership open to anyone
with responsibilities in personnel, counseling, and guidance; annual fee is $23,
$12.50 for students.
Placement services for members only.

AMERICAN PHILOSOPHICAL
  ASSOCIATION
WOMEN'S CAUCUS
c/o Mary Motherskill,
  Chairperson
Dept. of Philosophy
Barnard College
New York, N.Y. 10027
CC EmR ICH JP

AMERICAN SOCIETY FOR
  PUBLIC ADMINISTRATION
STANDING COMMITTEE OF
  WOMEN IN PUBLIC
  ADMINISTRATION
c/o June Martin, Chairperson
State Leg. Bldg., Rm. 830
Albany, N.Y. 12224
CC EmR TB

AMERICAN WOMEN IN
  RADIO & T.V.
1321 Connecticut Ave., N.W.
Washington, D.C. 20036
CC ICH
Members: women executives
and administrators in radio
and T.V., advertising, service
organizations, or government.
Sponsors seminars on careers
in broadcasting, women's
rights and the media
Education Foundation awards
scholarships.

ASSOCIATION OF FEMINIST
  CONSULTANTS
4 Canoe Brook Dr.
Princeton, N.J. 07550
609   799-0378
CC   ICH   LC
Network of feminist professionals providing management
consulting for business, government, institutions, and
community groups. Services
include: Affirmative Action
programs, m a n a g e m e n t
awareness seminars, career
workshops, and individual
counseling.
Fee: Varies with service.
Publication: Membership Directory, $2.50

BRANCH OF LABOR FORCE
  RESEARCH
DEPARTMENT OF LABOR
WOMEN'S BUREAU
Rm. 1322
Washington, D.C. 20210
202   961-2154
Offers information on oc-
cupational opportunities for
women.

CATALYST
14 E. 60th St.
New York, N.Y. 10022
CC   CL   EmR   TB
Nationwide resource pro-
gram. Aids college-educated
women with career planning
and job placement. Guidance
for continuing education, referrals for counseling and
data banks of résumés.
Publications: *Preparing for
Work* ($1.25), *Your Job
Campaign* ($1.25), Career
Opportunities Series. Write
for publications list.

CENTER FOR WOMEN IN
  MEDICINE
Medical College of
  Pennsylvania
330 Henry Ave.
Philadelphia, Pa. 19129
CC   JP

CENTRAL INTELLIGENCE
  AGENCY
FEDERAL WOMEN'S PROGRAM
Rm. 2E24
Headquarters Bldg.
Washington, D.C. 20505
202   351-5504

COLLEGE AND UNIVERSITY
  PERSONNEL ASSOCIATION
1 Dupont Circle, Suite 650
Washington, D.C. 20036
202   833-9080
EmR   ICH
Sponsors national referral and
placement service for higher-
education personnel and administrators.
Provides information, advice,
and t e c h n i c a l assistance

CC = Career Counseling
CL = Career Library
EmR = Employment
         Referral
ICH = Information
         Clearing House

JP = Job Placement
LC = Legal Counseling
TB = Talent Banks
VT = Vocational Training

236

through seminars, workshops, and conferences, and distributes publications.

Yearly institutional and individual membership dues.

COOPERATIVE COLLEGE
  REGISTRY
1 Dupont Circle, N.W.
Suite 10
Washington, D.C. 20036
202 223-2807
ICH JP
Membership open to accredited institutions on higher education and candidates invited to register for referral to positions in academic disciplines and administration.
Fee: $15 per year for candidates

DISTAFFERS RESEARCH AND
  COUNSELING CENTER
4625a 41st St., N.W.
Washington, D.C. 20016
202 362-9494
CC CL EmR ICH
Operates on-going career counseling workshops; publishes employment booklets.

FEDERALLY EMPLOYED
  WOMEN
621 National Press Bldg.
Washington, D.C. 20004
202 638-4404
EmR ICH LC
Organized to expand job opportunities for women in government; provides legal counseling in sex-discrimination cases; publicizes employment openings in newsletter.
Dues: $10 per year for gov-

ernment and nongovernment members.
Publications: *F.E.W. News and Views* (newsletter)

FEDERATION OF ORGANIZA-
  TIONS FOR PROFESSIONAL
  WOMEN
1346 Connecticut Ave., N.W.
Rm. 1122
Washington, D.C. 20034
202 833-1998
EmR ICH TB
Coalition of more than 40 women's organizations; promotes the advancement of c a r e e r opportunities for women in business and professions through seminars and publications.
Publication: *S u r v e y a n d Evaluation of Job Registries for Women in the Professions,* $5 for nonmembers, $2.50 for members. Also: "Federation Alert" (newsletter).

HIGHER EDUCATION ADMINIS-
  TRATION REFERRAL
  SERVICE (HEARS)
1 Dupont Circle, Suite 510
Washington, D.C. 20036
202 296-2347
EmR JP TB
National nonprofit referral service for professional administrative job opportunities in higher education. Open to anyone with an interest in nonfaculty positions in higher education. Fee for individual first-time registration: $25. Fees for institutions: $25–$100.

INFORMATION AND REFERRAL CENTER
WOMEN'S INFORMATION
U.S. Dept. of Labor
Wage-Hour Area Office
1022 Federal Office Bldg.
31 Hopkins Plaza
Baltimore, Md. 21201
301 962-2265
Provides both assistance for working women and current information on the employment rights of women.

INTERNATIONAL ASSOCIATION OF PERSONNEL WOMEN
Ropes & Gray
225 Franklin St.
Boston, Mass. 02110
617 423-6100
EmR ICH
Publication: *Careers in Personnel*

INTERSTATE ASSOCIATION OF COMMISSIONS ON THE STATUS OF WOMEN
Suite 1249
National Press Bldg.
Washington, D.C. 20004
202 347-8726
National coordinating agency for local commissions on the status of women. Write the Women's Bureau, U.S. Dept. of Labor, for local chapters that p r o v i d e employment services.

KNOW, INC.
P.O. Box 86031
Pittsburgh, Pa. 15221
412 621-4753
CC ICH
Publishes feminist materials including newsletters, books, and employment resources. Write for publication and price list.

NAACP
c/o Althea Simmons
Director of Training Programs
1790 Broadway
New York, N.Y. 10019
CC VT

NATIONAL ASSOCIATION FOR WOMEN DEANS, ADMINISTRATORS AND COUNSELORS
1028 Connecticut Ave., N.W.
Suite 922
Washington, D.C. 20036
202 659-9330
Offers job-placement services, a research award, and graduate fellowships.
Membership dues: $27 per year; $7.50 for graduate students.
Publication: Quarterly journal, $7.50 for four issues.

NATIONAL ASSOCIATION OF EDUCATIONAL BROADCASTERS

CC = Career Counseling
CL = Career Library
EmR = Employment Referral
ICH = Information Clearing House

JP = Job Placement
LC = Legal Counseling
TB = Talent Banks
VT = Vocational Training

238

1346 Connecticut Ave., N.W.
Washington, D.C. 20036
202   785-1100
ICH   JP
Specializes in professionals in telecommunications, but places people in all kinds of jobs.
Fee: $20–$30, depending on service.

NATIONAL ASSOCIATION OF SOCIAL WORKERS
2 Park Ave.
New York, N.Y. 10016
212   686-7128
ICH
Publication: *NASW News/ Personnel Information*

NATIONAL ASSOCIATION OF WOMEN IN CONSTRUCTION
Executive Office:
2800 W. Lancaster Ave.
Fort Worth, Tex. 76107
817   332-7635
Job Placement Plan:
1340 Kenwood Rd.
West Palm Beach, Fla. 33401
305   833-0391
JP   ICH   VT
Recruits women for careers in construction and promotes educational p r o g r a m s for members with a desire for career advancement.
Publication: *NAWIC Image*

NATIONAL COUNCIL OF ADMINISTRATIVE WOMEN IN EDUCATION
1815 E. Fort Myer Dr.
N. Arlington, Va. 22209
703   528-6111
CC   ICH   JP

NATIONAL COUNCIL OF NEGRO WOMEN
HIGHER EDUCATION COMMISSION
c/o Constance M. Carroll
Univ. of Maine/Portland
Gorham, Maine 04103

NATIONAL EDUCATION ASSOCIATION
WOMEN'S CAUCUS
1201 16th St., N.W.
Washington, D.C. 20036
202   833-5412
EmR   ICH   LC
See "Educational Opportunities—National"

NATIONAL ORGANIZATION FOR WOMEN (NOW)
5 S. Wabash
Suite 1615
Chicago, Ill. 60603
312   332-1954
National network of more than 800 local women's groups. Works to achieve equal status for women in government, industry, professions, political parties, labor unions. Local chapters provide employment seminars, legal counseling, and referral services.
Fee: Annual membership.
Publications: *Do It Now* (national newsletter); also local newsletters

NATIONAL SECRETARIES ASSOCIATION
(International)
2440 Pershing Rd.,
Suite G-10

Kansas City, Mo. 64108
CL
Membership open to secretaries and teachers of business education.
Dues: $10 per year.
Publications: Magazine and an on-the-job human relations book

NEW FEMINIST TALENT
ASSOCIATES
250 W. 57th St.
New York, N.Y. 10019
212 581-1066
TB
Talent bank of public speakers

SIX CITIES PROJECT
Vanguard Bldg., 1st Floor
1111 20th St., N.W.
Washington, D.C. 20036
202 872-8096
CC CL JP
Places people in jobs in Atlanta, Ga.; Richmond, Va.; Baltimore, Md.; B o s t o n, Mass.; Providence, R.I.; and White River Junction, Vt.

SOCIETY OF WOMEN
ENGINEERS
345 E. 47th St., Rm. 305
New York, N.Y. 10017
212 752-6800
EmR

SOCIOLOGISTS FOR WOMEN IN
SOCIETY
c/o Joan Huber, Chairperson
Dept. of Sociology
University of Illinois at
Urbana-Champagne
Urbana, Ill. 61801
217 352-5144
CC ICH JP

STOCKHOLDERS' ACTION
PROGRAM
P.O. Box 1267
San Francisco, Calif. 94101
Works for equal employment and representation of women in the investment field.

SYSTEMS EVALUATION
COMPANY
529 14th St., N.W.
Washington, D.C. 20004
202 628-6663
CC TB
Offers consulting services.

TOIL (TEACHING OPPOR-
TUNITIES INFORMATION
LISTING)
CSR Executive Office
Wilfred Laurier University
Waterloo, Ont.
Canada N2L3C5
CC EmR ICH JP

U.S. EQUAL EMPLOYMENT
OPPORTUNITY COMMISSION
1800 G St., N.W.

CC = Career Counseling	JP = Job Placement
CL = Career Library	LC = Legal Counseling
EmR = Employment Referral	TB = Talent Banks
	VT = Vocational Training
ICH = Information Clearing House	

240

Washington, D.C. 20506
202 343-5621
ICH LC

U.S. FEDERAL WOMEN'S
  PROGRAM
U.S. CIVIL SERVICE
  COMMISSION
1900 F St., N.W., Rm. 7540
Washington, D.C. 20415
202 632-6870
EmR JP TB

WOMEN IN COMMUNI-
  CATIONS, INC.
8305-A Shoal Creek Blvd.
Austin, Tex. 78758
512 452-0119
CL ICH
Membership open to women
with two years' professional
experience and currently employed in communications
and to students of high scholarship.
Publishes a national job-information bulletin for members and, on the local level,
provides vocational training
and career workshops.
Publications: *Careers Unlimited* (50¢); *Membership
Job and Salary Survey* ($1).

WOMEN IN COMMUNITY
  SERVICE
431 S. Dearborn St.
Chicago, Ill. 60605
312 427-1562
National coalition w h i c h
holds a contract with the
Dept. of Labor to recruit and
screen girls for Job Corps, to
refer girls who do not qualify
to other programs, and to

provide returnees with support services. Local organizations may provide services
for solo parents, unwed
mothers, or potential school
dropouts.

WOMEN IN COMMUNITY
  SERVICE
83 McAllister St.
San Francisco, Calif. 94102
415 863-2655
National organization of volunteers holding a contract
with the Labor Department to
screen and send disadvan-
taged women (those between
16 and 21) to Job Corps
training centers in Los Angeles and parts of Oregon.

WOMEN EDUCATORS (WE)
c/o Mary Craik
Psychology Department
St. Cloud State College
St. Cloud, Minn. 56301
Membership open to anyone
who considers herself a
woman educator, including
retired women.
Dues: $5, $2 optional information service.
Publication: Bimonthly newsletter

DOCTORAL PLACEMENT
  SERVICE
WOMEN'S THEOLOGICAL
  COALITION
Boston Theological Institute
210 Herrick Rd.
Newton Center, Mass. 02159
617 969-2946
EmR ICH JP TB
Nationwide placement service
for women with doctoral de-

241

grees in religion seeking teaching, administrative, or campus-ministry positions. Disseminates news of job openings throughout the country in bimonthly newsletter. Data bank of résumés.

Fee: $10 a year (free to members, $2 for others).

YWCA/YMCA AND
  YWHA/YMHA
Look into local branches for career-counseling services.

EAST

ADVERTISING WOMEN OF
  NEW YORK
153 E. 57th St.
New York, N.Y. 10022
Runs seminars on entering the advertising field. Provides informal referrals and free résumé counseling.

AFFIRMATIVE ACTION
  REFERRAL SYSTEM
COMMONWEALTH OF
  MASSACHUSETTS
294 Washington St., Rm. 743
Boston, Mass. 02108
617   727-7780-7380
EmR
State-wide referral agency for jobs in executive branch of the Massachusetts government. Priority given to hiring of minorities and women.

BOSTON PROJECT FOR
  CAREERS
83 Prospect St.
West Newton, Mass. 02165

617   969-0893-2339
CC   JP
Locates part-time job opportunities for women.
Fee: $10.

BOSTON YWCA
140 Clarendon St.
Boston, Mass. 02116
617   536-7940
CC
Maintains a job bulletin board.
Fee: $5.

CAREER AND VOCATIONAL
  ADVISORY SERVICE
CIVIC CENTER AND
  CLEARINGHOUSE, INC.
14 Beacon St.
Boston, Mass. 02108
617   227-1762-1763
CC CL EmR ICH JP TB
Job openings in the fields of human services and education, and in nontraditional

CC = Career Counseling	JP = Job Placement
CL = Career Library	LC = Legal Counseling
EmR = Employment Referral	TB = Talent Banks
	VT = Vocational Training
ICH = Information Clearing House	

women's roles and occupations.
$10 consultation fee;
no referral fee.

CAREER COUNSELING FOR
 WOMEN
P.O. Box 372
Huntington, N.Y. 11743
516 421-1948
CC CL
Feminist-oriented approach to career planning. Individual and group exercises, discussions, and assignments.
Fee: $100 for five-week program

CENTER FOR WOMEN AT
 MASSASOIT
290 Thatcher St.
Brockton, Mass. 02402
617 588-9100, ext. 223
CC LC ICH CL

EVE
Kean College of New Jersey
Morris Ave.
Union, N.J. 07083
201 527-2210
EmR CC CL ICH
Free walk-in counseling in group setting; $12 per hour for individual appointment with professional counselor.

FEMINIST FINANCIAL
 CONSULTANTS
115 W. 71st St., #7A
New York, N.Y. 10023
212 362-6962
CC ICH LC
Services include: Business and financial counseling, accounting, and tax preparation. Career planning and workshops in starting businesses, insurance, and investment.
Fee: Varies with service.

GEORGE WASHINGTON
 UNIVERSITY
CONTINUING EDUCATION
 FOR WOMEN
2130 H St., N.W.
Washington, D.C. 20037
202 676-7036
CL ICH

HARTFORD COLLEGE
 COUNSELING CENTER
 FOR WOMEN
50 Elizabeth St.
Hartford, Conn. 06105
203 236-5838
CC TB
Nonprofit organization devoted to helping women re-enter the job world. Conducts seminars on career development for women in business, a management training course, a training course for paralegal assistants, and group discussions to help women "find a focus" for their career aspirations.

HIGHER EDUCATION RE-
 SOURCE SERVICES (HERS)
Brown University
P.O. Box 1901
Providence, R.I. 02902
401 863-2197
EmR ICH

HOFSTRA UNIVERSITY
CAREER HORIZONS FOR
 WOMEN
Institute for Community Ed.
Hofstra University

Hempstead, N.Y. 11050
516 560-0500
CC EmR VT

HER—HUMAN EMPLOY-
MENT RESOURCES PLACE-
MENT SERVICE
Congress Bldg., Suite 512
142 High St.
Portland, Maine 04101
ICH JP

INDIVIDUAL RESOURCES
60 E. 12th St.
New York, N.Y. 10003
CC EmR ICH TB

INFORMATION AND COUNSEL-
ING CENTER FOR WOMEN
215 Park St.
New Haven, Conn. 06520
203 436-8242
CC CL
Sponsored by the Yale University Women's Organiza-
tion. Services include career
counseling, file of educational
opportunities, job listings,
library on women's topics,
day-care and domestic help
information, career symposia,
and contact group for di-
vorced and widowed women.
Fee: $10 annually.

JOB ADVISORY SERVICE
Chatham College

Woodland Rd.
Pittsburgh, Pa. 15232
412 441-8200
CC EmR ICH
Nonprofit community agency.
Obtains part-time professional
and semiprofessional employment for women in the Pittsburgh a r e a. Clearinghouse
for educational opportunities,
jobs, and creative volunteer
projects; place where employers and social service groups
can find skilled women to
fulfill their needs; free advisory center.

JANICE LAROUCHE
ASSOCIATES
333 Central Park West
New York, N.Y. 10025
212 663-0970
CC CL EmR
On-going career-counseling
workshops on job finding,
résumés, interviewing techniques, and strategies for
advancement. Also individual
job and résumé counseling
and assertiveness training.
Fee charged.

MASSACHUSETTS INSTITUTE
OF TECHNOLOGY
SPECIAL ASSISTANT TO THE
CHANCELLOR FOR WOMEN
AND WORK

CC = Career Counseling
CL = Career Library
EmR = Employment
Referral
ICH = Information
Clearing House

JP = Job Placement
LC = Legal Counseling
TB = Talent Banks
VT = Vocational Training

Cambridge, Mass. 02139
617 253-5925
CC

MERCY COLLEGE CAREER
COUNSELING AND
PLACEMENT
555 Broadway
Dobbs Ferry, N.Y. 10522
914 693-4500
CC CL JP
Fee: $25 for nonstudents.

MERLIN D. BISHOP CENTER
University of Connecticut
Storrs, Conn. 06208
203 486-3441
CC VT
Individual and group counseling for women who wish to re-enter the job market or return to school. Helps women find interesting part-time work. Offers noncredit courses in social work, interior design, etc. Not a placement service.

MONTGOMERY COLLEGE
OFFICE OF COMMUNITY
SERVICES
Rockville, Md. 20805
301 762-7400
CC ICH

MORE FOR WOMEN INC.
Gramercy Park Hotel
2 Lexington Ave.
New York, N.Y. 10010
212 674-4090
CC EmR
Career-counseling, workshops and individual sessions, emphasis on long-range vocational planning.
Fee charged.

NASSAU COUNTY VOCATIONAL
CENTER FOR WOMEN
33 Willis Ave.
Mineola, N.Y. 11501
516 535-4646
CC VT

NEW CAREERS
DEVELOPMENT CENTER
184 Fifth Ave.
New York, N.Y. 10010
212 598-7644
CC EmR ICH JP
Publication: *Human Services Newsletter*

NEW DIRECTIONS FOR
WOMEN
Maryland Dept. of Employment Security
330 N. Charles
Baltimore, Md. 21201
301 383-5579
CC CL EmR JP

NEW ENVIRONMENTS FOR
WOMEN ASSOCIATES
44 Bertwell Rd.
Lexington, Mass. 02173
617 862-0663
CC CL EmR
Counsels women on developing active job searches. Offers employment referrals and consulting service in women's education and employment.
Fee: $25 for first session; $15 per hour for additional sessions.

NEW JERSEY STATEWIDE
TASK FORCE ON CAREER
EDUCATION
549 Lenox Ave.

Westfield, N.J. 07090
201   232-0870
CC

NEW JERSEY TALENT
  BANK FOR WOMEN
Dept. of Community Affairs
363 W. State St.
Trenton, N.J. 08625
609   292-8622
JP   TB

NEWTON JUNIOR COLLEGE
Park Place
Newtonville, Mass. 02160
617   969-9570
CC   CL   EmR
Educational and career coun-
seling and group career work-
shops for women in Newton.

OPPORTUNITIES FOR WOMEN
c/o Professional Careers
  Information Center
144 Westminster St.
Providence, R.I. 02903
401   331-3315
CC   CL   EmR   JP
Federally financed project
that provides free job counseling and placement for
women.

OPTIONS FOR WOMEN
8419 Germantown Ave.
Philadelphia, Pa. 19118
215   Ch 2-4955
CC   CL   JP
Nonprofit employment agency

designed to find and create
job opportunities for women.
Affirmative Action consulting
arranges career-development
seminars for women and management-awareness   seminars
for employers and commu-
nity groups.
Fee varies with service.

PENNSYLVANIA GOVERNOR'S
  AFFIRMATIVE ACTION
  COUNCIL
Main Bldg., Rm. 611,
  South Wing
Harrisburg, Pa. 17120
717   787-4320
EmR

PHILADELPHIA OPPOR-
  TUNITIES FOR WOMEN
Strawbridge & Clothier
8th & Market Sts., 11th Floor
Philadelphia, Pa. 19105
215   925-4346
CC   CL   EmR   ICH

PROFESSIONAL SKILLS
  ROSTER
410 College Ave.
Ithaca, N.Y. 14850
607   256-3784
CC   JP   TB
Nonprofit e m p l o y m e n t
agency; seeks to provide
counseling based on women's
special job-market needs and
to create a local job-matching

CC = Career Counseling	JP = Job Placement
CL = Career Library	LC = Legal Counseling
EmR = Employment	TB = Talent Banks
Referral	VT = Vocational Training
ICH = Information	
Clearing House	

system for full- and part-time professionals.

RADCLIFFE INSTITUTE
3 James St.
Cambridge, Mass. 02138
617   495-8211
CL   ICH
Conducts research and seminars to expand women's opportunities in scholarships, the professions, business, and public service.

RESOURCES FOR WOMEN
Logan Hall
University of Pennsylvania
Philadelphia, Pa. 19104
215   243-5537
CC   CL   ICH   JP
Open to all women.
Small counseling groups discuss problems of women re-entering job market. Job bank set up with the university as largest employer to date and social-service organizations as second largest.

ROCKLAND COUNTY (N.Y.)
   GUIDANCE CENTER FOR
   WOMEN
10 N. Broadway
Nyack, N.Y. 10960
914   358-9390
CC   CL   VT

SUNY AT BUFFALO
PRESIDENT'S COMMITTEE ON
   RECRUITMENT AND
   PROMOTION OF WOMEN
192 Hayes Hall
Buffalo, N.Y. 14214
716   831-4019
JP   TB

TISHMAN MEMORIAL
   SEMINARS
Career Counseling and
   Placement.
Hunter College
505 Park Ave.
New York, N.Y. 10028
212   360-2872

VILLA MARIA COLLEGE
   CAREER COUNSELING
   CENTER FOR
   ADULT WOMEN
2551 West 8th St.
Erie, Pa. 16505
814   838-1966
CC   CL   ICH   JP
No fee.

VOCATIONS FOR SOCIAL
   CHANGE
353 Broadway
Cambridge, Mass. 02139
617   661-1570
CL   ICH
Program of the American Friends Service Committee. Serves as information clearinghouse on groups working for change in health, law, education, and other fields. Offers meeting space for social-action groups and discussion groups about work. Accepts donations according to ability to pay.
Publication: *People's Yellow Pages*, directory of Boston-area groups and individuals involved in social change, $1.50.

WASHINGTON OPPORTUNITIES
   FOR WOMEN (WOW)
1111 O St., N.W., Rm. 101

Washington, D.C. 20036
202 393-6151
CC CL EmR ICH JP

WHITE RIVER JUNCTION
   CENTER
5 N. Main St.
P.O. Box 397
White River Junction, Vt.
   05001
802 295-3136
CC CL EmR JP

WIDENING HORIZONS, INC.
115 Stow St.
Concord, Mass. 01742
617 369-9500
CC ICH
Information about education
and training programs, volunteer opportunities, selected
part-time employment, and
retirement planning.
Fees: $10 for counseling in-
terview, $15 for workshop.

WIDER OPPORTUNITIES
   FOR WOMEN
C. F. Hurley Bldg.
Government Center
Cambridge & Stamford Sts.
Boston, Mass. 02202
617 727-8979
CC CL EmR JP

WOMEN IN CITY
   GOVERNMENT UNITED
P.O. Box 1153
Church St. Station

New York, N.Y. 10008
212 222-9084
CL ICH TB
Memberhip open to any
woman who works for New
York City government or an
affiliate organization or
agency. Dues.

WOMEN'S EDUCATIONAL AND
   INDUSTRIAL UNION
   CAREER SERVICES
264 Boylston St.
Boston, Mass. 02116
617 536-5650
CC CL ICH JP
Counseling and placement for
full-time and part-time jobs.
Promotes positions with flexible hours. Special services for
recent college graduates and
women returning to work.
Counseling is free; job placement 5 percent fee.

WOMEN'S OPPORTUNITY RE-
   SEARCH CENTER (WORC)
Div. of Continuing Education
Middlesex Community
   College
Springs Rd.
Bedford, Mass. 01730
617 275-1590
CC CL EmR JP TB VT
Multifaceted service center
for women of all ages and
backgrounds. Programs focus
on personal growth and self-

CC = Career Counseling
CL = Career Library
EmR = Employment
       Referral
ICH = Information
      Clearing House

JP = Job Placement
LC = Legal Counseling
TB = Talent Banks
VT = Vocational Training

evaluation, career guidance and life planning, and exploration of job options in education, volunteer work, and paid employment.
Fees: $5 for counseling, $24 for six-week workshops, some programs and written materials free.

WOMEN'S RESOURCE CENTER
West Suburban YWCA
66 Irving St.
Framingham, Mass. 01701
617 653-4464
CC CL EmR JP

WOMEN'S UNIT
2 World Trade Center
New York, N.Y. 10047
212 488-5227
ICH LC TB
New York State government agency concerned with the rights of women in state government.

SOUTH

ATLANTA WOMEN ON
THE WAY
161 Peachtree St., N.E.
Rm. 310
Atlanta, Ga. 30303
404 656-5915
CC CL EmR JP

BLACK WOMEN EMPLOY-
MENT PROGRAM
Southern Regional Council
52 Fairle St., N.W.
Atlanta, Ga. 30303
404 522-8764
JP VT

CENTER FOR CONTINUING
EDUCATION OF WOMEN
(CCEW)
Miami-Dade College
300 N.E. Second Ave.
Miami, Fla. 33132
305 577-6840
CC CL EmR ICH TB

DUKE UNIVERSITY
CONTINUING EDUCATION
East Duke Bldg.
Durham, N.C. 27706
919 684-6259
CC CL ICH

LIFESPAN CENTER FOR
WOMEN
Salem College
SALEM STATION
Winston-Salem, N.C. 27108
919 723-7961, ext. 278
CC CL EmR
Counseling includes vocational testing, career-goal structuring, lifespan-planning seminars, and assertiveness training.
Fee: $5–$100, depending on the service.

PACE SERVICES
7220 S.W. 61st Court
South Miami, Fla. 33143
305 665-7611
Specializes in Affirmative Action consultation services.

RICHMOND WOMEN ON
THE WAY
318 E. Cary St.
Richmond, Va. 23219
703 770-6015
CC CL EmR JP

AFFIRMATIVE ACTION
  REGISTER FOR EFFECTIVE
  EQUAL OPPORTUNITY
  RECRUITMENT
10 S. Brentwood Blvd.
St. Louis, Mo. 63105
JP   LC

APPLIED POTENTIAL
P.O. Box 19
Highland Park, Ill. 60035
312   432-0620
CC   CL   EmR   ICH   TB
Offers personal, educational, and vocational counseling services. No job placement, but provides information on job opportunities, flexible work schedules, and volunteer work. Affirmative Action consulting for employers.
Fee: Depends upon services.

CAREER CLINIC FOR
  MATURE WOMEN
628 Nicollet Mall, Rm. 331
Minneapolis, Minn. 55402
612   335-8255
CC   EmR   JP   VT
Women thinking of going to work receive advice, training in some areas, and referrals to other training centers. Clinic offers c h a n c e for women to meet possible employers. Not an employment agency.
Publication: *Career Clinic Handbook*

CONTINUING EDUCATION
  FOR WOMEN
Western Michigan University
Kalamazoo, Mich. 49008
CC   CL   EmR   ICH
No fee for counseling; fee for workshops.

FLEXIBLE CAREERS
37 S. Wabash Ave., Rm. 714
Chicago, Ill. 60603
312   263-2488
CC   CL   ICH   TB
Offers women in the Chicago area a low-fee career-resource center. Promotes development of flexible opportunities in employment and related education and training.
Membership fee: $10.

FLEXIBLE OPPORTUNITIES IN
  ST. LOUIS FOR COLLEGE-
  EDUCATED WOMEN
School of Continuing
  Education
P.O. Box 1099
Washington University
St. Louis, Mo. 63130
314   863-0100, ext. 4261
CC   ICH   VT

CC = Career Counseling
CL = Career Library
EmR = Employment
        Referral
ICH = Information
        Clearing House

JP = Job Placement
LC = Legal Counseling
TB = Talent Banks
VT = Vocational Training

INDIANA UNIVERSITY
  CONTINUING EDUCATION
  FOR WOMEN
Owen Hall 302
Bloomington, Ind. 47401
812 337-1684
CC ICH TB VT
Fee for educational services;
counseling is free.

KANSAS UNIVERSITY
  WOMEN'S RESOURCE AND
  CAREER PLANNING CENTER
220 Strong Hall
Lawrence, Kans. 66044
CC CL

MINNESOTA WOMEN'S
  CENTER
301 Walter Library
University of Minnesota
Minneapolis, Minn. 55414
612 373-3850
CC EmR
Open to Minnesota women at
all levels of education. Provides advice, counseling, and
information on educational
and employment opportuni-
ties. Offers scholarships, child
care, job-placement services,
research on women, and undergraduate courses about
women.

NEW OPTIONS, INC.
2908 Book Bldg.
1249 Washington Blvd.
Detroit, Mich. 48226
313 961-8337
CC JP TB
Group of consultants providing job-placement and career-
counseling s e r v i c e s for

women and also working
with employers as Affirmative
Action consultants. Emphasis
on nontraditional jobs with
advancement potential.

NORTHERN ILLINOIS
  UNIVERSITY ACADEMIC
  WOMEN FOR EQUALITY
Northern Illinois University
DeKalb, Ill. 60115
815 753-0308
CC EmR ICH
Concerns include parity, dis-
crimination, and job oppor-
tunities.

OHIO AFFIRMATIVE ACTION
  OFFICERS ASSOCIATION
103 McGuffrey Hall
Ohio University
Athens, Ohio 45701
EmR ICH

PHI DELTA GAMMA
2752 N. Fefeber Ave.
Wauwatosa, Wis. 53210
414 964-3843
CC ICH

PROJECT EVE
Cuyahoga Community
  College
2900 Community College
  Ave.
Cleveland, Ohio 44115
216 241-5966, ext. 209
CC CL ICH JP VT
No fee for individual counsel-
ing, $10–$12 for group.

RESOURCE: WOMEN THE
  UNTAPPED SOURCE
13878 Cedar Rd.

251

University Heights, Ohio
44118
216   932-4546
CC   JP   TB

WOMEN IN REAL ESTATE
5702 N. Western
Chicago, Ill. 60612
312   561-9883
CC   ICH
Promotes educational pro-
grams and seminars on real
estate; provides professional
forum for women in real
estate to meet and arrange
cooperative real estate deals.

WOMEN'S, INC.
15 Spinning Wheel Rd.,
Suite 14
Hinsdale, Ill. 60521
312   325-9770
CC   CL   ICH   JP   TB
Provides vocational-counsel-
ing and job-placement services to women, management
consulting to business and
human development pro-
grams to assist schools and
groups in presenting new
career options for women of
all ages.
Fee variable.

WEST

ADVOCATES FOR WOMEN
593 Market St., Suite 500
San Francisco, Calif. 94105
415   495-6750
CL   ICH   JP   VT
Women's economic develop-
ment center which handles
job openings in management,
in business, professional sales,
marketing, and the skilled
trades. Also does apprenticeship recruitment.
Publication: *Advocates for
Women Newsletter*

BERKELEY CAMPUS, CENTER
    FOR CONTINUING EDUCA-
    TION FOR WOMEN

205 Women's Faculty Club
Berkeley, Calif. 94720
CC   CL   EmR   ICH

BETTER JOBS FOR WOMEN
1545 Tremont Place
Denver, Colo. 80202
303   244-4189
EmR   JP   VT
Places women in apprenticeship programs or other on-
the-job training positions in
such occupations as carpenter, cement mason, electri-
cian, plumber, roofer, forklift
operator, mechanic, and telephone installer. Developed
by the Bureau of Apprentice-

CC = Career Counseling	JP = Job Placement
CL = Career Library	LC = Legal Counseling
EmR = Employment Referral	TB = Talent Banks
	VT = Vocational Training
ICH = Information Clearing House	

ship and Training of the U.S. Dept. of Labor and operated by the YWCA.

CAREER PLANNING CENTER
1623 S. LaCienega
Los Angeles, Calif. 90035
213   273-6633
CC   ICH   JP   TB
Sponsored by the Soroptomist Club of Beverly Hills/Century City. Services include career counseling, job-search-strategy workshops, free job referrals.
Publication: *Career Planning Workbook for Women*, $10

COLORADO STATE UNIVERSITY WOMEN'S RESEARCH CENTER
Office of Women's Relations
Fort Collins, Colo. 80521
303   491-6383
CC   EmR

CONCENTRATED EMPLOY-
    MENT PROGRAM
730 Polk
San Francisco, Calif. 94109
415   771-7100
VT
Offers paid training programs in auto mechanics, electrical wiring, nursing, etc. Programs change every month.

FLAGG OPPORTUNITY
    CENTER
Rm. 306
1625 Main St.
Houston, Tex. 77002
713   228-2109
EmR   JP
Aims to help women over 40 obtain employment leading to self-support and independence.
No fee.

INDIVIDUAL DEVELOPMENT
    CENTER
1020 E. John
Seattle, Wash. 98102
206   329-5528
CC   CL   EmR   ICH
Individual and group career counseling; Affirmative Action consulting for businesses, school districts, and governmental agencies; career-development workshops for women employees; awareness seminars for male managers and supervisors.
Fee: $20 per hour for individual counseling; $90 for 15 hours of group counseling.

JOB SEARCH
WOMEN'S RESOURCE CENTER
YWCA
1111 S.W. 10th St.
Portland, Oreg. 97205
503   223-6281
EmR   ICH   JP

MONTCLAIR INSTITUTE
2063 Mountain Blvd.,
    Suite 5
Oakland, Calif. 94611
415   339-0485
CC   CL   EmR   ICH

ORGANIZATION OF
    WOMEN ARCHITECTS
1079 Broadway
San Francisco, Calif. 94133
ICH   TB
Schedules seminars and lectures for women in archi-

tecture and related fields. Operates a job bank.

PRESCOTT & PRESCOTT
   COUNSELING SERVICES
636 B St.
Davis, Calif. 95616
916   756-6041
CC   ICH
Concerned specifically with higher education, career planning, and Affirmative Action.

RESEARCH CENTER ON
   WOMEN
Loretto Heights College
3001 S. Federal Blvd.
Denver, Colo. 80236
303   936-8441, ext. 253
CC   CL
Sponsors research programming about past and present roles, behavior patterns, and life-styles of both women and men in their personal and professional lives.

RESOURCE CENTER FOR
   WOMEN
499 Hamilton Ave.
Palo Alto, Calif. 94301
415   324-1710
CC   CL   ICH   JP   TB
Minimal fee for workshops and individual counseling. Publications: *The 1974 Directory of Bay Area Colleges and Universities,* $3.00;

Talent Source, newsletter, $5.00 per year.

SEATTLE WOMEN'S
   COMMISSION
OFFICE OF HUMAN
   RESOURCES
885 Main St.
Seattle, Wash. 98104
Concerned with equal opportunity for women in the job market.

UCLA EXTENSION PROGRAM
   ADVISORY SERVICE
INFORMATION CENTER
   FOR WOMEN
10995 Le Conte Ave.,
   Rm. 215
Los Angeles, Calif. 90024
CC CL EmR ICH JP TB
Community service offered to residents of and visitors to the greater Los Angeles area. Explores education and vocational training as well as job opportunities.
No fee.

UCLA WOMEN'S RESOURCE
   CENTER
90 Powell Library
405 Hilgard Ave.
Los Angeles, Calif. 90024
213   825-3945
CC   ICH

CC = Career Counseling	JP = Job Placement
CL = Career Library	LC = Legal Counseling
EmR = Employment Referral	TB = Talent Banks
ICH = Information Clearing House	VT = Vocational Training

WOMANPOWER CONSULTANTS
2223B Roosevelt
Berkeley, Calif. 94703
415   834-8286
CC EmR ICH
Provides information on Affirmative Action for women: requirements and recommendations.

WOMEN FOR CHANGE CENTER
3220 Lemmon Ave.
Dallas, Tex. 75204
214   522-3560-3561
CC CL EmR JP LS TB
No fee for employment-information service; $10–$35 for in-depth personal counseling or courses.
Publication: Newsletter, contains supplemental information on jobs, $6 a year.

WOMEN'S OPPORTUNITIES
    CENTER
148 Admin. Bldg.
University Extension
Univ. of California
Irvine, Calif. 92664
714   833-7128

CC CL EmR ICH
Offers educational and vocational guidance, continuing-education services, and volunteer opportunities.
No fee.

WOMEN'S VOCATIONAL
    INSTITUTE
593 Market St., Suite 516
San Francisco, Calif. 94105
415   495-8044
CC CL-planning EmR ICH
Offers vocational counseling and awareness courses, workshops in problem solving, tutorials for employment or educational exams, management training courses, and special programs.
Fees: $15 for 12-hr. class, $8.50 for "economically disadvantaged"; $5 for workshops.

YOUNG CAREERIST
    COMMITTEE
13902 Fiji Way, No. 121
Mauna Del Rey, Calif. 90291
CC   CL   EmR

255

C

Educational Opportunities

Educational and extension programs at colleges and universities designed specifically for women are blossoming throughout the country. Courses, seminars, and informal workshops offer programs in many fields, including management, financial planning, and the skilled trades. The sources listed here are by no means comprehensive, but they should provide a starting point if you are seeking specialized training. For other programs, check colleges and universities in your area.

NATIONAL

ADULT EDUCATION
  ASSOCIATION
COMMISSION ON THE STATUS
  OF WOMEN IN ADULT
  EDUCATION
810 18th St., N.W.
Washington, D.C. 20036
CC EmR ICH

ADULT EDUCATION

ASSOCIATION
CONTINUING EDUCATION FOR
  WOMEN SECTION
810 18th St., N.W.
Washington, D.C. 20006
CC CL ICH

The Continuing Education for Women Newsletter and Adult Education Association Date-

---

CC = Career Counseling
CL = Career Library
EmR = Employment
        Referral
ICH = Information
        Clearing House

JP = Job Placement
LC = Legal Counseling
TB = Talent Banks
VT = Vocational Training

line ($7 for nonmembers) list openings for professional jobs in the continuing-education field.
Membership fee: $10–$50 per year.

ALPHA KAPPA ALPHA
  SORORITY, INC.
627 National Press Bldg.
Washington, D.C. 20004
202 347-7777
ICH
Black women's organization offering scholarships and related services to women students.

ALTRUSA INTERNATIONAL
  FOUNDATION
332 S. Michigan Ave.
Chicago, Ill. 60604
312 341-0818
ICH VT
Service organization of professional women. Provides scholarship awards to women for training or retraining. Focus on vocational education.
Publication: *International Altrusan*

ALUMNAE ADVISORY
  CENTER, INC.
541 Madison Ave.
New York, N.Y. 10022
212 758-2153
CC ICH
See "Career Counseling—National"

AMERICAN ASSOCIATION OF
  COMMUNITY AND JUNIOR
  COLLEGES
WOMEN'S CAUCUS

National Center for Higher
  Education
1 Dupont Circle
Washington, D.C. 20036
CC CL ICH VT
Operates a Career Staffing Center for women seeking jobs in two-year colleges and administrative openings.
Publications: *Community and Junior College Journal* and others; newsletters, pamphlets

AMERICAN ASSOCIATION OF
  UNIVERSITY WOMEN
AAUW Fellowships program
2401 Virginia Ave., N.W.
Washington, D.C. 20037
202 785-7700
ICH VT
Offers graduate fellowships to both American and foreign w o m e n; clearinghouse of women's educational opportunities.
Publications: *AAUW*, fact sheets

AMERICAN EDUCATIONAL
  RESEARCH ASSOCIATION
1126 16th St., N.W.
Washington, D.C. 20036
202 223-9485
Membership dues: $13–$25 per year.
JP—at annual meeting only

AMERICAN PERSONNEL AND
  GUIDANCE ASSOCIATION
WOMEN'S CAUCUS
1607 New Hampshire Ave.,
  N.W.
Washington, D.C. 20009
202 483-4633
CL ICH JP

257

Publications: *Guidepost* (newsletter), *Journal of College Student Personnel,* among others

AMERICAN SOCIETY FOR TRAINING AND DEVELOPMENT
WOMEN'S CAUCUS
c/o Katherine Kirkham
1718 P St., N.W.
#404
Washington, D.C. 20036
CL ICH JP TB
Membership: open to public. General job referrals; training and information programs for development of human resources.
Annual fee: $45.
Publications: *Training and Development Journal* a n d others, free to members

AMERICAN VOCATIONAL ASSOCIATION
1510 H St., N.W.
Washington, D.C. 20005
202 737-3722
CL ICH JP
Membership open to anyone interested in vocational-training education, manpower training, vocational guidance, administration a n d supervision, and to vocational-training instructors; fee $3–$20 per year.

Job openings listed in monthly journal; library of employment data on women, and vocational/technical training.
Publications: *The American Vocational Journal* (monthly) books and pamphlets, quarterly newsletter

ASSOCIATION OF AMERICAN COLLEGES
PROJECT ON THE STATUS AND EDUCATION OF WOMEN
1818 R St., N.W.
Washington, D.C. 20009
202 387-1300
CL ICH JP
Compiles and distributes resources on women and work in colleges and universities. Offers technical assistance for the promotion of Affirmative Action in colleges.

BUSINESS AND PROFESSIONAL WOMEN'S FOUNDATION
2012 Massachusetts Ave., N.W.
Washington, D.C. 20036
202 293-1200
CL ICH
Educational research foundation which operates a special library with general information on occupations and job-search skills; researches areas of interest to women, gives management seminars, and

---

CC = Career Counseling
CL = Career Library
EmR = Employment Referral
ICH = Information Clearing House

JP = Job Placement
LC = Legal Counseling
TB = Talent Banks
VT = Vocational Training

awards fellowships for doctoral research and Career Advancement Scholarships to women over 26 who need money to learn job skills or relearn skills. List of publications available on request.

DANFORTH FOUNDATION
Graduate Fellowships for Women
222 S. Central Ave.
St. Louis, Mo. 63105
Provides graduate fellowships for women pursuing teaching careers. Grants up to $4,000. Write for requirements.

DELTA KAPPA GAMMA
P.O. Box 1589
Austin, Tex. 78767
512 478-5748
Women's honorary society; offers eighteen scholarships to women.
Publication: *The News*

GENERAL FEDERATION OF WOMEN'S CLUBS
1734 North St., N.W.
Washington, D.C. 20036
Scholarships awarded through local or state chapters to women of all ages.

INFORMATION AND REFERRAL CENTER
WOMEN'S INFORMATION
U.S. Dept. of Labor
Wage-Hour Area Office
1022 Federal Office Bldg.
31 Hopkins Plaza
Baltimore, Md. 21201
301 962-2265
Established to provide special assistance for working women

and current information on the employment rights of women.

INTERNATIONAL INSTITUTE OF WOMEN STUDIES
1615 Myrtle St., N.W.
Washington, D.C. 20012
202 726-6674
Membership open to anyone interested; dues $3 per year. Promotes research and disseminates information on the nature and b e h a v i o r of women.
Publication: *Journal of the International Institute of Women Studies*—$9 per year in U.S. and Canada.

NAACP
c/o Althea Simmons, Director for Training Programs
1790 Broadway
New York, N.Y. 10019
CC VT

NATIONAL ASSOCIATION FOR WOMEN DEANS, ADMINISTRATORS AND COUNSELORS
1028 Connecticut Ave., N.W.
Suite 922
Washington, D.C. 20036
202 659-9330
ICH JP
See "Career Counseling—National"

NATIONAL ASSOCIATION OF BANK WOMEN
c/o Anne L. Bryant
NABW Educational Foundation
111 E. Wacker Dr.

Chicago, Ill. 60601
Developing a pilot project for funding women pursuing banking c a r e e r s. Contact NABW for details.

NATIONAL ASSOCIATION OF COLLEGE WOMEN
c/o Lillian W. McDaniel
417 S. Davis Ave.
Richmond, Va. 23220
Negro women college students awarded annual scholarships by local chapters.

NATIONAL BLACK FEMINIST ORGANIZATION
370 Lexington Ave., Rm. 601
New York, N.Y. 10017
212 685-0800
Membership open to all black women.
Set up to help black women in their struggles against both sexism and racism. Concerned with such issues as child-care centers, job training programs for black women, ending forced sterilization, the fight of the household worker, black female addiction. Information a n d bibliography available.

NATIONAL COALITION FOR RESEARCH OF WOMEN'S EDUCATION AND DEVELOPMENT, INC.

160 Harper Hall
10th & College Ave.
Claremont, Calif. 91711
Membership open to colleges and universities interested in sharing i n f o r m a t i o n on women's educational needs.

NATIONAL COUNCIL OF NEGRO WOMEN
HIGHER EDUCATION COMMISSION
c/o Constance M. Carroll
University of Maine
Portland-Gorham, Me. 04103
CC

NATIONAL EDUCATION ASSOCIATION
WOMEN'S CAUCUS
1201 16th St., N.W.
Washington, D.C. 20036
202 833-5412
CC EmR ICH
Concerned with the status of women and job opportunities for women in education.

NATIONAL HOME STUDY COUNCIL
1601 18th St., N.W.
Washington, D.C. 20009
202 234-5100
CC ICH VT
Membership includes 150 accredited home-study schools. Services as clearing-house of information about home-study

---

CC = Career Counseling	JP = Job Placement
CL = Career Library	LC = Legal Counseling
EmR = Employment Referral	TB = Talent Banks
ICH = Information Clearing House	VT = Vocational Training

260

field and as accrediting agency for private correspondence schools.

Publication: *Directory of Accredited Private Home Study Schools*

NATIONAL ORGANIZATION FOR WOMEN
LEGAL DEFENSE AND EDUCATION FUND
9 W. 57th St.
New York, N.Y. 10019
212 688-1715

THE NEWSPAPER FUND
P.O. Box 300
Princeton, N.J. 08536
609 452-2000
CC CL EmR ICH VT
Purpose is to encourage talented young people to enter the newspaper profession. Provides professional training programs, internships for college students, training programs for journalism teachers, assistance in educational efforts, and information on journalism careers. Supported by Dow Jones & Co., Inc.

Publications: *A Newspaper Career and You, Journalism Scholarship Guide*, and other related materials.

PHI CHI THETA
718 Judah St.
San Francisco, Calif. 94122
Professional development and leadership training in business and economics. Also provides scholarships.

PHI DELTA GAMMA
2752 N. Fefeber Ave.

Wauwatosa, Wis. 53210
414 964-3843
CC ICH
Membership requires B.A. or B.S. Encourages information exchange among professional women and offers scholarships.

SEARS ROEBUCK FOUNDATION LOANS
c/o Business and Professional Women's Foundation
2012 Massachusetts Ave., N.W.
Washington, D.C. 20037
Provides loans to women pursuing graduate business degrees.

SOROPTIMIST FEDERATION OF THE AMERICAS
1616 Walnut St.
Philadelphia, Pa. 19103
Provides scholarships for vocational training. Fifteen annual a w a r d s distributed through local chapters.

WOMEN'S BUREAU
EMPLOYMENT STANDARDS ADMINISTRATION
U.S. Dept. of Labor
14th and Constitution
Washington, D.C. 20210
202 961-2036
CL ICH
Distributes publications on all aspects of women and work, provides technical and advisory services to organizations, and cosponsors, with other groups, group career workshops.

WOMEN'S COLLECTION

Special Collections Dept.
Northwestern University
  Library
Evanston, Ill. 60201
312 492-3635
CL
Material on every facet of
the women's movement, in-
cluding women in the job
market, surveys and analyses
of job discrimination, and
federal and state legislation
pertaining to job discrimination.
Publication: *Women's
Collection Newsletter,*
free of charge

WOMEN'S DOCTORAL
  PLACEMENT SERVICE
WOMEN'S EQUITY ACTION
  LEAGUE
538 National Press Bldg.
Washington, D.C. 20004
202 638-4560
LC
See "Legal Services"

WOMEN'S HISTORY RESEARCH
  CENTER, INC.
2325 Oak St.
Berkeley, Calif. 94708
415 524-7710
ICH

The only international ar-
chive of the women's movement. Microfilm, publications,
and bibliographies and other
resources on women and employment are available. Write
for publications information.

WOMEN'S INSTITUTE FOR
  FREEDOM OF THE PRESS
3306 Ross Place, N.W.
Washington, D.C. 20008
202 966-7783
EmR
Nonmembership organization
that does research in communications.

WOMEN'S THEOLOGICAL
  COALITION
Boston Theological Institute
210 Herrick Rd.
Newton Center, Mass. 02159
617 969-2946
CC EmR ICH JP TB

ZONTA INTERNATIONAL
59 E. Van Buren St.
Chicago, Ill. 60605
312 939-3850
Executive women in business
and the professions. Offers
Amelia Earhart Fellowships
to women in aerospace field.

CC = Career Counseling	JP = Job Placement
CL = Career Library	LC = Legal Counseling
EmR = Employment	TB = Talent Banks
Referral	VT = Vocational Training
ICH = Information	
Clearing House	

EAST

ACADEMIC ADVISORY CENTER
   FOR ADULTS
c/o Laura O. Kornfield
Turf Ave.
Rye, N.Y. 10580
914 967-1653
CC CL ICH
Provides educational and career counseling, information on academic programs and continuing education courses. Consultant to businesses, institutions, and individuals.

BOSTON WOMEN'S
   COLLECTIVE, INC.
490 Beacon St.
Boston, Mass. 02115
617 261-1561, 547-9104
Emphasizes the "growth and development of women during a time of transition." Currently developing a program focusing on materials for women's studies in elementary and s e c o n d a r y schools.
Publication: *Women's Yellow Pages*

CAREER AND VOCATIONAL
   ADVISORY SERVICE
Civic Center Clearing House
14 Beacon St.
Boston, Mass. 02108
617 221-1762
CC CL EmR ICH JP TB
$10 consultation fee;
no fee for referrals.

CARNEGIE-MELLON
   MID-CAREER

WOMEN'S FELLOWSHIP
   PROGRAM
Admissions Officer
Graduate School of Public
   and International Affairs
Bruce Hall, Rm. 202
University of Pittsburgh
Pittsburgh, Pa. 15213
Offers fellowships in urban affairs or public administration to women aged thirty to fifty.

CENTER FOR WOMEN AT
   MASSASOIT
290 Thatcher St.
Brockton, Mass. 02402
617 588-9100 ext. 223
CC CL ICH LC

EDUCATIONAL EXCHANGE OF
   GREATER BOSTON
17 Dunster St.
Cambridge, Mass. 02138
617 876-3080
ICH—in adult education

GEORGE WASHINGTON
   UNIVERSITY
CONTINUING EDUCATION
   FOR WOMEN
2130 H St., N.W.
Washington, D.C. 20037
202 676-7036
CL ICH

HARTFORD COLLEGE
   COUNSELING CENTER
   FOR WOMEN
50 Elizabeth St.
Hartford, Conn. 06105
203 236-5838
CC TB

HOFSTRA UNIVERSITY
CAREER HORIZONS
  FOR WOMEN
Institute for Community
  Education
Hofstra University
Hempstead, N.Y. 11050
CC   EmR   VT

INFORMATION AND
  COUNSELING CENTER
  FOR WOMEN
215 Park St.
New Haven, Conn. 06520
203   436-8242
CC   CL
Fee: $10 annually.

MARYMOUNT MANHATTAN
  COLLEGE
221 East 71st St.
New York, N.Y. 10021
212   861-4200
CL   ICH
Offers special management
program for women, employ-
ment-related courses, and career information.

MASSACHUSETTS INSTITUTE
  OF TECHNOLOGY
SPECIAL ASSISTANT TO THE
  CHANCELLOR FOR WOMEN
  AND WORK
Cambridge, Mass. 02139
CC

MERLIN D. BISHOP CENTER
U-56

University of Connecticut
Storr, Conn. 06268
203   486-3441
CC   VT

MONTGOMERY COLLEGE
  OFFICE OF COMMUNITY
  SERVICES
Rockville, Md. 20805
CC

NEW CAREERS
  DEVELOPMENT CENTER
184 Fifth Ave.
New York, N.Y. 10010
212   598-7644
CC   EmR   ICH

NEW DIRECTIONS
Pace University
1 Pace Plaza
New York, N.Y. 10038
212   285-3688-3689
CC   CL   ICH

Arranges special class schedules, registration, and counseling for college women with
families.

NEW ENGLAND SCHOOL
  FOR PEDIATTS
67 Newbury St.
Boston, Mass. 02116
617   536-7257
EmR   VT

Training program for para-
professional child-care workers. Admission requirements:

CC = Career Counseling	JP = Job Placement
CL = Career Library	LC = Legal Counseling
EmR = Employment Referral	TB = Talent Banks
ICH = Information Clearing House	VT = Vocational Training

high-school diploma and aptitude for child care.
Application and testing fee: $25. Tuition: $750.

NEW JERSEY STATEWIDE
TASK FORCE ON CAREER
EDUCATION
549 Lenox Ave.
Westfield, N.J. 07090
201   232-0870
CC   ICH

NEW SCHOOL FOR
SOCIAL RESEARCH
HUMAN RELATIONS
WORK-STUDY CENTER
66 W. 12th St.
New York, N.Y. 10011
212   675-2700

OPTIONS FOR WOMEN
8419 Germantown Ave.
Philadelphia, Pa. 19118
215   CH 2-4955
CC   CL   JP
Fee varies with service.

PHILADELPHIA OPPOR-
TUNITIES FOR WOMEN
Strawbridge & Clothier,
11th Fl.
8th & Market Sts.
Philadelphia, Pa. 19105
215   925-4346
CL   EmR   ICH

RADCLIFFE INSTITUTE
3 James St.
Cambridge, Mass. 02138
617   495-8211
CC   CL

ROCKLAND COUNTY (N.Y.)
GUIDANCE CENTER
FOR WOMEN
10 N. Broadway

Nyack, N.Y. 10960
914   358-9390
CC   CL   VT

SUFFOLK UNIVERSITY
WOMEN'S PROGRAM
COMMITTEE
Ridgeway Lane Bldg.
Rm. 18
Boston, Mass. 02114
617   723-4700
CL   ICH

TRADE UNION WOMEN'S
STUDIES
New York State School of
Industrial and Labor
Relations
Cornell University
7 E. 43rd St.
New York, N.Y. 10017
212   697-2247
CL   ICH   VT

Program of education in labor studies. Represents most occupations and industries with labor unions.

Publications: "First New York Trade Union Women's Conference," Jan. 1974, $1; "Women in the International World of Work," $1; book, *Trade Union Women*, Wertheimer and Nelson, Feb. 1975, Praeger, $12.50

WASHINGTON OPPOR-
TUNITIES FOR WOMEN
Rm. 101, 1111 20th St., N.W.
Washington, D.C. 20036
202   393-6151
CC   EmR   CL   ICH

Publication: *Washington Opportunities for Women — A Guide to Work and Study*

WOMEN'S ACTION
ALLIANCE, INC.
370 Lexington Ave.
New York, N.Y. 10017
212 685-0800
Communications l i n k for
local projects designed to help
women improve their status.
Currently developing a general referral network of feminist lawyers, doctors, psychologists, and other professionals.
Publications: I n f o r mation
packets of sex discrimination in work, organizing
multiservice women's centers,
the women's movement, and
how to organize a child-care
center. Write for publications
and price list.

WOMEN'S LAW CENTER
1414 Ave. of the Americas
Suite 1100
New York, N.Y. 10019
212 838-8118
ICH LC
See "Legal Services"

WOMEN'S OPPORTUNITY
RESEARCH CENTER
(WORC)
Division of Continuing
Education
Middlesex Community
College
Springs Rd.
Bedford, Mass. 01730
617 275-1590
CC CL EmR ICH JP TB VT

SOUTH

CENTER FOR CONTINUING
EDUCATION OF WOMEN
(CCEW)
Miami-Dade Community
College
300 N.E. Second Ave.
Miami, Fla. 33132
305 577-6840
CC CL EmR ICH TB
Offers classes for women and
a consulting agency.
No charge for assessment in-
terview; $15 for nine-week
course.

DIUGUID FELLOWSHIP
PROGRAM
c/o Executive Director
Council of Southern
Universities
705 Peachtree St., N.E.
Suite 484
Atlanta, Ga. 30308
Provides scholarships for one

CC = Career Counseling
CL = Career Library
EmR = Employment
        Referral
ICH = Information
        Clearing House

JP = Job Placement
LC = Legal Counseling
TB = Talent Banks
VT = Vocational Training

year of retraining, independent or university study. Preference given to women whose careers are delayed by family, etc. Grants only for Southern schools.

DUKE UNIVERSITY
  CONTINUING EDUCATION

East Duke Bldg.
Durham, N.C. 27706
919 684-6259
CC CL ICH

EMORY UNIVERSITY
  COMMUNITY EDUCATION
  SERVICES
Atlanta, Ga. 30322

MIDWEST

APPLIED POTENTIAL
P.O. Box 19
Highland Park, Ill. 60035
312 432-0620
CC CL EmR ICH TB

ASSOCIATION FOR
  CONTINUING HIGHER
  EDUCATION
1700 Asp Ave.
Norman, Okla. 73069
405 325-1021
Membership open to individuals, agencies, and institutions involved in continuing education programs. Dues: $20 for individual, $30 for agency, $100 for institution per year.
Publications: Newsletter, $7.50 per year; other relevant materials

CAREER CLINIC FOR
  MATURE WOMEN, INC.
628 Nicollet Mall
Minneapolis, Minn. 55402
612 335-8255
CC

CENTER FOR WOMEN'S AND
  FAMILY LIVING EDUCATION

University of Wisconsin,
  Extension
428 Lowell Hall
610 Langdon St.
Madison, Wis. 53706
608 262-1411

CHICAGO WOMEN'S
  LIBERATION UNION
852 W. Belmont
Chicago, Ill. 60657
312 348-4300
LC
Operates legal clinic, women's g r a p h i c s collective, rape crisis line, and employment-rights project, among others. Work groups plan programs around such issues as health care, pregnancy testing, and community outreach.
Publications: Newsletter distributed to members, and newspaper, *Womankind*, publicizes issues and events of interest to women.

CONTINUING EDUCATION
  FOR WOMEN
Western Michigan University
Kalamazoo, Mich. 49008
CC CL EmR ICH

No fee for counseling;
fee for workshops.

DRAKE UNIVERSITY
  CONTINUING EDUCATION
  FOR WOMEN
Center for Continuing
  Education
Des Moines, Iowa 50311
515 271-2183
CC EmR ICH VT
Organized to help women
realize personal, educational,
and career goals. Offers programs in career development,
credit and noncredit courses,
and a legal assistant training
program.

FLEXIBLE OPPORTUNITIES
  IN ST. LOUIS FOR
  COLLEGE-EDUCATED
  WOMEN
School of Continuing
  Education
P.O. Box 1099
Washington University
St. Louis, Mo. 63130
314 863-0100, ext. 4261
Seminars and workshops for
women to acquire or update
skills in fields with flexible
part-time and full-time oppor-
tunities. Courses include land-
scape, design, communica-
tions and writing, medical-
historian training, etc.

INDIANA UNIVERSITY
  CONTINUING EDUCATION
  FOR WOMEN
Owen Hall 302
Bloomington, Ind. 47401
812 337-1684
CC ICH TB VT
Fee for educational services;
counseling is free.

MIDWEST CONTINUING
  PROFESSIONAL EDUCATION
  FOR NURSES
1401 S. Grand Blvd.
St. Louis, Mo. 63104

MIDWEST WOMEN'S
  LEGAL GROUP
56 W. Randolph St.
Chicago, Ill. 60601
312 641-1906
LC
Trains paraprofessionals.

MINNESOTA PLANNING AND
  COUNSELING CENTER
  FOR WOMEN
University of Minnesota
301 Walter Library
Minneapolis, Minn. 55455
CC

PHILIP MORRIS
  SCHOLARSHIP FUND
c/o Carole Johnson
Manager of Urban Affairs
Philip Morris, Inc.
100 Park Ave.

CC = Career Counseling	JP = Job Placement
CL = Career Library	LC = Legal Counseling
EmR = Employment Referral	TB = Talent Banks
ICH = Information Clearing House	VT = Vocational Training

New York, N.Y. 10017
Scholarships to women
twenty-five or older completing undergraduate program
at a community or four-year
college in southwestern
Michigan.

PROJECT EVE
Cuyahoga Community
  College
2900 Community College
  Ave.
Cleveland, Ohio 44115
216   241-5966, ext. 209
CC   CL   ICH   JP   VT

UNIVERSITY OF WISCONSIN
  OFFICE OF ADULT
  EDUCATION
Green Bay, Wis. 54302
414   465-2102
Group career workshop once
a year.

WISCONSIN COORDINATING
  COUNCIL FOR WOMEN IN
  HIGHER EDUCATION
University of Wisconsin
Stevens Pt., Wis. 55481
ICH   LC
Membership limited to faculty
women.

WEST

ASSOCIATION FOR WOMEN'S
  ACTIVE RETURN TO
  EDUCATION (AWARE)
5820 Wilshire Blvd.
Suite 605
Los Angeles, Calif. 90036
213   476-3146
ICH   VT
Activities centered in Cali-
fornia, Texas, and Arizona.
Small scholarships awarded to
undergraduate women return-
ing to school.
Publications: *The Minerva
Quarterly*, Membership
Directory

CENTER FOR CONTINUING
  EDUCATION FOR WOMEN,
  BERKELEY CAMPUS
205 Women's Faculty Club
Berkeley, Calif. 94720
CC   CL   EmR   ICH

COLLEGE OF SAN MATEO,
  CALIF.

DISTAFF DISCOVERY
  PROGRAM
San Mateo, Calif. 94402
CC   CL   ICH
Concerned with communica-
tions skills and leadership
positions in communications.

CONCENTRATED EMPLOY-
  MENT PROGRAM
730 Polk
San Francisco, Calif. 94109
415   771-7100
ICH   VT
Paid training programs in
auto mechanics, electrical
wiring, nursing, etc. Programs
change every month.

INDIVIDUAL DEVELOPMENT
  CENTER
1020 E. John
Seattle, Wash. 98102
206   329-5528
CC   CL   EmR   ICH

OREGON STATE SYSTEM OF
  HIGHER EDUCATION
DIVISION OF CONTINUING
  EDUCATION
WOMEN'S PROGRAMS
P. O. Box 1491
Portland, Oreg. 97207
503   229-4849
ICH

PEPPERDINE COLLEGE
  WOMEN'S PROGRAM
8035 S. Vermont Ave.
Los Angeles, Calif. 90044
Offers a B.S. in Administrative Science to prepare
women for executive positions.

RESEARCH CENTER ON
  WOMEN
Loretto Heights College
3001 S. Federal Blvd.
Denver, Colo. 80236
303   936-8441, ext. 253
CC   CL

UCLA EXTENSION PROGRAM
INFORMATION CENTER FOR
  WOMEN
10995 Le Conte Ave.,
  Rm. 215
Los Angeles, Calif. 90024
CC   CL   EmR   ICH   TB

WOMEN'S OPPORTUNITIES
  CENTER
University of California

Irvine, Calif. 92664
714   833-7128
CC   CL   EmR   ICH
Continuing education services

WOMEN'S RE-ENTRY
  EDUCATION PROGRAMS
DeAnza College
21250 Stevens Creek Blvd.
Cupertino, Calif. 95014
Academic programs in sixteen
Bay Area community colleges for women re-entering
school. Focus on practical
education and skill development.

WOMEN'S VOCATIONAL
  INSTITUTE
593 Market St., Suite 516
San Francisco, Calif. 94105
415   495-8044
CC   CL   EmR   ICH
Offers vocational counseling
and awareness courses, workshops   in   problem-solving,
tutorials for employment or
educational exams, management-training   courses,   and
special   programs   for   gay
women, Third World women,
and ex-offenders.

Fees: $15 for 12 1-hour
classes; $8.50 for "economically disadvantaged"; $5 for
workshops.

CC = Career Counseling
CL = Career Library
EmR = Employment
          Referral
ICH = Information
          Clearing House

JP = Job Placement
LC = Legal Counseling
TB = Talent Banks
VT = Vocational Training

D

Government Publications and Services

WOMEN'S BUREAU PUBLICATIONS

The Women's Bureau of the Department of Labor is a clearinghouse of information on a variety of subjects related to employment, including vocational programs, continuing education, career planning, and nontraditional fields.

The publications listed below for which no price is indicated and single copies of other publications may be obtained free from the Women's Bureau, Wage and Labor Standards Administration, U.S. Department of Labor, Washington, D.C. 20210.

Publications for which a price is listed may be purchased from the Superintendent of Documents, U.S. Government Printing Office, Washington, D.C. 20402, with a discount of 25 percent on orders of 100 copies or more of the same publication. A check or money order made payable to the Superintendent of Documents should accompany orders.

Women's Bureau Regional Offices
Region I—1612-C JFK Bldg., Boston, Mass. 02203
Region II—1515 Broadway, New York, N.Y. 10036
Region III—3535 Market St., Philadelphia, Pa. 19104
Region IV—1371 Peachtree St., N.E., Atlanta, Ga. 30309
Region V—230 S. Dearborn St., Chicago, Ill. 60604
Region VI—1100 Commerce St., Dallas, Tex. 75202
Region VII—911 Walnut St., Kansas City, Mo. 64106
Region VIII—1961 Stout St., Denver, Colo. 80202

Region IX—450 Golden Gate Ave., P.O. Box 36017, San Francisco, Calif. 94102

Region X—506 Second Ave., Seattle, Wash. 98104

Bureau of Labor Statistics Regional Offices

Women's Bureau publications may be purchased also from the Regional Offices, Bureau of Labor Statistics, U.S. Department of Labor, at any of the following addresses:

Region I—1603 JFK Bldg., Boston, Mass. 02203

Region II—1515 Broadway, New York, N.Y. 10036

Region III—P.O. Box 13309, Philadelphia, Pa. 19107

Region IV—1371 Peachtree St., N.E., Atlanta, Ga. 30309

Region V—300 S. Wacker Dr., Chicago, Ill. 60606

Region VI—1100 Commerce St., Rm. 6B7, Dallas, Tex. 75202

Regions VII and VIII—911 Walnut St., Kansas City, Mo. 64106

Regions IX and X—450 Golden Gate Ave., P.O. Box 36017, San Francisco, Calif. 94102

About the Women's Bureau

Functions and Services of the Women's Bureau. 1969

A Doughty Lady Turns 50. Reprint from *Manpower*, March 1970.

About Women Workers

Why Women Work. 1974

The Myth and the Reality. 1974

Women Workers (by State). (Reports for 50 states, Puerto Rico, Virgin Islands, the District of Columbia, and the Washington, D.C., Standard Metropolitan Statistical Area)

Highlights of Women's Employment and Education. 1974

Twenty Facts on Women Workers. 1974

Women Workers Today. 1973

Facts about Women Heads of Households and Heads of Families. 1973

A Guide to Sources of Data on Women and Women Workers for the United States and for Regions, States, and Local Areas. 1972

Calling All Women in Federal Service: Know Your Rights and Opportunities. Leaflet 53. 1972. 35¢.

Who Are the Working Mothers? Leaflet 37. 1972. 25¢
Women Workers in Regional Areas and in Large States and
  Metropolitan Areas, 1971. 1972
Guide to Conducting a Consultation on Women's Employ-
ment With Employers and Union Representatives. Pamphlet
12. 1971
Automation and Women Workers. 1970
Facts About Women's Absenteeism and Labor Turnover. 1969
Household Employment—New Careers in an Old Business.
  Reprint from *Word Magazine*, February 1969
Charts: (8 x 10½ inches, black and white):
  Women Are Underrepresented as Managers and Skilled
    Craft Workers. 1974
  Most Women Work Because of Economic Need. 1974
  Fully Employed Women Continue to Earn Less than Fully
    Employed Men of Either White or Minority Races. 1974

CAREER OPPORTUNITIES FOR WOMEN

Steps to Opening the Skilled Trades to Women. 1974
Careers for Women in the 70's. 1973. 50¢
Counseling Women for Careers in Business. Reprint from
  The Personnel Woman, July/August 1973
Help for the Woman Breadwinner. Reprint from *Manpower*,
  February 1973
Look Who's Wearing Lipstick! Reprint from *Manpower*,
  December 1972
Why Not Be—
  an Apprentice? Leaflet 52. (In press)
  an Engineer? Leaflet 41. 1971. 25¢
  a Medical Technologist? Leaflet 44. 1971
  a Technical Writer? Leaflet 47. 1971. 25¢
  an Urban Planner? Leaflet 49. 1970. 25¢
  an Optometrist? Leaflet 42. 1968

Education and Training
Get Credit for What You Know. Leaflet 56. 1974. 25¢
Career Planning for High School Girls. Reprint from *Occu-
pational Outlook Quarterly*, Summer 1973
Continuing Education Programs and Services for Women.
  Pamphlet 10. 1971. $1.55
Help Improve Vocational Education for Women and Girls
  in Your Community. 1971. 25¢

Child-Care Services

Day Care Facts. Pamphlet 16. 1973. 60¢

Day Care: An Employer's Plus. 1973

Employer Personnel Practices and Child Care Arrangements of Working Mothers in New York City. 1973

Children on Campus: A Survey of Pre-Kindergarten Programs at Institutions of Higher Education in the United States. 1973

Federal Funds for Day Care Projects. Pamphlet 14. 1972. $1.40

Day Care Services: Industry's Involvement. Bulletin 296. 1971. $1.00

Child Care Services Provided by Hospitals. Bulletin 295. 1970

Special Groups

Facts on Women Workers of Minority Races. 1974

Fact Sheet on Women of Spanish Origin in the United States. 1972

How You Can Help Reduce Barriers to the Employment of Mature Women. 1969

Women in Labor Unions. Reprint from *Monthly Labor Review*, February 1971

Negro Women in the Population and in the Labor Force. 1967

College Women Seven Years After Graduation: Resurvey of Women Graduates—Class of 1957. Bulletin 292. 1966

Standards and Legislation Affecting Women

Steps to Advance Equal Employment Opportunity for Women. 1974

A Working Woman's Guide to Her Job Rights. Leaflet 55

State Hours Laws for Women: Changes in Status Since the Civil Rights Act of 1964. 1974

State Equal Rights Amendments. 1973

Brief Highlights of Major Federal Laws and Orders on Sex Discrimination. 1974

Laws on Sex Discrimination in Employment: Federal Civil Rights Act, Title VII—State Fair Employment Practices Laws—Executive Orders. Reprinted 1973 with new appendixes.

New Law Liberalizes Child Care Deductions. Legislative
Series 1. 1972

Education Act Extends Sex Discrimination and Minimum
Wage Provisions. Legislative Series 2. 1973

Divorce Laws as of October 1, 1973. (Table) (In press)

Marriage Laws as of October 1, 1973. (Table) (In press)

Conozca Sus Derechos. Leaflet 39-A. 1967. (Spanish translation of "Know Your Rights")

ADDITIONAL GOVERNMENT PUBLICATIONS

Virtually every department of the government publishes its
own newsletter and/or magazine. Here are a few examples:

Occupational Outlook Quarterly: $3 for a 2-year subscrip-
tion, which can be obtained from the Bureau of Labor
office nearest you. This quarterly covers:
- Career prospects in traditional and nontraditional fields
- Training opportunities
- Educational assistance available
- New "manpower" (some day the name will change)
  developments

The locations of Bureau of Labor offices are as follows:

1603 Federal Bldg.
Boston, Mass. 02203

P.O. Box 13309
Philadelphia, Pa. 19101

300 South Wacker Dr.
Chicago, Ill. 60606

1100 Commerce St., Rm. 6B7
Dallas, Tex. 75202

1515 Broadway
New York, N.Y. 10036

1371 Peachtree St., N.E.
Atlanta, Ga. 30309

911 Walnut St.
Kansas City, Mo. 64106

450 Golden Gate Ave.
San Francisco, Calif. 94102

Manpower is the official monthly magazine of the Department of Labor's Manpower Administration, which administers
80 percent of the manpower programs funded by the federal
government. The magazine is designed for officials in industry, labor, and government who want to know what is
being done about employment. Apparently it isn't designed
for people working or looking for jobs—which makes it all

the more interesting for you to read. It costs $7.50 a year, but it might be worth it for a foxy view from inside the chicken coop.

To order:

> *Manpower*
> Superintendent of Documents
> Government Printing Office
> Washington, D.C. 20402

Occupational Outlook Handbook, published each year by the U.S. Department of Labor, Bureau of Labor Statistics, is available at any public library.

The *Handbook* has the basics on 800 occupations and 30 major industries gathered from labor unions, government agencies, colleges, universities, trade associations. Look up the job or field you're exploring and you'll find description of work, future labor demands, the actual work a person on the job does, and other statistics.

FEDERAL JOB INFORMATION CENTERS

Alabama

BIRMINGHAM
Federal Bldg., Rm. 259,
1800 5th Ave. North 35203;
(205) 325-6091

HUNTSVILLE
806 Governors Dr. S. W.
Southerland Bldg.,
  35801;
(205) 539-3781

MOBILE
First National Bldg.,
107 St. Francis St. 36602;
(205) 433-3581 (Ext. 237)

MONTGOMERY
Arnov Bldg.,
Rm. 357,
474 South Court St. 36104;
(205) 265-5611 (Ext. 321)

In other Northern Alabama locations dial 1-800-572-2970.
In other Southern Alabama locations dial 1-800-672-3075.

Alaska

ANCHORAGE
Hill Bldg.,
632 Sixth Ave. 99501;
(907) 272-5561 (Ext. 751)

FAIRBANKS
Rampart Bldg., Suite 7,
529 Fifth Ave. 99701;
(907) 452-1603

In other Alaska locations dial the operator and ask for Zenith 1600.

Arizona

PHOENIX
Balke Bldg.,
44 West Adams St. 85003;
(502) 261-4736

TUCSON
Federal Bldg., Rm. 105,
Scott and Broadway Sts.
  85702;
(602) 792-6273

In other Arizona locations
dial 1-800-352-4037.

Arkansas

LITTLE ROCK
Federal Bldg., Rm. 1319,
700 W. Capitol Ave. 72201;
(501) 378-5842

In other Arkansas locations
dial 1-800-482-9300.

California

FRESNO
Federal Bldg.,
1130 O St. 93721;
(209) 487-5062

LONG BEACH
1340 Pine Ave. 90813;
(213) 591-2331

LOS ANGELES
Eastern Columbia Bldg.,
851 South Broadway 90014;
(213) 688-3360

OAKLAND
Post Office Bldg., Rm. 215,
13th and Alice Sts. 94612;
(415) 273-7211

SACRAMENTO
Federal Bldg., Rm. 4210,
650 Capitol Mall 95814;
(916) 449-3441

SAN BERNARDINO
380 West Court St. 92401;
(714) 884-3111 (Ext. 395)

SAN DIEGO
Suite 100,
1400 Fifth Ave. 92101;
(714) 293-6165

SAN FRANCISCO
Federal Bldg., Rm. 1001,
450 Golden Gate Ave.,

Box 36122, 94102;
(415) 556-6667

SANTA MARIA
Post Office Bldg., Rm. 207,
120 West Cypress St. 93454;
(805) 925-9719

Colorado

COLORADO SPRINGS
Cascade Square, Suite 108,
228 N. Cascade, 80902;
(303) 633-0384

DENVER
Post Office Bldg., Rm. 203,
18th and Stout Sts. 80202;
(303) 837-3506

In other Colorado locations
dial 1-800-332-3310.

Connecticut

HARTFORD
Federal Bldg., Rm. 716,
450 Main St. 06103;
(203) 244-3096

In other Connecticut locations dial 1-800-842-7322.

Delaware

WILMINGTON
U.S. Post Office and
   Courthouse Bldg.,
11th and King Sts. 19801;
(302) 658-6911 (Ext. 540)

In other Delaware locations
dial 1-800-292-9560.

District of Columbia

METROPOLITAN AREA
U.S. Civil Service Com-
   mission, Rm. 1416,
1900 E Street, N.W. 20415;
(202) 737-9616

277

Florida

MIAMI
Federal Bldg., Rm. 804,
51 S.W. First Ave. 33130;
(305) 350-5794

ORLANDO
3101 Maguire Bldg. 32803;
(305) 894-3771
In other locations West of the
Apalachicola River dial
1-800-633-3023

In other locations East of the
Apalachicola River dial
1-800-432-0263.

Georgia

ATLANTA
Federal Bldg.,
275 Peachtree St. N.E.
30303;
(404) 526-4315

MACON
Federal Bldg.,
451 College St. 31201;
(912) 743-0381 (Ext. 2401)
In other Northern Georgia
locations dial
1-800-282-1670.

In other Southern Georgia
locations dial
1-800-342-9643.

Hawaii

HONOLULU AND OTHER
  OAHU LOCATIONS
1000 Bishop St.,
Suite 1500 96813;
(808) 546-8600

From other Hawaiian Islands
dial the operator and ask for
the FJIC's "Enterprise 8052"
number (toll-free).

Idaho

BOISE
Federal Bldg.,
U.S. Courthouse, Rm. 663,
550 W. Fort St. 83702;
(208) 342-2711 (Ext. 2427)

In other Idaho locations dial
1-800-632-5916

Illinois

CHICAGO
Dirksen Bldg., Rm. 1322,
219 South Dearborn St.
  60604;
(312) 353-5136

ROCK ISLAND
208 18th St., 61201;
(309) 788-6396

WAUKEGAN
2504 Washington St. 60085;
(312) 336-2770

In other Illinois locations dial
*800-972-8388.

Indiana

INDIANAPOLIS
Century Bldg., Rm. 102,
36 South Pennsylvania St.
  46204;
(317) 633-8662

In other Indiana locations
dial *800-382-1030.

Iowa

DES MOINES
191 Federal Bldg.,
210 Walnut St. 50309;
(515) 284-4546

In other Iowa locations dial
1-800-362-2066.

Kansas

WICHITA
One-Twenty Bldg., Rm. 101,
120 S. Market St. 67202;
(316) 267-6311 (Ext. 106)

In other Kansas locations
dial 1-800-362-2693.

Kentucky

LOUISVILLE
Federal Bldg., Rm. 167,
600 Federal Pl. 40202;
(502) 582-5130

In other Kentucky locations
dial 1-800-292-4585.

Louisiana

NEW ORLEANS
Federal Bldg. South,
600 South St. 70130;
(504) 527-2764

In other Louisiana locations
dial 1-800-362-6811.

Maine

AUGUSTA
Federal Bldg., Rm. 611,
Sewall St. & Western Ave.
  04330;
(297) 622-6171 (Ext. 269)

In other Maine locations dial
1-800-452-8732.

Maryland

BALTIMORE
Federal Bldg.,
Lombard St. and Hopkins Pl.
  21201;
(301) 962-3822

D.C. METRO. AREA
U.S. Civil Service Com-
  mission, Rm. 1416,

1900 E. St. N.W. 20415;
(202) 737-9616

In other Maryland locations
dial *800-492-9515.

Massachusetts

BOSTON
Post Office and Courthouse
  Bldg., Rm. 1004, 02109;
(617) 223-2571

In other Massachusetts locations dial 1-800-882-1621.

Michigan

DETROIT
Lafayette Bldg. Lobby,
144 W. Lafayette St. 48226;
(313) 226-6950

In other Michigan locations
dial *800-572-8242.

Minnesota

TWIN CITIES
Federal Bldg., Rm. 196,
Fort Snelling, Twin Cities,
  55111;
(612) 725-3355

In other Minnesota locations
dial 1-800-552-1244.

Mississippi

JACKSON
802 N. State St. 39201;
(601) 948-7821 (Ext. 594)

In other Mississippi locations
dial 1-800-222-8090.

Missouri

KANSAS CITY
Federal Bldg., Rm. 129,

601 E. 12th St. 64106;
(816) 374-5702

ST. LOUIS
Federal Bldg., Rm. 1712,
1520 Market St. 63103;
(314) 622-4285

In other Western Missouri
locations dial
1-800-892-7650.

In other Eastern Missouri
locations dial
1-800-392-3711.

Montana

HELENA
IBM Bldg.,
130 Neill Ave. 59601;
(406) 442-9040 (Ext. 3388)

In other Montana locations
dial *800-332-3410.

Nebraska

OMAHA
U.S. Court and Post Office
 Bldg., Rm. 1014,
215 N. 17th St. 68102;
(402) 221-3815

In other Nebraska locations
dial 1-800-642-9303.

Nevada

LAS VEGAS
Federal Bldg., Rm. 1-614,
300 Las Vegas Blvd. South,
 89101;
(702) 385-6345

RENO
Federal Bldg., Rm. 1004,
300 Booth St. 89502;
(702) 784-5535

In other Nevada locations
dial *800-992-3080.

New Hampshire

PORTSMOUTH
Federal Bldg., Rm. 104,
Daniel and Penhallow Sts.
 03801;
(603) 436-7720 (Ext. 762)

In other New Hampshire
locations dial
1-800-582-7220.

New Jersey

NEWARK
Federal Bldg.,
970 Broad St. 07102;
(201) 645-3673

In other New Jersey locations
dial 1-800-242-5870.

New Mexico

ALBUQUERQUE
Federal Bldg.,
421 Gold Ave. S.W. 87101;
(505) 843-2557

In other New Mexico loca-
tions dial *800-432-6837.

New York

NEW YORK CITY
Federal Bldg.,
26 Federal Plaza 10007;
(212) 264-0422

THE BRONX
590 Grand Concourse 10451;
(212) 292-4666

BROOKLYN
271 Cadman Plaza, East
 11201;
(212) 624-1000 (Ext. 256)

JAMAICA
Marine Midland Bank Bldg.,
89-64 163rd St. 11432;
(212) 526-6192

SYRACUSE
O'Donald Bldg.,
301 Erie Blvd. W. 13202;
(315)   473-5660
In Upstate N.Y. locations
dial *800-962-1470.
In the Downstate N.Y. counties of Suffolk, Dutchess,
Rockland, Orange, Putnam,
and N. Westchester, dial
800-522-7407; in the counties
of Nassau and S. Westchester
dial (212) 264-0422.

North Carolina

RALEIGH
Federal Bldg.,
310 New Bern Ave.,
  P.O. Box 25069, 27611;
(919)   755-4361
In other North Carolina locations dial 1-800-662-7720.

North Dakota

FARGO
Federal Bldg., Rm. 200,
657 Second Ave. N. 58102;
(701)   237-5771 (Ext. 363)
In other North Dakota locations dial *800-342-4781.

Ohio

CINCINNATI
Federal Bldg., Rm. 10503,
550 Main St. 45202;
(513)   684-2351
CLEVELAND
Federal Bldg.,
1240 Ninth St. 44109;
(216)   522-4232
COLUMBUS
Federal Bldg., Rm. 237,

85 Marconi Blvd. 43215;
(614)   469-5640
DAYTON
Grant-Deneau Bldg.,
  Rm. 610,
40 West 4th St. 45402;
(513) 451-4830 (Ext. 5540)
In other Northern Ohio locations dial 1-800-362-2910.
In other Southern Ohio locations dial *800-762-2435.

Oklahoma

OKLAHOMA CITY
210 Northwest Sixth St.
  73102;
(405)   231-4948.
In other Oklahoma locations
dial 1-800-522-3781.

Oregon

PORTLAND
Multnomah Bldg. Lobby,
319 Southwest Pine St.
  97204;
(503)   221-3141
In other Oregon locations
dial *800-452-4910.

Pennsylvania

HARRISBURG
Federal Bldg., Rm. 168,
  17108;
(717)   782-4494
PHILADELPHIA
Federal Bldg.,
6th and Market Sts. 19106;
(215)   597-7440
PITTSBURGH
Federal Bldg.,
1000 Liberty Ave. 15222;
(412)   644-2755

In other Eastern Pennsylvania locations dial 1-800-462-4050.

In other Central and Western Pennsylvania locations dial 1-800-242-0588.

Rhode Island

PROVIDENCE
Federal and Post Office Bldg., Rm. 310,
Kennedy Plaza 02903;
(401)   528-4447

South Carolina

CHARLESTON
Federal Bldg.,
334 Meeting St. 29403;
(803)   577-4171 (Ext. 328)

COLUMBIA
Main Post Office Bldg., Rm. 426 29201;
(803)   765-5387

In other South Carolina locations dial 1-800-922-3790.

South Dakota

RAPID CITY
Dusek Bldg., Rm. 118,
919 Main St. 57701;
(605)   348-2221

In other South Dakota locations dial *800-742-8944.

Tennessee

MEMPHIS
Federal Bldg.,
167 N. Main St. 38103;
(901)   534-3956

In other Tennessee locations dial 1-800-582-6291.

Texas

CORPUS CHRISTI
Downtown Postal Station, Rm. 105,
701 N. Upper Broadway 78401;
(512)   883-5511 (Ext. 362)

DALLAS
Rm. IC42,
1100 Commerce St. 75202;
(214)   749-3156

EL PASO
National Bank Bldg.,
411 N. Stanton St. 79901;
(915) 533-9351 (Ext. 5388)

FORT WORTH
819 Taylor St. 76102;
(817)   334-3484

HOUSTON
702 Caroline St. 77002;
(713)   226-5501

SAN ANTONIO
Post Office and Courthouse Bldg.,
615 E. Houston St. 78205;
(512) 225-5511 (Ext. 4343)

In other Northern Texas locations dial 1-800-492-4400.

In other Gulf Coast Texas locations dial
1-800-392-4970.

In other South Central Texas locations dial
1-800-292-5611.

In other Western Texas locations dial *800-592-7000.

Utah

OGDEN
Federal Bldg., Rm. 1413,
324 25th St. 84401;
(801)   399-6854

SALT LAKE CITY
Federal Bldg.,
Annex, 135 S. State St.
  84111;
(701)   524-5744
In other Utah locations dial
1-800-662-5355.

Vermont

BURLINGTON
Federal Bldg., Rm. 317,
Elmwood Ave. and Pearl St.
  05401;
(802)   862-6501 (Ext. 259)
In other Vermont locations
dial 1-800-642-3120.

Virginia

NORFOLK
415 St. Paul's Blvd. 23510;
(703)   625-6515
RICHMOND
Federal Bldg.,
400 N. 8th St. 23240;
(703)   782-2732

D.C. METRO. AREA
U.S. Civil Service Com-
  mission, Rm. 1416,
1900 E. St. N.W. 20415;
(202)   737-9616

In other Virginia locations
dial *800-582-8171.

Washington

SEATTLE
Federal Bldg.,
First Ave. and Madison St.
  98104;
(206)   442-4365

SPOKANE
U.S. Post Office, Rm. 200,

904 Riverside 99210;
(509)   456-2536
TACOMA
Washington Bldg., Rm. 610,
1019 Pacific Ave. 98402;
(206)   627-1700
VANCOUVER
Call 693-0541
In other Washington locations
dial *800-552-0714.

West Virginia

CHARLESTON
Federal Bldg.,
500 Quarrier St. 25301;
(304)   343-6181 (Ext. 226)
In other West Virginia locations dial *800-642-9027.

Wisconsin

MILWAUKEE
Plankinton Bldg., Rm. 205,
161 West Wisconsin Ave.
  53203;
(414)   224-3761
In other Wisconsin locations
dial 1-800-242-9191.

Wyoming

CHEYENNE
Teton Bldg., Rm. 108,
1805 Capitol Ave. 82001;
(307) 778-2220 (Ext. 2108)
In other Wyoming locations
dial 1-800-442-2766.

Puerto Rico

SAN JUAN
Pan Am Bldg.,
255 Ponce de Leon Ave.
Hato Rey 00917;
(809)   765-0404 (Ext. 209)

BUREAU OF APPRENTICESHIP AND TRAINING

Regional Offices

REGION I (serves Connecticut, Maine, Massachusetts, New Hampshire, Rhode Island, Vermont)
John F. Kennedy Federal Bldg., Room 1703-A
Government Center
Boston, Mass. 02203

REGION II (serves New Jersey, New York, Puerto Rico, Virgin Islands)
1515 Broadway, 37th Floor
New York, N.Y. 10036

REGION III (serves Delaware, Maryland, Pennsylvania, Virginia, West Virginia)
P.O. Box 8796
Philadelphia, Pa. 19101

REGION IV (serves Alabama, Florida, Georgia, Kentucky, Mississippi, North Carolina, South Carolina, Tennessee)
1371 Peachtree Street, N.E., Room 700
Atlanta, Ga. 30309

REGION V (serves Illinois, Indiana, Michigan, Minnesota, Ohio, Wisconsin)
300 South Wacker Drive, 13th Floor
Chicago, Ill. 60606

REGION VI (serves Arkansas, Louisiana, New Mexico, Oklahoma, Texas)
1512 Commerce Street, Room 704
Dallas, Tex. 75201

REGION VII (serves Iowa, Kansas, Missouri, Nebraska)
Federal Office Bldg., Room 2107
911 Walnut Street
Kansas City, Mo. 64106

REGION VIII (serves Colorado, Montana, North Dakota, South Dakota, Utah, Wyoming)
Republic Bldg., Room 232A
1612 Tremont Place
Denver, Colo. 80202

REGION IX (serves Arizona, California, Hawaii, Nevada)
450 Golden Gate Avenue, Room 9001
P.O. Box 36017
San Francisco, Calif. 94102

REGION X (serves Alaska, Idaho, Oregon, Washington)
Arcade Plaza Building, Room 2055
1321 Second Avenue
Seattle, Wash. 98101

STATE APPRENTICESHIP AGENCIES

(Including the District of Columbia, Puerto Rico, and the Virgin Islands)

ARIZONA

Arizona Apprenticeship Council
1623-B West Adams
Phoenix 85007

CALIFORNIA

Division of Apprenticeship Standards
Department of Industrial Relations
455 Golden Gate Avenue
P.O. Box 603
San Francisco 94102

COLORADO

Apprenticeship Council
Industrial Commission Offices
200 East Ninth Avenue, Room 216
Denver 80203

CONNECTICUT

Apprenticeship Training Division
Labor Department
200 Folly Brook Boulevard
Wethersfield 06109

DELAWARE

State Apprenticeship and Training Council
Department of Labor and Industry
618 North Union Street
Wilmington 19805

DISTRICT OF COLUMBIA

D.C. Apprenticeship Council
555 Pennsylvania Avenue, NW, Room 307
Washington 20212

FLORIDA

Bureau of Apprenticeship
Division of Labor
State of Florida Department of Commerce
Caldwell Building
Tallahassee 32304

HAWAII

Apprenticeship Division
Department of Labor and Industrial Relations
825 Mililani Street
Honolulu 96813

KANSAS

Apprentice Training Division
Department of Labor

401 Topeka Boulevard
Topeka 66603

KENTUCKY

Kentucky State Apprentice-
ship Council
Department of Labor
Frankfort 40601

LOUISIANA

Division of Apprenticeship
Department of Labor
State Capitol Annex
P.O. Box 44063
Baton Rouge 70804

MAINE

Maine Apprenticeship
Council
Department of Labor
and Industry
State Office Building
Augusta 04330

MARYLAND

Maryland Apprenticeship
and Training Council
Department of Labor
and Industry
203 East Baltimore Street
Baltimore 21202

MASSACHUSETTS

Division of Apprentice
Training
Department of Labor
and Industries
State Office Building
Government Center
100 Cambridge Street
Boston 02202

MINNESOTA

Division of Voluntary
Apprenticeship
Department of Labor
and Industry
110 State Office Building
St. Paul 55110

MONTANA

Montana State
Apprenticeship Council
1331 Helena Avenue
Helena 59601

NEVADA

Nevada Apprenticeship
Council
Department of Labor
Capitol Building
Carson City 89701

NEW HAMPSHIRE

New Hampshire
Apprenticeship Council
Department of Labor
State House Annex
Concord 03301

NEW MEXICO

New Mexico
Apprenticeship Council
Labor and Industrial
Commission
1010 National Building
505 Marquette, NW
Albuquerque 87101

NEW YORK

Bureau of Apprentice
Training
Department of Labor
The Campus, Building #12
Albany 12226

NORTH CAROLINA

Division of Apprenticeship
Training
Department of Labor
Raleigh 27602

OHIO

Ohio State Apprenticeship
Council
Department of Industrial
Relations
220 Parsons Avenue,
Room 314
Columbus 43215

OREGON

Apprenticeship and
Training Division
Oregon Bureau of Labor
Room 115, Labor and
Industries Building
Salem 97310

PENNSYLVANIA

Pennsylvania Apprenticeship
and Training Council
Department of Labor
and Industry
Room 1547
Labor and Industry Building
Harrisburg 17120

PUERTO RICO

Apprenticeship Division
Department of Labor
414 Barbosa Avenue
Hato Rey 00917

RHODE ISLAND

Rhode Island Apprenticeship
Council
Department of Labor
235 Promenade Street
Providence 02908

UTAH

Utah State Apprenticeship
Council
Industrial Commission

431 South 6th East
Room 225
Salt Lake City 84102

VERMONT

Vermont Apprenticeship
Council
Department of
Industrial Relations
State Office Building
Montpelier 05602

VIRGIN ISLANDS

Division of Apprenticeship
and Training
Department of Labor
Christiansted, St. Croix 00820

VIRGINIA

Division of Apprenticeship
Training
Department of Labor
and Industry
P.O. Box 1814
9th Street Office Building
Richmond 23214

WASHINGTON

Apprenticeship Division
Department of Labor
and Industries
314 East 4th Avenue
Olympia 98504

WISCONSIN

Division of Apprenticeship
and Training
Department of Labor,
Industry and Human
Relations
Box 2209
Madison 53701

E

Women's Centers

Prepared by the Project on the Status and Education of Women Association of American Colleges, 1818 R Street, N.W., Washington, D.C. 20009.

Alabama

Women's Center
Office of Woman's Affairs
Miles College
5500 Ave. G
Birmingham, 35208

The Association for
  New Women
P.O. Box U-27
307 Gaillard Dr.
Mobile, 36688

Alaska

Fairbanks Women's Coop
University of Alaska
c/o Student Activities
Fairbanks, 99701

Arizona

Associated Women Students
Jeanne Rice, AWS President
Arizona State University
Memorial Union 252-C
Tempe, 85281
602 965-3438

Tempe Women's Center
1414 S. McAllister
Tempe, 85281
602 968-0743

Tucson's Women's Center
838 North 4th Ave.
Tucson, 85705

Women's Collective
829 N. 5th Ave.
Tucson, 85705
602 792-1890

Arkansas

Women's Center of
  Fayetteville
c/o Mary Cochran, Billie
  Traynam, Nancy Sindon
University of Arkansas
902 W. Maple St.
Fayetteville, 72701

California

Women's Studies Program
c/o Kathy Marshall

California State University
Arcata, 95521

Center for Continuing
   Education for Women &
   Women's Center
c/o Diana Gong
University of California
Building T-9, Room 100
Berkeley, 94720
415   642-4786

Female Liberation
University of California
516 Eshelman Hall
Berkeley, 94720

Men's Center
2700 Bancroft Way
Berkeley, 94704
415   845-4823

Women's Center
Addison Street
Berkeley, 94720

Women's Center
Graduate Theological Union
2378 Virginia Avenue
Berkeley, 94709

Women's Center
2134 Allston (downstairs)
Berkeley, 94704
415   548-4343

Women's Coffee House
Unitas House
2700 Brancroft
Berkeley, 94704

Chico Women's Center
c/o Marilyn Murphy
932 Alder St.
Chico, 95926

Women's Studies Center
California State University,
   Chico
Chico, 95926

Women's Center
Orange Coast College
2701 Fairview Road
Costa Mesa, 92626

Women's Center Office
Costa Mesa
1926 Placentia #15
Costa Mesa, 92627

Davis Women's Center
c/o Sandi McCubbin,
   Coordinator
University of California,
   Davis
TB-124
Davis, 95616

Women's Educational Center
c/o Cindi Conway
California State College of
   Dominguez Hills
1000 East Victoria
Dominguez Hills, 90246

Women's Task Force
c/o Hessel Flitter
Ohlone College
P.O. Box 909
Fremont, 94537

Women's Center
c/o Doris N. Deakins,
   Assoc. Dean of Students
Fresno City College
1101 University Ave.
Fresno, 93741
209   262-4721

Women's Center
c/o Diane Reeves
California State University
Fullerton, 92634

Women's Education Program
   Director, Women's Center
c/o Kathleen M. Zanger
Ganilan Community College

5055 Santa Teresa
Gilroy, 95020

Women's Center
c/o Pat Lienhard
Glendale Community College
1500 N. Verdugo Rd.
Glendale, 91208

Isla Vista Women's Center
6504 Pardall Rd., #2
Goleta, 93017

Women's Center
c/o Lynne Tuscono
Community Projects Office
University of California
Irvine, 92664

Women's Opportunities
  Center
University of California
Irvine, 92664
714   833-7128

Women's Programs—
  Extension
c/o Dr. Mary Lindenstein
  Walshok
University of California
  Extension
P.O. Box 109
La Jolla, 92037

Continuing Education
  Center for Women
c/o Beverly O'Neill, Director
Long Beach City College
4901 E. Carson Blvd.
Long Beach, 90815

Women's Center
c/o Karen Johnson

California State University
6407 Bayard Street
Long Beach, 90815

Center for Women's Studies
c/o Lucile Todd, Director
Pepperdine University

1121 W. 79th St.
Los Angeles, 90044

Los Angeles Women's
  Liberation Center
c/o Margo Miller
746 S. Crenshaw
Los Angeles, 90005
213   936-7219

Womanspace
11007 Venice Blvd.
Los Angeles, 90034

Women's Resource Center
Carol Adams, Director
UCLA Powell Library
  Rm. 90
405 Hilgard Ave.
Los Angeles, 90024
213   825-3945

Women's Center
P.O. Box 1501
Monterey, 93940

YWCA of Los Angeles
East Valley Center
5903 Laurel Canyon Blvd.
North Hollywood, 91607

Women's Studies Research
  Institute
c/o Myra Strober
Stanford University
Graduate School of Business
Palo Alto, 94305

Women's Information and
  Counseling Center
c/o Stephanie Coles
Contra Costa College
405 Santa Fe Ave.
Point Richmond, 94801

Women's Center
Diane LeBow, Advisor
Canada College
4200 Farm Hill Blvd.
Redwood City, 94061

Riverside Women's Center
3122 Panorama St.
Riverside, 92506

Women's Center
4459-2 Orange Grove
Riverside, 92501

Women's Survival Center
c/o Dr. Janice Wilson,
   Director
California State University,
   Sonoma
1801 E. Cotati Ave.
Rohnert Park, 94928

Continuing Education
   for Women
Sacramento State University
Sacramento, 95819

Sacramento Women's Center
YWCA Building
17th and L
Sacramento, 95819

Women's Studies—CSUS
California State University,
   Sacramento
6000 J St.
Sacramento, 95819

Monterey County Peace
   Center (Women's Center)
P.O. Box 1364
Salinas, 93901

Valice
205 Laurel Ave.
San Anselmo, 94960

Woman's Way
412 Red Hill Ave., Suite 9
San Anselmo, 94960

Center for Women's
   Studies and Services
California State University
908 F St.
San Diego, 92101

Center for Women's
   Studies and Services
4004 39th St.
San Diego, 92105

Women's Liberation
Aztec Center,
   Organizational Center
San Diego State College
San Diego, 92105

American Indian
   Women's Center
227 Valencia
San Francisco, 94103

Bay Area Consortium of
   Continuing Education of
   Women
c/o Dr. Mary Janet,
   Prof. of Chemistry
Lone Mountain College
San Francisco, 94118

Haight-Ashbury
   Women's Center
#10 Ryan St.
San Francisco, 94117

Intersection Women's Night
756 Union St.
San Francisco, 94133

San Francisco Women's
   Switchboard
c/o YWCA
620 Sutter St.
San Francisco, 94102
415   771-8212

Women's Center for
   Creative Counseling
San Francisco:
   415   648-1509
San Mateo: 342-0278
Daly City: 756-4736

Women's Legal Center
558 Capp St.
San Francisco, 94110

Women's Need Center
558 Clayton St.
San Francisco, 94117

San Jose Women's Center
9th & San Carlos Bldg.
San Jose, 95114

Women's Center
San Jose State University
San Jose, 95114

Women's Center
c/o Ms. Elizabeth Burdash,
  Coordinator
College of San Mateo
1700 W. Hillsdale Blvd.
San Mateo, 94402

Women's Center and
  Emergency Housing,
  YWCA
1618 Mission St.
San Raphael, 94901
415   456-0782

Feminist Women's Health
  Center of Orange County
429 S. Sycamore St.
Santa Ana, 92701

Continuing Education for
  Women
c/o Myrtle Blum
Department of Psychology
University of California
Santa Barbara, 93107

Women's Center, Santa Cruz
314 Laurel St.
Santa Cruz, 95060

Stanford Women's Center
P.O. Box 2633
Stanford, 94305
415   321-2300, ext. 314

West Side Women's Center
218 W. Venice Blvd.
Venice, 90291
213   823-4774

Women's Center
2914 Grand Canal
Venice, 90291

Women's Center
c/o Angela Lask
El Camino College
16007 Crenshaw Blvd.
Via Torrence, 90506

Colorado

Resource Center for Women
Adams State College
San Luis Ranch
Allamosa, 81101

University of Colorado
  Women's Center
c/o Darcy Sease
UMC 334
Boulder, 80302

Women's Center
1520 Euclid
Boulder, 80302

Gay Women's Center
c/o Debby Squires
2460 S. Ogden
Denver, 80210

Research Center on Women
Loretto Heights College
3001 S. Federal Blvd.
Denver, 80236

Virginia Neal Blue Center
Colorado Women's College
1800 Pontiac St.
Denver, 80220

Women's Center
1452 Pennsylvania, #17
Denver, 80203

Women's Resource Center
c/o Joann Albright
University of Denver
University Park
Denver, 80210

Women's Studies Program
c/o Dr. Barbara Blansett
Metropolitan State College
Denver, 80210

Women's Crisis &
  Information Center
c/o Carol Gillespie, Director
Colorado State University
629 S. Howes St.
Ft. Collins, 80521
303   493-3888

Women's Research Center
c/o Mary Leonard
Office of Women's Relations
112 Student Services
Colorado State University
Ft. Collins, 80521
303   491-6383

Center for Women
c/o Meg Nichols
Mesa College
Mesa Junior College Dist.
Grand Junction, 81501

Virginia Neal Blue
  Women's Resource Center
c/o Nancy Frank
Southern Colorado State
  College
Pueblo, 81001

Connecticut

Every Woman's Center
YWCA of Greater Bridgeport
c/o Lillie Margaret Lazaruk
968 Fairfield
Bridgeport, 06606
203   334-6154

Asnuntuck Community
  College
c/o Michael J. Moran,
  Director of Library
  Services

P.O. Box 68
Enfield, 06082

Women's Center
c/o Barbara Crossea
87 Ridgefield St.
Hartford, 06112

Women's Liberation Center
  of Greater Hartford, Inc.
c/o Lynn Gall
11 Amity St.
Hartford, 06106
203   523-8949

Wesleyan Women's Center
Wesleyan University
High St.
Middletown, 06520

Women's Center
115 College St.
Middletown, 06457
203   346-4042

Union Theological Women's
  Center
3438 Yale Station
New Haven, 06520

University Women's
  Organization and Information Counseling Center
Yale University
215 Park St.
New Haven, 06520
203   436-0272

Women's Center
Yale University
Divinity School
Bacon Bldg.
New Haven, 06520

Women's Center
198 Elm St.
New Haven, 06520

Counseling Center for
  Women

c/o Ms. Marlene Adelman,
    Director
Norwalk Community College
33 Wilson Ave.
Norwalk, 06854

Women's Liberation Center
11 N. Main St.
South Norwalk, 06856

Women's Center
c/o Teri Eblen, Donna
    MacDonnell-Johnson
University of Connecticut
U-8 Student Union
Storrs, 06268

Continuing Education for
    Women
c/o Elizabeth Roper
University of Connecticut,
    Torrington Branch
University Dr.
Torrington, 06790

Delaware

Education Services for
    Women
c/o Mae R. Carter,
    Program Specialist
University of Delaware
John M. Clayton Hall
Newark, 19711
302   738-2211

Women's Center
c/o Episcopal Student Center
University of Delaware
57 E. Park Pl.
Newark, 19711

District of Columbia

Black Women's Institute
National Council of Negro
    Women
1346 Connecticut Ave. N.W.
Washington, 20036

Continuing Education for
    Women
c/o Dr. Ruth Osborn,
    Assistant Dean
GWU College of General
    Studies
George Washington
    University
2029 K St. N.W.
Washington, 20006

Institute for Continuing
    Education for Women
c/o Dr. Beverly B. Cassara,
    Acting Director
Federal City College
1424 K St. N.W.
Washington, 20001
202   727-2824

Trinity College Women's
    Center
Trinity College
Michigan Ave. N.E.
Washington, 20002

Washington Area Women's
    Center, Inc.
1736 R St. N.W.
Washington, 20009
202   232-5145

Women's Center
Catholic University
Michigan Ave. N.E.
Washington, 20017

Women's Phone
c/o Community Bookstore
2028 P St. N.W.
Washington, 20036

Florida

Women's Commission
c/o Dr. Evelyn Helmich
    Hireley
University of Miami
Coral Gables, 33124

Career Planning for
  Disadvantaged Women
c/o Ms. Chloe Atkins
Santa Fe Community College
P.O. Box 1530
3000 N.W. 83rd St.
Gainesville, 32601

Options (Women's Center)
1825 Hendricks Ave.
Jacksonville, 32207
904   398-7728

Council for Continuing
  Education for Women
c/o Betty Kaynor,
  Coordinator
Miami-Dade Junior College
141 N.E. 3rd Ave.
Miami, 33132

Institute for Women
c/o Charlotte R. Tatro,
  Director
Florida International
  University
Tamiami Trail
Miami, 33144

Women's Information Center
6255 S.W. 69th St.
South Miami, 33143

Women's Center
2554 1st Ave., N.
St. Petersburg, 33713
813   822-1856

Tallahassee Women's Educational and Cultural Center
c/o Debora K. Patterson
Florida State University
212 Mabry Heights,
  FSU Box 6826
Tallahassee, 32306
904   599-4049 or 559-3281

Tampa Women's Center
P.O. Box 1350
Tampa, 33601

Tampa Women's Center
214 Columbia Dr., #3
Tampa, 33606

Women's Center
c/o Joyce Davis
3215 Walcraft Rd.
Tampa, 33611

The Women's Center
405 Grand Central Ave.
Tampa, 33604

Women's Center
University of South Florida
Student Organizations Office
Box 438 University Ctr.
Tampa, 33620

Georgia

A Woman's Place
140 Marion Dr.
Athens, 30601

Atlanta Woman's Center
c/o Jane Kelley
1315 Stillwood Dr., N.E.
Atlanta, 30306

Women's Center
Midtown YWCA
45-11th St.
Atlanta, 30303

Hawaii

CEW, University of Hawaii
c/o Marion Saunders
931 University Ave., #205
Honolulu, 96914

Women's Center
University YWCA
1820 University Ave.
Honolulu, 96822

Women's Studies
c/o Doris Ladd
University of Hawaii, Manoa
Spalding 252
Honolulu, 96822

Idaho

University of Idaho
  Women's Center
c/o Jane E. Langenes,
  Student Advisory Services
108 Administration Bldg.
Moscow, 83843
208 885-6616

Women's Center
Idaho State University
Pocatello, 83201

Illinois

Women's Center
c/o Ms. Sue Palmer
Aurora College
Aurora, 60507

Carbondale Women's Center
c/o Rita Moss
1202 W. Schwartz
Carbondale, 62901

Continuing Education for
  Women
c/o Edith C. Spees, Director
Southern Illinois University
Pulliam Hall, Room 110
Carbondale, 62901

Women's Center
404 W. Walnut
Carbondale, 62901

Student Personnel Office for
  Continuing Education for
  Women
Betty L. Hembrough,
  Assistant Dean
University of Illinois
130 Student Services
610 E. John St.
Champaign, 61820
217 333-3137

Chicago Ecumenical
  Women's Center
c/o Janet H. Miller

5751 S. Woodlawn, #111
Chicago, 60637

Chicago Women's
  Liberation Union
852 W. Belmont
Chicago, 60657
312 348-4300

Ecumenical Women's Center
  in Chicago
Northside Center
1653 W. School
Chicago, 60657

Loop Center, YWCA
37 S. Wabash
Chicago, 60603
312 372-6600

M.O.R.E. for Women
5465 South Shore Dr.
Chicago, 60615

Sister Center
United Church of
  Rogers Park
Morris at Ashland
Chicago, 60626

The Sisters Center
Northside Women's
  Liberation
7071 Glenwood
Chicago, 60626

Women's Center
  North Area
1016 N. Dearborn St.
Chicago, 60610
312 337-4385

Women's Center
  Southwest Area
3134 W. Marquette Rd.
Chicago, 60629
312 436-3500

Women's Center
  South Suburban
45 Plaza, Park Forest

Chicago, 60466
312 748-5660

Women's Center
  Uptown
4409 N. Sheridan Rd.
Chicago, 60640
312 561-6737

Women's Center
  West Side
5082 W. Jackson Blvd.,
  2nd Floor
Chicago, 60644
312 379-8332

Women's Center
6200 S. Drexel St.
Chicago, 60637
312 955-3100

Women's Center
3322 N. Halsted St.
Chicago, 60657
312 935-4270

Women's Center
436 E. 39th St.
Chicago, 60653
312 285-1434

Women's Studies Center
535-3 Lucinda
Northern Illinois University
Chicago, 60625

Women's Studies
  Committee
Mundelein College
6363 N. Sheridan Rd.
Chicago, 60620

Women's Institute
20 E. Jackson, Rm. 902
Chicago, 60657
312 922-6749

Women's Studies Center
c/o Mary Siegler
Northern Illinois University
540 College View Court

Dekalb, 60115
815 752-0110

Kendall College
  Women's Center
2408 Orrington
Evanston, 60201

Women of Northwestern
c/o Ms. Carol Slatkin,
  Ms. Carol Owen
Northwestern University
Evanston, 60201

Women's Liberation Center
  of Evanston
2214 Ridge St.
Evanston, 60201
312 471-3380 (A.M.)

Prelude
c/o Ms. Vicki Kessler
Knox College
Galesburg, 61401

Student Services
College of Lake County
19351 W. Washington St.
Grayslake, 60030

Women's Center
  West Suburban
1 S. Park St.
Lombard, 60148
312 629-0170

Association of Women
  Students
c/o Ms. Ayn Crowley
Monmouth College
Monmouth, 61462

Greenerfields, Unlimited
c/o Sonja T. Mast, Carol R.
  Godwin, Nancy C. Robin-
  son, Katrina Johnson
318 Happ Rd.
Northfield, 60093
312 446-0525

"A Woman's Place"
401 W. California
Urbana, 61801

Indiana

Office for Women's Affairs
Indiana University
Memorial Hall, East
Bloomington, 47401
812   337-3849

Women's Center
414 N. Park
Bloomington, 47401
812   366-8691

Continuing Education for
    Women
c/o Janet R. Walker
University of Evansville
P.O. Box 329
Evansville, 47701

Span Plan
c/o Cecilia Zissis, Director
Purdue University
Office of Dean of Women
Lafayette, 47907

South Bend Women's Center
1125 Thomas St.
South Bend, 46625

Purdue Women's Caucus
c/o Joyce Field,
    Corresponding Secretary
Purdue University
Krannert Graduate School of
    Industrial Administration
West Lafayette, 47906
317   463-1736

Iowa

Dean of Women's Office
c/o Anne Doolin
Mt. Mercy College
1330 Elmhurst Dr., N.E.
Cedar Rapids, 52402

Continuing Education for
    Women Section
c/o Betty Durden,
    Vice-chairperson
Drake University
Des Moines, 50311

Women's Information Center
YWCA
8th and Grand
Des Moines, 50309
515   244-8961

University of Iowa
    Women's Center
3 E. Market St.
Iowa City, 52240
515   353-6265

Women's Committee
c/o Barbara Fassler, Director
Central College
Pella, 50219

Kansas

Lawrence Women's Center
University of Kansas
1314 Oread
Lawrence, 66044

University of Kansas
    Commission on the
    Status of Women
Dean of Women's Office
Lawrence, 66044

Women's Resource Center
Kansas State University
Manhattan, 66506

A.W.A.R.E.
Wichita State University
Wichita, 67208

Kentucky

Lexington Women's Center
120 Kentucky Ave.
Lexington, 40502

Women's Center Director
Brescia College, Lafiat Hall
120 W. 7th St.
Owensboro, 42301

Louisiana

New Orleans
  Women's Center
1422 Felicity St.
New Orleans, 70130

Women's Liberation Center
P.O. Box 19001
New Orleans, 70119

Maine

Women's Center
University of Maine, Augusta
University Heights
Augusta, 04330

Women's Center
P.O. Box 914
Bangor, 04401

Brunswick/Bath
  Women's Center
136 Main St.
Brunswick, 04011

Maryland

Woman Center
c/o Susan Dubrow
University of Maryland
9010 Riggs Rd., Apt. 205
Adelphi, 20783

Baltimore Women's
  Liberation
101 E. 25th St., Suite B2
Baltimore, 21218
301   366-6475

Continuing Education
  for Women
Morgan State College
Baltimore, 21239

Towson Women's Center
c/o Annette Flower,
  English Department
Towson State College
Baltimore, 21204
301   823-7500, ext. 826

Women's Center
Towson State College
P.O. Box 203
Baltimore, 21204

Women's Center
Essex Community College
P.O. Box 9596
Baltimore, 21237

Women's Center
Johns Hopkins University
Box 1134, Levering Hall
Baltimore, 21218
301   235-3637 or 336-3300,
  ext. 529

Women's Center
St. Mary's College of
  Maryland
Baltimore, 21210

Women's Law Center
P.O. Box 1934
Baltimore, 21203
301   547-1653

Women's Union
University of Maryland,
  Baltimore County
5401 Wilkens Ave.
Baltimore, 21203
301   455-2446

Women's Center
Catonsville Community
  College
800 S. Rolling Rd.
Catonsville, 21228
301   747-3220, ext. 355

Women's Center
University of Maryland
1127 Student Union

College Park, 20742
301   454-5411

Women's Information Center
4110 School of Library and
  Information Services
College Park, 20742
301   454-5441

Women's Resource Center
c/o Valerie Kitch
8905 Footed Ridge
Columbia, 21045
301   454-5411

Women's Center
c/o Judy Gray and
  Nancy Hume
Essex Community College
Rm. 17, Red Temporaries
Essex, 21221
301   682-6000

Women's Center
c/o Carol Blimline,
  Counselor
Montgomery College
Rockville, 20830

St. Mary's Women's Center
c/o Nancy Schniedewind
St. Mary's College
St. Mary's City, 20688

Women's Center
Goucher College
P.O. Box 1434
Towson, 21204

GYN Clinic
Western Maryland College
Westminster, 21157

Massachusetts

Everywoman's Center
c/o Pat Sackrey
University of Massachusetts
Munson Hall, Room A
Amherst, 01002
413   545-0883

Men's Center
Jones Library
Amherst, 01002

Southwest Women's Center
University of Massachusetts
John Quincy Adams Lobby
Amherst, 01002

Southwest Women's Center
c/o Judith Katz
Southwest, University of
  Massachusetts
c/o Washington Lobby
Amherst, 01002
413   545-0626

Third World Women's Center
University of Massachusetts
Amherst, 01002

The Women's Caucus
University of Massachusetts
School of Education
Amherst, 01002

Andover Women's Center
224 Lowell St.
Andover, 01810

Women's Opportunity
  Research Center
Middlesex Community
  College
Division of
  Continuing Education
Springs Road
Bedford, 01730

Boston University Female
  Liberation
George Sherman Union
775 Commonwealth
Boston, 02215

Boston University
  Women's Center
c/o Sue McKeon
211 Bay State Rd.
Boston, 02215
617   353-4240

Pregnancy Counseling Service
  of Boston
3 Joy St.
Boston, 02108

Women's Center
Boston State College
174 Ipswich St.
Boston, 02115

Women's Center
P.O. Box 286
Prudential Center
Boston, 02199

Women's Center
Simmons College
300 The Fenway
Boston, 02115

Crittenston Hastings House
10 Perthshire Rd.
Brighton, 02135

Female Liberation
639 Massachusetts Ave.
Cambridge, 02139

Library Collective
492 Putnam Ave.
Cambridge, 02139

Radcliffe Institute
c/o Alice K. Smith, Dean
Radcliffe College
3 James St.
Cambridge, 02138
617   495-8211

Women and Work
c/o Dr. Mary Potter Rowe
Massachusetts Institute
  of Technology
Cambridge, 02139

Women's Center
46 Pleasant St.
Cambridge, 02139
617   354-8807

Women's Research Center

123 Mt. Auburn
Cambridge, 02139

Women's Center
c/o Ms. Margaret Fletcher
Bristol Community College
64 Durfee St.
Fall River, 02720

Simon's Rock Early College
Great Barrington, 02130

Community Women's Center
c/o Rebecca Winburn
208-310 Main St.
Greenfield, 01301
413   773-7519

Greenfield Women's Center
Federal St.
Greenfield, 01301

Women's Caucus
c/o Janet Levine,
  Coordinator
1 Kennedy Dr.
Hadley, 01035

Lowell Women's Center
Lowell YWCA
50 Elm St.
Lowell, 01852
617   445-5405

Continuing Education for
  Women
Suzanne Lipsky,
  Office of the Dean
Jackson College
Tufts University
Medford, 02155

YWCA Women's
  Resource Center
2nd Floor Recreation Room
Sears Roebuck & Co.
Natick Mall
Natick, 01760

New Bedford
  Women's Center

241 Reed St.
New Bedford, 02747

Women's Resource Center
Andover-Newton
  Theological School
215 Herrick Rd.
Newton Centre, 02159

Southeastern Massachusetts
  University Women's Center
Southeastern Massachusetts
  University
North Dartmouth, 02747
617 997-9321, ext. 698

Sophia Sisters: Smith College
  Lesbian Liberation
c/o Annie Korn
Clark House, Smith College
Northampton, 01060

Valley Women's Center
c/o Cheryl Schaffer
200 Main St.
Northampton, 01060
413 586-2011

Women's Center
6 Goswald St.
Provincetown, 02675
617 487-0387

Eastern Nazarene College
c/o Ann Kiemel,
  Dean of Women
23 E. Elm
Quincy, 02170

North Shore Women Center
Pat Watson
58 High St.
Rockport, 01966

Women's Center
Salem State College
Salem, 01970

Somerville Women's
  Health Project
326 Somerville Ave.
Somerville, 02143

Women's Center
Mt. Holyoke College
3 Brigham
South Hadley, 01075

Springfield Women's Center
451 State St.
Springfield, 01101
413 732-7113

Women's Health
  Counseling Service
115 State St.
Springfield, 01103

Brandeis University
  Women's Center
c/o Rona Shribman
20 Stanley Rd.
Swampscott, 01907
617 598-2188

Lowell Women's Center
c/o Ruth Yaw
90 10th St.
Tewksbury, 01876

Women's Center
Clark University
Worcester, 01610

Worcester
  Pregnancy Counseling
52 Burncoat St.
Worcester, 01603

Worcester Women's Center
905 Main St.
Worcester, 01610
617 753-9622

Worcester Women's
  Resource Center
Worcester YWCA
2 Washington St.
Worcester, 01608
716 791-3183

Michigan

Office of Women's Programs
c/o Barbara Zikmund,

Co-director
Albion College
Albion, 49224

Center for
  Continuing Education
c/o Jean Campbell, Director
University of Michigan
330 Thompson St.
Ann Arbor, 48108

Feminist House
225 E. Liberty, Rm. 203
Ann Arbor, 48104

Gay Advocate Office
Michigan Union
530 S. State
Ann Arbor, 48104
313   763-4186

Women's Resource Center
Kellogg Community
  Collective Library
Battle Creek, 49016

The Women's Center
Lake Michigan College
Benton Harbor, 49022

Alternative Resource Center
c/o Mandella
16261 Petoskey
Detroit, 48221

Detroit Women's Liberation
415 Brainard
Detroit, 48201

Women's Action and
  Aid Center
103 W. Alexandrine
Detroit, 48201

East Lansing Women's Center
223½ E. Grand River
East Lansing, 48823

ENCORE Program
Aquinas College
Grand Rapids, 49506

Women's Resource Center
c/o June Mochizuki,
  Director CEW
Western Michigan University
Kalamazoo, 49001

Women's Center for
  Continuing Education
Northern Michigan
  University
Marquette, 49855

Continuum Center for
  Women
c/o Eleanor Driver, Director
Continuing Education
  Division
Oakland University
Rochester, 48063

Chrysallis Center
c/o Dr. Margaret Cappone,
  Director
Saginaw Valley College
University Center, 48710

Women's Center
Delta College
University Center, 48710

East Michigan University
c/o Bette C. White, Assistant
  Dean of Students
Ypsilanti, 48197

Minnesota

Duluth Women's Center
University of
  Duluth Medical School
EPIC, Rm. 5
Duluth, 55812

Woman to Woman Center
University of Minnesota
101 Kirby Student Center
Duluth, 55812

Grace High School
  Women's Center

1350 Gardena Ave., N.E.
Fredley, 55432

Mankato Women's Center
Mankato State College
426½ N. 4th St.
Mankato, 56001

Lesbian Resource Center
710 W. 22nd St.
Minneapolis, 55405
612   374-2345

Minnesota Women's Center
c/o Anne Truax, Director
University of Minnesota
306 Walter Library
Minneapolis, 55455

Women's Clearinghouse
c/o Experimental College
1507 University Ave., S.E.
Minneapolis, 55414
612   376-7449

Women's Counseling Service
621 W. Lake St.
Minneapolis, 55408

Women's Center
c/o Joletta Crooks
Concordia College
Moorhead, 56560

St. Olaf Women's
   Resource Lounge
St. Olaf College
Northfield, 55057

Mississippi

Gay Counseling & Ed.
   Projects, Anne de Bary
Mississippi Gay Alliance

Box 4470 Mississippi
   State Union
State College, 39762

Women's Action Movement
Mississippi State University

P.O. Box 1328
State College, 39762

Missouri

CEW
Margot Patterson,
   Coordinator
Univ. of Missouri
Coop. Extension Services
Carthage, 64836

Women's Center
501 E. Rollins
Columbia, 65201

Women's Liberation Union
5138 Tracy
Kansas City, 64110

Women's Resource Service
Univ. of Missouri
Div. for Continuing
   Education
1020 E. 63rd St.
Kansas City, 64110

Women's Resource Center
c/o Esther M. Edwards
William Jewel College
Liberty, 64068

CEW
c/o Mrs. Jean M. Pennington
Washington University
P.O. Box 1095
St. Louis, 63130

St. Louis University
   Women's Center
Hussleip Hall
3801 W. Pine
St. Louis, 63108

St. Louis Women's Center
c/o Margaret C. Fagin,
   CEW Director
University of Missouri
8001 Natural Bridge Rd.
St. Louis, 63121

St. Louis Women's Center
1411 Locust St.
St. Louis, 63103

Women's Center
c/o Ms. Helen Dieterich
Florissant Valley
   Community College
3400 Pershall Rd.
St. Louis, 63135

Montana

Women's Action Center
Venture Center
University of Montana
Missoula, 59801

Nebraska

Women's Study Group
c/o Dr. Evelyn Haller
Doane College,
   New Dorm 108
Crete, 68333
402   826-2161

Women's Resource Center,
   Lincoln
Rm. 116, Nebraska Union
14th and R Sts.
Lincoln, 68506

Nevada

Women's Resource Center
University of Nevada
Reno, 89507

New Hampshire

Concord Women's Center
130 N. Main St.
Concord, 03103

Franconia Women's Center
Franconia College
Franconia, 03580
603   823-8460

Women's Center of the
   Upper Valley
19 South Main St.
Hanover, 03755
603   643-5981

Laconia Women's Center
c/o Carol Pierce
21 Shore Dr.
Laconia, 03246

Manchester Women's Center
Unitarian Church
Mrytle and Union Sts.
Manchester, 03106

The Women's Center
104 Middle St.
Manchester, 03102

Women's Center
c/o Lissi Savin
P.O. Box 172
Warner, 03278

New Jersey

YWCA Women's Center
Upsala College
Administration Annex 11
East Orange, 07019
201   266-7213

Together
7 State St.
Glassboro, 08028

Women's Center of
   Bergen County
166 Main St.
Hackensack, 07601
201   342-8958

Middlesex County NOW
P.O. Box 94
Iselin, 08830

Women's Center
c/o N. Klein, Director
Brookdale Community
   College

Newman Springs Rd.
Lincroft, 07738

Center for Women's Studies
c/o Dr. Mara M. Vamos
Fairleigh Dickinson
    University
285 Madison Ave.
Madison, 07940
201   377-4700, ext. 369

Drew Women's Collective
c/o Diana Stewart
Drew University
Madison, 07940

AWE Women's Center
c/o Ethel Smyth
P.O. Box 583
Maple Wood, 07040
201   467-1422

Women's Center
Montclair-North Essex
    YWCA
159 Glenridge Ave.
Montclair, 07042

Women's Center
15 W. Main St.
Moorestown, 08057
609   235-9297

Center for the American
    Woman and Politics
Rutgers, The State University
Eagleton Institute of Politics
New Brunswick, 08901
201   247-1766, ext. 1384

Women's Center
Douglass College
New Brunswick, 08903

Women's Center of
    New Brunswick
2 Easton Ave.
New Brunswick, 08901
201   246-9637

Monmouth County NOW
11 Aberdeen Terrace

New Monmouth, 07748
201   671-3213

YWCA Women's
    Center of the Oranges
395 Main St.
Orange, 07052
201   674-1111

Morristown Area NOW
c/o Elizabeth C. Cieri
3379 Route 46, Apt. 16-E
Parsippany, 07054
201   334-6135

Princeton Seminary
    Women's Center
c/o Ms. Martha Bellinger
Princeton Theological
    Seminary
Princeton, 08540

Woman's Place
14½ Witherspoon St.
Princeton, 08540
609   924-8989

Somerset County NOW
147 Stony Brook Rd.
Somerville, 08876
201   722-3866

Summit NOW
34 Canoe Brook Pkwy.
Summit, 07901
201   277-0135

EVE
c/o Betsy Brown, Director
Kean College
Kean Bldg.
Union, 07083

Women's Center
c/o Constance Waller,
    Director
Montclair State College
Upper Montclair, 07405
201   893-5106

Passaic County NOW
P.O. Box 1051 Valley Station

Wayne, 07470
201   274-5042

Women's Center
c/o Viola Wilbanks
Tombrock College
West Paterson, 07424

New Mexico

Albuquerque
    Women's Center
University of New Mexico
1824 Las Lomas
Albuquerque, 87106
505   277-3716

Santa Fe Women's Liberation
c/o Guin Reyes
Santa Fe, 87501
505   982-1225

New York

Astoria Women's Center
44-03 28th Ave.
Astoria, 11102
212   932-5130

Women's Research and
    Resource Center
c/o Dr. Elinor Pam
Queensborough
    Community College
222-03 Garland Dr.
Bayside, 11364
212   423-0666

The Women's Center
Lehman College, CUNY
2468 Jerome Ave.
Fordham Center
Bronx, 10468

Women's Center
Sarah Lawrence College
Bronxville, 10708

Women's Center
c/o Lois Chafee

915 Washington Ave.
Brooklyn, 11225

Women's Studies College
SUNY, Buffalo
108 Winspear Rd.
Buffalo, 14214
716   831-3405

Kirkland College
    Women's Center
Kirkland College
Clinton, 13323

Women's Information Center
P.O. Box 268
Dewitt, 13224

Queens Women's Center
153-11 61 Rd.
Flushing, 11367

Hofstra Women's Center
Hofstra University
Rm. 106, Phillips Hall
Hempstead, 11550

Women's Center,
    Nassau County
14 W. Columbia St.
Hempstead, 11550

Hewlett Women's Center
1007 Broadway
Hewlett, 11557

Women's Center, Islip
1 Grant Ave., off Main St.
Islip, 11751
516   581-2680

Ithaca Women's Center
140 W. State St.
Ithaca, 14850

Women's Center
Cornell University
Willard Straight Hall
Ithaca, 14850

Women's Studies Program
c/o Jennie Farley, Director
Cornell University

431 White Hall
Ithaca, 14850

Westchester Women's Center
S. 6th St. and W. 2nd St.
Mount Vernon, 10550

AIR Gallery
97 Wooster St.
New York, 10012

Barnard Women's Center
c/o Jane S. Gould, Director
Barnard College
606 W. 120th St.
New York, 10027

Career Information Center
c/o Dolores Kaminski
Baruch College, CUNY
17 Lexington Ave.
New York, 10010

N.Y. Theological Seminary
  Women's Center
c/o Ms. Payne
235 E. 49th St.
New York, 10017

N.Y. Women's Center
36 West 22nd St.
New York, 10010

N.Y. Women's Law Center
351 Broadway
New York, 10013
212   431-4074

NOW Center
47 E. 19th St.
New York, 10003

Resource Center on Women
c/o Dr. Claire Fulcher
YWCA
600 Lexington Ave.
New York, 10022
212   753-4700

Upper East Side
  Women's Center
c/o Carol Hardin

359 E. 68th St.
New York, 10021

West Side Woman's Center
210 W. 82nd St.
New York, 10024

Women Photographers
The Midtown Y Gallery
Midtown YM-YWCA
344 E. 14th St.
New York, 10018

Women's Center
N.Y.C. Firehouse
243 West 20th St.
New York, 10011
212   255-9802

Women's Center for Occupation and Educational
  Development
167 East 67th St.
New York, 10021
212   861-0931

Women's Inter-Arts Center
549 W. 62nd St.
New York, 10019
212   246-6570

Northport Women's Center
  (Suffolk)
144 Bayview Ave.
Northport, 11768
516   757-6564

Women's Information Center
Old Westbury
Oyster Bay, 11771

Rockland City Women's
  Liberation Women's Center
St. Stephen's Episcopal
  Church
Pierce Hwy. and
  Eberhardt Rd.
Pearl River, 10965
914   354-7442

Mid-Hudson Women's Center
27 Franklin St.
Poughkeepsie, 12601
914   473-1538

Poughkeepsie
  Women's Center
96 Market St.
Poughkeepsie, 12601
914   454-9487

Rochester Women's Center
139 Raleigh St.
Rochester, 14620

Suffolk Community College
  Women's Group
533 College Rd.
Selden, 11784

Staten Island Women's Center
121 Van Duzen St.
Staten Island, 10301

Women's Center
SUNY at Stony Brook
Stony Brook, 11790

Women's Center for
  Continuing Education
University College
610 E. Fayette St.
Syracuse, 13202

Women's Information Center
104 Avondale Pl.
Syracuse, 13210

Women's Center,
  Academic Center
c/o Sister Margaret Farrara,
  Dean of Students
Elizabeth Seton College
1061 N. Broadway
Yonkers, 10701

North Carolina

Female Liberation
P.O. Box 954
Chapel Hill, 27514

Women's Center
1616 Lyndhurst Rd.
Charlotte, 28203
704   334-9655

Disadvantaged Women in
  Higher Education
1 Incinerator Rd.
Durham, 23824

Women's Center
Guilford College Campus
Greensboro, 27410

Women's Center
c/o Vicki J. Tolston
Chowan College
Murfreesboro, 27855

North Dakota

None Reported

Ohio

Continuing Education Group
University of Cincinnati,
  Raymond Walters College
Cincinnati, 45236

Educational Resource and
  Women's Center
c/o Dean of Women
Xavier University
Cincinnati, 45207

University of Cincinnati
  Women's Center
412 Tuc Woman Affairs
  Council
Cincinnati, 45221

Women's Center
c/o Martha Brown
6728 Alpine Ave.
Cincinnati, 45236

Women's Center
Case Western
  Reserve University
Thwing Study Center

11111 Euclid Ave.
Cleveland, 45118

Columbus Women's
  Liberation
Lutheran Student Center
38 E. 12th Ave.
Columbus, 43201

Dayton Women's Center
1203 Salem Ave.
Dayton, 45400

Office of Special Programs
  for Women
c/o Ms. Verna Graves,
  Coordinator
Wright State University
Dayton, 45431

Women's Center
University of Dayton
P.O. Box 612
Dayton, 45469

Cleveland Women's Center
P.O. Box 2526
East Cleveland, 44112

Women's Center
c/o Ms. Betty Kirschner
Kent State University
Kent Women's Project
Kent, 44242

Women's Center
Oberlin College
Wilder Hall
Oberlin, 44074

AWS Women's
  Resource Center
c/o Anne Bush
Miami University
225 Warfield Hall
Oxford, 45056

Miami University Women's
  Information Center
Miami University
P.O. Box 13, Bishop Hall
Oxford, 45056

Women's Liberation,
  USN Center
410 E. High
Oxford, 45406

Women's Center
c/o Linda J. Headrich
Wittenberg University
966 Pythian Ave.
Springfield, 45504

Women's Programs
c/o Jean Parke, Consultant
The University of Toledo
2801 W. Bancroft St.
Toledo, 43606

Antioch College
  Women's Center
Antioch College
Yellow Springs, 45387
513 767-7331, ext. 311

Oklahoma

Women's Resource Center
University of Tulsa
600 S. College
Tulsa, 74104

Oregon

Office of Women's Studies
c/o Dr. Jeanne Dost
Oregon State University
Corvallis, 97331

Women's Research and
  Study Center
University of Oregon
c/o Sociology Department,
  Joan Acker
Eugene, 97403
503 686-5002

The George House
c/o Mrs. Laura Crockett
Western Baptist Seminary
5511 S.E. Hawthorne
Portland, 97215

Women's Institute and
    Resource Center
Portland State University
Portland, 97207

Pennsylvania

Career-Counseling Center
    for Adult Women
c/o JoAnne Painter,
    Director
Villa Maria College
2551 West Lake Rd.
Erie, 16505

Women's Center
230 W. Chestnut St., 1st fl.
Lancaster, 17603

Bucks County
    Community College
Women's Caucus
c/o Marlene Miller
Hicks Art Center
BCCC
Newton, 18940

Center for Women in
    Medicine
c/o Nina B. Woodside,
    Director
Medical College of
    Pennsylvania
3300 Henry Ave.
Philadelphia, 19129
215   849-0400

Continuing Education for
    Women
c/o Jean McBryde Swanson
Temple University
Mitten Hall, Room 207
Philadelphia, 19122

Philadelphia Women's
    Liberation Center
P.O. Box 19826
Philadelphia, 19143

Women's Center
c/o Cathy Balsley,
    Coordinator
Temple University
Mitten Hall, 1st fl.
Philadelphia, 19122
215   787-7990

Women's Center
c/o Sharon Grossman,
    Coordinator
University of Pennsylvania
3533 Locust Walk
Philadelphia, 19104

Women's Center
4634 Chester Ave.
Philadelphia, 19104
215   729-2001

Women's Resource Center
YWCA Philadelphia
Kensington Branch
174 W. Allegheny Ave.
Philadelphia, 19133

Women's Center
Community College of
    Allegheny County
Allegheny Campus
Pittsburgh, 15212

Women's Liberation House
Pennsylvania State University
245 E. Hamilton Ave.
State College, 16801

Swarthmore Gay Liberation
c/o Christina Crosby
Swarthmore College
Swarthmore, 19081

Rhode Island

Kingston Women's Liberation
University of Rhode Island
Memorial Union
Kingston, 02881

Resource Center for Women
in Higher Education
c/o Dr. Jacqueline Mattfeld,
Director
Brown University
Providence, 02912

Women's
Liberation Umbrella
59 Olive St.
Providence, 02906

Women's Liberation Union
of Rhode Island
P.O. Box 2302,
East Side Station
Providence, 02906

YWCA Women's Center
Jackson St.
Providence, 02903

South Carolina

Women's Center
1106 Hagwood Ave.
Columbia, 29205

Women's Center
Winthrop College
Winthrop Coalition Group
P.O. Box 6763
Rock Hill, 29730

South Dakota

None Reported

Tennessee

Nashville Tennessee
Women's Center
1112 19th Ave. S.
Nashville, 37212
615   327-1969

Women's House
The University of the South
Sewanee, 37375

Texas

Women's Liberation
1106 W. 22nd St.
Austin, 78705

Women for Change Center
20001 Bryan Tower,
Suite 290
Dallas, 75201
214   741-2391

Women's Center
c/o Sandra I. Tinkham,
Director
3118 Fondrell Dr.
Dallas, 75205

Women's Center
c/o Office of the Dean of
Student Programs
Southern Methodist
University
Dallas, 75275

Women's Center
North Texas State University
Denton, 76203

Women's Center
3602 Milam
Houston, 77002

Women's Resource Center
YWCA of Houston
1521 Texas Ave.
Houston, 77002

Austin Women's Center
1208 Baylor St.
West Austin, 78103

Utah

Women's Environ Institute
c/o Jan W. Tyler, Director
and Dean of Women
Weber State College
Harrison Blvd.
Ogden, 84403
801   399-5941

Women's Center
Brigham Young University
Provo, 84601

Women's Resource Center
c/o Shauna M. Adix,
   Director
University of Utah
293 Union Bldg.
Salt Lake City, 84112
801   581-8030

Vermont

Women's Center
217 N. Winooski
Burlington, 05404

Women's Union
c/o Lisa DeMauro,
   Chairperson
Middlebury College
Middlebury, 05753

Feminist Studies
Goddard College
Aiken Dorm
Plainfield, 05667
802   454-8311, ext. 273

Women's Center
c/o Ellen Dorsh/Mary
   Boyle, Directors
Windham College
Putney, 05346

Virginia

None Reported

Washington

Women's Center
c/o Mary Robinson
Women's Commission and
   Occupational Resource
   Center
Western Washington State
   College
Bellingham, 98225

Lesbian Resource Center
YWCA
4224 University Way N.E.
Seattle, 98105
206   632-4747, ext. 3

Seattle Counseling Center
   for Sexual Minorities
1720 16th Ave.
Seattle, 98134
206   329-8737-8707

Women's Center
University of Washington
Seattle, 98195

Women's Guidance Center
Alene H. Moris, Director
1209 N.E. 41st St.
Seattle, 98195

Women's Center
c/o Hallien Johnson
Office of Women's Programs
Spokane Falls Community
   College
3410 W. Fort George
   Wright Dr.
Spokane, 99204

Tacoma Women's Center
c/o Debbie Jordan
1108 N. Fife St.
Tacoma, 98406

Women's Center
Chris Smith, Director
University of Puget Sound
Tacoma, 98416

Women's Center
Tacoma Community College
Tacoma, 98465

Women's Center
c/o Marcia Weidig
Whitman College
Walla Walla, 99362

West Virginia

Women's Center
Beckley College
S. Kanawha St.
Beckley, 25801

Women's Center
Appalachian
    Bible Institute
Bradley, 25818

Women's Information Center
West Virginia University
Bennett House
221 Wiley St.
Morgantown, 26506

Wisconsin

Women's Action Group
c/o Ms. Joan Smith
Northland College
Ashland, 54806

Women's Center
University of Wisconsin
Green Bay, 54302

Center for Women's and
    Family Living Education
430 Lowell Hall
610 Langdon St.
Madison, 53706

Scarlet Letter Collective
University of Wisconsin
    YWCA
306 N. Brooks
Madison, 53715

Women's Center

836 E. Johnson
Madison, 53703

Research Center on Women
c/o Kathleen C. Gigle,
    Coordinator
Alverno College
3401 S. 39th St.
Milwaukee, 53215
414   671-5400

The Women's Center
2110 W. Wells St.
Milwaukee, 53208

The Women's Coalition
c/o Ellen Guiseppi
2211 E. Kenwood Blvd.
Milwaukee, 53211
414   964-7535

Women's Information Center
University of Wisconsin,
    Milwaukee
P.O. Box 189
Milwaukee, 53201

Oshkosh Women's Center
Wisconsin State University
Oshkosh Student Association
Oshkosh, 54900

Women's Center
University of Wisconsin,
    Oshkosh
312 Dempsey Hall
Oshkosh, 54901

Wyoming

None Reported

F

Newsletters and Magazines

The print medium has literally exploded with newsletters and magazines written by women for women and covering every aspect of women's lives. We have selected here those nationally based newsletters that are most immediately concerned with employment and equal rights for women. Reading these newsletters will give you information on job openings, Affirmative Action, legislation, and clues to companies seeking women.

In addition to the groups listed here, many of the listings in the "Occupational Organizations" section also publish newsletters in their field. Contact them for samples and subscription rates.

At the end of this list, you'll find information on other newsletters and magazines that may contain employment information.

Advocates for
  Women Newsletter
564 Market St., Suite 218
San Francisco, Calif. 94104

Extremely informative newsletter on current economic trends, fields o p e n i n g to women, career and employment counseling, and apprenticeship programs. Published monthly.

American Association of
  University Women Journal
2401 Virginia Ave., N.W.
Washington, D.C. 20007

Articles on the status of women in education, industry, government, and the professions. Also general news columns and job-opportunity information. Published seven times a year.

Breakthrough
Interstate Association of
  Commissions on the
  Status of Women
District Bldg., Rm. 204
14th and E Sts., N.W.
Washington, D.C. 20004
News of state and federal
enforcement of equal opportunity laws and legislation
related to enforcement of
equal opportunity public service. Published bimonthly.

Do It Now
National Organization for
  Women (NOW)
1957 E. 73rd St.
Chicago, Ill. 60649
Newsletter of the main headquarters of NOW. News on
activities in the field of equal
rights, state and federal legislation, women, and the media.
Local chapters also publish
newsletters.

The Executive Woman
747 Third Ave.
New York, N.Y. 10017
Information on women in
management, personal interviews, and articles on banking, credit, and legislation.
Often publishes bibliography,
news on women's conven-
tions, as well as job openings.
Published monthly. Subscription: $20.

F.E.W. News and Views
Federally Employed Women
487 National Press Bldg.
Washington, D.C. 20004

Articles on job opportunities
for women in government
and legislation, federal government progress on the Affirmative Action front. Good
inside view of what's happening in the Capitol. Subscription: $10.

The Federation "Alert"
4818 Drummon Ave.
Washington, D.C. 20015
Published by the Federation
of Organizations for Professional Women. Provides information on current political
and economic trends, equal
rights for women, and the
progress of female professionals.

The Feminist Bulletin
262 Scarborough Ave.
Westchester, N.Y. 10510
Articles of general interest to
the women's movement. News
on current legislation, equal
employment, and Affirmative
Action.

*Human Rights for
  Women Newsletter*
1128 National Press Bldg.
Washington, D.C. 20004
Legal information on major
sex-discrimination i s s u e s.
News on the educational and
equal-employment progress of
women.

Know News
Know, Inc.
P.O. Box 86031
Pittsburgh, Pa. 15221

News related to the printing industry from a feminist perspective. Information of interest to female writers seeking a publishing outlet for their work.

Media Report to Women
3306 Ross Place, N.W.
Washington, D.C. 20008

News of women's actions and achievements in the broadcasting, film, radio, and print media. Personal interviews, articles on books, publications, and programs of interest to women in every field. Subscription: $10. Also publishes a Media Directory (see Bibliography under "Employment"). Subscription.

National Committee on Household Employment News
1625 I St., N.W.
Washington, D.C. 20006

News on the committee's efforts to improve the working conditions and status of household employees. Articles on wage and employment legislation.

New Directions for Women
P.O. Box 27
Dover, N.J. 07801

On Campus with Women
Project On the Status and Education of Women
Association of American Colleges
1818 R St., N.W.

Washington, D.C. 20007

Concise reports on the educational and legal status of women. Information on employment discrimination, women's activities and organizations. Excellent background builder. Free. Also write for other publication information.

Prime Time
264 Piermont Ave.
Piermont, N.Y. 10968

Main focus of the newsletter is on the needs and rights of older women. Information on social-security and pension benefits and employment opportunities. Also general information on employment discrimination and women's activities. Subscription rates: $3.50–$5.00 monthly.

Pro Se: National Law Women's Newsletter
79 Dartmouth St., #2
Boston, Mass. 02116

Concerned mainly with legal aspects of equal-employment issues. News on current legislation and sex-discrimination cases.

The Spokeswoman
5464 South Shore Dr.
Chicago, Ill. 60615

Reports on women's rights, conventions, economic trends, and political activities of women. Also regularly publishes a section on job opportunities for women in management, education, and other fields. Excellent general background. Subscription: $9.

Union W.A.G.E.
(Union Women's Alliance
 to Gain Equality)
2135 Oregon St.
Berkeley, Calif. 94705
Articles on equal pay for women union workers, current economic trends, and f e m a l e unionist activities. Also information on maternity leaves, advancement, and legal status of union women.

Weal Washington Report
621 National Press Bldg.
Washington, D.C. 20004
Published by the Women's Equity Action League. Information on women and employment discrimination, political opportunities for women, and federal legislation.

Woman Today
Today Publications & News
 Service
National Press Bldg.
Washington, D.C. 20004
News on the projects and research of the women's movement, and the legal, political, and employment status of women. Valuable overview of women's network. Subscription: $18.

*Womanpower: A Monthly
 Report on Fair Employ-
 ment Practices*

Betsy Hogan Associates
222 Rawson Rd.
Brookline, Mass. 02146
Background information on current legislation, economic trends, women in management, and the progress of Affirmative Action programs. Also gives news on publications and activities of women. Subscription: $35.

Women and Work
c/o Shelley Nopper, Editor
Rm. 2138
U.S. Dept. of Labor
14th and Constitution Ave.,
 N.W.
Washington, D.C. 20210
Free p u b l i c a t i o n giving women-oriented analysis of labor trends and information on government activities and publications c o n c e r n i n g women. Often focuses on trends in specific occupations.

Women's Lobby Quarterly
1345 G St., S.E.
Washington, D.C. 20003
News of the activities of the Women's Lobby in Washington. Currently working for pension reform, credit legislation, and minimum wage laws as well as ratification of Equal Rights Amendment.

*Women's Rights Law
 Reporter*
180 University Ave.
Newark, N.J. 07102
Journal of developments in the fields of sex discrimination, legal rights, and equal

employment for women. Also prints articles of general interest to the women's movement. Semiannual. Subscription: $12 for 6 issues.

Women's Studies Newsletter
Clearinghouse on Women's
  Studies
P.O. Box 334
SUNY
Old Westbury, N.Y. 11568

Information on resources and projects related to women. Articles on women's studies,

financial support for women, and news on publications, media activity, and job openings.

Women's Work
Washington Opportunities
  for Women
Suite 101, Vanguard Bldg.
1111 20th St., N.W.
Washington, D.C. 20036

News about job openings and new fields, legal counseling, and Affirmative Action. Bimonthly: Subscription: $5.

The publications listed below are more regionally oriented than the newsletters listed above, and they are less likely to focus on employment or equal rights alone. Often they are run by volunteers or on small budgets, and many of them may be short-lived. However, a look through these publications can often give you insights into the particular problems women face in a local area, and so we have chosen to give a cross-section of these magazines and newspapers here.

Awake and Move
c/o Women's Center
4634 Chester Ave.
Philadelphia, Pa. 19104

*Berkshire Women's
  Liberation Newsletter*
P.O. Box 685
Lenox, Mass. 01240

Best Friends
Women's Center
1824 Las Lomas
University of New Mexico
Albuquerque, N. Mex. 87106

Change
968 Valencia St.
San Francisco, Calif. 94110

The Changing Woman
705 S.E. 46th Ave.
Portland, Oreg. 97215

*Cold Day in August:
  Newsletter of Baltimore
  Women's Liberation*
101 E. 25th St., Suite B-2
Baltimore, Md. 21218

Country Women
P.O. Box 51
Albion, Calif. 95410

Female Liberation Newsletter
P.O. Box 344
Cambridge A
Cambridge, Mass. 02139

Feminist Art Journal
41 Montgomery Pl.
Brooklyn, N.Y. 11215

*Feminist Newsletter of
Chapel Hill*
P.O. Box 954
Chapel Hill, N.C. 27514

Feminist Quarterly Journal
1520 New Hampshire Ave.,
N.W.
Washington, D.C. 20036

Feminist Studies
Ann Calderwood, Editor
417 Riverside Dr.
New York, N.Y. 10025

The Feminist Voice
2745 North Clark
Chicago, Ill. 60614

Front Page
Bloomington Women's Center
414 North Park
Bloomington, Ind. 47401

Goodbye to All That
P.O. Box 3092
San Diego, Calif. 92103

*Her-Self: A Community
Women's Newspaper*
225 E. Liberty St., Suite 200
Ann Arbor, Mich. 48108

*Indianapolis Women's
Liberation Newsletter*
P.O. Box 88365
Indianapolis, Ind. 46208

Inforwomen
P.O. Box 1727

Chicago, Ill. 60690

*Jackson Women's
Coalition Newsletter*
P.O. Box 3234
Jackson, Miss. 39207

Mainely Now
P.O. Box 534
Kennebunkport, Maine 04046

Majority Report
74 Grove St.
New York, N.Y. 10014

Marin Women's Newsletter
P.O. Box 1414
San Rafael, Calif. 94902

Matrix
P.O. Box 4218
North Hollywood, Calif.
91607

*Momma: The Magazine for
Single Mothers*
926 Marco Place
Venice, Calif. 90291

New Hampshire Sisters
6 Rumford St.
Concord, N.H. 03301

New Womankind
P.O. Box 18102
Buechel, Ky. 40218

New Women
P.O. Box 24202
Fort Lauderdale, Fla. 33302

*Newsletter of the Kansas City
Women's Liberation Union*
5138 Tracy
Kansas City, Mo. 64110

Notes from the Third Year
P.O. Box AA

Old Chelsea Station
New York, N.Y. 10011

Off Our Backs
1724 20th St.
Washington, D.C. 20009

On the Way
Anchorage Women's
   Liberation
7801 Peck Ave.
Anchorage, Alaska 99504

Quest: A Feminist Quarterly
c/o Diana Press
12 W. 25th St.
Baltimore, Md.

*Right-On, Sister: Newsletter
   of Isla Vista Women's
   Center*
6304 Pardell Road
Isla Vista, Calif. 93017

*Santa Fe Women's
   Community Magazine*
520 Jose St., #5
Santa Fe, N. Mex. 87501

Sister
c/o Westside Women's
   Center
218 S. Venice Blvd.
Venice, Calif. 90291

Sister
c/o New Haven
   Women's Liberation
Women's Center
3438 Yale Station
New Haven, Conn. 06520

Sojourner
Sojourner Collective
Women's Interart Center
549 W. 52nd St.
New York, N.Y. 10019

Speakout: A Feminist Journal
184 Washington Ave.
Albany, N.Y. 12210

Tell-a-Woman
c/o Women's Liberation
   Center
4634 Chester Ave.
Philadelphia, Pa. 19143

Texan Woman
1208 Baylor St.
Austin, Texas 78703

Up from Under
339 Lafayette St.
New York, N.Y. 10009

US (United Sisters)
4213 West Bay Ave.
Tampa, Fla. 33616

Whole Woman
The Women's Center
836 E. Johnson
Madison, Wis. 53703

*WICA: The Ames Feminist
   Newspaper*
Women's Coalition
Rm. 6-S, Memorial Union
University of Iowa
Ames, Iowa, 50010

Woman
Campus Women's Forum
University of California
Berkeley, Calif. 94704

Woman
2621 Beechwood Dr.
Los Angeles, Calif. 90068

*Woman Activist: An Action
   Bulletin for Women*
2310 Barbour Rd.
Falls Church, Va. 22043

Woman Becoming
6664 Woodwell St.
Pittsburgh, Pa. 15217

Woman/News
c/o *The Spokeswoman*
5464 South Shore Dr.
Chicago, Ill. 60615

Womankind
c/o Chicago Women's
Liberation Union
852 W. Belmont
Chicago, Ill. 60615

The Woman's Journal
Valley Women's Center
200 Main St.
Northampton, Mass. 01060

Womanspace Journal
11007 Venice Blvd.
Los Angeles, Calif. 90034

*Women: A Journal of
Liberation*
3028 Greenmount Ave.
Baltimore, Md. 21218

Women and Film
2802 Arizona Ave.
Santa Monica, Calif. 90404

Women in the Arts
P.O. Box 4476
Grand Central Station
New York, N.Y. 10017

*Women Speak Out for Peace
and Justice*
P.O. Box 18139
Cleveland Heights, Ohio
44118

*Women's Action Movement
Newsletter*
Box 4770 Mississippi State
Starkville, Miss. 39762

*The Women's Center
Newsletter*
27 Franklin St.
Poughkeepsie, N.Y. 12601

Women's Journal of the Arts
c/o Jan Oxenberg
School of Art
California Institute of
the Arts
24700 McBean Parkway
Valencia, Calif. 91355

*Women's Liberation
Newsletter*
3800 McGee
Kansas City, Mo. 64111

Women's Newsletter
Portland State University
Women's Union Office
450 Smith Center
Portland, Oreg. 97203

Women's Newspaper
P.O. Box 7418
North End Station
Detroit, Mich. 48202

The Women's Page
1227 37th Ave.
San Francisco, Calif. 94122

Women's Press
P.O. Box 562
Eugene, Oreg. 97401

*Women's Studies: An
Interdisciplinary Journal*
Gordon and Breach Science
Publishers
440 Park Ave. South
New York, N.Y. 10016

Women's Studies Abstracts
P.O. Box 1
Rush, N.Y. 14543

Women's Yellow Pages
Sanctuary
1151 Massachusetts Ave.
Cambridge, Mass. 02138

Worcester Women's Press
903 Main St.
Worcester, Mass. 01610

The Working Mother
Maternal Information
  Services, Inc.
46 W. 96th St.
New York, N.Y. 10025

G

Books

Dozens of employment handbooks and studies for women are now on the market. The following bibliography, although by no means complete, lists a wide variety of books on finding a job, choosing a career, educational opportunities, and legal rights. The bibliography is divided into four sections: Employment, Legal Rights, Education, and Other Reference Sources. Prices are subject to change.

EMPLOYMENT

Absent from the Majority: Working Class Women in America, Nancy Seifer, Middle America Pamphlet Series, c/o Institute of Human Relations, 165 E. 56th St., New York, N.Y., 1973, $1.25.
> Survey of the job discrimination and social problems blue-collar women face and their recent efforts to organize through trade unions and coalitions.

After College . . . Junior College . . . Military Service . . . What?: The Complete Career Exploration Handbook, Newall Brown, New York, Grosset & Dunlap, Inc., 1971, $3.95.
> Primer on career choices; useful background on traditional fields and job types.

Breakthrough: Women into Management, Rosalind Loring and Theodora Wells, New York, Van Nostrand & Reinhold Co., 1974, $7.95.
> Survey of women's recent move into management and the impact of executive women on business.

Career Awareness Project, Business and Professional Women's

Foundation, 2012 Massachusetts Ave., N.W., Washington, D.C. 20036, 1973.

Study of the knowledge and career choices of women today.

Career Choices for Women in Medicine, The American Medical Women's Association, 1740 Broadway, New York, N.Y. 10010, 2 vols., $2.

Explores the work options opening to women in medical field; encourages women's entrance into specialized practice.

Career Opportunity Series, Catalyst, 14 E. 60th St., New York, N.Y.

Series of pamphlets on career options in a variety of fields, including banking, finance, engineering, health care, and many others. Provides case histories, salaries, and background on jobs. Write for full publication list. Cost per pamphlet: 95¢.

Careers for Women in Uniform, Grover Heiman and Virginia Myers, Philadelphia, J. B. Lippincott Co., 1970, $4.95.

Basics on women entering public service in police work, military, etc.

Corporate Lib: Women's Challenge to Management, Eli Ginzberg and Alice M. Yohalem, editors, Baltimore, Johns Hopkins University Press, 1973, $2.50.

Study of women's role in the work force, inroads into management and the problems of discrimination, dual careers.

Creative Careers for Women, Lee McGrath and Joan Scobey, New York, Simon & Schuster, 1968, $1.

Nontraditional approach to the job market; exploration of new careers in the professions, business, and industry.

Everything a Woman Needs to Know to Get Paid What She's Worth, Caroline Bird, New York, David McKay Co., 1973, $8.95.

A handbook for women on moving into men's careers, interviewing for jobs, detecting and combating discrimination, exploring apprenticeships and business ownership.

The Executive Suite—Feminine Style, Edith M. Lynch, American Management Association, Inc., 135 W. 50th St., New York, N.Y. 10019, 1973, $10.50.

An insider's view of women in management and the myths, realities, and success stories of women in the corporate world.

The Female Labor Force in the United States: Demographic and Economic Factors Governing Its Growth and Changing

Composition, Valerie Kincaid Oppenheimer, Berkeley, The Institute of International Studies, 1970, $2.50.

Statistical study of women in the labor force and the job market.

Five Hundred Back-to-Work Jobs for Housewives, Barbara A. Prentice, New York, Macmillan, 1971, $1.50 (paperback).

Guide for women returning to job market with limited or rusty skills.

Getting Yours, Letty Cottin Progrelsin, New York, David McKay Co., 1975, $8.95.

Tips on overcoming the inequities and other problems women face in employment.

Go Hire Yourself an Employer, Richard K. Irish, New York, Doubleday, Anchor Press, 1973, $2.95 (paperback).

Nontraditional approach to the job hunt; though little attention is given to the special problems of female job seekers, the book has a good section on résumés and interviews.

Handbook on Women Workers, Women's Bureau, Bulletin 194, U.S. Dept. of Labor, Washington, D.C. 20210, 1969, $1.50.

Basic, though dated reference source; data on labor trends, income, educational opportunities, and women's organizations.

How to Go to Work When Your Husband Is Against It, Your Children Aren't Old Enough, and There's Nothing You Can Do Anyhow, Felice W. Schwartz, Margaret H. Schifter, and Susan S. Gillotti, New York, Simon & Shuster, 1972, $2.95 (paperback).

Emphasis on job seeking for the woman combining career and family, plus valuable basics on organizing a job campaign. Gives a career survey of job types, salaries, and requirements.

How to Return to Work in an Office, Mary Ralston and Wilbur Cross, New York, Harper & Row, 1972, $6.95.

Suggestions for women readjusting to clerical work.

Introduction to the Woman's Movement, The Woman's Action Alliance, 370 Lexington Ave., New York, N.Y., 1975, $5.

Practical and informative guide to resources of women's movement, including publications, employment services, history, and health care.

Job-Finding Techniques for the Mature Woman, U.S. Dept. of Labor, Superintendent of Documents, U.S. Government Printing Office, Washington, D.C. 20402, 30¢.

A pamphlet outlining basic pointers on finding and interviewing for jobs.

Job Ideas for Today's Woman, Ruth Lembeck, Englewood Cliffs, 1974, $6.95.

Suggestions for women interested in breaking away from, or readjusting to, traditional work goals.

Media Report to Women Index/Directory, compiled by Media Report to Women Newsletter, 3306 Ross Pl., N.W., Washington, D.C. 20008, 1975, $6.

Comprehensive directory of women's publications, presses, media groups, and job-lead sources for women in publishing, film, etc.; also listings of individual media women.

Medicine—A Woman's Career, The American Medical Women's Association, 1740 Broadway, New York, N.Y., 10010, 50¢.

Moving Up, Eli Djeddah, Philadelphia, J. B. Lippincott Co., 1971, $5.95.

Strategies for advancement, based on proved management techniques.

The New Woman's Survival Catalog, edited by Kirsten Grimstak, Fannette Pollack, Susan Rennie, and Ruth Smith, New York, Coward, McCann & Geoghegan, 1973, $5.

Compendium of women's movement progress and resources in key areas; media, employment, legal rights, day care.

The New York Woman's Directory, Womanpower Project, New York, Workman Publishing Co., 1973, $2.95.

Resource book geared to New York; also provides excellent general guidelines on job seeking, financial management, choosing medical and legal assistance.

No Experience Necessary: A Guide to Employment for the Female Liberal Arts Graduate, Sande Friedman and Lois C. Schwartz, New York, Dell Publishing Co., 1971, $1.25.

Handbook on careers for college women in a variety of fields, including publishing, banking, and the film and broadcast media; somewhat dated but readable and helpful in matching interests to jobs.

Non-traditional Careers for Women, Sarah Splaver, New York, Julian Messner, 1973, $5.95.

Explores new fields and work patterns now opening up for women, with emphasis on creative approach to job choices.

The Occupational Outlook Handbook, U.S. Dept. of Labor, Superintendent of Documents, U.S. Government Printing Office, Washington, D.C. 20402, 1974–75, $6.85.

Standard work, updated annually and available at most public libraries. Gives background, labor statistics, and detailed descriptions of salaries, advancement, and requirements of over 800 job types.

Paraprofessions: Careers of the Future and the Present, Sarah Splaver, New York, Julian Messner, 1972, $4.95.

Study of the new back-up, technical jobs now attracting many women, from legal assistant to exhalation therapist.

Personal and Professional Success for Women, Jan Dunlap, Englewood Cliffs, Prentice Hall, 1972, $6.95.

Practical guide to gaining visibility, planning for advancement, and developing management skills.

Preparing for Work, Catalyst, 14 East 60th St., New York, N.Y., 1974, $1.25.

A pamphlet providing guidelines for women in the job market; basics of job hunting, locating openings, preparing résumés.

The Professional Woman, Athena Theodore, editor, Cambridge, Schenkman Publishing Co., 1971, $5.95 (paperback).

Survey of the characteristics of female professionals and the range of their participation and problems in the work force.

Rooms With No View: A Woman's Guide to the Man's World of the Media, compiled by Media Women's Association, New York, Harper & Row, 1974, $5.95.

Realistic insiders' views of the supporting role women play in the media industry, including publishing, broadcasting, and film.

Saturday's Child: 36 Women Talk about Their Jobs, Suzanne Seed, New York, Bantam Books, 1974, $1.25.

Interviews and discussions of women and work, with insiders' views on success and failure in wide range of fields from medicine to media.

Sex in the Marketplace: American Women at Work, Juanita Kreps, Baltimore, John Hopkins University Press, 1971, $1.95.

Basic study of women and their role in the work force; statistics on earnings, sex discrimination, and job choices.

The Shortchanged: Minorities and Women in Banking, Rodney Alexander and Elizabeth Sapery, New York, Dunellen Publishing Co., Inc., 1972, $5.95 (paperback).

Research report on the job discrimination and lack of progress in the banking industry.

380 Part-Time Jobs for Women, Ruth Lembeck, New York, Dell Publishing Co., 1968, 95¢.

Brief descriptions of part-time employment from sales to sewing.

The Two Career Family, Holstrom and Lynda Lytle, Cambridge, Schenkman Publishing Co., 1972, $3.50 (paperback).

Survey of the experiences of families in which both male and female are self-supporting.

What Color Is Your Parachute? Richard Nelson Bolles, Berkeley, Ten-Speed Press, 1974, $4.95 (paperback).

Nontraditional survival and strategy manual for modern job seekers, male and female; emphasis on locating and using new resources and creative approach to pavement pounding.

Woman's Place: Options and Limits in Professional Centers, Cynthia Fuchs Epstein, Berkeley and Los Angeles, University of California Press, 1971, $2.45.

Examines the problems and possibilities women face in the professional marketplace.

Women, Work and Volunteering, Herta Loeser, Boston, Beacon Press, 1974, $8.95.

Practical guide for women seeking full- or part-time volunteer work; listings of volunteer organizations, women's groups, and literature on volunteer work.

Women's Almanac, Armitage Press, 1430 Massachusetts Ave., Cambridge, Mass. 02138.

Series of local resource almanacs prepared for more than 20 cities, including Houston, Washington, Philadelphia, Boston, and New York. Articles and local listings for employment, education, and legal services. 1975 Almanac Series: $1.95 per issue.

Women's Organizations and Leaders, 1973 Directory, Myra E. Barre, editor, Today Publications and News Service, Inc., National Press Bldg., Washington, D.C. 20004, $25.

Comprehensive directory of women's groups and individual women in wide range of areas: employment, education, legal services.

Women's Rights Almanac 1974, Nancy Gager, editor, Bethesda, Elizabeth Cady Stanton Publishing Co., $4.95 (paperback).

Information-filled state-by-state directory of resources for women. Includes articles and listings in employment, legal, government fields, and literature, and background data on women's movement.

329

Women's Yellow Pages, Boston Women's Collective, Inc., 490 Beacon St., Boston, Mass. 02115, 1974, $1.50 (paperback).

Local resource booklet, with general information on employment, legal rights, and health-care services.

The Working Mother's Guide to Her Home, Her Family and Herself, Ann Skelsey, New York, Random House, 1971, $6.95.

Supportive guide for women seeking dual careers.

Your Job Campaign, Catalyst, 14 East 60th St., New York, N.Y. 10028, 1974, $1.25.

Booklet outlining the basics of job finding, including locating job openings, researching fields, and preparing a résumé.

LEGAL RIGHTS

Affirmative Action and Equal Employment, A Guidebook for Employers, vols. 1 and 2, U.S. Equal Employment Opportunity Commission, 1800 G St., N.W., Washington, D.C. 20506, free.

Detailed survey of equal-employment laws and Affirmative Action requirements for employers.

Legal Remedies Against Sex Discrimination, Woman's Action Alliance, 370 Lexington Ave., New York, N.Y., 1974, $3.50.

Comprehensive resource booklet on equal-employment laws, filing job-discrimination complaints, and locating legal services.

The Rights of Women: An American Civil Liberties Union Handbook, Susan Ross, New York, Avon Books, 1973, $1.25.

Pocketbook reference guide to legal rights for women in employment, education, and divorce fields, and other areas of current concern; clear and well-organized.

Step by Step: Affirmative Action for Women, Woman Power Publishers, Betsy Hogan Associates, 222 Rawson's Rd., Brookline, Mass. 02146, 1973, $2.50.

Informative explanations of Affirmative Action programs, equal-employment laws, and policies for increasing women's role in management.

Women Law Reporter, 1541 Massachusetts Ave., Washington, D.C. 20016. Legal service for employers, government, and institutions. Annual fee: $275.

Monitors all areas of sex discrimination and publishes complete texts of key cases, as well as other material related to women's rights.

A Working Woman's Guide to Her Job Rights, Women's Bureau, Employment Standard Administration, U.S. Dept. of Labor, Washington, D.C., Leaflet 55, 1974, single copies free.
Concise handbook outlining women's rights and laws covering equal pay, maternity benefits, social-security and pension payments; an excellent ready-reference guide. See also other Women's Bureau publications on job rights.

EDUCATION

Continuing Education Programs and Services for Women, The Women's Bureau, Pamphlet 10, 1971, 70¢.

Status of Women in Higher Education: A Selected Bibliography, Harmon, Iowa State University, Iowa State University Press, 1972 (The Library; Attn.: Photoduplication Center, Ames, Iowa 50010), $3.50.

Women's Higher and Continuing Education: An Annotated Bibliography with Selected References on Related Aspects of Women's Lives, Esther Manning Westervelt and Deborah A. Fixter, Publications Order Office, College Entrance Examination Board, P.O. Box 592, Princeton, N.J. 08540, 1971, $1.50.

OTHER REFERENCE SOURCES

Career Counseling: New Perspectives for Women and Girls, A Selected Annotated Bibliography, Business and Professional Women's Foundation, 2012 Massachusetts Ave., N.W., Washington, D.C. 20036, 1972, 50¢ (paperback).

Women: A Bibliography, Lucinda Cisler, P.O. Box 240, Planetarium Station, New York, N.Y. 10024, 1970, 60¢.

Women: A Bibliography on Their Education and Careers, Helen S. Astin, Nancy Suniewick, and Susan Dweck, The Human Service Press, Suite 160, 4301 Connecticut Ave., N.W., Washington, D.C. 20008, 1971, $5.95.

Women at Work: An Annotated Bibliography, Mei Liang Bickner, Manpower Research Center, Institute of Industrial Relations, Los Angeles: University of California, 1974, $6.

Women Executives: A Selected Annotated Bibliography, Business and Professional Women's Foundation, 2012 Massachusetts Ave., N.W., Washington, D.C. 20036, 1970, 50¢ (paperback).

Women's Work and Women's Studies, 1971: An Interdisciplinary Bibliography, Kirsten Drake, Dorothy Marks, Mary Wexford. Available from KNOW, Inc., P.O. Box 86031, Pittsburgh, Pa. 15221, $4.25.

Working Mothers: A Selected Annotated Bibliography, Business and Professional Women's Foundation, 2012 Massachusetts Ave., N.W., Washington, D.C. 20036, 1968, free.

VI

KNOWING YOUR JOB RIGHTS

Besides providing new job opportunities through Affirmative Action, equal-employment laws also offer job applicants protection against discrimination. As a job applicant, it is important that you know about these laws, how effective they are and what your rights really are. It will be helpful to know how these laws are enforced and how they can affect you, employers, and the labor market itself. Once you know your rights under the law, you're in a better position to identify and cope with discriminatory hiring practices. New legal precedents are continually being set as employers enter into forced or voluntary compliance with laws barring discrimination. Some key laws and agencies are outlined here as a quick reference guide. A more detailed discussion of each law and agency is provided later in this chapter.

Key Laws

Title:	*Prohibits Discriminatory Hiring on the Basis of:*	*Applies to:*
Equal Pay Act (1963) (Educational Amendments, 1972)	Sex in salaries and fringe benefits	All private and public employers
Civil Rights Act of 1964	Race, religion, national origin, sex	All employers with 15 or more employees; state/local government; employment agencies; corporations

Title:	Prohibits Discriminatory Hiring on the Basis of:	Applies to:
Executive Order 11246 (1965) (Amended by Exec. Order 11375, 1968)	Age, sex, race	Any employers with a federal contract of $10,000 or more—virtually all major U.S. corporations
Revised Order #4 (1971)	Sex in recruiting, training and advancement. Requires active recruitment of women.	All federal contractors
Equal Employment Opportunity Act (1972)	Sex, race	All employers with 15 or more employees

Key Agencies

Agency:	Functions:	Regulates:
Office of Federal Contract Compliance (OFCC)	Reviews Affirmative Action plans of individual employers; may cancel or suspend federal contracts for non-compliance.	All federal contractors and subcontractors
Equal Employment Opportunity Commission (EEOC)	Reviews employment practices, charges of discrimination in recruitment, training, advancement. May bring suit directly in cases of discrimination.	All employers

How do all these laws translate into job-market realities? What are *your* rights as a job applicant?

- First, you may not be discriminated against in hiring by any institution with fifteen or more employees, including state or local governments, employment agencies, school systems, labor unions, and corporations.
  —Civil Rights Act of
  1964 (Amended by Equal Employment
  Opportunity Act, 1972)
- You may not be discriminated against in hiring by any institution with a federal contract or subcontract of $10,000 or more. Virtually all "Fortune 500" corporations (those U.S. companies with the largest

334

annual sales volume) are included in this category. In simple terms, nine out of ten companies hold federal contracts which make them responsible for pursuing equal-employment policies.

  —Executive Order 11246
   (1965) (Amended by Executive
   Order 11375 and Revised Order #4)

- As a job applicant, you have the right to compete on an equal basis with men for jobs in every phase and at every managerial level of operation in any institution that holds a federal contract or subcontract. This applies to recruitment as well as to inhouse discrimination by an employer.

  —Revised Order #4 (1972)

- You may not be discriminated against in salaries or fringe benefits on the basis of sex. A man and a woman applying for the same job (or working for the same employer) with basically equal skills, education, and responsibility must be offered the same salary. In practice, this means that it is unlawful for a potential employer to offer you $9,000 per year while offering the same job to a man at $10,000 per year. This also applies to on-the-job salary discrimination.

  —Equal Pay Act of 1963

- All of these laws and regulations also apply to discrimination once you are on the job. You must receive equal consideration in training, promotion, and company benefits.

As an aid in identifying illegal practices on the part of employers, the Equal Employment Opportunity Commission suggests that women check themselves on the following statements:

Any employer can legally:	True	False
1. refuse to hire women who have small children at home.	_____	_____
2. generally obtain and use an applicant's arrest record as the basis for nonemployment.	_____	_____
3. prohibit employees from convers-		

ing in their native language on the job. _____ _____

4. rely solely upon word-of-mouth to recruit new employees if his employees are mostly white or male. _____ _____

5. refuse to hire women to work at night, because he wishes to protect them. _____ _____

6. require all pregnant employees to take a leave-of-absence at a specified time before delivery date. _____ _____

7. establish different benefits—pension, retirement, insurance, and health plans—for male and female employees. _____ _____

8. hire only males for a job if state law forbids the employment of women in that capacity. _____ _____

9. refuse to adjust work schedules to permit an employee time off for religious observance. _____ _____

10. disobey the Equal Employment Opportunity laws only when he is not acting intentionally or with malice. _____ _____

The answer to *each* of these questions is FALSE, and if your present employer or a potential employer has clearly violated your rights under equal employment, you may want to consider filing a complaint as an individual or with a group of others whom the action has affected.

FILING A COMPLAINT

Although this system is considered by many women to be slow and unwieldy and although you may never have reason to file such a complaint, you should be aware of the procedures involved.

The Equal Employment Opportunity Commission (EEOC) regulates Title VII of the 1964 Civil Rights

Act, which prohibits discrimination on the basis of color, religion, age, sex, etc. If you believe you have been discriminated against by a present employer, potential employer, an employment agency, or a labor union, then contact:

The Equal Employment Opportunity Commission
1800 G St., N.W.
Washington, D.C. 20506

Ask for a "Charge of Discrimination" form, fill it out, and have it witnessed by a notary.

When you send a complaint to the EEOC, here's what happens:

- If your state has a fair-employment practices law, the EEOC will refer your case to the proper state agency for 60 days and tell you of the referral.
- If the EEOC is not notified by the state that the complaint has been resolved by the state, or if 60 days have passed, the EEOC will begin to handle the case.
- The EEOC will notify the employer of the charge filed and send an investigator to discuss the case with you and the employer. *The employer cannot discharge or take any punitive action against an employee who has filed a complaint.*
- If the investigator determines that an agreement cannot be reached by the employer and employee(s) and the discrimination charge appears to be valid, the EEOC can file against the employer in the U.S. District Court.
- If the EEOC fails to take action within 180 days after your charge is received (and with the backload of cases on file, the EEOC has often been unable to process a case within six months), you can bring action against the employer yourself.

The Office of Federal Contract Compliance (OFCC) enforces the nondiscrimination laws affecting federal contractors and subcontractors. When a complaint is lodged against a contractor with the OFCC, the EEOC usually investigates the charge. If the charge is judged valid and an agreement is not reached by the employee and employer, either office may handle the legal proceedings. For further information, contact:

The Office of Federal Contract Compliance
Employment Standards Administration
U.S. Department of Labor
Washington, D.C. 20201

or the government agency charged by the OFCC with compliance enforcement in your field. (In the education area, for instance, you would contact the Department of Health, Education, and Welfare for further information or enforcement.)

The Equal Pay Act is regulated by the Wage and Hour Division of the Labor Department, as is the Age Discrimination Act. If you feel you and/or your fellow workers can prove a case of unequal pay for equal work, you should file your complaint with the Wage and Hours Division. The procedure once your charge is received is similar to that of the EEOC. For further information, write:

The Wage and Hour Division
Employment Standards Administration
U.S. Department of Labor
Washington, D.C. 20201

If you do file a complaint, your identity will not be revealed by the government during its investigation, and your employer will be allowed to comply voluntarily with the law; more than 95 percent of complaints based on the Equal Employment Act are handled in this informal way.

THE EQUAL PAY ACT OF 1963
(as amended in 1972)

This Act prohibits discrimination in salaries and fringe benefits on the basis of sex. All workers, including professionals, administrators, executives, and labor-union members, are protected under this law, and all private and public employers are affected by it. The law states that a man and woman working for the same employer under equal conditions with basically equal skills, education, and responsibility must be paid equally. The Act is regulated by the Wage and Hour Division of the Department of Labor, and all private and public employers are affected. This Act was upheld recently (6/74) by the Supreme Court in a historic decision against Corning Glass Works. Women at Corning were awarded $1 million in back wages for doing the same work at a lower base pay than their male co-workers. This decision could affect employers in every field: education, publishing, manufacturing, even the government itself—any industry in which it can be proved that women are receiving lower salary rates for the same work and skills than a man.

TITLE VII OF THE CIVIL RIGHTS ACT OF 1964
(Amended by the *Equal Employment Opportunity Act* of 1972)

Title VII prohibits employment discrimination on the basis of race, religion, national origin, or sex. The law extends to all phases of employment, including recruitment, training, promotion, and company benefits.

All institutions with fifteen or more employees (state and local governments, employment agencies, school systems, labor unions, corporations) are covered by this law as amended in 1972.

The Equal Employment Opportunity Commission (EEOC) investigates all charges of employment discrimination in cooperation with the Office of Federal Contract Compliance (OFCC). Exactly what happens when a complaint is brought to the EEOC against an employer?

In theory, the EEOC notifies the employer that a complaint has been filed within ten days after it is received. The EEOC then conducts an investigation; if discriminatory practices are found, then the EEOC attempts to work out a program with the employer to end unfair employment policies. If this program is not put into action, or if it clearly fails to end unfair treatment of employees, the EEOC may file a suit against an employer.

In practice, however, the system is painfully slow; some investigations don't begin until six months after a complaint is filed, with the case-load backlog becoming larger every year.

339

EXECUTIVE ORDER 11246 (1965)
(Amended by *Executive Order 11375* in 1968 and
Revised Order #4)

This Order prohibits any institution with a federal contract or subcontract of $10,000 or more from practicing employment discrimination. The word "contract" is broadly defined to include any grants indirectly related to government work (subcontracts).

Any employer covered by the Order cannot discriminate in hiring, promoting, training, or providing company benefits for women, minorities, or older workers. As a further government requirement, any employer with federal contracts of $50,000 and more than fifty employees, must design a written Affirmative Action plan. These government-regulated plans spell out concrete numerical goals for hiring, promoting, and training of women.

AFFIRMATIVE ACTION PLANS

The Office of Federal Contract Compliance (OFCC) was created within the Department of Labor to enforce this order and to monitor the practices of all federal contractors and subcontractors. The OFCC has set up five divisions with several government agencies in each division to review the Affirmative Action plans of individual employers.

Along these lines, *Revised Order #4* (1971) is a key law for women in their drive for equal employment. This order spells out goals for compliance. The order specifically requires all federal contractors to include women in their Affirmative Action programs and to develop numerical goals for actively recruiting, training, and advancing women within 120 days after employers submit a written Affirmative Action Plan to their compliance agency.

This means that Affirmative Action plans cannot be limited to ending existing, in-house discrimination by an employer. That employer also has the responsibility for actively locating and training women to take over jobs in every phase and at every managerial level of operation.

How is one of these Affirmative Action programs set up? Let's take a hypothetical corporation and see how it operates.

First, the corporation would appoint an Equal Opportunity Manager or Affirmative Action Director who would supervise recruitment and training policies. Or hire an outside consulting firm to set up a compliance program. Reports from company plants and divisional headquarters could provide raw data on the age, sex, and race of all employees. What types of jobs is the company moving women into? What percentage of women are managers? These are some of the questions an Affirmative Action might raise.

Once the figures have been studied, the company would begin to plan numerical goals for bringing women and minorities into high-level jobs and moving them out of dead-end positions. For instance, within five years the company might plan to increase the number of women in management to 15 percent of the total company labor force, or raise 10 percent of the total number of female employees to the level of manager.

Once these data are gathered, the company would set up an actual plan for translating them into reality. Reports from every plant or division on job openings, job referrals, and promotions would be forwarded to the main Affirmative Action headquarters; training programs might be created, management-awareness seminars run, and interviewers coached on the types of questions they may or may not ask a woman.

In addition, career-path programs which outline the types of company jobs available and job requirements would be publicized. All openings within the company would be advertised freely on bulletin boards and in company newsletters. Employers might also go outside their own ranks in order to recruit qualified women for job openings; they might contact professional women's groups, advertise in women's newsletters, or set up internship programs with colleges to gain a source of female trainees.

LEGAL SERVICES

The federal government's move to enforce Affirmative Action programs has resulted in a whole new field of legal counseling, as more and more women seek legal information about the specifics of employment discrimination.

The legal counseling services represented here offer a range of services, from helping women identify subtle forms of discrimination on a job interview to filing charges of employment discrimination and handling these cases in the event that they go to court.

ACADEMIC WOMEN ALLIED
  FOR RIGHTS AND EQUALITY
Box 1137
Washington University
St. Louis, Mo. 63130
314   863-0100, ext. 4110
ICH   LC
An organization of women involved in research and teaching and engaged in gathering data on the status of women at Washington University. Informs women of their rights under antidiscrimination laws.
Publication: Newsletter

AFFIRMATIVE-ACTION
  REGISTER FOR EFFECTIVE
  EQUAL OPPORTUNITY
  RECRUITMENT
10 S. Bentwood Blvd.
St. Louis, Mo. 63105
CC   CL

AMERICAN CIVIL LIBERTIES
  UNION
WOMEN'S RIGHTS PROJECT
156 Fifth Ave.
New York, N.Y. 10010
212   675-5990
Check also into local ACLU chapters.

AMERICAN FEDERATION OF
  STATE, COUNTY AND
  MUNICIPAL EMPLOYEES
COMMITTEE ON SEX
  DISCRIMINATION
1155 15th St., N.W.
Washington, D.C. 20005
202   223-4460

CLINICAL LAW PROGRAM IN
  EMPLOYMENT
  DISCRIMINATION
Wayne State University
  Law School

CC = Career Counseling	JP = Job Placement
CL = Career Library	LC = Legal Counseling
EmR = Employment Referral	TB = Talent Banks
ICH = Information Clearing House	VT = Vocational Training

342

Rm. 192-3 Law School Annex
Detroit, Mich. 48202
313   577-3983-4816

Serves two functions: (1) to provide clinical experience in employment-discrimination cases for law-school students; (2) to assure compliance in Detroit area with Equal Employment Opportunity laws. Women clients represented are chosen on basis of meritorious cases and desire to maintain wide range of cases to serve teaching function. No fee.

CLINICAL PROGRAM ON SEX
   DISCRIMINATION IN
   EMPLOYMENT
1983 East 24th St.
Cleveland, Ohio 44115
216   687-2528

Legal help for women discriminated against in seeking employment or in conditions of employment once hired. Law students in this program work with lawyers at the Women's Law Fund, Inc. No fee.

COMMISSION ON CIVIL
   RIGHTS FEDERAL
   WOMEN'S PROGRAM
1405 I St., N.W.
Washington, D.C. 20573
202   382-4145

COORDINATING COMMITTEE
   ON WOMEN'S RIGHTS IN
   NEW JERSEY
NEW DIRECTIONS
   FOR WOMEN
P.O. BOX 27

Dover, N.J. 07801
201   366-6036

COUNCIL FOR UNIVERSITY
   WOMEN'S PROGRESS
University of Minnesota
68 Morrill Hall
Minneapolis, Minn. 55455
612   373-7501
ICH   LC

Concerned with improvement in the status of women at the University of Minnesota. Filed discrimination charges against the university with the Department of Health, Education, and Welfare.

DIRECT ACTION FOR RIGHTS
   IN EMPLOYMENT (DARE)
Chicago Women's
   Liberation Union
852 W. Belmont
Chicago, Ill. 60657
312   348-4300

Helps women organize for their rights on the job and file sex-discrimination complaints. Developing an information and referral service to offer legal counseling to women.

EMPLOYMENT TASK FORCE
8000 E. Jefferson
Detroit, Mich. 48211

HUMAN RIGHTS FOR WOMEN
1128 National Press Bldg.
Washington, D.C. 20004
202   737-1059
Publication: *Job Discrimination Handbook*

INSURANCE EMPLOYEES FOR
   EQUAL RIGHTS

593 Market St., Rm. 223
San Francisco, Calif. 94105
415   495-0923
ICH   LC

Membership open to current or recent employees in the insurance industry.

Files complaints against companies on behalf of members or educates them as to legal action. Works with other groups to bring outside pressure on organizations with discriminatory employment practices.
No fee.

INTERNATIONAL FEDERATION
  OF WOMEN LAWYERS
150 Nassau St.
New York, N.Y. 10038
212   227-8339

LAW WOMEN'S CAUCUS
Condon Hall
University of Washington
Seattle, Wash. 98105
206   525-6106

LEFCOURT, KRAFT & ARBER
150 Nassau St.
New York, N.Y. 10038
212   233-8920

Women's law firm working with sex-discrimination cases.

MEXICAN AMERICAN LEGAL
  DEFENSE AND

EDUCATIONAL FUND
145 Ninth St.
San Francisco, Calif. 94103

Law-reform agency funded largely by foundation grants. Does test-case litigation in women's employment. Chicana Rights Project specializes in problems of Chicana women.
No fee.

MIDWEST WOMEN'S
  LEGAL GROUP
56 W. Randolph St.
Chicago, Ill. 60601
312   641-1906

NATIONAL ORGANIZATION FOR
  WOMEN LEGAL DEFENSE
  AND EDUCATION FUND
9 West 57th St.
New York, N.Y. 10019
212   688-1751
LC

Concerned with all forms of discrimination against women.

PENNSYLVANIANS FOR
  WOMEN'S RIGHTS
Women's Center
230 W. Chestnut St.
Lancaster, Pa. 17603
717   299-5381

A statewide organization working for equal employment, child-care programs,

---

CC = Career Counseling
CL = Career Library
EmR = Employment
        Referral
ICH = Information
        Clearing House

JP = Job Placement
LC = Legal Counseling
TB = Talent Banks
VT = Vocational Training

and the full rights of women in marriage, divorce, and financial affairs.
Dues: $5.

U.S. EQUAL EMPLOYMENT
  OPPORTUNITY COMMISSION
1800 G St., N.W.
Washington, D.C. 20506
202   343-5621
LC

WISCONSIN COORDINATING
  COUNCIL FOR WOMEN IN
  HIGHER EDUCATION
University of Wisconsin
Stevens Pt., Wis. 55481
ICH   LC

WOMEN EMPLOYED
37 S. Wabash St.
3rd fl., YWCA
Chicago, Ill. 60603
312   372-7822
Publicizes the situation of women workers and demands that employers make public plans for promoting women and for increasing wages. Public hearing held to expose illegal practices of Loop employers and to call on federal and state compliance agencies to enforce the law.

WOMEN FOR CHANGE CENTER
3220 Lemmon Ave.
Dallas, Tex. 75204
CC   CL   EmR   ICH   JP
  LC-referral   TB
Fee for LC set by attorney.
See "Career Counseling—West"

WOMEN FOR EQUAL
  OPPORTUNITY AT THE
UNIVERSITY OF
  PENNSYLVANIA
Houston Hall
Philadelphia, Pa. 19104
Acts as watchdog for equal opportunity for women at Penn and assists women who h a v e   b e e n   discriminated against by the university. Also presses for child care and women's studies.

WOMEN UNITED
Crystal Plaza 1, Suite 805
20001 Jefferson Davis
  Highway
Arlington, Va. 22202
Lobbies for legislation benefiting women, has worked to promote the Equal Rights Amendment, and serves as a clearinghouse for information on ERA topics.

WOMEN'S CENTER
1736 R St., N.W.
Washington, D.C. 20009
202   232-5145-7533
Headquarters and clearinghouse for several groups, including one on employment discrimination.

WOMEN'S EMPLOYMENT
  RIGHTS CLINIC
2437 Shattuck Ave., #20
Berkeley, Calif. 94704

WOMEN'S EQUITY
  ACTION LEAGUE
538 National Press Bldg.
Washington, D.C. 20004
202   638-4560
Membership open to women sympathetic to the organiza-

tion's goals; dues are $15. Thirty state chapters.

Devoted to improving the status of women through education, legislation, and litigation.

Advocates the Equal Rights Amendment and works to insure equal pay for equal work, equality in higher education, reform in family laws, and reform in credit systems. Publication: *WEAL Washington Report*, monthly newsletter with information on congressional issues and court actions of interest to women

WOMEN'S JOB RIGHTS
Rm. 318, 620 Sutter St.
San Francisco, Calif. 94102
415   771-1092
Puts out the *Women's Job Rights Advocate Handbook*, which outlines what constitutes sex discrimination in hiring and employment practices and the steps to take in case of discrimination.

Works to help women file effective complaint actions and provides access to legal help.

WOMEN'S LAW CENTER
P.O. Box 1934
Baltimore, Md. 21203
301   547-1653

Membership open to all persons interested in furthering women's rights through law. Provides advice, assistance, and representation to individual women encountering sex-based discrimination. Members handle cases concerning discrimination against women in employment, housing, credit extension, marriage and divorce laws, criminal law, and any other case dealing with sex-based discrimination.

WOMEN'S LAW CENTER
1414 Avenue of the Americas
Suite 1100
New York, N.Y. 10019
212   838-8118
ICH
Offers referral service for legal questions and assistance. Maintains collection of law books, publishes pamphlets on legal issues, sponsors lectures and discussion groups on current legal topics, conducts workshops on legal research skills for self-representation; clearinghouse for women lawyers engaged in women's rights work.
Publications: Fact sheets and booklets on legal issues of interest to women.

CC = Career Counceling
CL = Career Library
EmR = Employment
           Referral
ICH = Information
           Clearing House

JP = Job Placement
LC = Legal Counseling
TB = Talent Banks
VT = Vocational Training

WOMEN'S LAW FUND, INC.
620 Keith Bldg.
Cleveland, Ohio 44115
216 621-3443
LC
Nonprofit organization which handles litigation involving sex discrimination in employment, education, housing, government benefits. Also involved in education in these areas. Lawyers work with law students in the Clinical Program on Sex Discrimination in Employment.
No fee.

WOMEN'S LEGAL CENTER
558 Capp St.
San Francisco, Calif. 94110
415 285-5066
Operates a number of projects for women in the Bay Area: a divorce clinic (where legal workers teach women do-it-yourself divorce); an information and referral service for welfare women; and a directory of women lawyers. Prepares pamphlets dealing with the legal aspects of keep-ing one's own name after marriage, the ins and outs of divorce, and the community-property laws of California. The staff writes a column, "Women and the Law," in *The Conspiracy*, a National Lawyers Guild publication.

WOMEN'S RIGHTS
  LITIGATION CLINIC
Rutgers Law School
175 University Ave.
Newark, N.J. 07102
201 648-5637
LC
Law office, using student help, handles test cases in women's rights. Takes cases in New York and New Jersey.
No fee.

WOMEN'S RIGHTS PROJECT
Center for Law and
  Social Policy
1751 N St., N.W.
Washington, D.C. 20036
202 872-0670
LC
Public-interest law firm.
No fee.

HELP KEEP *WOMAN'S WORK BOOK* UP TO DATE.
FILL IN THE FOLLOWING QUESTIONNAIRE:
Questionnaire: Karin Abarbanel & Gonnie McC. Siegel, c/o
Information House, Inc., 211 E. 51st St., N.Y., N.Y. 10022

Name of organization_____

Address_____

Phone_____ Zip Code_____

_____

Director(s)_____

Please check each description that applies to your
organization:
☐ Professional   ☐ Association   ☐ Committee
☐ Educational
☐ Information clearinghouse
☐ Women's center/action group   ☐ Employment Agency
☐ Government agency
Other_____
This organization is: ☐ Local   ☐ Regional   ☐ National
If national, please give number of chapters and number of
members:

_____

_____

Is your organization: ☐ Profit?   ☐ Nonprofit?
Do you charge a fee for your services?   ☐ Yes   ☐ No
If yes, how much_____

If your organization is directly involved in helping women to
get jobs, please check the services you provide:
☐ Talent bank
☐ Vocational testing
☐ Individual career counseling
☐ Group career workshops
☐ Job-placement services
☐ Information clearinghouse
☐ Vocational training
☐ Résumé preparation
☐ Career-goal structuring
☐ Executive recruiting
☐ Legal counseling
Other_____

If you place women in jobs, what kind of jobs do you place them in:

- ☐ Entry level   Salary range _____
- ☐ Management-training programs   Salary range _____
- ☐ Affirmative Action programs   Salary range _____
- ☐ Management positions   Salary range _____
- ☐ Executive positions   Salary range _____

In which industries/occupations do you specialize?

_____

_____

If you are not directly involved in helping women to get jobs, do you refer them to other agencies or groups? ☐ Yes ☐ No
If yes, which groups (please give full name and address)

_____

_____

_____

Do you have a resource file of career information open to women?   ☐ Yes   ☐ No
If yes, please describe the contents.

_____

_____

_____

Are these publications available free?   ☐ Yes   ☐ No
If no, what is the price/subscription fee?_____

_____

What are the membership requirements of your organization (if any)?

_____

_____

_____

_____

If you are affiliated with any other organizations, please list them:

_____

_____

_____

Are there any other organizations, services, or publications you feel we should know about?   □ Yes   □ No
If yes, please list them (with name and address)

_____

_____

_____

Comments

THE BEST OF BESTSELLERS
FROM WARNER BOOKS!

AUDREY ROSE by Frank DeFelitta   **(89-100, $1.95)**
The novel on reincarnation. Soon to be a Major Motion Picture!
"Is it ever compulsive reading! The author . . . can unobtrusively gather up a fistful of our nerve ends, and squeeze. If **The Exorcist** was your cup of hemlock you'll be mad about **Audrey Rose.**"——Cosmopolitan

LILIANE by Annabel Erwin   **(79-941, $1.95)**
An unforgettable romantic saga similar in appeal to **Love's Tender Fury.** Liliane is the story of a passionate woman's search for peace and love.

A STAR IS BORN by Alexander Edwards   **(84-214, $1.75)**
A novel based on the Warner Bros. movie starring Barbra Streisand and Kris Kristofferson. **A Star Is Born** is the love story of two musical superstars, one on the rise, the other on a long spiral down.

SYBIL by Flora Rheta Schreiber   **(79-403, $1.95)**
Over 5 million copies in print! A television movie starring Joanne Woodward, Sally Field and Martine Bartlett! A true story more gripping than any novel of a woman possessed by sixteen separate personalities. Her eventual integration into one whole person makes this a "fascinating book."——Chicago Tribune

 A Warner Communications Company

Please send me the books I have checked.

Enclose check or money order only, no cash please. Plus 35¢ per copy to cover postage and handling. N.Y. State residents add applicable sales tax.

Please allow 2 weeks for delivery.

WARNER BOOKS
P.O. Box 690
New York, N.Y. 10019

Name ....

Address ....

City .... State .... Zip ....

_____ Please send me your free mail order catalog

THE BEST OF BESTSELLERS
FROM WARNER BOOKS!

WITHOUT FEATHERS by Woody Allen   **(89-035, $1.95)**
A major N.Y. Times bestseller; Woody Allen's funniest book
since **Getting Even.** This new collection of short pieces and
plays "crackles with droll remarks . . . mixing the comic with
the cosmic"—**Hartford Courant**

GETTING EVEN by Woody Allen   **(88-244, $1.50)**
Getting Even is the first collection by one of America's last
serious humorists, Woody Allen. **Getting Even** represents Woody
Allen as psychologist, historian, philosopher and sex maniac.
"The funniest book I've read since **Portnoy's Complaint.**"
                                        —The National Observer

ROUGHING IT EASY by Dian Thomas   **(89-119, $1.95)**
A great new idea book for camping and cooking—the best book
ever published on America's fastest-growing leisure activity!
More than 130,000 copies in print in the trade edition!
Crammed with diagrams, drawings and photographs, many in
full color, and "just bursting with practical, inventive solutions
to everyday and special camping needs."—**Family Weekly**

MAN IN BLACK by Johnny Cash   **(89-086, $1.95)**
A "moving and often punishingly honest reading experience"
(**Publishers Weekly**) in which Johnny tells the true story of how
he was saved from drugs by his religion. **16 pages of photographs.**

 A Warner Communications Company

Please send me the books I have checked.

Enclose check or money order only, no cash please. Plus 35¢
per copy to cover postage and handling. N.Y. State residents
add applicable sales tax.

Please allow 2 weeks for delivery.

WARNER BOOKS
P.O. Box 690
New York, N.Y. 10019

Name ....

Address ....

City .... State .... Zip ....

_____ Please send me your free mail order catalog